Human Significance in Theology
and the Natural Sciences

Princeton Theological Monograph Series

K. C. Hanson, Charles M. Collier, and D. Christopher Spinks,
Series Editors

Recent volumes in the series:

Chris Budden
*Following Jesus in Invaded Space:
Doing Theology on Aboriginal Land*

Gale Heide
*System and Story: Narrative Critique
and Construction in Theology*

Linden J. DeBie
*Speculative Theology and Common-Sense Religion: Mercersburg
and the Conservative Roots of American Religion*

David Paul Parris
Reception Theory and Biblical Hermeneutics:

Ilsup Ahn
*Position and Responsibility: Jürgen Habermas, Reinhold Niebuhr,
and the Co-Reconstruction of the Positional Imperative*

Jeanne M. Hoeft
*Agency, Culture, and Human Personhood: Pastoral Thelogy
and Intimate Partner Violence*

Lisa E. Dahill
*Reading from the Underside of Selfhood: Bonhoeffer
and Spiritual Formation*

Charles Bellinger
The Trinitarian Self: The Key to the Puzzle of Violence

Human Significance in Theology and the Natural Sciences

An Ecumenical Perspective with Reference to Pannenberg, Rahner, and Zizioulas

CHRISTOPHER L. FISHER

◆PICKWICK *Publications* • Eugene, Oregon

HUMAN SIGNIFICANCE IN THEOLOGY AND THE NATURAL SCIENCES
An Ecumenical Perspective with Reference to Pannenberg, Rahner, and Zizioulas

Princeton Theological Monograph Series 128

Copyright © 2010 Christopher L. Fisher. All rights reserved. Except for brief quotations in critical publications or reviews, no part of this book may be reproduced in any manner without prior written permission from the publisher. Write: Permissions, Wipf and Stock Publishers, 199 W. 8th Ave., Suite 3, Eugene, OR 97401.

Pickwick Publications
An Imprint of Wipf and Stock Publishers
199 W. 8th Ave., Suite 3
Eugene, OR 97401

www.wipfandstock.com

ISBN 13: 978-1-60608-053-5

Cataloging-in-Publication data

Fisher, Christopher L.

    Human significance in theology and the natural sciences : an ecumenical perspective with reference to Pannenberg, Rahner, and Zizioulas / Christopher L. Fisher.

    xvi + 352 p. ; 23 cm. Includes bibliographical references and indexes.

    Princeton Theological Monograph Series 128

    ISBN 13: 978-1-60608-053-5

    1. Theological anthropology. 2. Religion and science. 3. Pannenberg, Wolfhart, 1928–. 4. Rahner, Karl, 1904–1984. 5. Zizioulas, John, 1931–. I. Title. II. Series.

BD450.F5 2010

Manufactured in the U.S.A.

Unless otherwise indicated, all scripture quotations are from the Holy Bible, New Revised Standard Version Bible: Anglicized Edition, copyright © 1989, 1995, Division of Christian Education of the National Council of the Churches of Christ in the United States of America. Used by permission. All rights reserved.

For Elizabeth, Luke, Mercy, Raquel, and Evangelina

Contents

List of Tables / viii

Acknowledgments / ix

Preface / xi

Abbreviations / xv

Introduction / 1

PART ONE: Human Significance in Theology

1. Wolfhart Pannenberg: The Human Divine Representative / 23

2. Karl Rahner: Human Evolutionary Transcendence and Its Incarnational Fulfillment / 86

3. John Zizioulas: The Correlation of Divine and Human Personhood / 143

PART TWO: Human Significance in the Natural Sciences

4. Some Boundary Issues between Science and Theology / 187

5. Human Uniqueness in the Natural Sciences / 203

6. Cosmic Evolution and Human Existence: Providence in Science and Theology / 246

7. Critical Anthropocentrism and Ecological Concerns / 278

Conclusion: The Anthropocentric Cosmos / 294

Bibliography / 307

Subject Index / 335

Author Index / 347

Tables

1. Vocal Utterances of Some Primates Classified by Design Features of Language / 208

Acknowledgments

THERE ARE MANY PEOPLE AND COMMUNITIES I WISH TO THANK FOR help in accomplishing this work.

I am very grateful to my supervisors David Fergusson and Michael Fuller at New College, University of Edinburgh, for their help, insight, and guidance throughout the process. I also thank the faculty, staff, and students of New College, as well as the staff of the New College Library and the National Library of Scotland in Edinburgh.

I am grateful to the Women's Division of the General Board of Global Ministry of the United Methodist Church, and to the Eastern Pennsylvania Conference of the UMC and Bishop Peter D. Weaver, for granting me permission and assistance to take study leave, and to the Faculty Scholarship Committee of New College for their assistance. I also want to thank the people of West Lawn and Fritz Memorial United Methodist churches, in the Eastern Pennsylvania Conference, and Priestfield Parish Church of Scotland in Edinburgh, for their support, encouragement, and hospitality. Members and friends from all three churches helped make this project possible.

Thanks to Ian McDonald, Joseph Pan, and Eun Chul Kim for their helpful insights, and to Gregory R. Peterson for graciously lending me his PhD dissertation.

I am very grateful to my parents, John and Nelda Fisher, for their support and help in the process. I thank my brother Nevan Fisher and brother-in-law Peter Larson for their research assistance "from afar" in the United States when I needed help with a source. I especially thank my wife Elizabeth, and my children Luke, Mercy, and Raquel, for their constant support and encouragement, for the wonderful sense of adventure we have shared together, and for the love that has made such an endeavor possible and delightful. I also thank God for our fourth child, Evangelina Grace, who arrives as this work finally comes to publication.

I wish also to thank my publisher, Wipf and Stock, for believing in this project and giving me the chance to bring it to a wider audience. Thanks to Charles Collier, Nathan Rhodes, Patrick Harrison, Chris Spinks, and the other editorial staff at Wipf & Stock in Eugene, Oregon. Thanks also to Dawn Housel for her help with indexing and editorial corrections.

The monograph before you is substantially a presentation of my 2004 doctoral dissertation in systematic theology at New College, University of Edinburgh, with minor revisions, updates, and corrections. Portions of chapter 2 have been adapted with David Fergusson and published in the article "Karl Rahner and the Extra-Terrestrial Intelligence Question," in *The Heythrop Journal* 47 (2006). Portions of chapter 5 have been adapted and published in the article "Animals, Humans and X-Men: Human Uniqueness and the Meaning of Personhood," in *Theology and Science* 3, no. 3 (2005). All work here is my own, and I bear sole responsibility for it.

Finally, I wish to give glory to God the Father and thanks to the Lord Jesus Christ, who has picked me up by the Spirit many times in the course of this study and been the ever-faithful friend who is "closer than a brother." To Father, Son, and Holy Spirit, I give my eternal thanks and praise.

Preface

I WAS ORIGINALLY INSPIRED TO PURSUE THIS SUBJECT WHILE READING Stephen Hawking's *A Brief History of Time*. While mostly concerned with physical aspects of time, the big bang, and the physical history of the cosmos, Hawking cannot help but make an occasional theological comment. His efforts to get around the initial beginning problem, "which smacks of the divine," are now legendary.

But what caught my attention was Hawking's admission—in an almost throw-away line—that from our observational standpoint, it really looks like we—that is, Earth, our solar system, and indeed our entire galaxy (on a grand cosmic scale, they are all one tiny spot)—are at *the center of the universe!* More than that, Hawking confessed that it was possible—based on Edwin Hubble's astronomical observations—that we actually *are* at the center of the universe, although we could never verify this without leaving our local galactic frame of reference.[1] While he was quick to qualify and downplay this observation, I was fascinated by his admission that a special cosmic status for our planet was possible—even from the perspective of modern science.

And that brings me to the relevance of all this to human beings—to human significance. Hawking's confession led me to an investigation that revealed, regardless of where one comes out on the question of our cosmic location, the sense in which the medieval worldview may have got it right after all. Not right in its nascent scientific knowledge, its vestiges of ancient Greek philosophy, or the particulars of its pin-pricks-on-a-celestial-sphere version of the heavens, but right in its grasp that the Earth is at the center of the cosmos in a profound kind of way, and at the center of something wonderful God is doing in the entire created realm, *through* human beings. Picture John Milton's vision in *Paradise Lost* of the new world God makes after the great rebellion in heaven. It looks small and insignificant, but the lovely garden Earth is destined to

---

1. Hawking, *Brief History of Time*, 44–45.

be the home of mysterious, terrible, and wonderful events, events with cosmic and eternal significance.

All this unfolded for me in the course of my doctoral study, which I have revised and present to you here. I've been following aspects of the discussion between theology and science since my undergraduate days in engineering physics at Lehigh University, but my work at New College, University of Edinburgh, opened up new vistas for me. My advisor, Professor David Fergusson, encouraged me to pursue my initial question, naïve as it was to begin with, and helped me along the way to see the riches of theology in consideration of human significance. My second advisor, Rev. Dr. Michael Fuller, canon of St. Mary's Episcopal Cathedral in Edinburgh, with his doctorate in chemistry, challenged me to take the hard path of concrete scientific evidence on the subject. Conversations with fellow students were also helpful, especially my talks with Ian MacDonald, who helped me grasp the importance of *contingency*. Many thanks to them all.

As a Christian, I was already convinced that Jesus had conquered death and is the Messiah, the Christ, and that this alone foretold something amazing in a finite and mortal universe. What I did not expect was the coherent picture that would emerge between contemporary natural science and modern Christian theology, in terms of Earth's special cosmic status, human uniqueness, and human significance. Unpacking the implications of the creature made to image God's own self in the cosmos, through whom God has deigned to join with his creation in the incarnation, was and remains a grand and exciting project. Indeed, as I was to discover, any Trinitarian theology that takes the incarnation seriously must have a very high view of human significance.

What was a bit more suprising is that modern, twenty-first century natural science agrees in its own way that humans are special and unique in the cosmos. Popular dehumanizing and downgrading stereotypes of human importance from science and science fiction abound. If sci-fi is the aesthetic expression of our culture's scientific imagination, you can hardly name a modern sci-fi movie that doesn't somehow degrade humans in the cosmic scheme (think *Aliens*, *X-Men*, or *X-Files*). Yet the real contemporary scientific data tells a very different and much more amazing story of human uniqueness.

In what follows, I have tried to lay out the case for what I call *critical anthropocentrism*—which is just a fancy scholarly way to label this vital human cosmic significance. After the introduction, which is standard organizational and definitional stuff, I lay out the case in part 1 for this vital significance in modern theology. There I examine some key, well-respected ecumenical theologians, each representing different traditions in the Christian faith, who are sensitive to questions raised by science. Each of these takes the incarnation seriously in Trinitarian perspective. Lutheran Wolfhart Pannenberg, Roman Catholic Karl Rahner, and Greek Orthodox John Zizioulas occupy chapters 2, 3, and 4, respectively. The Christian faith has a profound understanding of human beings as made in the image of God, and of God having become a human in the incarnation of the Son to redeem humanity along with all of creation. Needless to say, God figures prominently in the discussion, so that any version of anthropocentrism we arrive at can only be as a derivative—a received gift. We are the recipients, not the creators, of our significance. Each of these Christian thinkers provides nuanced insights on these theological realities.

The second part of this work begins with a bridge, chapter 4, on scientific and religious epistemology—how we can know truth in these areas—for those who are skeptical that science and religion can talk to each other. A common move in the religion-science dialogue has been to limit science to the domain of facts and relegate theology to the realm of values. My aim is to show, at least in outline form, how contemporary philosophy has moved beyond this simplistic view, why religion may have more to say about concrete reality than our Western rationality has been willing to allow it for several hundred years, as well as how often scientists have overstated the capacity of science to *see* all of reality.

The rest of part 2 engages the scientific data. To keep the project within bounds, I lay out the case in contemporary natural science by focusing on two questions: chapter 5 tackles what science sees as truly unique about humanity. This is a fun romp through animal intelligence, decision making, and communication, Neanderthal intelligence, artificial intelligence (AI) and its promises, and even through the possibility of extra-terrestrial or "alien" intelligence. Without giving away the store here, these highlight some clearly unique aspects of human nature. Chapter 6 inquires into the relationship between human existence and the unfolding of the cosmos. This is where Stephen Hawking and the big bang come back into play, along with the implications of the so-called *anthropic principle*, emergent complexity, the possibility of multiple universes, and the import of cosmic evolution leading to life on Earth. I even look at Earth's special "location" in the universe.

Chapter 7 examines the implications of a renewed anthropocentrism for our environment, since people have been concerned for a while that humans are running amok. I want to make the case that a proper view of human significance includes a strong sense of human responsibility and stewardship in the creation, and that a humble version of anthropocentrism that takes its cues from the One we are made to image is actually the best way forward in regard to Earth's ecological well-being.

Finally, the conclusion is a wrap-up summary. If you want to get the *Reader's Digest* version, that is the place to go. But you will miss the meat of the project, so I hope you will not settle for that. Although much of the language here is technical, I believe that with a little perseverance you will be able to follow the argument and reap the rewards. Enjoy.

Abbreviations

AARDS	American Academy of Religion Dissertation Series
AB	Anchor Bible
BAR	*Biblical Archaeological Review*
CC	Continental Commentaries
CD	Barth, Karl, *Church Dogmatics*, 5 vols. (Edinburgh: T. & T. Clark, 1956–69)
EvT	*Evangelische Theologie*
FT	*First Things*
IBC	Interpretation: A Biblical Commentary for Teaching and Preaching
JES	*Journal of Ecumenical Studies*
JR	*Journal of Religion*
JRE	*Journal of Religious Ethics*
JTS	*Journal of Theological Studies*
KD	*Kerygma und Dogma*
LCC	Library of Christian Classics
LXT	Rahlfs, Alfred, editor, *Septuaginta: Id est Vetus Testamentum Graece Iuxta LXX Interpretes*, 2 vols. (Stuttgart: Deutsche Bibelgesellschaft, 1935)
NICOT	New International Commentary on the Old Testament
NIGTC	New International Greek Testament Commentary
OiC	*One in Christ*
OTL	Old Testament Library
PRSt	*Perspectives in Religious Studies*
RelS	*Religious Studies*

SJT	*Scottish Journal of Theology*
TS	*Theological Studies*
WTM	Groves, J. Alan, Dale Wheeler et al., *Westminster Hebrew Morphology*, release 3 (Philadelphia: Westminster Theological Seminary, 1998)

Introduction

> What are human beings that you are mindful of them, mortals that you care for them? Yet you have made them a little lower than God, and crowned them with glory and honor.
>
> —Psalm 8:4–5

Introduction and Statement of Thesis

SINCE THE SUCCESS OF THE COPERNICAN REVOLUTION IN ASTRONOMY, humanity's cosmic self-understanding has been undergoing radical revision. While the medieval worldview generally thought the earth was the center of the universe, and humans the pinnacle of creation on earth, the Copernican revolution began a process completed with Darwin of decentering humanity on the cosmic scale. The earth circles the sun, which is just a medium size star, two-thirds of the way out from the center of a medium size galaxy composed of billions of stars, just one among billions of other galaxies in the universe.[1] Darwin's evolutionary theory extended the process to biology, seeming to eliminate humanity's categorically unique position among living creatures. The dominant paradigm of special creation gave way to the evolutionary paradigm of human existence rising from chance and natural necessity—seemingly transitory, impermanent, and meaningless. With the loss of these centering references, humanity has had its self-image gravely altered. Paul Davies observes that these scientific revolutions "had the effect of marginalizing, even trivializing, human beings. People were no longer cast at the center of the great scheme, but were relegated to an incidental and seemingly pointless role in an indifferent cosmic drama, like unscripted extras" on a vast movie set.[2]

---

1. Stannard, *God Experiment*, 103–4.
2. P. Davies, *Mind of God*, 20.

This project proposes, however, that this "Copernican" stereotype is problematic; that in fact humans are cosmically significant in some clear and precise ways that are visible to both theology and the natural sciences. While the former medieval alliance between theology and Ptolemaic-Aristotelian thought in support of anthropocentrism is obsolete, it is the contention of this thesis that a related form of anthropocentrism is still viable and can be maintained in the face of the theological, scientific, and ecological objections.

Contemporary theology and natural science will each be explored to support this contention, with a goal of coherence rather than cross-disciplinary proof. The aim is to show that it is reasonable to believe, on the basis of theological and scientific considerations, that humanity *is* special in some specific and non-trivial ways in the cosmic scheme; that the universe may be said to be *critically anthropocentric*. This is not meant to anthropomorphize the universe, or to divinize humanity. Rather it is to suggest that, in a theological framework, it is reasonable to believe that human beings are cosmically significant because in some sense they enable certain values to be expressed in creaturely terms in the cosmos. This is not accidental, but is part of the divine plan in creating the world. Further, this is consistent with contemporary science. It will be argued that *critical anthropocentrism* is intrinsic to many streams of contemporary Christianity, and is coherent with the scientific portrait of human significance. It will also be argued that this understanding is sensitive to some contemporary issues in epistemology and ecology. If true, it should help revise the modern self-understanding of what it means to be human.

Definition of Terms

Uses of Anthropocentrism in Scholarly Literature

Anthropocentrism has been defined and used in a variety of ways in scholarly literature. In order to frame a more precise definition of *critical anthropocentrism*, other uses of the terms will be demarcated here. This is a representative rather than exhaustive study, limited in scope to theological, ethical, and scientific discourse, and intended as descriptive, not evaluative.

A few basic dictionary definitions are in order. *The Oxford English Dictionary* defines *anthropocentrism* as (1) "A view or doctrine centering in man," and (2) "The assumption that man is the center of all things," and "to which all surrounding facts have reference." The *Merriam-Webster Collegiate Dictionary* adds (1) "Considering human beings as the most significant entity of the universe," and (2) "Interpreting or regarding the world in terms of human values and experiences." The *Academic Press Dictionary of Science and Technology* adds (1) "Of or relating to the belief that humans are the center of the universe." Finally, the *Macquarie Dictionary* adds (1) "regarding human beings as the central fact of the universe" and (2) Assuming human beings to be the final end and aim of the universe."

The scholarly literature generally uses *anthropocentrism* in some variation of these definitions. It may refer to anything having to do with humanity, the human world, or the byproducts of human existence. The "anthropocentric environment"[3] or anthropocentric architecture means here, more or less, "that which pertains to or concerns humans."

Anthropocentric is sometimes used in theological and historical literature to refer to aspects of the medieval synthesis, which found a three-fold support for its elevation of humanity in theology, philosophy, and contemporary science. Theological support came from Christianity's high view of human status in light of the incarnation, philosophical support came from Aristotelian philosophy's high regard for humanity, and proto-scientific support came from widespread belief in the Ptolemaic geocentric universe. The earth was at the center of the universe, humans the focus of earth's history, and all things revolved around them in the cosmos. The synthesis was not simplistic: human status, centrality, and dominion were subservient, guarded against hubris by the relationship of humans to God.[4] Human self-confidence was tempered by an awareness of the limitations imposed by human sinfulness and the need for illumination and revelation from God, yet humanity remained central in the cosmos and in God's plans. Ernst Haeckel pejoratively described this worldview as "the anthropocentric error, that Man is the premeditated aim of the creation of the earth, for whose service alone all the rest of nature is said to have been created."[5] Abraham Heschel comments, "in science the *anthropocentric* view of

---

3. Senesi et al., "Preface," 165.
4. Gibellini, "Theological Debate on Ecology," 126.
5. Haeckel, *History of Creation*, 1:38–39.

the earth as the center of the universe and of man as the purpose of all being has long been discarded."[6]

Anthropocentrism may denote a philosophical frame of reference for understanding reality, located on humanity. Wolfhart Pannenberg uses the term in this sense when describing "the growing anthropocentrism of modern theology," which is shaped by "the philosophical concentration on the human person as subject of all experience and of philosophical reflection itself."[7] Kevin Vanhoozer refers to the shift that took place following the turn towards human subjectivity by Rene Descartes and Immanuel Kant: "There is no knowledge of God except through knowledge of self."[8] Here, the word represents the conscious choice of a human frame of reference on which to anchor all knowledge. It describes a chosen perspective, centered on human subjectivity.

Anthropocentrism may describe a belief in the ultimate superiority of humanity, and of human reason and empirical experience. Alfons Auer describes the "radical anthropocentrism inaugurated by Descartes" and followed by other thinkers all the way through the end of the nineteenth century.[9] Rosino Gibellini says this view "subordinates nature to human beings and generates an anthropocentric arrogance and an imperialistic conception of nature."[10] Following Bacon and Descartes, human knowledge and the foundation of the human sense of self were established independently from theology, finding their justification in experience and self-reference.[11] For instance, John Morgan uses *anthropocentric* to describe the theological milieu of liberal nineteenth-century theology, "which placed man and culture at the center of attention at the expense of God's deity." He says the atrocities of world wars and genocides in the twentieth century caused the decline of this type of anthropocentrism with its ideological optimism, and shattered belief in humanity's inherent goodness and the infallibility of its knowledge, and disinte-

---

6. Heschel, *Man Is Not Alone*, 186.

7. Pannenberg, *Anthropology*, 12.

8. Vanhoozer, "Human Being," 159.

9. Auer, *Ethics of the Environment*, quoted in Gibellini, "Theological Debate on Ecology," 127.

10. Gibellini, "Theological Debate on Ecology," 127.

11. Descartes' "I think, therefore I am/*cogito ergo sum*" inaugurated this non-theological anthropocentrism (though himself viewing human reason as evidence for God), which de-absolutized theology, and made human subjectivity supreme. See ibid., 126–27; Descartes, *Discourse*, pt. 4, 75; Pannenberg, *Anthropology*, 11.

grated the illusions of human ethical and religious superiority.[12] Here, *anthropocentrism* indicates an ideological sense of human superiority and self-confidence.

Anthropocentrism may designate any judgment made by a human being that is necessarily dependent on "human values, interests and preferences."[13] A judgment is anthropocentric if it reveals any evidence of dependence on these, on human location in the cosmos, or on human scale. This has been called "epistemic anthropocentrism,"[14] "cosmic anthropocentrism,"[15] as well as "inevitable anthropocentrism."[16] Because of our nature as human beings, we are limited to an understanding of the cosmos that is from the human perspective, in contrast to some other perspective that might exist, such as God's, that of another animal—a bat for instance,[17] or that of the natural order. Bruce Morito describes this as "a limiting condition," a boundary from which all human activity must proceed.[18] This is not necessarily a negative concept, but simply describes the inevitable result of the human perspective.

A related use, however, is negative, signifying not only this sense of human knowledge limits, but also the understanding that this judgment is one-sided or flawed. Some of our observations of the universe are necessarily flawed, according to John Barrow and Frank Tipler, because of our unique position as *Homo sapiens*. These observations are a matter of appearance only, and are to be separated from those features that "are genuinely determined by the action of physical laws."[19] This observational limitation results from the finite, local, and relative position of human beings on the earth. For instance, to the ordinary observer, the sun appears to go around the earth. This perspective offers problems only when making detailed observations of planetary and stellar motion. Copernicus' achievement was to disengage from an

---

12. Morgan, "Karl Barth in Pursuit," 327–29.
13. Grey, "Anthropocentrism and Deep Ecology," 473.
14. Kazlev, "Anthopocentrism," online: http://www.kheper.net/topics/worldviews/anthropocentrism.html.
15. Plumwood, "Androcentrism and Anthropocentrism," 329.
16. Gruen, "Revaluing Nature," 369.
17. See Nagel, "What is it like to be a bat?" 165–180.
18. Morito, "Value, Metaphysics, and Anthropocentrism," 31.
19. Barrow and Tipler, *Anthropic Cosmological Principle*, 4.

anthropocentric perspective in order to contemplate a simpler explanation of planetary motion: the earth and planets went around the sun.

Such a limited or prejudiced view of things is similar to the anthropological concept of *ethnocentrism*. Paul Hiebert explains: "Human beings are at the center of their own perceptual worlds, resulting in a basic egocentrism in which everything is judged in terms of the self... On another level, people everywhere seem to look on their own culture as most suitable or best, and on those of others as less civilized. This becomes the source of 'ethnocentrism,' the tendency of people to judge other cultures by the values and assumptions of their own culture."[20] Val Plumwood, representing the ecofeminist position, refers to "the liberation model of anthropocentrism, based on extending to the human/nature case the understanding of centrism drawn from liberation concepts such as androcentrism, ethnocentrism, and Eurocentrism."[21] John Templeton describes this as "egotism": "Egotism caused men to think that the stars and the sun revolved around them. Egotism is still our worst enemy."[22] John Seed has labeled this "human chauvinism" or "homocentrism"; "the idea that humans are the crown of creation, the source of all value, the measure of all things."[23] Here, note that he has conflated several uses of anthropocentrism, which in this analysis will be separated. The "selfish" dimension denotes the tendency to judge the universe and other living species by values and assumptions from a biased, self-centered human perspective.

In related use, *anthropocentrism* may denote "a system of thought which emphasizes the priority of humans over other species."[24] This prejudicial perspective reads onto the universe or other creatures a false human character, or a false prioritization of humanity. For example, humans sometimes treat animals and computers as if they were "human-like" entities, as opposed to living beings or machines "that happen to possess human-like characteristics."[25] It may represent "the

---

20. Hiebert, *Cultural Anthropology*, 38.
21. Plumwood, "Androcentrism and Anthropocentrism," 335.
22. Templeton, *Humble Approach*, 11.
23. Seed, "Beyond Anthropocentrism," 35, 37. He says of his own "non-anthropocentric" position, "we act because life is the only game in town, and actions from a disinterested, less attached consciousness may be more effective."
24. Southgate, *God, Humanity, and the Cosmos*, 203.
25. Nass, et al, "Anthropocentrism and Computers," 229.

attitude that only humans matter, or only humans have intrinsic value, while everything else in the world is valued only insofar as it serves, or may serve, human interests."[26] Lori Gruen calls this "pernicious anthropocentrism."[27] Lynn White Jr. describes Western Christianity as "the most anthropocentric religion the world has seen,"[28] seeking to lay the blame for the ecological crisis at the feet of the church and Christian teaching in medieval Europe. A variation of this definition is apparent in A. B. Masao's comments from an Eastern religious perspective. He contends that Western (pernicious) anthropocentrism is rooted in the Western religious conception of the self. Eastern religions such as Buddhism offer a corrective by seeking to reduce or eliminate the self in favor of the communal, of the natural order, or of nothing at all.[29]

Used neutrally in ethical discourse, *anthropocentrism* may represent intentionally choosing a course of action that is most favorable to humanity, in contrast to some other non-human creature it might favor (e.g., earth, or another animal species). For example, Michael Northcott examines the ethical implications of animal extinctions caused by humans. "Looked at purely anthropocentrically, the more pressing import of accelerated humanly originated species extinction may be the significance of the reduction of biodiversity for the human use of the environment, for example in the quest for new pharmaceutical preparations or new genetic strains of staple foods."[30] This type of anthropocentrism has been divided into *strong* and *weak* forms. In *strong* form, human interests alone are valuable; in *weak* form, human stewardship of other non-human beings (who have intrinsic value) is emphasized. Environmental political policy that reflects decisions for reasons of human economic, spiritual, or psychological good fit either usage. Strip-mining might represent *strong* anthropocentrism. Conservationism and preservationism are examples of the *weak* form.[31] Such views are contrasted with "ecocentric" philosophies like Seed's, which reverse "the man-nature relationship and make . . . nature the dominant or predomi-

26. Troxell, "Environmental Ethics."
27. Gruen, "Revaluing Nature," 369.
28. White, "Historic Roots of the Ecologic Crisis," 25–26.
29. Masao, "Problem of Self-Centeredness," 15–25.
30. Northcott, *Environment and Christian Ethics*, 21–22.
31. Landa, "Humans and the Environment"; Michaels, "Ecocentrism vs. Anthropocentrism."

nant actor,"[32] or "biocentric" philosophies, which emphasize the priority of life in general.

In animal-rights ethics, *anthropocentrism* and *non-anthropocentrism* are flags indicating a position on the moral standing of humans and non-humans. Per Ariansen uses the term to discuss the nature of morals. Recognizing morals as intrinsically human is *anthropocentrism*, or what Stan Godlovitch calls "normative anthropocentrism." Non-anthropocentrists hold that "certain classes of non-humans hold rights that are on a prima facie level with human rights. Accordingly, by proxy or guardian, nature can and ought to be represented on the moral scene. The direct moral standing of (some parts of) nature should be recognized and respected"[33] (see chapter 7).

Finally, the *anthropocentric hypothesis* is an expression referring to a somehow justified and privileged position for *Homo sapiens* in the cosmos. Carl Sagan says, on the possibility of extra-terrestrial life, "[If ETI is not found], it would be the first instance in the long series of historical scientific debates in which the *anthropocentric hypothesis* had proved even partly valid."[34] This hypothesis comes quite close to the anthropocentrism of the medieval synthesis, although with unstated rather than explicit theological implications. The hypothesis, if validated, implies that humanity is unique in the universe, that we are the only physical intelligence in all the vast reaches of space, or more simply: "we are alone." John Leslie is using the phrase in this way when he says that the *anthropic principle* (see below, pages 9–10; 60) is "not anthropocentric."[35]

To summarize, *anthropocentrism* has a variety of meanings and nuances in the scholarly literature, with modifiers like "radical," "cosmic," or "pernicious." In the medieval view, it describes the central importance attributed to humanity in the cosmos and in God's plans. In philosophy, *anthropocentric* may describe a chosen perspective—

32. Michaels, "Ecocentrism vs. Anthropocentrism."

33. Ariansen, "Anthropocentrism with a Human Face," 154; Godlovitch, "Descriptive and Normative Anthropocentrism."

34. Quoted by Barrow and Tipler, *Anthropic Cosmological Principle*, 601. Italics added.

35. Leslie, *Universes*, 19–21, 223. The anthropic principle concerns "the nature not of manhood [(anthropos, *Homo sapiens*, mankind)] but of *observerhood*... The key point is . . . that *intelligent life of any plausible kind* seems crucially dependent on [certain] natural conditions."

that of a concentration on the human person. It is sometimes used in scientific discourse to mean that which pertains to or concerns humans or human culture. It may denote the tendency to judge the universe and other living species by values and assumptions from a biased, self-centered human perspective. In ethics, it may describe a course of action that is most favorable to humanity for pragmatic reasons, or may be a flag indicating something about the moral standing of humans vs. non-humans. *Radical anthropocentrism* describes belief in the ultimate superiority of humanity, and of human reason and empirical experience. *Cosmic* or *epistemic anthropocentrism* refers to dependency on a human location in the cosmos, or on human scale, preferences, or values. *Pernicious anthropocentrism* indicates a prejudicial, egotistical perspective, which falsely prioritizes humans, or reads onto the universe or other creatures a false human character. In what might be regarded as a modern scientific incarnation of the medieval view, the anthropocentric hypothesis asks whether a privileged position for humanity in the cosmos is justified by scientific research.

Types of Anthropocentrism That Will Not Be Defended

A spectrum of meaning is evident in these uses of the term *anthropocentrism*, ranging from a positive or justifiable focus on humanity, to a negative judgment regarding human arrogance. Most of these variations are not particularly contentious, and will not be defended in this thesis; these include the neutral, purely descriptive, and pejorative variations. Hence the philosophical concentration on the human person as subject, and the technical scientific use referring to whatever has to do with humans or human culture, are not of interest. The descriptive sense in pragmatic ethics of a course of action that is most favorable to humanity is not relevant. Radical anthropocentrism, with its belief in the ultimate superiority of human reason and experience, and pernicious anthropocentrism, with its self-centered perspective, will not be defended. Indeed, an awareness of the dangers of these types of egocentrism should help correct whatever form of anthropocentrism one may care to support.

The concept of cosmic (or epistemic) anthropocentrism will not be defended. As it stands for a conception of human knowledge and understanding that seems inevitable for human beings, it might be said that this acknowledges the limits of objectivity. There is a school of thought, represented by such works as Seeds' *Think Like a Mountain*, that seeks to make the world part of a non- or anti-anthropocentric dialogue, particularly in ecological discourse. But as Lori Gruen observes, "While it may be useful in certain instances to speak metaphorically of the subjectivity of nature, the literal suggestion to 'think like a mountain' only serves to obfuscate and confuse."[36] No matter how hard we may try to put ourselves in the shoes of whatever other entity or reference frame we choose, it will still be us doing the trying, with all our limitations. "To know the world from another species point of view is beyond us, although sympathetic imagination may help to bridge that gap. Human language and experience are the sources of both our opportunities and our limitations, our possibilities and our constraints."[37] Cosmic or epistemic anthropocentrism gives label to this limitation, and no effort will be made here, even if it were possible, to overturn it. At the same time, this calls for wariness of the type of anthropocentrism characterized by the geocentric observation error: faulty perception based on a limited perspective.

A note on the *anthropic principle*: the focus of the thesis is not simply on observerhood, as most versions of the anthropic principle seem to imply. Rather it is upon humanity—*Homo sapiens*, mankind. On the other hand, the anthropic principle may have much to contribute to some form of legitimate anthropocentrism. As Barrow and Tipler elaborate, "Although we do not regard our position in the Universe to be central or special in every way [viz. the Copernican Principle], this does not mean that it cannot be special in *any* way."[38] John Polkinghorne emphasizes the point when he says, "the anthropic principle represents a kind of anti-Copernican revolution in our cosmological thinking. We do not live at the center of the universe, but neither do we live in just 'any old world.' Instead, we live in a universe whose constitution is precisely adjusted to the narrow limits that alone would make it capable of being our home."[39] This principle will be examined in more detail in relation to human significance in the course of the thesis.

---

36. Gruen, "Revaluing Nature," 368–69.
37. Page, *God and the Web of Creation*, 111.
38. Barrow and Tipler, *Anthropic Cosmological Principle*, 1.
39. Polkinghorne, *Serious Talk*, 39–40.

Critical Anthropocentrism Defined

We are now in a position to define *critical anthropocentrism*. It includes aspects of the medieval synthesis combined with the modern idea of the *anthropocentric hypothesis*. It is explicitly theological, though sensitive to contemporary scientific issues. The thesis is that human beings do in fact occupy a significant position in the cosmos. They are cosmically significant because in them, certain eternal purposes and values are uniquely realized in creation. This is not accidental, but is part of the divine plan in creating the world. If human existence is not *the* goal of the universe, something like it may at least be regarded as *a* goal of the universe. While acknowledging that the support that made anthropocentrism reasonable in the medieval synthesis is now absent, *critical anthropocentrism* postulates that a related but contemporary version of that synthesis may still be justified.

Why retain "anthropocentrism" as part of the definition at all? Why not "human-centered" or some other formulation? "Human-centered" is included in the intended meaning of *critical anthropocentrism*, with some qualifications to be developed later. However, the term "anthropocentrism" is chosen because it is commonly used in the scientific and ecological literature to talk about the supposedly outmoded view, as in Sagan's theory of the "anthropocentric hypothesis." The phrase has historical depth. Though criticized, reformed, and cleaned up, what is nonetheless being offered is a position that has an ancient heritage, going back at least to the ancient Greeks. In Protagoras' dictum "man is the measure of all things," we have an early expression of the concept, which has continued in use and understanding through much of Western history, granted the errors and arrogances of the position that must be addressed. "Anthropocentrism" is retained in deference to this lineage.

However, this conception will not be a reworking of Greek philosophy. Rather, the essential milieu for establishing the contemporary truthfulness of an *anthropocentric* universe will be modern Christian theology in dialogue with modern science. This thesis will seek to show that humans are significant on a cosmic scale in both contemporary disciplines. On the other hand, Judeo-Christian theology must be uncomfortable with any conception of humanity that puts it at the center of the universe without qualifications. Only in light of and subordinate to God does humanity find any place at all. So Jürgen Moltmann suggests giving theology and ethics a theocentric focus as a solution to the problems of anthropocentrism.⁴⁰ From a theological perspective, this concept of theocentric dependence will be acknowledged as valid and helpfully corrective.

This brings us to the use of the modifying term *critical*. Several sensitivities are intended by the use of this word. First, as just mentioned, it acknowledges the centrality of God to any adequate theological approach to human being. Second, the physical or scientific naivety of the pre-Copernican vision will be avoided. While there are scientific and hence "physical" considerations that play a role, they may not be amenable to simplistic interpretations. Third, the *critical* approach acknowledges that in the past, theology has sometimes been guilty of an *uncritical* anthropocentrism. This is evident in post-Augustinian thought that tends to under-emphasize nature and dichotomize it from humans. It is found in Thomas Aquinas' extreme elevation of human rationality and relative denigration of the animals, which are "naturally enslaved and accommodated" to our use.⁴¹ It is evident in the radical anthropocentrism of post-Enlightenment theology, which accepted with Scholasticism and Descartes "the idea that the *imago Dei* consists in the *reason* of man."⁴² It is present, according to Gibellini and Ruth Page, even in the modern tendency to prioritize humans ahead of the rest of creation,⁴³ which brings us to a fourth sensitivity: the excesses and errors that have become especially clear in recent decades in the human relationship to the environment. A careless attitude toward the environment may lead to frightening developments that are beyond our control, possibly dangerous, or even lethal to humanity. Douglas John Hall notes the theological ambiguity that Christianity historically has tended to have towards the world, the question of who governs the world (God or humans), and about what aspects of human nature constitute the image of God and place them "above Nature."⁴⁴

Sensitivity to ecological issues is coupled with the need to avoid what has often been a barely disguised androcentrism, manifest in the

---

40. Moltmann, *God in Creation*, 31.

41. Thomas Aquinas *Summa Theologica* III.2b.64.1 ad. 2; Linzey, *Animal Theology*, 23–25.

42. Zizioulas, "Preserving God's Creation (1)," 3–4.

43. Gibellini, "Theological Debate on Ecology," 126–28; Page, "Theology and the Ecological Crisis," 109–10.

44. Hall, *Imaging God*, 16, 25–58.

systematic underprivileging and oppression of women in a majority of cultures throughout the world. As Michael Welker puts it, "ecological concerns and feminist consciousness have brought to an end the naïve or self-satisfied assumption of the preeminent position of 'man.'"[45] The thesis will attempt to engage with these objections, and seek to incorporate appropriate sensitivities, criticisms, and nuances into any justified form of anthropocentrism.

The project will attempt to show that theology can regard the cosmos as *critically anthropocentric* because humans play a vital role in the cosmos, forming a key part of God's plans for the universe. Consider a metaphor: the lead role in a play *is* the center of physical attention on the stage, wherever he or she happens to be. Now, whether humanity really has the lead role, is a co-star, plays a supporting role, or just has a bit part is something that bears closer scrutiny. Uncovering this role will engage the heart of the theological research. A vital role for humans, if it is found, does not exclude the possibility of other divine plans and goals for the cosmos. Consider another metaphor: the importance parents place on their children. Do parents only join together to have children? Can the family be said to exist solely for the sake of the children? Are they its goal? Children clearly are an important part of family life. But other important functions and goals could be elucidated. Similarly, evaluating humanity's cosmic priority may be difficult or impossible. It will be enough to discover that humanity plays *a* vital role in God's plans for the universe, without insisting that they have the *only* role, in order to justify *critical anthropocentrism*.

Epistemological Foundations

The epistemological model of this thesis might be called *postfoundational*,[46] in that it accepts the philosophical critique of foundationalism, without resorting to postmodern relativism, which remains rooted in the foundationalist rejection of the transcendent realm (see chapter 4).[47] My epistemology can be outlined in terms of the four couplets of F. LeRon Shults' postfoundationalist model: (A) experience and belief—belief

---

45. Welker, *Creation and Reality*, 60.
46. Van Huyssteen, *Essays*; Shults, *Postfoundationalist Task*.
47. Without a transcendent or "absolute" source of truth, relativism seems inevitable. See Graham, "Playing God."

informs experience, and interpreted experience informs belief; (B) truth and knowledge—there must be an objective unified truth in reality to make the search for knowledge intelligible, but our knowledge is fallible and subjective; (C) individual and community—rationalities are defined by communities that use them, and are used by "socially situated individuals"; and (D) explanation and understanding—explanation aims for cross-disciplinary universal understanding, while understanding is dependent upon the particular context of explanations.[48]

(A) Since foundational assumptions in human knowledge are by their nature not provable, the epistemological model of this thesis accepts the "fiduciary rootedness" of all explanations and understanding.[49] In this sense, the thesis accepts that belief is a precondition to understanding. I take as my absolute starting points the assumption of God and faith in God revealed in Jesus Christ, as witnessed in Scripture—what Nicholas Lash describes as "a standpoint shaped by recognition of God's uttered Word and outpoured Spirit."[50] Miracles are therefore regarded as possible, and the authority of Scripture as the written Word of God and normative boundary of Christian theology is accepted. Final faith is not placed in human reason apart from God; rather, faith is regarded as a gift of God.[51] Such faith is not simply categorical and epistemological, but first and foremost relational and personal, initiated by God himself.[52] It is therefore "basic" and foundational.[53] It informs experience, and allows it to be interpreted, while itself growing through experience.

(B) The model accepts that there is an objective reality outside of human mental construction, but that this reality is only accessible

---

48. Shults, *Postfoundationalist Task of Theology*, 43, 38–76.

49. Van Huyssteen, *Essays*, 44; Shults, *Postfoundationalist Task*, 38–43, 81.

50. Lash, *Beginning and End of "Religion"*, 170.

51. See Ratzinger (Pope Benedict XVI), *In the Beginning*, 24, where he says that the creation account in Genesis "put human reason firmly on the primordial basis of God's creating Reason, in order to establish it in truth and in love, without which an [independent human] 'enlightenment' would be exorbitant and ultimately foolish." See also Del Colle, "'Person' and 'Being' in Zizioulas," 82. Del Colle presumes "the doctrine of creation, lest it be misunderstood that I venture these suggestions on the basis of reason alone.... the thinking together of being and person, or, even 'person as the most perfect instance of being' (paraphrasing Aquinas, ST 1a.29.3), presupposes the reception and participation in being which the 'creature' possesses."

52. Eph 2:8.

53. Plantinga, "Reason and Belief in God," 6–93.

to humans via their own subjective knowledge apparatus, colored as they are by cultural limitations and parochial worldview assumptions. Acknowledging that science is gradually uncovering more and more of the truth about material reality, it also supposes that science is unable to access those features of reality that are beyond its methodological and cultural perceptual limits, since it is *a priori* seeking to describe reality within those limits.[54] Thus, science does not engage with certain facets of reality that are visible to theology, nor is it able to disprove basic theological presuppositions, such as the possibility of miracles, the truthfulness of Jesus Christ as God's revelation, or the scriptural witness to God's acts in history (see chapter 4). Since human knowledge is imperfect and fallible, a form of *critical realism* is also appropriate in theology—we see "through a glass, darkly." While some theological truths are foundational, and form part of the accepted faith structure of reason,[55] critical realism implies that, in general, theological truth is subject to investigation, critical analysis, possible refutation, as well as possible confirmation. Therefore, with J. Wentzel Van Huyssteen, John Polkinghorne, and others I agree that a critical realist approach is to be preferred in both science and theology.[56]

(C & D) It will already be clear from my faith presuppositions that the epistemology of this thesis stands in a certain community stream within contemporary Christian theology. At the same time, this stream is not isolated. Because of the unity of truth, it must be able to engage in reasonable interdisciplinary dialogue. For this reason, an apologetic approach to dialogue with the natural sciences will be undertaken. Though neither discipline is expected to prove conclusions in the other discipline, coherence between the theological and the scientific views will be sought, with the aim of a cross-disciplinary universal integration of understanding. It is acknowledged that theological and scientific criteria for explanation are not the same. Further, theological explanation is about more than simply understanding and meaning. With Van Huyssteen, the model accepts that "both the scope and content of

---

54. I agree with Karl Rahner that theology transcends science because it can already show the limitations of scientific methodology in the human orientation towards the transcendent/infinite. Rahner, *Theological Investigations*, 21:42.

55. In contrast to the faith structure of naturalism or atheism. See Plantinga, "Reason and Belief in God," 73–91.

56. Van Huyssteen, *Essays*, 41–44; Polkinghorne, *Science and Theology*, 16–17.

theological explanations may set them apart from explanations in other areas" (see chapter 4).[57] It may have things to say about objective reality that move between explanation and understanding. The dialogue will, for these reasons, attempt to go beyond mere coherence to some level of integration.

This summarizes the epistemological approach of this thesis. I take my starting point as faith in God in Jesus Christ, and believe this faith is coherent with the unity of all truth. A critical realist approach to reality will be used in both theology and science, admitting the need for ongoing and continual correction and refinement of beliefs and knowledge in both domains. Coherence between and within the two domains will be sought as the data from each are evaluated for evidence of human significance.

The Theological Perspective—Criteria, Problems, Representatives

Many Christian doctrines might provide evidence for human significance. Here, two key doctrines will be examined for this evidence: (1) the *imago Dei*—the doctrine that God has created human beings in his own image and likeness; and (2) the incarnation—the doctrine that God has taken on human form, and fully become one of us in the human being Jesus of Nazareth. These two closely related doctrines will be examined together for evidence of human significance in theological perspective. The doctrine of the *imago Dei* is chosen because, as Hall notes, it is the shorthand encapsulation of all Christianity believes about what is "*essential* as distinct from *existential*" to humanity: humanity is meant to image God.[58] The doctrine of the incarnation is chosen because it is the shorthand expression in Christianity for the meaning of the life of Jesus Christ to humanity: *God has become one of us*, with all that implies. This project will attempt to deduce a renewed or *critical anthropocentrism* from the contemporary ecumenical interpretation of these two doctrines. It will not be suggested in any way that human significance transcends God's own significance. The former can only be derived from the latter. Therefore, a theocentric universe is assumed from the beginning, with humanity located within that context.

57. Van Huyssteen, *Essays*, 4–5, 231–32; Shults, *Postfoundationalist Task*, 68–72.
58. Hall, *Imaging God*, 61.

The two doctrines will provide the focus for examining the work of three theologians representing different traditions, in order to obtain an ecumenical perspective: Lutheran Wolfhart Pannenberg, Roman Catholic Karl Rahner, and Eastern Orthodox John Zizioulas. These theologians have been chosen for investigation because each wrestles with the subject of human nature from a Trinitarian and incarnational perspective, and each is sensitive to related issues in contemporary thought and in the natural sciences. The investigation is not intended to be a thorough survey or critique of their thought, but rather an appraisal of its anthropocentric character. To that end, the accompanying critical analysis will focus on problems related to the question of human significance and the validity of their anthropocentric conclusions. It is hoped by this to show that ecumenical Christianity, at least as represented by these three leading modern thinkers, remains very much *critically anthropocentric.*

There are several theological problems that might possibly threaten the thesis. To many theologians, the Sabbath rest of Genesis 1 appears to be the crown of creation, not the creation of humanity. Some believe the image of God is to be found elsewhere than in the totality of human nature, perhaps in the human mind or in nature, as they image rationality or creativity. Is the image of God separable in creation from human nature? Others suppose that humans cannot be alone in the universe—that there must be many other sentient species with rational consciousness. Would these creatures also be an image of God, in need of their own incarnation for salvation? Is the revelation of God in Christ just about our local human needs, or does it have larger scope? Many believe there can be no conceivable connection between the origin and fate of the universe and human existence. Does theology really make a sound connection between these two? Some believe human beings are an artifact of nature, a product of purely natural processes, however complexly and non-reductively understood. Does this picture measure up to a theological portrait of the transcendent human spirit? Is that portrait just fluff on top of what we know to be true from science? Some see human dominion of nature as an ecological problem motivated by bad theology. Is this a fair assessment? These issues will be examined primarily in part 1 of the thesis, though part 2 may give them some consideration.

The Scientific Perspective—Foundations, Issues, Problems

Part 2 will consider human significance from the perspective of the natural sciences. The fields of science to be considered include cosmology, comparative and evolutionary biology, the cognitive sciences, and some related fields, but not the social sciences. The discussion will be introduced with an examination of the boundary of science with theology, where the use of science's methodological naturalism impinges on the question of theological rationality. This section will attempt to establish some boundaries for dialogue between the two disciplines (chapter 4). Then human uniqueness will be assessed in relation to the non-human creation, with particular reference to animal and (extinct) hominid intelligence, artificial intelligence, and extra-terrestrial intelligence (chapter 5). The anthropic principle and the processes of cosmic evolution will be examined to determine if these could be coherent with the theological dogma of God's providence leading to human existence (chapter 6). Finally, some arguments purporting to show that ecological concerns require us to de-anthropocentrize our theology will be examined (chapter 7). It will be suggested that *critical anthropocentrism* is coherent with contemporary science's position on human significance, and is sensitive to ecological concerns.

There are several scientific problems that might conceivably threaten such a conclusion. Some suppose that modern humans can no longer believe in foundational features of theology like incarnation and resurrection in any realist sense. Is this modern reductionistic naturalism the ultimate rationality it claims to be? Is human significance purely metaphoric or symbolic? Some insist that humans are only different in degree from animals, and that natural science has eliminated the absolute barrier separating humans from the non-human creation. Has humanity lost its unique cosmic status in any substantive sense? The natural sciences are supposed to show that humans are nowhere near the center of the universe, either physically or metaphorically. Is this the real import of contemporary science? Science suggests to some that humans are just a cosmic accident, a fluke of nature occurring in a remote and unimportant corner of the universe. Is human *being* a cosmic triviality, a universal inevitability, or some third option? Can science be interpreted in any way as supporting the idea that God's providence has led to human existence? Finally, do contemporary ecological concerns require us to abandon any anthropocentric conclusions?

Throughout, the investigation will engage with the position of key writers in the science-theology dialogue, such as John Polkinghorne, Ian Barbour, Arthur Peacocke, and others. While the limitations of space prohibit their perspective being given the same depth of analysis as the ecumenical theologians, an effort will be made to give them representative voice. The project intends to show that, despite the objections of former generations, contemporary science is coherent with the theological conclusion of *critical anthropocentrism*.

Summary

This thesis proposes that human beings are of vital significance in the cosmos, and that this significance is visible to both theology and science, though in respectively different ways. If this is true, there should be some measure of coherence between the theological and scientific views, despite stereotypes to the contrary. The scope and nature of human significance will be unpacked in what follows, suggesting that contemporary theology may reasonably hold a position of *critical anthropocentrism*, and that though this is not necessarily *required* by a scientific viewpoint, it is coherent with one. There should be noticeable consequences for theology and other disciplines from such a positive appraisal of human cosmic significance.

PART ONE

Human Significance in Theology

1

Wolfhart Pannenberg

The Human Divine Representative

> It is when we look at Jesus Christ that we know decisively that God's deity does not exclude, but includes His humanity . . . [In Jesus Christ] the fact is once for all established that God does not exist without man.
>
> —Karl Barth[1]

Introduction to Pannenberg's Thought

WOLFHART PANNENBERG (1928–) IS ONE OF THE PREEMINENT GERMAN Lutheran theologians of the twentieth century. He is now retired, though continuing to write and engage with contemporary issues. A brief introduction to his thought will serve to illuminate his specific approach to the anthropological theme. After analyzing his theology for its support of the thesis of *critical anthropocentrism*, a critique of aspects that might endanger the thesis will be undertaken.

Pannenberg's basic position is that all truth is one. All components of truth, whether theological, historical, philosophical, or scientific, must ultimately be coherent with each other, or else they are rendered self-negating. These components must also correspond to reality—they must be shown to be valid in the actual world. Thus coherence and correspondence to reality are Pannenberg's tests of truth.[2] He believes the truth of all reality comes from God, and that this truth is testable. Theological truth in particular is testable using the method of historical research, rather than the scientific method of theory, experiment,

---

1. Barth, *Humanity of God*, 49–50.
2. Pannenberg, *Introduction to Systematic Theology*, 8.

and observation. Because of its testability, he believes the Christian understanding of truth can show itself to be true in the context of modern thought.[3] He insists that theology must be able to listen to and synthesize the insights gained by the secular sciences in nature, history, and life; truth from those realms must ultimately be coherent with theological truth. Christian theology must have a "sound claim to universal validity"—that is, be true for everyone, everywhere—if it is to be credible at all.[4] In keeping with such universal claims, Pannenberg maintains that the idea of God, if true, must provide the "unity of all reality."[5] Human truth claims are provisional, and subject to revision short of their ultimate confirmation at the end of time, so that an open and critical approach is essential.

According to Pannenberg, history is the main medium of God's revelation to humanity. The truths of Christian faith are in the historical events of God's interaction with the world, particularly in Israel, and focused and consummated in the life, death, and resurrection of Jesus Christ, the final revelation of God, and the center of Pannenberg's theology. He contends that the history of Jesus has to be real history, "not in its details, but in its core," if Christian faith is to be regarded as valid.[6] The core event of that history is the resurrection, which verifies him as God's final revelation.[7] It is Christianity's central truth. It is so important that it even establishes for humanity the reality of God the Father:

> [It is as] constitutive for the Godhead of the Father, as it is for the divine Sonship of Jesus. Without Jesus being raised from the dead, the one whom Jesus announced as his father would not be God.[8]

Only in light of Jesus' actual resurrection are his divinity verified and the christological doctrines of the incarnation and God's fulfilled revelation in him disclosed and made credible.[9]

---

3. Buller, *Unity of Nature and History*, 48.
4. Pannenberg, *Anthropology in Theological Perspective*, 15, 18.
5. Grenz, *Reason for Hope*, 8.
6. Pannenberg, *Introduction to Systematic Theology*, 5.
7. Pannenberg, *Systematic Theology*, 1:213.
8. Pannenberg, "Der Gott der Geschichte," 87. My translation.
9. Galloway, *Wolfhart Pannenberg*, 71, 77–78.

Since history is the domain of God's self-revelation to humanity, Pannenberg proposes that the events of history recorded in Scripture cannot be regarded simply as stories about spiritual or moral truths whose facticity is secondary. They must be seen as intending to capture the real historical events of God's actions to and for the cosmos, the world, and humanity in the creation, the history of Israel, and especially the history of Jesus of Nazareth.[10] The remembrance of these may have been passed on in a flawed manner, subject to historical and critical investigation, but the record nevertheless points to real history. Pannenberg maintains that divine revelation is historically testable, in sharp contrast to "fideistic" theologians such as Barth, Brunner, or Bultmann. In the previous generation, these had posited a kind of salvation history that is accessible only through faith, either separate from or unrelated to the secular history accessible to all.[11] Pannenberg insists that revelation history is real history, universally accessible and testable using the critical methods of the historian. Hence, historical-critical study of Scripture is vital to discovering the real events of revelation that took place in the human history they record or attempt to remember; those human events *were* the revelation.[12]

The resurrection is verified by "the historical evidence yielded by a rigorously critical use of the documents," and could only be dismissed by someone who has decided on *a priori* grounds that a resurrection is

---

10. Pannenberg, *Jesus*, 99.

11. Galloway, *Wolfhart Pannenberg*, 43–44; Buller, *Unity of Nature and History*, 47; Pannenberg, "Response to My American Friends," 316.

12. Pannenberg modifies the historical-critical method to allow supernatural events. He inverts its "principle of analogy," which defines the boundary of past experience by analogy with present experience and excludes miraculous events *a priori*. Pannenberg insists that since present experience often contains unique and particular events, by analogy, the historical study of the past must be open to the presence of the unique and particular in any part of human history. To hold otherwise conflicts "with the nonexchangeable individuality and contingency of individual events." Nature need not be violated during the occurrence of miracles, because contrary to the Enlightenment belief in a closed, mechanistic cosmos, nature in contemporary understanding is elastic, open, and contingent. Miracles can happen as unusual cases within the bounds of as-yet-unknown and provisional natural laws. The historian, not the scientist, must determine the truth of historical events. The historicity of the resurrection is thus intelligible in the contemporary context. Craig, *Reasonable Faith*, 168; Holwerda, "Faith, Reason, and the Resurrection," 283–84; Pannenberg, *Basic Questions*, 1:42–47; *Jesus*, 98; "Resurrection," 259; "Concept of Miracle," 762.

inherently impossible.[13] This event has validity in both the real world of facts—the supposedly hard "what" of the scientist—and what has sometimes been characterized as the "subjective" world of faith. It destroys the separating prejudice that has mistakenly isolated the theologian in the soft realm of values, beliefs, and interpretation, and provides the objective grounds for Christian faith. In support of his position, Pannenberg sites what he believes are the evidences and proofs for the resurrection that stand up to rigorous historical-critical scrutiny. The witnesses of the event, recorded by the Gospels and listed by Paul in 1 Corinthians 15:3–8, provide the weightiest testimony. The empty tomb is another evidence, although less weighty than the eyewitnesses. The post-resurrection appearances of the risen Lord and the change in the disciple's character from a depressed state following the crucifixion to a confident and joyful state after seeing the risen Lord, are otherwise inexplicable. Since it is difficult to categorize the resurrection using ordinary language because it belongs to the new creation, Pannenberg describes it with metaphorical or spiritual language. He does not mean by this that the event is untrue, ghostly, or simply a matter of faith. Neither vision, nor physical body, nor any other this-worldly description is adequate to capture its meaning, because words are insufficient to describe this cosmically crucial yet next-worldly event.[14]

Pannenberg maintains that fact and interpretation are inseparable, and believes the proper interpretation of historical events is objectively available to all, given sufficient information and research into events. The resurrection's occurrence within the apocalyptic milieu of intertestamental Judaism thus forms part of its interpretation. With the resurrection, the special character of God's revelation in Israel and finally in Jesus is revealed and verified. It is contained in the historical events themselves, "not in the attitude or inspiration with which one confronts them."[15] Revelation *as* history is therefore a key motif for Pannenberg. Jesus of Nazareth is revealed by the resurrection as the incarnate Word of God active in history, the ultimate historical revelation of God. The resurrection is an actual event in history, subject to investigation like

---

13. Galloway, *Wolfhart Pannenberg*, 75–76. He insists we must reject the assumption that "the dead do not rise."

14. Pannenberg, *Jesus*, 75. For some objections to Pannenberg's proof of the resurrection, see Grenz, "Appraisal of Pannenberg," 22–23.

15. Galloway, *Wolfhart Pannenberg*, 48, 52.

any other historical event. There are enough witnesses and evidences to support its facticity that, though doubt is possible, Pannenberg believes we are rationally justified in accepting its truthfulness, and therefore also justified in putting our faith in the risen Lord Jesus. This is the heart of his theology.[16] He desires to reintroduce critical rationalism into theological thinking, to replace what he perceives as the irrational subjectivity of faith divorced from facts, with reason, critical inquiry, and historical investigation. This corrects the modern privatization and marginalization of Christian theology that comes from the fideist dichotomy between fact and faith.[17]

Pannenberg believes that all events in Jesus' life should in principle be open to the same historical and critical investigation given to other non-religious historical events. Lesser events such as the virgin birth are regarded as peripheral and dispensable non-core details, secondary because everything is secondary in light of the resurrection.[18] He is not convinced the evidence requires us to accept the facticity of these secondary events, nor that they are crucial for verifying the truth of Christ as God's revelation in the same way that is true of the resurrection. He views the Scriptures as participatory in witness of God's historical acts, while subjecting them in their entirety to historical-critical research. For instance, he believes the Genesis creation account is in mythological and archaic language with some now-outdated scientific features,[19] while acknowledging the truthfulness—particularly the historical truthfulness—of the core theological ideas. Those core truths are that God is "the normative and abiding basis of creaturely reality"—he is responsible for the creation of the world, humanity is made in God's image, and humanity is estranged from God.[20] Pannenberg is willing

---

16. Pannenberg, *Jesus*, 88–106. This section details the historical proof referred to here.

17. Pannenberg, "Response to My American Friends," 316.

18. Pannenberg, *Systematic Theology*, 2:318–19.

19. Ibid., 116–17. For example, Pannenberg regards some features in the account as scientifically obsolete: the creation of fixed creature types, the separation of waters from the firmament, or the stars' origin on the forth day. These were consistent at the time of their writing with the theological milieu of ancient cosmology to which they were addressed, but are now obsolete (e.g., the creation of stars on day four was aimed at countering the obsolete Babylonian tendency to divinize the stars, by placing their creation nearer the beginning).

20. Ibid., 34.

to accept evolutionary processes as the scientific explanation for life,[21] even for human life, while affirming the theological truth that God is the creator and sustainer of the cosmos.[22] Evolutionary causation does not ultimately guide the cosmos to its fulfillment, but rather the eschatological rule of God. This rule of God guides all history from and to its end.[23]

Truth in general and theological truth in particular has this eschatological character: history will only be completely understandable at its fulfillment and end. God's revelatory truths in the life of Jesus Christ are to be confirmed at his return, though his resurrection is a downpayment on that confirmation. The end of history guarantees its final verification. Thus Pannenberg holds that the anticipatory expectation of the end of history with the final judgment, when all the dead will be raised, is an essential part of Christianity. Likewise, the historicity of the resurrection and its promise for redeemed humanity are of central importance. Apart from this promise, the event of Jesus as God's ultimate revelation remains incomprehensible.[24] Pannenberg supposes that this eschatological understanding in Christianity's truth claims demonstrates a realization of the disputability of religious truth claims in general, and acknowledges the need for proof of those claims, which requires the attempt to verify them in the actual world.[25] Because the medium of this verification is history, its final seal of authenticity will come at the end of history. Truth is contingent upon history, open-

---

21. Pannenberg appears to follow Augustine on God's Sabbath rest, supposing it means an end to the creation of new creature types rather than a cessation from labor (see *Systematic Theology*, 2:36). Why he bothers to deal with the Sabbath as a "protoscientific" description is unclear, since he rejects the story's claim to be real history. See also his *Anthropology*, 57.

22. The Genesis creation accounts need not be in complete enmity with evolutionary theory. Welker points to the fecundity of the created order called forth by the word of God: the land and sea produce living creatures at God's command (Gen 1:11–12, 20–21, 24). Genesis does not say *how* the land or sea produces them, but rather that God's command makes the creation fruitful and creative in its own right. Nahum Sarna also draws attention to creation's generative power, which is not inherent or divine, but is given at God's command. There is room for scientific speculation about the how. Welker, *Creation and Reality*, 9–11, 40–44; Sarna, *Genesis*, 9–10. See Pannenberg, *Systematic Theology*, 2:121 n. 314, 315, for further attempts to synthesize creation and evolutionary theory.

23. Pannenberg, *Metaphysics*, 105–9.

24. Pannenberg, *Jesus*, 82–83.

25. Grenz, *Reason for Hope*, 27.

ended in the sense that the final meaning of reality is contestable and provisional until the end of history.[26] Thus Pannenberg argues for the "ontological priority of the future" in disclosing the fullness of truth.[27] Truth encompasses facts and meaning, explanation and evaluation, the what and the why of understanding.

Throughout much of his career, Pannenberg has been concerned to bring theology and science into constructive dialogue with each other, based on his belief in the unity of truth. He rejects the dualism that exists between nature and history in modern thought, as evidenced in the problematic discussion between the natural sciences and the historical sciences: he believes the Christian conception of creation decisively unifies them.[28] He rejects the Greek notion that truth is something to be discovered behind and transcending the events of history in unchanging essences and constants. All truth is essentially historical in its character. Even the truths of nature have about them a contingency that binds them to history (see page 56). While he does not believe scientific data must prove the existence of God, or believe God's activity will necessarily be evident scientifically, he is willing to admit God's acts may be open to scientific confirmation.

Since God is only indirectly detected in history,[29] theological and scientific statements are essentially made on "different methodological levels."[30] He is "dubious about turning to scientific data, instead of religious experience, tradition, and scripture, for primary theological evidence for God."[31] His larger agenda is to show that scientific and theological truths are coherent with each other: "there need be no rivalry between scientific and theological statements."[32] He wants to show that Christian theology has a significant contribution to make to a holistic understanding of reality, even for the modern scientist. That contribution is real knowledge, though perhaps of a philosophical or

---

26. Ibid. 14.

27. Buller, *Unity of Nature and History*, 66.

28. Ibid., 48. When the laws of nature are given ultimate truth status, their intelligibility is unexplained. The Christian concept of creation provides them a rational metaphysical foundation. See chapter 6.

29. Grenz, "Appraisal of Pannenberg," 21.

30. Pannenberg, *Systematic Theology*, 2:70, 106.

31. Pannenberg, "Anthropic Principle."

32. Pannenberg, *Systematic Theology*, 2:70, 106.

metaphysical rather than physical kind.[33] A universal understanding requires theology, and cannot be achieved solely with the natural sciences.[34] Later in this chapter we will take a closer look at his engagement with science as it bears on the anthropocentric focus, in such issues as the anthropic principle, the possibility of extra-terrestrials, and the significance of human rationality.

To summarize, Pannenberg maintains that revelation is God's action in history. Truth is fundamentally historical in character, and is now provisional and contestable. All its dimensions, whether theological, scientific, philosophical, or otherwise, must ultimately be coherent with each other, for truth is a unified entity. Truth can only be understood in its entirety, and its provisional and contestable nature disappeared into certainty, at the end of the historical process. The man Jesus of Nazareth is the ultimate manifestation of God's historical action and therefore the ultimate word of God. His truth claims, including his authority and divinity as incarnate Son, are verified by his resurrection. That event verifies not only Christ's own history and person, but also "every event of history."[35] This is because Christ's resurrection is the breaking in now of the end of history, from whence history's meaning is finally and completely verified. The confirmation of incontestable truth at the end of history is the eschaton, when the kingdoms of the world become God's kingdom, and the specific resurrection of Christ becomes the general resurrection of all.

Pannenberg's theory of theological truth may thus be described as christocentric, critically historical, eschatological, and requiring coherence with other branches of human truth. This introduction to his thought has been necessarily brief and preliminary. However, it should give sufficient background for understanding aspects of his theology relevant to this thesis.

Incarnational Anthropocentrism

Is it reasonable to suppose that humans are the goal of creation, the final aim of all God has done in creating the cosmos? Pannenberg believes

---

33. Polkinghorne, "Fields and Theology"; Pannenberg, "Response to John Polkinghorne"; Hefner, "Role of Science in Pannenberg," 273.

34. Hefner, "Role of Science," 274, 283–84.

35. Galloway, *Wolfhart Pannenberg*, 83.

both the Old Testament creation stories and the incarnation imply this. The incarnation reveals that humanity can be called the goal of creation only because in it, "or more precisely in Jesus of Nazareth," the fellowship of the Creator with his creatures is fully realized, as the Son of God becomes a human being. From this perspective, the history of the entire cosmos is "a prehistory to the coming of humanity."[36]

Pannenberg speaks extensively on humanity's place in the universe in his *Anthropology in Theological Perspective* and in the *Systematic Theology* (vol. 2). His position is rooted in his reflections on the incarnation:

> The growing anthropocentrism that has marked the development of Christian theology has [had a] genuinely theological cause: the fact that Christian theology is a response to the human questions of salvation. The foundation for a concentration on the human person was already laid in the early Christian faith in the incarnation of God.[37]

He does not suppose that salvation is just about humanity. But humanity does occupy a primary role in the salvation of the cosmos. He addresses the question of whether humanity could be the goal of the creation directly, wrestling with both theological and scientific issues related to the subject. The incarnation is the strongest theological evidence for a human-centered creation. The goal of creation, according to Christian Theology, is the sharing of creatures in the divine Trinitarian fellowship. This is seen plainly, actualized and fulfilled in the incarnation in Jesus of Nazareth of the divine Logos. The goal of the incarnation is that all creation might be reconciled to God through the Son. This is achieved in and through humanity, though it will not be completed until the end of history.[38]

Cornelius Buller notes that for Pannenberg, just as there is a unity between the natural and theological sciences, so salvation and natural history are unified.[39] Salvation history and actual natural and human history coincide. It is not that one describes mythology (a story of symbolic rather than historical truth), and the other historical reality (such as is accessible to the secular historian). They are one and the same. A

---

36. Pannenberg, *Systematic Theology*, 2:74.
37. Pannenberg, *Anthropology*, 12.
38. Pannenberg, *Systematic Theology*, 2:73.
39. Buller, *Unity of Nature and History*, 122–23.

secularized history is therefore one-dimensional, blind to the reality of God at work in salvation history.

The Son of God is central to the entire creation in Pannenberg's unified vision of nature and history. While acknowledging that the Christian church has always credited God the Father as the Creator, he believes, also with the broad sweep of Christian tradition, that creation has always been mediated through the Son. Christoph Schwöbel sees here Pannenberg's development of Hegel's insight that the Son is the principle of otherness or difference in the Trinity, although Pannenberg rejects the logical necessity of God's action.[40] The Son's origin in and then distinction from God the Father provide the ground for all that is distinct from God, including the origin and existence of all creaturely reality. Further, the Son's relation to the Father is the model for the intention of all creaturely being for fellowship with God. In the human incarnation, Jesus' recognition of the Father as God in distinction from himself gives validity to "the independent existence of other creatures alongside himself."[41] When the Son surrenders his participation in the non-incarnate unity shared within the Trinity, and takes on creaturely form in the man Jesus, in whom his self-distinction from the deity of the Father takes concrete form, he gives validity to the otherness of creaturely existence from God himself. "The Son in his self-differentiating love for the Father *is* in *eternity* both one with the Father and the source of finite reality."[42] He is thus both the origin of the self-distinction of creation from Creator, and the link between them.

If not for the continued existence of this self-distinction of Son from Father in Jesus of Nazareth, there would be no eternal basis for the continuation of the creaturely world. "Creaturely reality would ... be no more than the emergence and extinction of a tiny light in God's eternity." Hence, the preservation of the cosmos is especially related to the Son. It maintains its continued existence only by participation in God. The incarnation brings the eternal life of God down into the otherwise finite and doomed life of the created cosmos, and allows it to share in eternity. It is through the Spirit that this life is communicated, but the Spirit comes to the world only through the Son. Since the lasting

40. Schwöbel, "Rational Theology," 508.

41. Pannenberg, *Systematic Theology*, 2:29–31.

42. Buller, *Unity of Nature and History*, 45. He is the Logos of God, the "Author of life." John 1:3–4; Acts 3:15.

self-distinction of creaturely reality from God, accompanied by fellowship with God, is finally accomplished in the incarnation of the Son in the man Jesus, the whole history of creation can be said to converge upon the incarnation. "Because the Logos who permeates the world of creation came to full manifestation in this man, all things in heaven and on earth are summed up in Him (Eph 1:10)." Thus the Logos is the "principle of unity" of the created order, and the incarnation provides the "integrating center of the world's historical order."[43]

Because of the cosmic centrality of the incarnation, creation may be said to find its fulfillment through the history of the cosmos, as it is *a history of preparation for the incarnation*. This is so from the laying of the cosmos' physical foundations, to the development of all life from simplest to most complex, to the "full manifestation of the divine likeness in humanity."[44] In this light it is impossible to see the incarnation as some kind of afterthought of God's, as if it were a reaction to Adam's sin, an "ornamental addition,"[45] or some kind of "external appendix" to the created order. Instead, it must be viewed as "*the crown*" (Pannenberg's own phrase) of God's created world order from the very beginning, the supreme concrete manifestation of "the active presence of the Logos in creation."[46] As will be apparent in chapter 3, Pannenberg is here following the Orthodox tradition. All of nature, all of the cosmos, has been engaged in a unified process, first in inorganic physical forms, then in the evolution of life, leading up to and centering upon the emergence of human history. Buller summarizes Pannenberg's position: the creation of reality is the process "of realizing the incarnation of the image of God, proleptically realized in the life and destiny of Jesus."[47] Humanity is not a separate feature independent of this unified cosmic process, but of one piece with it, so that the meaning of human history is inseparable and indeterminable apart from its place in the rest of creation.

So it may be said that creation finds its fulfillment in humanity, more precisely in the incarnation of God in the human being Jesus. The

---

43. Pannenberg, *Systematic Theology*, 2:32, 63–64.
44. Ibid. 34.
45. Peters, "Editor's Introduction," 12.
46. Pannenberg, *Systematic Theology*, 2:64.
47. Buller, *Unity of Nature and History*, 155–56.

universal process of history can only be "understood in anthropocentric terms."[48] There is no

> history of nature by itself apart from the human being; rather, it is a history of nature directed to the human being. The fact that the connection of the sequence of forms of the world process is demonstrated as a historical connection only from its end, from the human being backward, would correspond only to the manner in which historical connections as such can be constituted, that is, from the end.[49]

As new events illuminate earlier relationships and events, the arrival of humanity on the stage of cosmic history, and then the arrival and completed mission of Jesus of Nazareth on the stage of human history, reveal the unified whole history of nature directed to this human end. Colin Gunton agrees that the background scriptures of Genesis 1–3 and Romans 8 demonstrate that the natural realm has been ordered for or to the human race. "Whether or not this is 'anthropocentric' and ecologically incorrect, and whether indeed that matters, it seems to me the clear message of scripture."[50] The ontological priority of the future gives coherence and meaning to the entire past of nature's history, as it culminates in humanity, and in a certain sense comes to its end in the incarnation and the resurrection of Jesus Christ. To be sure, the eschatological end of all history has not yet come—an end that shall be fulfillment for the whole of creation, not just humanity. But that eschatological end has already been exposed for what it is in Jesus' resurrection, which is the proleptic end of history already revealed. Paul Van Buren wonders if this marginalizes history subsequent to the resurrection.[51] But rather than causing history to fade, the resurrection imparts to history as a whole its abiding significance, as the eschatological "end breaking in." Humanity is neither the unity of history, nor its sole focus: the nature and unity of history are found in God alone.[52] Yet this unity is revealed in God incarnate as the human Jesus of Nazareth.

48. Ibid. 67.
49. Pannenberg, *Toward a Theology of Nature*, 111–12.
50. Gunton, "Spirit Moved," 4.
51. Van Buren, *Discerning the Way*, 43.
52. Pannenberg, *Theology of Nature*, 112.

The *Imago Dei,* Human Uniqueness and Dominion

The *imago Dei* developed in Genesis 1:26–28 reveals, according to Pannenberg, something of humanity's cosmic significance. According to the Scripture, "Then God said, 'Let us make humankind in our image, according to our likeness; and let them have dominion over the fish of the sea, and over the birds of the air, and over the cattle, and over all the wild animals of the earth, and over every creeping thing that creeps upon the earth'" (Gen 1:26). The command is embellished further: "God blessed them, and God said to them, 'Be fruitful and multiply, and fill the earth and subdue it; and have dominion over the fish . . . the birds . . . and over every living thing that moves upon the earth'" (1:28). The psalmist echoes the idea: "You have given them [(human beings)] dominion over the works of your hands; you have put all things under their feet, all sheep and oxen, and also the beasts of the field . . ." (Psalm 8:6–7). Pannenberg claims the capacity for dominion and mastery of nature is particularly human, a unique feature of the *imago Dei*. Though now deformed and mired in sin, this capacity prepares humanity for its cosmic role.

Human Uniqueness and Mastery of Nature

Dominion is evident, according to Pannenberg, in humanity's ability to name things external to themselves. Such naming, first described in Gen 2:19–20, is part and parcel of human mastery of nature. Adam names the animals and finds in them no suitable partner for himself. Pannenberg suggests this human ordering and rational capacity is part of the *imago Dei*. There is clearly no other creature like the human: they are set apart from the rest of the created order. This locates humans in some measure on the side of God. Humans reach beyond the immediate horizon to which the other creatures are confined, and grasp the widest possible "horizon of meaning": this is "exocentric self-transcendence." They embrace all finite reality in their quest for meaning, and desire to reach beyond it towards the infinite.

> This process of defining the individuality of things has become the basis for all human mastery of nature. Precisely because human beings reach beyond the given, and therefore ultimately because human exocentricity is characterized by an impulse, inconceivable except in religious terms, to the unconditioned

do they have the ability to rule over the objects of their natural world.[53]

Human rule over nature is coherent only in a religion that sharply contrasts the divine reality with the reality of the world, not confusing God with the forces of nature. By placing humanity on the side of God, it sets them over against the world.

Exocentric self-transcendence is uniquely human. Humans are open *to* and *beyond* the world (*Weltoffenheit*), to the transcendent, the contingent, to what is novel in and beyond the world.[54] Animals seem to be aware of and respond only to their immediate environment, generally lacking the cognitive capacities to symbolically envision the future. Human beings live in a dynamic that encompasses the whole world, and are fundamentally open to the possibilities of the future; they can hope for, long for, and strive for that which is beyond experience.[55] Francisco J. Ayala notes that humanity's unique capacity for language and symbolic thinking enable this openness to the future. Without symbolic and representational reasoning, alternate potential future paths and true freedom of choice are impossible.[56] Pannenberg suggests "it is because man, in distinction from the beasts, has an open world that the question of God arises for him. The given world can never satisfy him."[57] Robert Jenson also identifies this as uniquely human, describing *Homo sapiens* as the first hominids who "were embodied" and open towards God and one another: we are "the praying animal," constituted corporately from the beginning with the "traces of the Trinity" in our capacity for "self-transcendence."[58] Van Huyssteen suggests that in light of modern oppression and abuse of persons, the concept of *imago Dei* as embodied relationality must fully incorporate the justice theme in its core to be

---

53. Pannenberg, *Anthropology*, 76–77.

54. Ibid. 69; idem., *What Is Man?*, 3–5; quoted in Galloway, *Wolfhart Pannenberg*, 14.

55. Stewart (*Reconstructing Science and Theology*, 50–69) critiques Pannenberg's development of *exocentricity* for using as foils now discredited biological theories like ethology and classic behaviourism. Something like it could be constructed using other means, as is clear in both Rahner and Zizioulas. See for example Eisenberg, "Human Nature," 123–28.

56. Ayala, "Human Nature," 41–45.

57. Pannenberg, *What Is Man?*, 10; Galloway, *Wolfhart Pannenberg*, 15.

58. Jenson, *Systematic Theology*, 2:59–65.

legitimate. With that correction, embodied, exocentric relationality can be fairly acknowledged as uniquely human.⁵⁹

Some challenge this claim to human uniqueness in the animal kingdom. This theme will be addressed systematically in chapter 5, but for now, it is sufficient to note that Pannenberg, writing during the upswing of hope in primate cognitive research prior to the 1990s, had already identified the uniqueness of human linguistic capacity at which that primate research has reluctantly arrived.⁶⁰ Humans are uniquely capable of responding to and fulfilling a call to exercise dominion. Linguistic capacity seems to be a foundationally unique feature of the *imago Dei*, supporting a suite of features that together comprise the totality of human uniqueness. This symbolic reasoning capacity is, according to Ayala, at the heart of humanity's unique capacity for moral choice and responsibility.⁶¹ This moral capacity figures prominently in the New Testament presentation of the *imago Dei* (see page 49). Van Huyssteen concludes that the modern sense of human uniqueness must acknowledge self-consciousness, moral responsibility, and yearning or capacity for religious fulfillment.⁶² Ayala points to religious belief and ethical behavior, along with "art, science, technology, and sociopolitical institutions" as distinctly human, "epigenetic outcomes of humankind's enhanced intelligence."⁶³ Humanity's relational exocentricity contributes to its unique role on the earth, and may suggest a unique role in the cosmos.

Dominion as Stewardship

The connection between the image of God and the dominion of humanity over the earth has been challenged on ecological grounds.⁶⁴ Typical objections include the apparent excuse this offers for the human rape of nature, and the patriarchal and imperialistic tendencies it appears to legitimate in the human treatment of the non-human world.⁶⁵ Gibellini

---

59. Van Huyssteen, "Rethinking the *Imago Dei*."
60. Tattersall, *Becoming Human*, 66.
61. Ayala, "Human Nature," 43–48.
62. Van Huyssteen, "Rethinking the *Imago Dei*."
63. Ayala, "Human Nature," 48.
64. E.g., Moltmann, *God in Creation*; Welker, *Creation and Reality*, 60–73.
65. Welker, *Creation and Reality*, 60.

and Page blame the problem in part on Christian theology's inclination to desacralize the world,[66] although Hall responds by reminding us that "refusal to consider the world divine does not necessitate ignoring or rejecting its sacredness."[67] Most famously, White attempted to show that the biblical concept of dominion has been a source of the current ecological crisis by giving to humanity permission to have a domineering and enslaving grasp of nature.[68]

Jacqui Stewart accuses Pannenberg of having small regard for ecological concerns, or for the place of animals and non-human creatures in his systematic theology. She claims that "the natural world appears to have little value in itself for Pannenberg, and he does not give much significance to human relationships with it in his anthropology."[69] But while Pannenberg's writings are not substantial on the ecological theme, he has given some attention to the issues raised, and his position is clearly delineated in light of the life of Christ. Buller suggests Pannenberg's theology addresses the ecological crisis because it is aimed at countering the destructive modern dualistic splitting of nature and spirit.[70] Nature is approached with a reductionistic and abusive attitude because spirit has been isolated and abstracted from nature. Pannenberg explicitly refutes White's critique by pointing out that it is precisely in the abandonment of worship of and submission to God that the command of dominion has been perverted into tyrannical domination. "Only the emancipation of the modern West from commitment to the God of the Bible has replaced the thought that we are God's stewards in our rule over his creation by the idea that we have a right to unrestricted exploitation of nature. It is illegitimate, then, to make the biblical picture of humanity responsible for the unrestricted exploitation of the earth by humanity today."[71] Fergus Kerr similarly notices the deeply anti-Christian causes of the environmental crisis: with the decline of the Christian worldview, "nature is no longer manifestly ordered and sacred . . . we no longer regard our natural environment with reverence, we treat it as raw material

---

66. Gibellini, "Theological Debate on Ecology," 126–28; Page, "Theology and the Ecological Crisis," 109–10.

67. Hall, *Imaging God*, 48.

68. White, "Historic Roots," 25–26.

69. Stewart, *Reconstructing Science and Theology*, 20–21.

70. Buller, *Unity of Nature and History*, 150–54.

71. Pannenberg, *Systematic Theology*, 2:131–32.

for technological exploitation."⁷² It is not "dominion" in and of itself that must be seen as ecologically or morally insensitive and evil, but rather the perversion that it has undergone in fallen and rebellious humanity. As van Huyssteen notes, dominion has degraded into oppression in both the human and non-human realms.⁷³

In light of the christological character of human destiny, the human calling to dominion as part of the *imago Dei* can only be understood as it has been realized in Jesus Christ. His rule consists "in reconciling to God what had been separated from God." His ministry is specifically directed to humanity, and not the non-human world. "Nevertheless we have to think about the cosmological dimension of his rule along the same line. The realization of the image of God in Jesus Christ calls for responsible stewardship of man in the creation . . ."⁷⁴ The servant life of Jesus illuminates and typifies the true nature of dominion as he surrenders himself in the care of his creatures. Dominion means acceptance of duty and responsibility in a sphere beyond one's own self-interest, rather than "unscrupulous exploitation and oppression" in rule over another sphere, purely for selfish, self-interested reasons.⁷⁵ As given by God, human power over nature implies responsibility for the world.⁷⁶

Pannenberg calls attention to John Cobb's idea of Christian responsibility in the environment as faith that needs to "substitute a vision of a healthy biotic pyramid with man as its apex for the absoluteness of man." Cobb's vision emphasizes human continuity with the biosphere in contrast to a position of absolute autonomy and tyranny. While Pannenberg points out the need to beware of obscuring the difference between the divine and nature in such responsibility, he notes that the advantage of Cobb's perspective is that it reminds us of the actual nature of the divine commission to be master in Genesis 1–2. Human representative rule on behalf of the creator is modeled after God's creative will.⁷⁷ Hall agrees that we are neither completely above nor completely within nature; our nature and vocation demand limits to mastery yet

---

72. Kerr, *Immortal Longings*, 163.
73. Van Huyssteen, "Rethinking the *Imago Dei*."
74. Pannenberg, *Human Nature, Election, and History*, 25.
75. Pannenberg, *Anthropology*, 80.
76. Galloway, *Wolfhart Pannenberg*, 15.
77. Pannenberg, *Anthropology*, 78; refers to Cobb, *Is It Too Late?*

also indicate "special responsibility" for nature.[78] The command of dominion is not an excuse for the wholesale and wanton abuse of nature, nor have humans been given "carte blanche for the selfish pillage and exploitation" of the non-human realm. Rather, dominion is a call to the opposite: nature's care and protection, God's appointment of his image to exercise responsibility for the preservation of creation.[79]

Humanity as God's Representative in the World

This balanced understanding of dominion reveals an important characteristic of what it means to be human. Humanity is not just made in the image of God, and then given a job to do: "rule over the . . . earth." Rather, *humanity is made in the image of God, and as such it represents God in the creation.* E. Frank Tupper notes this feature in Pannenberg: human beings are to mediate the rule of God to the world.[80] Gunton agrees that humanity represents and mediates the rule of God to the rest of creation; this is their vocation in the command of dominion.[81] The Old Testament teaches, according to Pannenberg, that "within the entire creation, man represents the sovereignty of God over against the other creatures of the earth."[82] Only *as* the image of God is humanity able to represent God in the creation. This nuance is illuminated by the preposition *in* from Gen 1:26: "*in* our image, *in* our likeness." The preposition *in* (Hebrew: בְּ, or Septuagint: κατ᾽)[83] may be translated as "according to" or "corresponding to."[84] Moltmann's translation is helpful: "Let us make human beings *as* our image, *as* our very form."[85] To be in the image of God is to be his image on the earth: to represent or correspond to God, to display his glory on the earth. Moltmann's insight is worth noting. "As his image, human beings represent God on earth; as his similitude, they reflect him . . . To be an image of some-

---

78. Hall, *Imaging God*, 51, 60.
79. Pannenberg, *Anthropology*, 78.
80. Tupper, *Theology of Wolfhart Pannenberg*, 242.
81. Gunton, "The Spirit Moved," 4.
82. Pannenberg, *Human Nature*, 24.
83. WTM; LXT.
84. Newman, *Concise Greek-English Dictionary*.
85. Moltmann, *God in Creation*, 215–16. Emphasis added.

thing always means letting that something appear, and revealing it."[86] Claus Westermann concludes that "image" in Gen 1:26 means "concrete representation."[87] He insists that Genesis emphasizes the uniqueness of God in contrast to his non-divine created universe. Humanity created in God's image is *the* unique expression of the unique God. This special emphasis enables us to understand "how this history leads ultimately to God becoming human."[88] Benedict XVI proposes a similar idea: "in the human being God enters into his creation." For humanity to be *imago Dei* means that it images and represents God to the world. This is not to impute incarnational status to general humanity, but rather to suppose that in humanity, God has a fitting ambassador for himself to his creation.[89]

Pannenberg's position on dominion and representation supports this understanding.[90] Humans not only aspire to "that which infinitely transcends the world," but also are representative of it.[91] Barth suggests that humanity is the place where, in and for all the cosmos, "the thoughts of its Creator are disclosed."[92] God has culminated his creative cosmic work in a creature that will be his image and his representative in and to the cosmos. This is what it means theologically to be human.[93] Westermann insists that the image of God "does not consist in any particular detail of the person but describes the human being as a whole without limiting itself to anything taken in isolation."[94] This holistic theological approach encompasses human spirituality, relational capacity, rationality, creativity, and moral freedom and freedom of will, among other things. Cosmic significance is found in all of these put together, because humanity is the unified platform that is personhood come into being in the cosmos, the image of God's personhood reflected in and

  86. Ibid. 219.
  87. Westermann, *Genesis 1–11*, 146.
  88. Ibid. 67–68.
  89. Benedict XVI (writing as Joseph Ratzinger), *In the Beginning*, 45; for *image* as manifestation of God see 47–48.
  90. Pannenberg, *Anthropology*, 78.
  91. Galloway, *Wolfhart Pannenberg*, 16.
  92. Barth, *Church Dogmatics* III/2: 18–19.
  93. Alter suggests that because humanity is the *imago Dei*, it also "shares a measure of God's transcendence of categories, images, and defining labels" (Alter and Kermode, *Literary Guide to the Bible*, 23).
  94. Westermann, *Genesis 1–11*, 149–51.

into the universe. Human cosmic significance is entailed in its cosmic representation of God.

Human and Cosmic Destiny in Light of the Incarnation

Human cosmic status as the image of God must be qualified. The fullness of the *imago Dei* is lost, marred, or never fully realized because of the fall. God's solution is the incarnation: it not only redeems humanity but also demonstrates their cosmic importance. Jesus Christ has come as the complete image of God, the last vestiges of that image's fallenness redeemed in his resurrection. Furthermore, he comes as "the firstborn within a large family," the firstborn among many children of God (Rom 8:29). He reveals what it means to be truly human. His perfected humanity is to be communicated and shared by the humanity he has redeemed, "the new humanity."[95] Only through communion with him does humanity achieve its true destiny.[96] Humanity obtains the fullness of the image of God when it is in Christ: "Just as we have borne the image of the man of dust, we will also bear the image of the man of heaven" (1 Cor 15:49). This is not only significant for the earth; the *whole of creation* "waits with eager longing" (Rom 8:19) for the sons of God to be revealed. Christ is the *cosmic* redeemer, not merely the savior of a small planet (see page 120). His resurrection "is the forerunner both present and to come, of the fulfillment of all creation with and in God."[97]

Being created as the *imago Dei* prepares humanity for a unique and vital role in the cosmos. First, this is the creature prepared for and with the potentiality to receive the incarnation. To be human is to be the vehicle wherein God may become one with his creation. No other creature, angel, or sphere is constituted *as* the form of God within his creation. Thus humanity is of central significance for the whole of the cosmos, because only it is the image of God wherein God can decisively incarnate himself. Further, humanity *in Christ* is of highest significance, because the cosmos cannot be fulfilled except in and through redeemed humanity. Barth also links the *imago Dei* and the incarnation to an exalted human cosmic status. Nature is prepared for the future union of God and humanity in Jesus Christ by the creation of humanity in the

---

95. Pannenberg, *Systematic Theology*, 2:304.
96. Pannenberg, *Anthropology*, 495.
97. Stewart, *Reconstructing Science and Theology*, 4.

image of God. Humanity was created as a being capable of real partnership with God even in its non-deity. Human beings are "capable of action and responsibility in relation to Him; to which His own divine form of life is not alien; which in a creaturely repetition, as a copy and imitation, can be a bearer of this form of life. Man was created as this being."[98] Thus humanity is a repetition, copy, and reflection of the life of God in the created realm, God's counterpart in the cosmos. It is because humanity is so imaged and called by the grace of God that it is capable of receiving the incarnation of the Son of God, of God himself. According to Pannenberg, this is made possible because "openness to God is the real meaning of the fundamental structure of being human, which is designated as openness to the world in contemporary anthropology, although this designation means an openness beyond the momentary horizon of the world."[99] Hence the definition of humanity as *imago Dei*, verified by the incarnation, guarantees an exalted and vital cosmic role. The incarnation confirms and guarantees humanity's cosmic importance by fulfilling the cosmos' destiny.

Humanity as Creation's Representative to God

Humanity represents God in the cosmos, but it also represents the creature and the cosmos to God. Pannenberg insists that the conviction that creation culminates in humanity can only be held as a result of the biblical insight that humanity is destined to fellowship with the Author of creation. This destiny is a fellowship meant for all creatures, but only realized and mediated through humanity, which is thus distinguished from all other creatures.[100] Similarly, T. F. Torrance maintains that humanity is "the focal point in the interrelations between God and the universe."[101] Ray Anderson describes this distinction as "a spiritual orientation to and personal relation with God as Creator."[102] Humans alone have such an orientation between the creation and Creator. Just because humanity is most able to consciously acknowledge God does not mean that they are separate from the rest of the created order; they

98. Barth, *Church Dogmatics* III/1:184–85.
99. Pannenberg, *Jesus*, 193.
100. Pannenberg, *Systematic Theology*, 2:175.
101. Torrance, *Divine and Contingent Order*, 129.
102. Anderson, "On Being Human," 180.

can best represent the cosmos because they are part of the creation. Buller points out that as the representative of the rest of creation, humanity has the unique role of acknowledging both the difference from and dependence on God of creaturely existence.[103] It represents the independence of creaturely existence from God, as well as being able to bring to full expression the "creaturely recognition of God as God."

Fellowship and relationship with God are realized only in light of the incarnation. Human beings discover who they were meant to be in relationship to God through the incarnate Son. He validates the claim that the creation's relationship to the Creator "finds its supreme and final realization in humanity," because only in humanity is intimate fellowship with God realized and fulfilled. This human participation in incarnate relationship with God can be legitimately regarded as ultimate, because no other form of relationship to God can transcend the relationships between the persons of the Trinity. So Pannenberg says,

> As the eternal God took form in man, and through him made acceptance as children of God accessible to all other men and women, the relation of the creature to the Creator has found in principle the highest fulfillment that we can possibly imagine.[104]

The creation has no self-contained powers of persistence apart from the Son's mediation of the love of God in the Spirit. Neither does human existence attain to the self-transcendence central to it apart from that mediation.[105] The creation finds its fulfillment only by the full manifestation of the divine likeness of the incarnate Son in humanity.[106] Galloway describes this eschatological fulfillment of the eternal essence of humanity as the disclosure of the glory of God.[107] Christ's union with humanity confers upon them both individually and corporately their destiny of fellowship with God. This fellowship raises humanity above the natural world, including its concomitant social relationships, and confers upon each human life a sacred inviolability and "inalienable dignity."[108] The good creation of humans as both body and soul, irre-

---

103. Buller, *Unity of Nature and History*, 48.
104. Pannenberg, *Systematic Theology*, 2:175–76.
105. Buller, *Unity of Nature and History*, 49.
106. Pannenberg, *Systematic Theology*, 2:34.
107. Galloway, *Wolfhart Pannenberg*, 133.
108. Pannenberg, *Systematic Theology*, 2:175–76.

vocably joined, yields the "eternal value of the individual," in contrast to the view offered by other religions or philosophies in which the soul or person is detachable from his or her bodily existence.[109] Thus the incarnation illuminates the eternal worth and dignity of every human person founded on the *imago Dei*.

Jesus Christ opens the way for the divine union of fellowship of Creator and creature. It flows from him, through humanity, to the rest of creation. Scripture makes clear that the redemption that Christ has accomplished, which will be fully realized at the end of the age, is not just for humanity. The destiny of the entire creation is at stake. The cosmos is therefore dependent upon the completion of humanity for its own fulfillment. So Pannenberg says, "All creation waits for the manifestation of divine sonship in the human race, for thereby the corruptibility from which *all creatures* suffer will be vanquished (Rom 8:19ff)."[110] The entire creation depends upon humanity in this sense; unless humanity is complete in its eschatological realization as children of God, neither is the cosmos complete. Unless humanity's sonship is fulfilled, the cosmos can but wait with "eager longing." Until humanity is fully redeemed, the rest of creation is "subjected to futility" (Rom 8:20), groaning and longing in frustration. Though the thematic scriptural focus is upon Christ as cosmic redeemer, humanity is central to cosmic redemption.

The *Imago Dei* in Canonical Perspective

A deeper look at the scriptural meaning of the *imago Dei* will be helpful here. The concept is largely an underground or indirect theme in the Old Testament after the opening chapters of Genesis, though the dimensions of relational righteousness and holiness are there. The concept comes into clearer focus in the New Testament in the person and work of Jesus Christ. The analysis of human dominion and transcendence has already uncovered some of its features. This section will briefly examine some Old Testament themes related to the image, and then focus on Jesus Christ and the nature of the community founded upon him as typifying the image.

---

109. Pannenberg, "Resurrection," 256. E.g., Plato's transmigration of souls, Nietzsche's eternal return, or Buddhist and Hindu notions of reincarnation.

110. Pannenberg, *Systematic Theology*, 2:73. Emphasis added.

The Imago Dei in the Old Testament

The Old Testament concept of the *imago Dei* has relational dimensions that are both vertical and horizontal. The creation account of Genesis 1 and 2 portrays the fullness of the image of God in both these dimensions, neither divisible from the other, each realizable only in conjunction with the other. The first humans are created male and female. Anderson notes that only with the joint existence of these complementary forms "is there a sense of completeness" of the human being.[111] Francis Watson suggests this is primarily a paradigm for human relationality rather than gender difference as constitutive of the *imago Dei*.[112] He maintains that a significant aspect of the image of God lies in the human ability to "engage in dialogical communication with one another and with God."[113] However, noting the complementarity and differences between the sexes need not endanger the concept of the *imago Dei*. Michael Novak insists that our human sexuality, however imperfectly (because we violate the will of our Creator by using each other, "wishing to put self in the place of God"), models the self-giving communion of God. The "experience of communion between woman and man, self-giving, in mutuality, and without either's dominance, is more like the inner life of God than anything else that we encounter in creation." Novak finds this insight in the thought of Karol Wojtyla (John Paul II), who insists that "God is more like the communion of persons than He is like anything else we know of. That, at least, is the way He has revealed Himself to us, not only in Scripture and in His Son, but also in the way our embodied selves are joined in matrimony."[114] The corporate creation of human beings as male and female indicates this essential fact: the image of God is a relational image, and God himself is a relational being. Whether or not one sees Trinitarianism in God's self-address in Genesis 1 ("Let *us* make humans in *our* image"), created human relational and corporate nature

---

111. Anderson, "On Being Human," 180.

112. Watson, *Text, Church and World*, 108, 115. Otherwise, only heterosexual marriage could be the norm for true personhood. This is repudiated by the New Testament. In Christ, there is neither male nor female (Gal 3:28); in the Kingdom of Heaven, there will be neither marrying nor giving in marriage (Matt 22:30; Mark 12:25; Luke 20:34–35). Yet marriage does function as a symbol of the *imago Dei* and of God's relational nature: e.g., the union of humanity and God at the end of time is depicted as the marriage between Christ and his Church (Eph 5:32; Rev 19:7–9).

113. Watson, *Text, Church and World*, 214.

114. Novak, "Embodied Self," 19–20.

supports such an interpretation.¹¹⁵ Stanley Grenz and Derrick Bailey both insist that "for the Christian, the *imago Dei* must have a Trinitarian reference... Man in the image of God is essentially a 'being-in-relation,' and human existence is essentially 'existence-in-community.'"¹¹⁶

Anderson notes the relational capacity opens up in two directions in humans expressed by the two great commandments, to love God and to love one's neighbor.¹¹⁷ The vertical relationships of the image are constituted between human beings and God, and between human beings and the rest of creation as typified by the charge of dominion. The horizontal relationships of the image are between themselves; in the initial instance male *and* female. The vertical relationship between humanity and the rest of creation is underlined in the Genesis account by the contrast between the method of creation for humanity and that used for all other living creatures. The earth, sea, and land bring forth the other creatures at God's command (Gen 1:11–12, 20–21, 24–25); God, planning a creature in his own image, determines to *make* this particular one, as "a new and transcendent event." They are related to the earth, for they are made of its dust. Yet humans are made directly by God, rather than springing indirectly from some other feature of creation as the other living creatures do.¹¹⁸ Further, as Walther Eichrodt points out, humans alone among the creatures are made alive when God breathes into them the breath of life (Gen 2:7).¹¹⁹ So Anderson observes

115. Modern scholars frequently deny a Trinitarian interpretation to the Genesis 1–3 *imago Dei*. Sarna suggests the divine address ("Let us") is God's address to the heavenly court. Westermann and Cassuto see it as the "plural of deliberation." Other scholars regard "Let us" as a "plural of fullness," which is closer to Trinitarianism without being directly so (e.g., Hamilton, *Book of Genesis*, 134). Pannenberg believes a new authoritative interpretative perspective on the Old Testament is valid in light of Christ, perhaps differing from the Old Testament's self-interpretive view. A Trinitarian interpretation of Genesis 1:26f is consistent with the eschatologically verified orientation of the whole creation towards the Logos manifested in the incarnation, and takes into account the object of action: the creation of human beings in corporate communion. Sarna, *Genesis*, 12; Westermann, *Genesis 1–11*, 144–46; Cassuto, *Commentary*, 1:55; Pannenberg, "Response to My American Friends," 318.

116. Grenz, *Social God*, 286–87; Bailey, *Man-Woman Relationship*, 267.

117. Anderson, "On Being Human," 181.

118. Watson, *Text, Church and World*, 144.

119. Eichrodt, *Theology of the Old Testament*, 2:121. Despite its use to describe the "breath," or life, of other creatures elsewhere (Gen 6:7; Eccl 3:19), the Gen 2:7 creation account draws a contrast between the "universal divine breath blowing through the whole of Nature" and humans, who receive their life "by a special act of God," and who

that "their origination as *human* creatures is qualitatively marked off from non-human creatures by the endowment of the divine image and the divine inbreathing."[120]

Martin Buber unpacks the significance of the image of God in terms of an I-Thou relationship. The I-Thou dialogue between human persons establishes the world of relation, in contrast to the I-It form that establishes the world of things and experience. Humans become persons because of a "You" with whom they relate. God is the source of personhood, the eternal "You/Thou" of relationship for the human "I."[121] Barth holds the analogy between God and humanity is evident in the "I and Thou" of God's creative fiat "Let us" (Gen 1:26), and also in the "confrontation and conjunction of man and woman."[122] As Welker puts it, to remove the "face to face existence of I and Thou . . . is tantamount to removing the divine from God as well as the human from man."[123] Alistair McFadyen notes the archetypal relationship thus made possible between Adam and Eve. Only in Eve does Adam find another "Thou" with whom he can relate as a human "I." Without their mutual belonging to one another, with Eve as an equal "I," Adam's "isolation would not be broken. He would then have only another animal being and not one for whom he may also become a Thou. Adam can only say 'I' in the recognition that Eve is a human Thou before him and therefore an 'I' for herself."[124] Human relationships are characterized by this mutual recognition of each other, by dependence upon and yet independence from one another as "related but distinct Thou-Is." God's image in humanity is distorted unless this individual and communal incomplete-

---

are "thus treated as an independent spiritual I, and accorded a closer association with God than the animals."

120. Anderson, "On Being Human," 180.

121. Buber, *I and Thou*, 56, 80, 180–81.

122. Barth, *Church Dogmatics* III/1:196. The corporate creation of male-female is a creaturely "repetition of the fact that the one God is in Himself not only I but also I and Thou. . . . for his part the man who corresponds to Him can know God and be the seeing eye at which all creation aims and which is 'the true and sole motive of the cosmic process.' . . . [T]he distinction of sexes found in man too is the only genuine distinction between man and man, in correspondence to the fact that the I-Thou relationship is the only genuine distinction in the one divine being. Hence it may be seen that the distinction has not only a special but a unique connection with the divine likeness."

123. Welker, *Creation and Reality*, 65, quoting Barth, *Church Dogmatics* III/1:207.

124. McFadyen, *Call to Personhood*, 33.

ness is recognized.[125] Further, this relational dimension makes the ethical paramount, as relationships are essentially constituted by love. Humans are given freedoms, duties, responsibilities, and limitations in relationship to God, each other, and the creation that flesh out this ethical dimension.

The Imago Dei in the New Testament

The New Testament is rich with references to Jesus as the full image of God, and the church as called to conform to that image. Pannenberg maintains that true humanity that displays the image of God "has been fully realized only in Jesus of Nazareth," who is the perfect image of God.[126] The Old Testament trajectory of meaning for the image is "brought to focus in the person of Jesus Christ."[127] Thus, of all human beings, only Jesus is fully and unbrokenly human. His full humanity surpasses even that of his pre-fall ancestors, since Christ is in type superior to the first Adam, having humbled himself, as St. Paul and others (e.g., Athanasius) note, to become one of us.[128] His complete and whole humanity is part of his qualification to manifest the perfect image of God in the creation.

The Gospels contain numerous references to Jesus as the image of the Father. John's Gospel emphasizes Christ as the image or representation of God, in such typical passages as John 12:45 ("Whoever sees me sees him who sent me") or John 14:9 ("Whoever has seen me has seen the Father"). This view pervades much of the New Testament. Christ is "the image of God" (2 Cor 4:4). He is the image of the invisible God, and the firstborn of creation (Col 1:15). Further, the church is described as the community of those being conformed to the image of God. The disciple will be like the teacher (Matt 10:25). The elect are those who are "predestined to be conformed" to the image of the Son (Rom 8:29). "All who are lead by the Spirit of God are children of God" (Rom 8:14). Believers are to put on "the new self, created according to the likeness of God in true righteousness and holiness" (Eph 4:24); they are to clothe

---

125. Ibid. 34.
126. Tupper, *Theology of Wolfhart Pannenberg*, 242–43.
127. Pannenberg, *Anthropology*, 75.
128. Phil 2:7–9; 1 Cor 15:45–49; Athanasius, *Select Treatisess*, 521.

themselves "with the new self, which is being renewed in knowledge according to the image of its creator" (Col 3:10).

The most comprehensive statement of the *imago Dei* in Christ is found in Col 1:15–20:

> He is the image of the invisible God, the firstborn of all creation; . . . all things have been created through him and for him. He himself is before all things, and in him all things hold together. He is the head of the body, the church; he is the beginning, the firstborn from the dead, so that he might come to have first place in everything. For in him all the fullness of God was pleased to dwell, and through him God was pleased to reconcile to himself all things, whether on earth or in heaven, by making peace through the blood of his cross.

In this passage, the *image* and *fullness* of God in Christ is not simply a fulfillment of his humanity, as if in him we have a second human Adam who happens to have luckily escaped a fall into sin. Rather, this is the Logos of creation of John 1:1, the divine Son of God, the only begotten Son of the heavenly Father. Christ is the image of God because he is one person of the Trinitarian God, perfectly representing to the creation the God who cannot be seen by humans. The fullness of God dwells in him, so that in him, God is physically present in his creation. As Son of God he exercises the full dominion of God over all creation, heaven and earth: a realization and fulfillment of the familiar Old Testament concept; the dominion over the earth given to humanity in Genesis is a pale reflection of this cosmic dominion exercised by the Son. Christ is "before all things," present *at* and an essential part *of* the creation process, having priority in both time and rank before the rest of creation.[129] The universe was "created through him," and "holds together" in him. Though part of the Godhead, he has appeared in the world as a human being, and so is the image and essence of God in the domain of humanity.

The vertical and horizontal brokenness of humanity's relational nature is only finally redeemed in the person and work of Christ. As the fullness of the *imago Dei*—God himself inhabiting his own image in humanity—Jesus brings to human beings a share in God's self. Jesus' existence in and for the world proclaims that God *is* love.

---

129. Barth and Blanke, *Colossians*, 200, 203, 212–13.

> Whoever does not love does not know God, for God is love. God's love was revealed among us in this way: God sent his only Son into the world so that we might live through him. (1 John 4:8–9)

The *imago Dei* is fulfilled in Christ in both vertical and horizontal dimensions. Relationships are restored, first between God and human beings, then within the human community. Christ exercises not just earthly, but universal dominion, and redeemed humanity becomes his co-rulers and heirs of the kingdom. They will reign with him (2 Tim 2:12; Rev 5:10; 22:5), they will sit as judges even of angels (1 Cor 6:3). Since the image of God in Christ is the image of love, then the restoration of that image in humanity must also include the restoration of love in them. So the image of God as it is restored and fulfilled in the church has a particularly relational and moral dimension. The new self, as conformed to the *imago Christi*, is the moral opposite of the rebellious old self, justifying van Huyssteen's insistence on recovering justice into the core of the *imago Dei*.[130]

In Colossians 3:10, the believer is called to put off that old self:

> But now you must get rid of all such things—anger, wrath, malice, slander.... Do not lie to one another, seeing that you have stripped off the old self with its practices and have clothed yourselves with the new self, which is being renewed in knowledge *according to the image of its creator*. In that renewal there is no longer Greek and Jew, circumcised and uncircumcised, barbarian, Scythian, slave and free; but Christ is all and in all! As God's chosen ones, holy and beloved, clothe yourselves with compassion, kindness, humility, meekness, and patience ... Above all, clothe yourselves with love, which binds everything together in perfect harmony. (Col 3:9–14; emphasis added)

This contrast of opposites between the new and the old self highlights the relational and moral nature of the image of God. Compassion, kindness, humility, meekness, patience, forbearance, forgiveness, and love are to replace anger, wrath, malice, slander, abusive language, and lying. Such human measures of identity and separation as ethnicity (Greek, Jew, or Scythian), religious commitment (circumcised and uncircumcised), socioeconomic status (barbarian or civilized, slave or free), or

---

130. Van Huyssteen, "Rethinking the *Imago Dei*."

even sexual identity (male or female, Gal 3:28) are to disappear before a unified identity as children of God.

The church is the community destined for the fellowship of love "for which human beings, made in the image of the triune God, are intended and destined."[131] The church is the gathering of those among humanity who are becoming the image of their Creator in Christ. They are to show forth the loving relational potential that may be realized in Christ. Those members of humanity who are being conformed to his likeness share in his imaging of God (Col 3:15). The image has been frustrated and ruined by sin, but now in Jesus Christ, redeemed humanity is being renewed in this hitherto lost image of God.

This brief study illuminates some prominent features of the *imago Dei* in both Old and New Testaments, and especially in Jesus Christ and the church. While the Old Testament hints at the meaning of the concept in vertical, horizontal, and moral dimensions, its thematic development occurs in the New Testament, where the person and work of Christ unveil its fullness. According to Stewart, this is the basis of "Pannenberg's interpretation of the image as destiny to fellowship with God." It is found in "the idea of Jesus Christ as the image of God in which believers share through the spirit (2 Cor 3:18)."[132] Personhood, relationality and righteousness, expressed as love of God and neighbor, justice, and authority, are its hallmarks. It is concrete, bodily, dependent upon human rational and linguistic capacity (naming, dominion, I-Thou dialogue), and involves both vertical and horizontal relationships with God, creation, and other persons. Christ is the fullness of the image, and calls the church to share in it. The *imago Dei* might be summarized as the manifestation of the *character* and *personhood* of God in the cosmos.

The Sabbath Day as Crown of Creation

Barth disputed somewhat a high position for humanity by claiming that humanity cannot be regarded as the crown of creation, since this honor belongs to the Sabbath day. Others have more recently expressed

---

131. Watson, *Text, Church and World*, 11.

132. Stewart, *Reconstructing Science and Theology*, 9; Pannenberg, *Systematic Theology*, 2:208.

similar misgivings.[133] Claus Westermann maintains that in the sweep of the entire Scripture, rooted in Genesis 1, the apocalyptic texts do not give a goal merely for human history, but point to a goal for the whole of the created realm. This is captured in the idea of the Sabbath, in which God's work does not come to an end with the creation—or even with the redemption—of humanity, but rather with the completion or redemption of the whole cosmos.[134] According to Barth, "it is only with reservation that [humanity] can be described as 'the crown of creation.' Strictly speaking, creation is crowned only when God in His joyful Sabbath rest looks back upon it and down on what He has created. But it is the work concluded and terminated on the sixth day with the creation of man that is the object of this completing divine rest and joy."[135] Gunton also says the creation of humanity cannot be claimed to "represent the goal of creation." That is to be found in the seventh day rest "and its ultimate goal in the reconciliation of all things."[136] David Fergusson echoes the point when he says, "the crowning moment of creation is not the creation of Adam and Eve but the Sabbath day of rest on which the whole creation glorifies its maker."[137] Walter Brueggemann elaborates on the significance of the Sabbath day as reflected in the year of Jubilee, that symbol of a future time when justice between all is perfect, when "God's way is fully established."[138] Moltmann has similar ideas of the Sabbath as a "prefiguration of the world to come," and as "crown of creation."[139] His theocentric version of the world forbids any anthropocentrism, and he insists that human beings are not the meaning and purpose of either the world or of evolution. He claims that the fulfillment of the creation is not to be found in humanity, but rather humanity will find its destiny in the fulfillment of creation, at the Sabbath "feast of creation."[140]

133. E.g., Brueggemann, *Genesis*, 35–36; Moltmann, *God in Creation*, 6, 197; Fergusson, *Cosmos and the Creator*, 17; Gunton, "Spirit Moved," 8.

134. Westermann, *Genesis 1–11*, 177.

135. Barth, *Church Dogmatics* III/1:181.

136. Gunton, "Spirit Moved," 8.

137. Fergusson, *Cosmos and Creator*, 17.

138. Brueggemann, *Genesis*, 36.

139. Moltmann, *God in Creation*, 6, 187, 197. Note: Moltmann has his exegesis incorrect on page 187. He says, "It is the Sabbath with which God crowns the creation which he beholds as 'very good.'" In fact, the creation is declared "very good" at the end of the sixth day, *not* the seventh day (Gen 1:31).

140. Ibid., 197.

On purely literary grounds, it might be said that the description given of the creation in Genesis 1 seems to place the events of the sixth day culminating in the creation of humanity at the climax of the creative process.[141] The seventh day is more like an epilogue to what has gone before than anything else. Christ's words, "The Sabbath was made for humankind, not humankind for the Sabbath" (Mark 2:27), seem to place an ordering on the relative value of humanity in relation to the simple Mosaic legal day of the Sabbath, and so perhaps in the larger overall concept of Sabbath. Brueggemann recognizes this, writing, "Sabbath as rest for God is the ground of a sweeping humanism. It exists for the well-being of humankind."[142] However, the Sabbath has several symbolic meanings within the Scripture beyond simply the last day of creation. Some of these symbolic meanings, such as the rule or peace of God, or the end of all labor at the consummation of the kingdom of God, deserve special emphasis.

A Sabbath priority does not necessarily compromise the key importance of humanity or the crowning status ascribable to the incarnation. A case can certainly be made for the Sabbath rest as the *telos* or crowning purpose of creation. But this is a Sabbath that is celebrated only in light of the fullness of the creation, which includes humanity as completion of all that has gone before. It includes the entire created order, and not just human beings. At the same time, this does not contradict the vital status of humanity. The worship of God offered by humans remains essential to the Sabbath. God creates everything and calls it good. But only after the creation of humanity on the sixth day is *all* the created order (not just humanity) declared "very good" (Gen 1:31). Only then does God declare the Sabbath rest. What is *not* being claimed in this thesis, contra Moltmann, is that humanity is *the* meaning and *the* purpose of the world (and of evolution). Nor is it being claimed here that because humanity *in the incarnation* is the crown of creation, that therefore the rest of creation is irrelevant and *not* good. Human praise of God "is also a participation in the whole of creation."[143] A vital role can be maintained for humanity in the cosmos, but need not imply that the cosmos can be entirely explained by the presence of humanity.

---

141. Westermann, *Genesis 1–11*, 80, 177.
142. Brueggemann, *Genesis*, 36.
143. Northcott, *Environment and Christian Ethics*, 181.

The best answer to such basic meaning-of-the-universe type questions, must, in theological perspective, be God himself. Sarna observes that while humanity is the pinnacle of creation, the Genesis seventh day is about God, the "solo performer" who has accomplished all that has gone before.[144] If the Sabbath is taken as a symbol of God, of his being the beginning and end of all things, then it would have to be the crown of creation since there is no creation without God. If, as in Pannenberg, the creation is only completed at the end of history at the fulfillment of all things in Christ, then the Sabbath might be taken as a symbol of that completion. The end of history has already broken into the present through Jesus' resurrection. He will bring creation to completion. Therefore it is appropriate in some sense to say that Jesus *is* the Sabbath in the new creation, expanding the meaning of his words, "the Son of Man is lord even of the Sabbath" (Mark 2:28).

The Sabbath as Jubilee is a related theme. The justice and love of this "day" have their consummation and fulfillment in humanity, albeit redeemed humanity. The fulfillment has cosmic dimensions, and includes the angels and other beings of the universe. The will of God shall be fully accomplished only in Christ; God's will is fully done only when humanity is complete in God's love. The Sabbath may describe God's perfect will for his creation, but that creation is only completed and fulfilled when God's family is completed and in order. The perfect way of justice and rest is not completed in the created order except in and through humanity. From this perspective, the perfect justice and will of God as imaged by the Sabbath/Sabbath Jubilee are not goals of creation separate from or in contradiction to the importance of humanity itself. In fact, the glory of the Sabbath does not imperil the vital priority of humanity in the cosmos, but is rather fulfilled when humanity is realized in its eschatological glory. These are interdependent, rather than contradictory or mutually exclusive categories of importance.

Thus the Sabbath as a teleological concept does not endanger human significance, nor is there a unilateral case for the priority of the Sabbath over humanity. Jesus Christ as the Lord of the Sabbath does not diminish the critical place of humanity in the whole of creation, but rather establishes the order and boundaries of its fulfillment in the human story. Since the worship of God offered by humans is an essential

---

144. Sarna, *Genesis*, 11, 14.

part of the Sabbath, even if the Sabbath is the *telos* of creation, a type of anthropocentrism is still implied.

Pannenberg's Response to some Scientific Issues

As outlined in the introductory section, Pannenberg sees coherence between scientific and theological knowledge, and holds that "there need be no rivalry between scientific and theological statements."[145] A constructive dialogue is possible between them on the philosophical common ground they share. He aims to show that theology has a necessary contribution to make to a holistic view of reality even for the natural sciences.

For example, Pannenberg believes the current understandings in modern science of nature's open character and the contingency of its laws are coherent with the Christian idea of the contingent, creative activity of God. "There is agreement that the laws of physics, as well as the reality [those] laws seek to describe, are contingent . . . From a theological point of view, the philosophical concept of contingency can be regarded as the creative activity of the God of love."[146] The modern understanding of reality emphasizes "the elasticity and openness" of the natural order. This understanding leaves room for such transcendent and miraculous events as the resurrection, in contrast to the closed, deterministic and mechanistic worldview of the Enlightenment already rejected by science. Thus theology can escape from the Enlightenment's materialistic naturalism.[147]

This is not to say that the different ways of describing reality in physics and in theology are the same, but rather that they are describing the same reality, from different points of interest.[148] If we admit that the descriptions offered by science are not "exhaustive explanations of events," and causal relations in reality are only possible because events are contingent, then a description of God's activity within the open systems of the laws of nature does not compete with the scientific description, but operates on a different level.[149] God's activity need

145. Pannenberg, *Systematic Theology*, 2: 70, 106.
146. Buller, *Unity of Nature and History*, 64–65.
147. Pannenberg, "Resurrection," 259.
148. Pannenberg, *Systematic Theology*, 2:83.
149. Ibid., 106. Explanation in music is multi-level. Music may be described using scientific laws, with studies of tone, rhythm, etc. However, such descriptions are not

not violate scientific laws, nor can God disappear as "gaps" in the understanding of those laws close. This is because God is not operating only in the gaps thus far unsolved by human understanding, but in all aspects of the operation of those laws, from their origin to their maintenance and preservation. Contingency and historicity mark all aspects of reality and attest to its creatureliness, and this demonstrates that God is the Creator, and continues to be so, not in the gaps, but in all of reality describable by science. Pannenberg's point is that God never did occupy the gaps, but resides in the entire contingent process from beginning to end.[150]

Pannenberg holds that the two views of reality are traceable to the same root philosophical origin, the same "metaphysical intuitions,"[151] with root motifs expressed on the one hand in theological statements, and on the other hand in formalized mathematical language in the realm of physics. The physicist seeks to discover the natural laws in the structure of reality. However, the existence of such laws and the intelligibility of the universe require explanation. Science, as Peacocke observes, cannot explain "*why* there are laws —*why* there is *anything*."[152] The physicist who has described the how of the Big Bang has not provided the whole picture of reality until it is combined with the theologian's knowledge of the who and why. God remains a coherent—and for many the best—metaphysical foundation upon which to build all knowledge, including that of science.[153] Theology contributes meaningful knowledge to the provisional understanding of the physicist, in that the physicist's cosmological descriptions are only partial until they are linked with the theological understanding.[154] A comprehensive picture of reality thus requires both disciplines.

---

complete explanations of the nature, meaning, and purpose of music, nor would the accuracy of the scientific description make such greater explanation less true, valid, or objective. A full *description* of a process is not the same as a fully satisfying *explanation* of it. Polkinghorne, "Friendliness of Science and Religion."

150. Pannenberg, *Systematic Theology*, 2:71.

151. Ibid., 83.

152. Peacocke, "End of All Our Exploring."

153. E.g., Rahner, who suggests God, as the background cause and "enabler" of all natural processes, is the best explanation. See Stanley, "Transcendental Method of Rahner," 200–202. Wicken agrees that science provides an "essentially incomplete epistemology for understanding nature" ("Theology and Science," 45–31).

154. Hefner, "Role of Science," 273.

Another fruitful example of coherence lies in the comparison of the Christian concept of the eschatological meaning of history with science's method for uncovering natural laws. Natural laws only become understandable from the endpoint of observation looking backward. The meaning of the data can only be discovered *after* it has all been collected and analyzed; if there is a relationship from A leading to B, it only becomes evident *after* B. Once a law-like feature of the universe has been uncovered, it seems that science might predict future relationships without any obvious dependence upon history or the future. Yet the actualization of these laws in the real world depends in every case on contingent conditions that must always be stipulated to describe their unfolding. Furthermore, while theoretically the laws appear timeless, in fact, time is irreversible—the universe only moves forward. This means that the laws that provisionally describe the universe, A to B, A_1 to B_1, A_2 to B_2 ... are not the self-contained timeless descriptions that some glosses on scientific knowledge suppose, but are rather always contingent and temporally bound. Their unfolding in reality always depends on the contingencies of the historical moment.

Since reality cannot be described non-historically or non-contingently, Pannenberg insists that "nature ought to be understood as historical."[155] Since reality is everywhere understood to be an ongoing and incomplete process, even partial projections of reality such as those in scientific descriptions are at best of only provisional value. As a result, the comprehension of reality "is open to continual revision until such time as reality is temporally completed."[156] This is the "ontological priority of the future": the fullness of the meaning of history can only be verified eschatologically at its end.[157] When combined with the contemporary understanding of nature as "elastic and open," such an approach permits Pannenberg to rationally posit the reality of such a unique event as the resurrection.[158] Pannenberg suggests science is here indebted to theology for its metaphysical foundations, since it contributes a foundation for understanding what the natural sciences must otherwise accept *a priori*, in the concept of the ontological priority of the future.

---

155. Pannenberg, *Theology of Nature*, 36–37; Peters, "Editor's Introduction," 9–10.

156. Peters, "Truth in History," 53.

157. Pannenberg, *Theology of Nature*, 105–8; Buller, *Unity of Nature and History*, 66.

158. Holwerda, "Faith, Reason, and the Resurrection," 283–85.

Pannenberg has made other forays into the science-theology dialogue, such as comparing the Holy Spirit to unified field theories in modern physics, and attempting to develop his anthropology from the social sciences. Some of these are problematic, but pursuing them is beyond the scope of this thesis.[159] His engagement with the question of extraterrestrial intelligence, the anthropic principle, and the relation between human personhood, body, and mind—three themes that will recur throughout this thesis—are somewhat less contentious, and bear on the question of human cosmic significance.

The Possibility of Extraterrestrial Life

Pannenberg asks whether the discovery of non-human intelligences in the cosmos would affect the key status of humanity. He observes that there is no consensus as to whether non-terrestrial life and intelligence will ever be found, some researchers supporting, others refuting the possibility, with no hard data available to decide the case. Further, Christian theology has always been able to address the issue of non-human intelligence in the creation, particularly in the angels, which assume many and varied forms. Some of these non-human intelligences have no need of redemption, while others are incapable of attaining to it, having rebelled against God. Christian tradition developed humanity's central place in the cosmos on the basis of the incarnation, despite acknowledging the existence of these other beings with superior intelligence. Pannenberg admits that the discovery of extraterrestrials would require a theological appraisal of their relationship to Jesus as the incarnate Logos, and therefore also to humanity. But given the currently questionable possibility of their real existence, he sees no threat to the traditional Christian interpretation.

> The as yet problematic and vague possibility of their [ETI] existence in no way affects the credibility of the Christian teaching

159. Pannenberg's "field-theory" theology has engendered much discussion and criticism in the science-theology literature, right up to the present. E.g., Buller, *Unity of Nature and History*, 53–56; Polkinghorne, "Fields and Theology," 795; Wicken, "Theology and Science," 45–55. Wicken thinks Pannenberg has gone too far by claiming historical particularity and temporality belong to theology, "begging the wrong question of where science ends and theology begins" (45–51); Stewart believes Pannenberg has lost a "proper critical distance" between science and theology in his apologetic effort to require coherence between the two, particularly in his use of the social sciences (*Reconstructing Science and Theology*, 146).

that in Jesus of Nazareth the Logos who works throughout the universe became a man and thus gave to humanity and its history a key function in giving to all creation its unity and destiny.[160]

Human cosmic uniqueness may be a provisional claim, in that time may disclose higher life forms on other planets. But with no consensus as to the likelihood of its discovery in the future, the current SETI yielding a null conclusion, and other scientific considerations suggesting no ETI will ever be found (see page 237),[161] it is hard to see why theology ought to make significant changes based on speculation.

The Anthropic Principle

Pannenberg asks whether humanity's lofty position can be maintained in light of scientific objections such as those raised by the Copernican principle. Recall that the Copernican principle is "the idea that we are not in a special place"[162] in the universe, that we are at best a "marginal phenomenon in the cosmos."[163] He points to certain gains in scientific understanding that have only been recently achieved, which can be seen as "anti-Copernican" in their import.[164] "Only the scientific cosmology of the twentieth century and its calculations of the age and development of the universe have shown us what cosmological data are indispensable for the emergence of life, and therefore of human life, in the world." These data are collectively known as the *anthropic principle*. It expresses, in its various versions, the "otherwise inexplicable" correlation of the constants of nature required for the universe's particular form, and for life and particularly human life to have emerged.[165]

While the anthropic principle is about intelligence, rather than humanity *per se*—the kind of intelligence that reflects upon the universe and through which the universe becomes conscious of itself—the anthropic conditions may suggest a more specialized focus upon human origins and significance. Since human beings are currently the only known intelligent beings of this type in the physical universe, and

---

160. Pannenberg, *Systematic Theology*, 2:75–76.
161. Pannenberg, *Metaphysics*, 75–76.
162. Rowan-Robinson, *Nine Numbers of the Cosmos*, 25.
163. Pannenberg, *Systematic Theology*, 2:74.
164. From Polkinghorne, *Serious Talk*, 39–40.
165. Barrow and Tipler, *Anthropic Principle*, 15–17.

represent the highest known form of physical and rational complexity, there may be a connection between the principle and the significance of humanity. While Pannenberg admits that the anthropic principle is not an explanation for the phenomenon it observes, he points to the fact that it reveals a very tight connection between the large- and small-scale structures of the universe. Humanity, once thought insignificant in the overall scheme of cosmic things, may have tremendous significance in light of this connection. The serious discussion "devoted to the idea that the goal of the universe and the normative details of its construction are the producing of human life" reveals that there is room in science for the truth revealed by the incarnation, that humans are the goal of creation.[166]

While many theologians and scientists are willing to see God only as the cosmic initiator or sustainer, Pannenberg insists on God's involvement with creation throughout cosmic history. He maintains that cosmic processes, whether described by fine-tuning, self-organizing principles or by various evolutionary pathways, have an underlying causation in the form of the eschatological rule of God. The creation is not simply the beginning of things, but an entire process with a beginning, ongoing upholding, and final realization or fulfillment at the end of history. Natural processes appear to be incomprehensible (or meaningless) until the resurrection of Jesus breaks in to reveal a foretaste of the eschatological end, disclosing the whole of creation for what it is—a creation destined for consummation and fulfillment. *Therefore, with the resurrection, natural processes can no longer be taken simply as brute facts unrelated to cosmic destiny.* God's eschatological rule guides the cosmos to its fulfillment, leading it towards an incarnational and therefore human climax.[167] Thus the idea that humanity might be the goal of the creation is coherent with scientific discourse on the anthropic principle, though is itself a theological conclusion.

Page, whose thought will be explored in detail in chapter 7, maintains that this incarnational reading of the creation process makes the created order too dependent upon humanity, and ignores the fact that God has had a real relationship with the creation apart from humanity. Humans are, after all, only recent arrivals on the stage of universal

---

166. Pannenberg, *Systematic Theology*, 2:75.
167. Pannenberg, *Metaphysics*, 105–9.

history.¹⁶⁸ Pannenberg agrees that the rest of the cosmic order with its living creatures is not simply a means to the end of humanity. But taken "as a whole, they form the basis for [human] emergence." The rest of creation has a relationship with God, but that relationship only finds its fullness in humanity, specifically in and through the incarnation.¹⁶⁹ Biblical eschatology portrays an ultimate cosmic purpose and destiny for the whole creation: it is to be redeemed, to be saved from its slavery to decay and death. But the incarnation is the direct and principal means whereby this redemption takes place. God's ongoing relationship to the cosmos, as its evolutionary history unfolds in the life-friendly matrix of finely tuned physical laws, is not at odds with a fulfillment of the cosmos mediated by humanity.

Stewart summarizes Pannenberg's theological anthropology as largely dependent on the theological datum of the incarnation, with little help from the realm of science. "Biology can do no more than hint; only a biblically and religiously based knowledge can reveal the purpose and direction of humanity."¹⁷⁰ Pannenberg's analysis of the anthropic principle shows some possible scientific themes that run contrary to the Copernican principle, and partially overturns the marginalizing of humanity implied by that latter principle. He agrees that ultimate meaning is to be found theologically, not scientifically.¹⁷¹ But if the scientific data is coherent with that ascribed meaning, theology is strengthened.

Many others have commented on the significance of the anthropic principle as a point of contact between theology and science. For instance, T. F. Torrance concludes that its real import is "not only that the universe is a home for humanity, but that the personal nature of humankind belongs to the very nature of nature." Human personhood that comprehends the intelligibility of the cosmos is reflective of the "personal Author," God the Creator, who is stamped upon nature— James Clerk Maxwell's moral and personal boundary cause of the universe's "existence, nature and structure."¹⁷² Gunton observes that "at the very least [the principle] suggests a necessary relatedness of the cosmos to human intelligence." "Recent discussions encourage us to conceive

---

168. Page, "Animal Kingdom," 2.
169. Pannenberg, *Systematic Theology*, 2:115.
170. Stewart, *Reconstructing Science and Theology*, 11.
171. Pannenberg, *Systematic Theology*, 2:175.
172. Torrance, "Transcendental Role of Wisdom," 142–44.

a positive relation between human rationality and the structure of the universe." He thinks it is a mistake to take the principle as "evidence that the world is created for the production of human life," yet he admits that this "may as a matter of fact be the case." In theological perspective, because of God's intention to bring creation into fellowship, the exact ordering of creation through time—described by the scientific concept of the anthropic principle—can be seen as the way to make humanity, and hence the incarnation, possible.[173] The relationship between the anthropic principle, human existence, and God's providence will be examined more fully in chapter 6.

Rationality, Human Nature, and the Imago Dei

Is the universe's fine-tuning for life simply about consciousness or *mind*, rather than humanity? Some take this as an implication of the anthropic principle, which Brandon Carter explicitly claimed was designed to illuminate the rise of *conscious* life, rather than specifically *human* life.[174] The word *anthropic* has been regarded as unfortunate and misleading, since it seems to indicate a special status for humans not intended by the principle.[175] A thought experiment might posit something analogous to the *imago Dei* in some other speculative intelligent creature type. Could Neanderthals, for instance, if they had survived and dominated instead of *Homo sapiens*, have become the *imago Dei* and therefore also the creaturely vessel for the incarnation? What if another evolutionary path had yielded a creature quite different from humans that was nevertheless self-conscious and "humanly" intelligent? Would that creature have been the image of God, the goal of creation?

There are several related issues here that will be addressed in other chapters. The question on Neanderthal capacity will be examined in chapter 5. The historical contingency of human existence in relation to the anthropic principle and God's providence will be examined in chapter 6. This section will examine whether the *imago Dei* and the incarnation could have been realized in the universe apart from particularly human form. The question will be framed in terms of *rationality*: is the image of God reducible to rationality? Could only humans represent

---

173. Gunton, "Trinity," 57, 115.
174. Carter, "Anthropic Principle," 348.
175. P. Davies, *Mind of God*, 200.

God in creation and the creation to God, or could any rational being do the job? It will be suggested here that Pannenberg's concept of the embodied nature of the *imago Dei* in humanity, with some corrections, helps put rationality in perspective.

It is clear that rationality is critical and foundational to the *imago Dei*. This is implied at least by God's own rationality in the creation account (as Logos, or ordering principle), by the command of dominion, and by Adam's naming of the animals. It is evident in human symbolic reasoning (see chapter 5). The New Testament analysis of the *imago* has already shown the importance of ethical capacity and responsibility, each rooted in human reason (page 49). Symbolic and moral reasoning enables a unique level of communication, grounding the ability to be in personal relationship, in communion. A purely material or bodily interpretation of the *imago Dei*—as though human beings were in *physical* appearance like God—is therefore inadequate.[176] The human physical body alone cannot be proffered as the image of God, as if God could be described in physical terms without reference to his character, nature, and personhood. Umberto Cassuto insists such a physicalist interpretation is deficient because it does not do justice to the lofty spiritual and non-corporeal nature of God revealed by the Genesis 1 context. The God of Israel cannot be reduced to physical imagery, a habit common to the ancient pagan religions but ultimately shown to be idolatry. He maintains that what delineates us as closest to God in distinction from the animals is our thinking and our conscience.[177]

But while rationality is an important part of the image, it cannot be taken in isolation. Cassuto's vision of human thought fails to take into account the bodily and social rootedness of the human mind. Even the natural sciences have come to understand that human rationality arises within its bodily and social context, intimately bound to the physical nature and development of the brain and body.[178] Gregory Peterson notes

---

176. Westermann, *Genesis 1–11*, 146.

177. Cassuto, *Commentary*, 56.

178. See page 226. Human nature is increasingly understood in modern scientific research as a mind-brain-body unity with personal, biological, social, and moral dimensions, rather than solely in terms of *mind*. Clark and Herzfeld point out that cutting edge AI research abandons the Cartesian notion of disembodied mind and recognizes the embodied, social nature of intelligence. W. S. Brown observes that in the neurological sciences, "the unity of the body-mind-soul is clear" in such phenomena as religious and moral breakdown in some patients with Alzheimer's disease, or in "spiritual de-

that as the cognitive sciences have developed, it has become clearer "that a full understanding of the human person requires a radically integrative approach." We must acknowledge "not only that we have minds and brains but that the brain/mind is itself intricately tied to the biology of our bodies as well as to our physical and social environments."[179] In other words, human rationality itself arises in the context of embodied relationships with other persons. Pannenberg does well to emphasize human embodiment, insisting that we cannot separate the soul from the body, as if one could exist without the other: "the soul (*nephesh*) is not another component part of a human being over and above the body, as in Cartesian or Platonic dualism. It is simply the bodily being as living." The body *is* the person, not simply some kind of dispensable or temporary shell through which reality is experienced by the *imago Dei* resident in the mind. An adequate description of human being must reject such dualism.[180] Anderson agrees that human nature can only be understood as a holistic physical, spiritual, and personal unity.[181] It is an integrated "psychophysical" unity, according to David Braine. He suggests that both dualist Cartesian and modern materialistic philosophies of human nature suffer from the same flaw of isolating mental states from the physical body.[182] Philip Mellor and Chris Shilling describe "the stubborn enfleshment of humans; they cannot be dissolved into thought, nor can they be reduced to a Foucauldian notion of discourse."[183] A. Synott suggests that because the Cartesian heritage separated mind and body, Western philosophy has been unable "to deal comprehensively or consistently with the human body."[184]

The judgment of a supreme value for rationality has a long history in the West. Descartes' redefinition of *being* in the perspective of *cogito ergo sum* has an older theological root, in the third-century theology of Origen, who described the nature of God as infinite mind (*nous*), or intellect and will. Origen's concept can in turn be linked to the Hellenistic

---

pression secondary to physical disorders." See A. Clark, *Being There*, xi–xiii, 218, 220; Herzfeld, *In Our Image*, 51; Brown, "Scientific and Biblical Portraits," 220.

179. Peterson, *Minding God*, 30.
180. Pannenberg, *Anthropology*, 523.
181. Anderson, "On Being Human," 193.
182. Braine, *Human Person*, 23–35, 172–77.
183. Mellor and Shilling, *Re-forming the Body*, 4–5.
184. Quoted in ibid., 6.

cosmology that maintained the superiority of mind over matter, which Maurice Wiles insists must be rejected by Christian theology at least on the grounds of the goodness of creation (Genesis 1).[185] Origen's description of God as mind or *nous* has some significant problems. Pannenberg suggests it is overly anthropomorphic, and does not properly capture the biblical Hebrew and Greek concept of *spirit*.[186] The emphasis on rationality has led to a kind of "intellicentric" arrogance, rendering a flawed and incomplete picture of God's image that neglects its moral dimensions. Humans can act with great rationality to perpetrate great evil, such as in the methodical engineering of genocides, or the systematic rape of nature. Indeed, the most rational and clever creature in the creation account might well be seen as the serpent. So Pannenberg insists that the biblical picture of God's rationality focuses on *wisdom*, not mere *intellect*. The one who displays the image of God is the one who is oriented towards the transcendent, who seeks after God; it is the one who does good, whose deeds are holy, in contrast to the abominable.[187]

Liberation theology also critiques Western theology for overemphasizing rationality: true Christian spirituality must be a spirituality of experience and action, not just words and reason. Theology that is doctrinal, deductive, and purely explanatory—i.e., a theology of *mind*—is inadequate: it simply has not captured the fullness of the *imago Dei*, either in Christ or in the church as it is to be molded to the image of Christ. Jon Sobrino blames this error on the Enlightenment spirit, which reduces to and defines everything by Descartes' *cogito* plumb line.[188] A proper theology of the *imago Dei*, if it is to be realized and displayed in creation in a way that does justice to the biblical concept, must also be more than talk and reason, the fruit of the focus on *mind*. The full biblical understanding of the *imago Dei* must be taken into account to arrive at a balanced understanding of its significance.

Such a holistic approach to God's image emerges in both the Old and New Testaments. Human beings created male and female relate to each other not merely dialogically, but bodily, emotionally, and intimately—"This at last is bone of my bones, and flesh of my flesh" (Gen 2:23). The man relates to his *rational* Creator God, but is lonely

185. Wiles, Review of *The Triune Creator*, 220.
186. Pannenberg, "Theology and Science," 306.
187. Pannenberg, *Anthropology*, 76–77.
188. Sobrino, "Spirituality and the Following of Jesus," 234.

without the woman. In New Testament perspective, Jesus is the primary model of the full image of God. His life is a union of words and actions: in his praxis he not only preached the gospel, he *is* the good news, he *is* the gospel. This was manifest as he laid hands to heal the sick, freed the demon-possessed, gave sight to the blind, died for humanity, and ultimately conquered death on their behalf. Pannenberg insists that the gospel as the revelation of God stems not primarily from what was *spoken*, but from what *happened*.[189] In his *body*, Jesus is the ultimate medium of the restoration of a right and whole relationship between humanity and God, irreducible to mental states or communications.

Lars Thunberg observes that many early church fathers noticed the problem of neglecting the bodily dimension of the image, rejecting both Origenian tendencies to see something "lacking in created humanity as such," and to see the mind as alone carrying the divine image as if it is "bound down through its relationship to the body and has to free itself through ascetic efforts in order to gain the divine likeness."[190] In Wojtyla's terms, the human person is inseparable from the body: we are "embodied selves."[191] A Platonic ideal of disembodied pure thought or mind as the ultimate form of existence is also contrary to the Christian hope for the resurrection.[192] Jesus' own resurrection demonstrates that the embodied, social, and ethical dimensions of God's image in human nature remain in the new creation. He is embodied not merely on earth, but for all eternity in a recognizably human body complete with his stigmata.[193] The Christian promise is that all human beings will share in the bodily resurrection in the eschaton—some in everlasting life, others in everlasting contempt. Thus human personhood is embodied both in this world and the next.

If there is a failure in Pannenberg, it is his limited interaction with the social and communal aspects of human nature and mind. Stewart notices that he evades "emotion, affect and mood," and he tends to avoid

---

189. Pannenberg, *Revelation as History*, 13.
190. Thunberg, "Human Person," 298.
191. Novak, "Embodied Self," 20.
192. Brown, "Conclusion," 226.
193. See page 116. Personal identity is not erased or forgotten in eternity. The redeemed nature springs from what the person has been and become in *this* life, with all its bodily, social and relational aspects (e.g., Matt 17:1–5; 1 Cor 13:12; Job 19:26–27). See McArthur, "Memory at the Eschaton."

the psychology of human relationships in favor of individualist and rationalist leanings, blaming this on his "lack of emphasis on the relational aspects of the cross."[194] Welker criticizes the modern understanding of personhood as *autonomy* because it fails "to grasp the authenticity of the unique corporal and sensual person. It also underestimates the contextuality of morality and the mutability of rationality." Since modernity has been fixated on the "disembodied person behind the mask," it has been unable to categorize the way in which humanity is shaped by social and cultural processes of differentiation. As a result, modern concepts of morality and rationality have been "unable to prevent entire societies that appealed to these governing powers from being possessed by chauvinist, fascist, racist and ecologically brutal mentalities."[195] Jay Budziszewski criticizes rationality-centered and functionalistic definitions of human nature for being inadequate to protect the whole meaning of "person" in the categorical thinking of natural law. He observes that the modernist's "functional method allows him to know only what he wants [human beings] to be—and different modernists want them to be different things":

> One thinker has greater regard for sentience, another for cognition, another for self-awareness. One thinks the important thing is sociality, another the capacity to make plans. With each different criterion of personhood, a different set of beings is welcomed through the gates of other's regard. This writer says that higher mammals are persons, but human babies are not. That one says that human babies are persons, but Grandma not. The one over there says that *some* human babies are persons, but only if their mothers think they are.[196]

Redefining humanity in reductionistic terms does violence to the *imago Dei*. It must be found in the totality of human nature, not in a

---

194. Stewart, *Reconstructing Science and Theology*, 88–89, 102–3, 116–27, 152–53, 158.

195. Welker, "Autonomous Person?" 104–11. Welker proposes a model of personhood based on *faith*, as a subjective relationship with God constructed upon objective certainties (e.g., Jesus' resurrection) and experienced and built in community. God "constitutes the complex unity of the person and the complex interdependence of the creatures. Without addressing God's creative activity, appreciated by faith, we do not gain a perspective on the unity of the public person and the unity of creation" (110–11).

196. Budziszewski, "Second Tablet Project," 31.

singular feature. As God's character and nature are inviolable, so human nature made in his image is inviolable. All aspects contribute to the holistic unity of human being: upright posture and the socially mediated mind, face-to-face communication and moral capacity, freedom from instinct and the capacity for intimate male-female sexual union, artistic creativity and the biological necessity of live birth, symbolic reasoning and emotional-physical bonding needs, even the simple abilities to take a walk, kneel in prayer, embrace, and hold hands. This is not to say that disembodied or alternately embodied rationality are a theoretical impossibility (e.g., God, biblical angels). It does suggest that these fall short of truly imaging God *in creation*. When God as transcendent mystery becomes incarnate, uniting once and forever with his creation, it is not as an angel or other sentient being, but as a *human* being. So Barth insisted that because of the incarnation, we could decisively assert the *humanity* of God.[197] Thus Pannenberg maintains that the *imago Dei*, the incarnation, and the divine fellowship offered humanity in Christ provides the grounds for a sweeping humanism: they guarantee the dignity and inviolability of all human beings.[198]

Pannenberg insists that human nature is what it is by God's intention, to reflect Godself in the cosmos. It can only be known for what it is in light of God's own nature and being. The *imago Dei* in Jesus is more than rationality: it is an inviolable whole representing God's self in the cosmos. Fergus Kerr observes, "being the image of God is not something extra added on from outside to a life lived in accordance with natural or secular principles." Such a dualist view is a byproduct of secular humanism.[199] Without its holistic, embodied, social, and essentially theological meaning as the *imago Dei*, human personhood and dignity inevitably suffers violation and degradation.[200]

---

197. Barth, *Humanity of God*, 49–50: "It is when we look at Jesus Christ that we know decisively that God's deity does not exclude, but includes His *humanity* . . . God requires no exclusion of humanity, no non-humanity, not to speak of inhumanity, in order to be truly God . . . His deity *encloses humanity in itself* . . . [In Jesus Christ] the fact is once for all established that God does not exist without man."

198. Pannenberg, *Systematic Theology*, 2:175–76.

199. Kerr, *Immortal Longings*, 167.

200. Budziszewski, "Second Tablet Project," 24–25, 30–31. Budziszewski's point is that no purely natural system devoid of the presence of God could maintain the inviolability of human nature. "A godless natural law would revere the laws of human nature only insofar as we continued to be human. Denying that our humanity is a creation,

Some Relevant Problems in Pannenberg's Theology

Several problems that are relevant to this thesis surface in Pannenberg's theology. Some of his philosophical presuppositions may be problematic, including an excessive reliance on questionable Hegelian notions. Also, his attempt to establish rational grounds for faith may be vulnerable in a postmodern setting. His hermeneutic appears to have some inconsistencies. His historical version of the resurrection has been attacked. His presentation of Jesus' divinity is contentious: he has been accused of presenting Jesus too much "from below," neglecting the transcendent aspects of the Christ revelation—those "from above." These accusations, if true, might compromise the thesis of dependent or critical anthropocentrism. Are his philosophical presuppositions too uncertain to sustain his program? If Pannenberg's hermeneutic is flawed, is the version of Jesus he arrives at reliable? Can the resurrection be held as a true event in either a modern or postmodern rationally critical setting? If Christ's divinity is improperly portrayed, is his cosmic significance challenged? These issues will be addressed in what follows.

Philosophical Challenges

There are several philosophical challenges to Pannenberg's thought. These include a detrimental reliance upon Hegel, a challenge from philosophical (materialistic) naturalism, and an examination of Pannenberg's rationalism in light of postfoundational issues.

Gunton proposes that because of his use of historical criticism, Pannenberg is too reliant upon Hegel's thought to establish a meaning for the resurrection. His hermeneutic leads to the rejection of the traditional gospel picture that establishes the pre-incarnate divinity of Jesus as the Son of God. Pannenberg's critical hermeneutic forbids him to follow Scripture's assertions about Jesus' divinity. Gunton insists that Pannenberg's rationality is not thoroughgoing, because it begins with a divine premise in the Hegelian assumption that there *is* a universal horizon of meaning. Therefore his theology must operate from the beginning in an unfounded "Hegelian matrix."[201] Paul Molnar agrees that Pannenberg's reliance on Hegelian and Heideggarian anticipation,

---

it would have no reason to preserve this humanity, and no objection to its abolition" (25).

201. Gunton, *Yesterday and Today*, 18, 20–23.

and his grounding reality in "limited human experience" (the idea that there is "a mysterious ground of all reality transcending one's own and all other finite existence"), leads to subjectivity rather than ultimate rationality.[202] Gunton insists Pannenberg's interpretative use of the apocalyptic milieu only works by insisting that historical facts and their interpretation are inseparable. But what if the witnesses were simply wrong in their apocalyptic interpretation, as a given culture's take on any historical event may be rejected or reinterpreted by succeeding generations?[203]

Roger Olson and others point out Pannenberg's indebtedness to Hegel,[204] which Pannenberg acknowledges, insisting all modern Christian theology is similarly indebted: "Indeed, none of the great thinkers of modernity has done half as much as Hegel to put the Christian religion back on the throne it lost because of the Enlightenment."[205] Pannenberg uses Hegel's idea of the "field of universal truth" as the only domain in which the idea of God could last.[206] But he agrees that Christian theology for the most part bypassed Hegel because of various perceived flaws in his program, and insists on his independence from Hegel.[207] Philip Clayton suggests Pannenberg's program of "anticipation" (the anticipation of the "apocalyptic horizon") is not just a Hegelian inspiration, but is a natural derivative of the resurrection, which is the anticipation of God's ultimate future. The resurrection, in its apocalyptic milieu, points to and demands a reckoning with the end of history. This anticipatory vision moves beyond Hegel's "insistence on truth and reality as the final whole of experience."[208] For Pannenberg, there is a "strictly theological root of the concept of anticipation . . . if Jesus' person and history are to be understood as final revelation of the divine Logos."[209] He accepts Julius Müller's critique of Hegel's insistence upon the logical necessity

202. Molnar, "Problems," 315, 325.

203. Gunton, *Yesterday and Today*, 18, 20–23.

204. Olson, "Human Self-Realization of God," 207–323; Westphal, "Hegel, Pannenberg, and Hermeneutics," 276; Galloway, *Wolfhart Pannenberg*, 64.

205. Pannenberg, "Die Bedeutung des Christentums," 112 (my translation); see also 78–113, esp. 93–94. See also Welker, "Das theologische Prinzip," 234.

206. Pannenberg, *Basic Questions Vol. 3*, 159.

207. Pannenberg, "Response to my American Friends," 320.

208. Clayton, "Anticipation and Theological Method," 129, 134; Galloway, *Wolfhart Pannenberg*, 64.

209. Pannenberg, "Response to my American Friends," 319–20.

of God's creation of the world, as well as his concept of God as *Mind*. Hegel's thought leads to a type of pantheism, in that God and the world are inextricably bound by God's dependence on the creation for his self-realization. Proper contingency also disappears from Hegel's version of the freedom of God and human beings, and cannot do justice to Christianity, which is—among all religions—*the* religion of freedom.[210] He rejects Hegel's version of history as overly deterministic; the historical notion of being is freed from rational necessity and embedded in the actual changes of human history. Thus Clayton concludes Pannenberg is not fatally Hegelian.[211] Merold Westphal even suggests that Pannenberg is the "most articulate anti-Hegelian since Kierkegaard."[212]

Galloway and Buller note the flaws in Hegel's dialectic of the historical process with the triune life of God, which particularly in Feuerbach led to the conflation of humanity and the infinite, and the replacement of God by Hegel's eternal human spirit.[213] Pannenberg is influenced by the original dialectic, but moves beyond it in his concept of the eschatological futurity of God and of history in their mutual distinction. Humanity's finiteness is preserved, while the potential relationship with the infinite in the persons of God is maintained, hence humanity's essentially religious or spiritual nature. Because of this correction to Hegel, he has an answer to the Feurbachian atheistic tendency in such thinkers as Nietzsche, Marx, and Freud. Pannenberg's notion that God only becomes God at the end of history is not Hegelian, because God is eschatologically realized only in relationship to the creation, not in his inter-Trinitarian relations. The invisible and transcendent God exists independently of creation and history, and becomes the visible and present God in relationship to creation at the eschaton. He is the hidden God of Israel's faith; yet even in his hiddenness, he has revealed himself in Israel and in Jesus.[214] Stewart also notes that Pannenberg moves away

---

210. Pannenberg, *Basic Questions*, 3:169–77. Pannenberg refers to Müller, *Die Christliche Lehre von der Sünde*, 552.

211. Clayton, "Anticipation and Theological Method," 132–36.

212. Westphal, "Hegel, Pannenberg, and Hermeneutics," 276.

213. Galloway, *Wolfhart Pannenberg*, 113; Buller, *Unity of Nature and History*, 15–16.

214. Tupper, *Theology of Wolfhart Pannenberg*, 187.

from Hegel by accepting Gadamer's assertion of the provisional, time-conditioned nature of knowledge.[215]

Another dispute arises over the issue of philosophical naturalism. Martin Buss regards "apocalyptic expectation" as belonging to a mythical category. He says the expected end of history, both in Christ's resurrection and in the general resurrection, cannot be regarded as historical in nature, and as a result cannot provide an interpretive framework for something claiming to be within history.[216] Those like Buss who continue to adhere to materialistic naturalism will be unsatisfied with Pannenberg's modification of historical criticism to allow unusual events such as resurrections. They will insist on philosophical grounds that human beings simply do not conquer death. Pannenberg's rejection of absolute naturalism and his insistence on the possibility of unusual past events that are outside our normal experience anticipates contemporary postfoundationalist thought (see chapter 4).[217] Although he rejects naturalism in his evaluation of the resurrection, he often tacitly returns to it in his evaluation of other events in Scripture.

David Holwerda wonders if Pannenberg's definition of revelation as history, rather than as verbal transmission, can really hold up, given that he uses Israel's verbal apocalyptic expectation to ground the meaning of the resurrection. He suggests that Pannenberg's claim to historical objectivity may in fact have some subtle faith precommitments hidden within it, so that the success of his effort to establish the resurrection solely by reason is dubious.[218] Molnar notices a similar problem in Pannenberg's philosophical approach, which grounds faith in God ultimately in human subjective experience and rationality.[219] Shults observes that in the postfoundational setting, every epistemology has an element of "fiduciary rootedness," even those taking a critical realist stance.[220] Pannenberg in later writing admits his own subjectivity before the Christ event, in the sense that he believes it to be so all-determining for the meaning of history that everyone must be subjective before it.[221]

215. Stewart, *Reconstructing Science and Theology*, 28.
216. Buss, "Meaning of History," 150–51.
217. Shults, *Postfoundationalist Task of Theology*, 111.
218. Holwerda, "Faith, Reason, and the Resurrection," 304–11.
219. Molnar, "Some Problems," 338–39.
220. Shults, *Postfoundationalist Task of Theology*, 38–43, 81.
221. Pannenberg, "Response to My American Friends," 315.

This suggests vulnerability or the need for qualification in his program of critical rationalism.

Pannenberg's Hermeneutic

Pannenberg's hermeneutic of the resurrection differs from his treatment of other aspects of Jesus' life. The resurrection confirms that in Jesus the end of the world has begun, that Jesus "is the 'Son of Man' who will come again," that God confirms Jesus' pre-resurrection ministry, and that Jesus is God's final revelation. The witness of the early church "is to be understood as an exposition of the significance of the resurrection." The resurrection is more than brute fact: there is a "unity of event and word in the resurrection appearances" that helps establish faith.[222]

John Hick observes that modern New Testament scholarship takes it as basic that our access to the life of Jesus comes only through the memories and interpretation of the post-Easter church.[223] Even though a true resurrection seems to entail a fairly high view of the Gospel testimony, Pannenberg does not consistently follow this conclusion. His method often seeks the historical truth *behind* the resurrection witnesses and their record. Although theoretically he believes in miracles, his analysis often looks very much like that of his naturalistic colleagues, even at times relying upon them.[224] He rules many other significant supernatural Gospel events and presuppositions invalid in the name of rationalism, using the original historical-critical filter. The miraculous often continues to be legendary, even including actual resurrection appearances in the Gospels. This appears to be bait-and-switch tactics, claiming freedom from naturalism, but submitting to it for much of the analysis.

---

222. Pannenberg, *Jesus*, 67–73.

223. Hick, *Metaphor of God Incarnate*, 15. The recent discovery of the ossuary of "James, son of Joseph, brother of Jesus" may send some cracks through this standard view, even though charges of forgery against the inscription remain currently unsettled. In principle, there is no reason to reject the possibility that other archaeological evidence of aspects of Jesus' pre-Easter life will surface. See Lemaire, "Burial Box of James," 24–33.

224. E.g., Pannenberg's dismissal of Jesus' self-consciousness as Messiah and Son of God (*Jesus*, 252) looks much like Bornkamm's *Jesus of Nazareth*, 169–78. He explicitly follows Wrede and Marxsen in declaring the passion predictions later church inventions (*Jesus*, 245).

For example, he rejects the virgin birth, the pre-incarnate existence of Christ, Jesus' foreknowledge of the cross, and his self-identity as Messiah or Son of God. Some of the resurrection accounts are deemed "legendary" because of their corporeal aspect.[225] In practice, the resurrection is the main transcendent event to pass through Pannenberg's historical-critical filter. By accepting the part of the apostolic witness touching directly upon the resurrection while rejecting much of the rest, he calls into question the connection that allows us to know the same Jesus the apostles knew. Why should the resurrection, for example, be seen as any less "mythological" than a pre-incarnate existence? If the resurrection was a bodily phenomenon, a real historical event with some aspect occurring in space and time, why should a "corporeal" description of it be deemed "legendary"? If the resurrection is true, why is Pannenberg in a better position to judge the nature of the resurrected Jesus than the Gospel witnesses? Why should a virgin birth or a messianic self-understanding or prophetic predictions of future events be regarded as any more incredible or unlikely than a man conquering death?[226] If the modern historical and scientific consciousness can be induced to swallow the one, then why not the rest? Or if not the rest, why the one?

Pannenberg offers a system theoretically free from the limitations of naturalism. By expanding the bounds of possibility, and recognizing the provisional understanding of reality in contemporary science as open and elastic, he opens the way to establish the resurrection as a real transcendent event in history through critical historical investigation. He begins from the historical-critical method as an apologetic move, in an effort to make the resurrection a credible basis of faith for a critical generation. To that extent, his use of those methodological tools is a submission to the needs of his target audience: he wants to answer for them why, in the midst of the currently contested details of Jesus' life, they should put faith in Jesus because of his resurrection. He

225. E.g., the Emmaus road account is "legendary"; Jesus must have been surprised by the cross, to protect his limitation as Son of God to his incarnate existence, so that our conception of Jesus does not fall "back into the mythological realm." Pannenberg, *Systematic Theology*, 2:318–19; *Jesus*, 89, 160–69, 224, 246, 394–95.

226. Stewart notices the disjoin here sometimes extends even to the rejection of New Testament ethical teaching (e.g., on the valuation of people before property) in the interest of philosophical coherence. *Reconstructing Science and Theology*, 123; Pannenberg, *Anthropology*, 424.

develops a theological program built throughout with this approach, which Schwöbel has called "rational orthodoxy."[227] This is a reasonable move to the extent that it answers the problem of subjective experience as the basis of scriptural authority.[228] It appears, however, to be internally inconsistent; for while Pannenberg agrees that the nature of the resurrection is truth-establishing, at the same time he forbids that fact to demonstrate the truth of Christ's whole life.[229] It may also mean Pannenberg's claims of critical rationalism are overstated in light of his own admission of fiduciary subjectivity. While admitting the failure of Enlightenment rationality, he is frequently bound by it.[230]

The Resurrection as Ground of Truth

Does the importance Pannenberg places upon an objective resurrection leave his theology vulnerable? This is the position of Buss and others, who see in the violation of naturalism an irrational return to premodern thinking. A deeper analysis of just how rational materialistic naturalism of this type actually is will take place in chapter 4, though as noted previously, many philosophers reject naturalistic epistemology as fundamentally irrational. If a faith stance is taken based upon a precommitment to materialistic or ontological naturalism, then no amount of evidence will be adequate to prove a resurrection. Without a real resurrection, Pannenberg's historically rooted theology would likely collapse.

Postmodern thought sometimes suggests that events like the resurrection can only be relevant to the particular community that has accepted them *a priori*.[231] In this critique, however, there is no objective reality independent of particular communities available to *anyone*. Every community is dependent upon its own subjective narrative, and objectivity is a myth. The gospel and resurrection phenomenology would therefore be acceptable as the narrative of the church, but would have no intrinsic authority over the narrative of any other community. If the resurrection was merely an idea, an ideology, or a philosophical concept, then it might thus be relevant only to its own community. Then

---

227. Schwöbel, "Rational Theology in Trinitarian Perspective," 499.

228. Pannenberg, *Systematic Theology*, 1,:33–36.

229. Grenz, "Appraisal of Pannenberg," 25.

230. Pannenberg, "Resurrection," 259; Stewart, *Reconstructing Science and Theology*, 114.

231. This is very similar to Barth's position.

the arguments presented here for *critical anthropocentrism* would have a similar status to that given the resurrection. At best, it could have only metaphorical, symbolic, or mythical meaning, or be important only within its own narrative community.

Such a relativistic conclusion ought to be questioned on the grounds that postmodern relativism continues to be based on the Enlightenment rejection of the transcendent realm. This is anticipating arguments to be developed later, but the contention of this thesis is that such naturalism must be set aside as an "absolute" worldview, even by postmoderns (see chapter 4, page 196). Further, Pannenberg would sharply disagree with the idea that the truthfulness of an event applies only to the particular community that constitutes the given historical record. This is the opposite of the meaning of history. Some events are only locally interesting, while others have universal significance, but all are universally true to the degree that they actually happened. The modern historical sensibility even of relativists is that "there are basic facts which are the same for all historians."[232] While the resurrection is unique, trust in its authenticity could be based on a critical evaluation of basic facts pertaining to it, particularly if the naturalistic bias against it were set aside. When historical-critical research rejects the resurrection, it is on the grounds of philosophical naturalism. As William P. Alston observes, such findings are ideological in character, not "a *result of historical investigation*."[233] If one accepts miracles as possible, there is in principle nothing barring the confirmation of the truth of the resurrection.

Pannenberg is explicitly not interested in scriptural authority for its own sake.[234] Rather, he appropriates the scriptural record as a flawed historical document, yet one which the historian must take seriously, and which has enough data to verify the historicity of the resurrection, which in turn places Jesus in a unique category. Other religions have claimed divinity for various persons throughout history, but those claims are not offered as objectively verifiable events such as Pannenberg claims for the resurrection.[235] It happens decisively in history, thus mak-

---

232. Carr, *What is History?*, 8. Carr identifies himself as a historical relativist.

233. Alston, *Perceiving God*, 244–45.

234. Pannenberg, "Response to the Discussion," **226**; Holwerda, "Faith, Reason, and the Resurrection," 279.

235. Hindu avatars, claims for divine inspiration by prophets such as Muhammad,

ing God's claims open to doubt, possible refutation, investigation, and ultimately to the possibility of historical verification.[236] So Pannenberg claims that Judeo-Christian revelation is as testable as any other historical event. The resurrection, witnessed by doubting, incredulous, ordinary women and men who nevertheless became convinced of its reality, is the watershed event that defines—or redefines—all history. If true, it confirms the deity and incarnation of God in Jesus Christ.[237] No competing claims to ultimate authority can be successful without equivalent credentials.

The Nature of Jesus' Divinity

Pannenberg's version of the incarnation differs from the traditional understanding offered by patristic and classical Christology. This is clear already in his hermeneutic separation of the resurrection from other events that might confirm a different type of divinity for Jesus, e.g., one with a pre-incarnate existence. Jenson agrees that the early Pannenberg has followed Rahner's move of declaring that "the immanent Trinity *is* the economic Trinity."[238] Jesus' earthly relationship to the Father *is* the content of his relationship as Son of God to the Father. Galloway sees something similar: the eternal Father-Son relationship seems reduced to just what happened between God and Jesus in the history recorded by the Gospels.[239] His presentation in *Jesus—God and Man* does seem to underemphasize the existence of the Son of God independently of the man Jesus of Nazareth.

> Jesus is the Son of the eternal Father only in his complete dedication to the will of the Father . . . The absolute, real unity of Jesus' will with the Father's, as was confirmed in God's raising

---

Joseph Smith, or Sun Yung Moon, or the divinity ascribed to Buddha (in certain traditions, e.g., Theravāda and folk Buddhism), are faith claims effectively beyond historical investigation, and are philosophical, subjective, or experiential in their method of verification. See Bowker, ed., *Oxford Dictionary of World Religions*, 171–77; Powers, *Concise Encyclopedia of Buddhism*, 134; Carlyon, *Guide to the Gods*, 121.

236. Pannenberg, *Systematic Theology*, 1:48–50, 151–53, 244–45; "Der Gott der Geschichte," 87; *Anthropology*, 15–16.

237. Pannenberg, *Jesus*, 321.

238. Jenson, "Jesus in the Trinity," 197.

239. Galloway, *Wolfhart Pannenberg*, 104.

him up from the dead, is the medium of his essential unity with God and the basis of all assertions about Jesus' divine Sonship.[240]

It is precisely in and through Jesus that the Son of God manifests that relationship to the Father that characterizes him as the Father's Son. The Son seems to exist only within the temporal order, and the creation's origin in the Son as Logos is neglected, as if he does not become the Son of God until he appears in the man Jesus.[241] How can the Son be the co-author of creation in this understanding? Ted Peters maintains that this makes the Logos contingent upon history, rather than vice versa, because it is found in the concrete and contingent order of the creation, rather than in the abstract laws of nature.[242]

If the Son of God's existence is so contingent upon historical reality, does this threaten our understanding of the Trinitarian nature of God? To put it crudely, how can the Son be begotten in this framework, rather than made? Roger Olson asks whether the character of Jesus Pannenberg derives from his bounded version of the resurrection is in fact a type of adoptionism, rather than the classical understanding of Jesus' incarnation.[243] Pannenberg has, according to Olson, rejected the traditional doctrine of the immanent Trinity as flawed because it violates the contingency and openness of history. An immanent Trinity "thought of as previous to all historical relations of God to the world [implies] that the incarnation was something supplementary and exterior to the eternal life of the Trinitarian God."[244] Nicholas Lash sees in this position a departure from classical Christology to the extent that it no longer takes the pre-incarnate existence as a given of faith.[245]

Pannenberg suggests the idea of Christ's pre-incarnate existence is to be rejected as a "Hellenistic infiltration."[246] But Gunton notes that

---

240. Pannenberg, *Jesus*, 349.

241. Galloway, *Wolfhart Pannenberg*, 128–30.

242. Peters, "Editor's Introduction," 12. Pannenberg might answer that in the created realm, there *are* no abstract laws, only contingent ones.

243. Olson, "Human Self-Realization of God," 221.

244. Olson, "Trinity and Eschatology," 223.

245. Lash, "Up and Down in Christology," 31–46.

246. Pannenberg rejects the defining of the Logos as active in creation separately from or prior to the historical Jesus (*Jesus*, 160–69, 394–95, n. 65 on 394). He insists Jesus' divinity and identity as Logos is guaranteed by the fact that Jesus is God's full revelation. His christological interpretation of the Old Testament downplays theophanies that have been taken as early revelations of the Son of God in traditional Christian

St. Paul's pre-incarnation references show that belief in a divine and co-eternal Christ was an early phenomenon in the church, already taken for granted by Paul and the Corinthians at an early date, and not a gradual development, as some have portrayed the Johannine material to represent. In classical incarnational theology both Old and New Testament references are regarded as part of the unified witness to Christ's pre-incarnate existence. Although shaped by awareness of Hellenistic culture, and the need to make the gospel comprehensible to it, both John's logos Christology and Paul's kenotic Christology are parts of the general New Testament acknowledgment of Jesus' pre-incarnate divinity. Gunton observes that as a result of his position, Pannenberg is forced to rely upon a dubious philosophical model to ground his incarnational theology. He suggests that what Pannenberg really offers in his Christology is a "divinized man," rather than the eternal and only-begotten Son of God.[247]

James Cone objects that Pannenberg's version of Jesus not only cuts him off from a pre-incarnate existence, but from an ongoing post-resurrection presence in the church. Speaking from the Black-American church tradition, Cone insists that the contemporary experience of "the historical Jesus as the Crucified and Risen Lord who is present with us in the struggle of freedom" must be taken into account in any holistic portrayal of Jesus. He cannot accept Pannenberg's delineation of such experiences as untestable, purely subjective, or emotional.[248] Stewart agrees he overemphasizes rationality and neglects love, emotion, experience, and aesthetic sensation. Here, she may have indirectly uncovered the parallels between Pannenberg's version of Trinitarian relations and his approach to human nature as individual rather than communal or social (which she blames on his neglect of the cross).[249] Daniel Hardy

---

theology (Josh 5: 13–15; Judg 6:20–22; 13:17–22; Ps 2; Prov 30:4; Dan 7:13–14; 10:1–11). He also rejects the New Testament teaching on the Son's pre-incarnate existence, explicitly in John's Logos present in the beginning *with* and *as* God and in Paul's kenotic references, and implicitly elsewhere (John 1:1, 30; 8:42, 56, 58; Phil 2:6–11; Col 1:17; 1 Cor 10:4). (E.g., following Barth and Blanke, *Colossians*, 203). Pannenberg's departure from Paul here is particularly surprising, since Paul is his most authoritative apostolic witness.

247. Gunton, *Yesterday and Today*, 18, 73, 79.

248. Cone, *God of the Oppressed*, 121–22.

249. Stewart, *Reconstructing Science and Theology*, 88–89, 102–3, 116–27, 152–53, 158.

observes that social Trinitarian thought helps ground and explain the "being-with" condition of humanity. Human social nature, including in the church, ought to be traced to the truth of the Logos "of God present in creation." "This divine ordering is what ultimately implants in the human condition the 'being-with' which is natural to it," which itself reflects "the sociality of God present for humanity in created society."[250] Pannenberg's philosophical rationalism fails him for being unable to properly acknowledge either divine or human social nature.

Pannenberg's later writings do not seem to restrict the life of the Son of God solely to his existence in the historical man Jesus of Nazareth. He agrees the Logos must have some kind of eternal character to be internally consistent. He says a complete christological doctrine cannot be developed "solely from the perspective of Jesus' humanity," because truths about God "can never be derived from anthropology alone." He suggests that the Logos as organizing principle and Word of God is the origin of the information which science reveals to be present throughout the cosmos.[251] Jesus' recognition of the Father as God in distinction from himself gives validity to "the independent existence of other creatures alongside himself"; he provides the ground for all that is distinct from God, including the origin and existence of all creaturely reality.[252] In more recent writings, he maintains that Jesus' communion with the eternal God, confirmed by Easter, "is itself eternal," and appears to tacitly agree with the early church's belief in Jesus' preexistence as "immediately following" from this eternal communion.[253]

Pannenberg's version of God's relationship to time attempts to reconcile views from "below" and "above."[254] If God is present in eternity to all time, then the appearance of the Son of God only in the particular space-time of Jesus of Nazareth is still not inconsistent with his co-presence in eternity.[255] The Logos stands with God on the side

---

250. Hardy, *God's Ways with the World*, 202.

251. Pannenberg, *Systematic Theology*, 2:4–5, 112; Grenz, *Reason for Hope*, 113.

252. Pannenberg, *Systematic Theology*, 2: 29–30. The Logos must be the foundation upon which all of history is built, not merely an order that arises simultaneously with history, to be properly regarded as governing the process. If it is the ground of natural law, it cannot be merely a result of natural law's contingent operation within history.

253. Pannenberg, "Concept of Miracle," 762; "Resurrection," 261.

254. Buller, *Unity of Nature and History*, 37.

255. Pannenberg, "Theological Questions to Scientists," 74.

of eternity, and so in direct relationship to *all* time, not just the time beginning with the historical birth of Jesus. So the world can be said to have been created through and by the Logos, the Son of God. He is then manifest completely as the Son of God in Jesus of Nazareth without either compromising his deity or denying his humanity, because of his all-time-embracing character. The Logos will be shown to have been the founding principle and cause of creation all along, as revealed from the retrospective position of the eschatological end of history.

> The statement that all things and beings are created through Jesus Christ means that the *eschaton* that has appeared beforehand in Jesus represents the time and point from which the creation took place. According to the Biblical understanding, the essence of things will be decided only in the future. What they are is decided by what they will become. Thus the creation happens from the end, from the ultimate future.[256]

It is a three-fold process: origin or beginning, ongoing maintaining through "immanent divine self-involvement," and completion or perfection from and at the end.[257] Pannenberg thus asserts the predestination of all things toward Jesus: "their eschatological summation" through him "is identical with their creation through" him.[258] The universe is contingent, not the persons of God. The Trinitarian relationships are *eternal*, hidden until revealed by the resurrection. Here there seems to be room for a richer Trinitarian understanding of the Son's divinity, transcendent and immanent, rather than purely economic.[259]

Conclusion

Despite what might be perceived as de-anthropocentrizing flaws, Pannenberg still arrives at the unique divinity of Jesus and at a clear version of the incarnation. This must be credited to the strength that the resurrection has for Pannenberg: once having accepted it as historical fact, he must find some way to make sense of it. He insists that to understand the real meaning of Jesus requires wrestling with the real history;

---

256. Pannenberg, *Jesus*, 169.
257. Buller, *Unity of Nature and History*, 72.
258. Pannenberg, *Jesus*, 378–97; 391.
259. Grenz, *Reason for Hope*, 113; Gunton, *Yesterday and Today*, 29–30; Pannenberg, *Jesus*, 53–55.

its meaning is to be found within it, and there is something *objective* there to be found. In turn, this search for the objective puts Pannenberg on a track that takes him away from Hegel, for Hegel's Christology "tends to swallow up into philosophical abstraction the historical reality of Jesus."[260] Pannenberg, like the Gospel writers, moves first from the objective fact of the resurrection to the conclusion that "Jesus is Lord." Though he may have difficulty with other important features of Christology due to his methodology, he nevertheless is able to see those key aspects. Perhaps his could be described as a "core theology" of the incarnation and resurrection, reliable for the broad sense, rather than the detailed exposition.

Pursuing this discussion into a deeper critique is beyond the scope of this project. The fundamental importance of the incarnation for all of cosmic reality is not compromised by these potential problems. Whether the Son of God has an independent existence in relation to creation and time prior to Jesus of Nazareth, or only appears with certainty in him, the incarnation, as demonstrated by the resurrection, is the decisive event of cosmic unity and destiny, and is the fulfillment of God's revelation through the whole history of Israel. Pannenberg's essential and positive point is that the appearance in history of the loving relationship of the Father to the Son in the person of Jesus is the "actual mode" for the drawing of creaturely existence into the divine love of the inner-Trinitarian relationship.[261] Therefore, even if it is only revealed to the cosmos for what it is at the end of history, the incarnation *is* the keystone of the cosmos. The creation is still ordered to the Logos in his incarnation, and ordained to fulfillment in and through his humanity, appearing in history as it does in Jesus Christ. From the retrospective position of the eschatological end of history, all things are created through and by the Son of God, the Logos made flesh in Jesus of Nazareth. The history of creation from its beginning to its ending receives its meaning, fulfillment, and crowning in him.

If anything, Pannenberg's "rational orthodoxy" leads him to understate the scope and significance of the incarnation. The fact that his hermeneutic tends to reduce everything to the least common denominator, and yet he nevertheless arrives at a strong doctrine of the incarnation in light of the resurrection, is an indication of the strength

---

260. Grenz, *Reason for Hope*, 47.
261. Buller, *Unity of Nature and History*, 49.

of the claim. Thus, a critical evaluation of Pannenberg's thought does not undermine its anthropocentric aspects.

Summary of Pannenberg's Perspective

This analysis of Pannenberg's thought has shown just how deeply anthropocentric is his theological program. According to him, God has created the universe with incarnation as its chief crown and goal. The universe is focused towards and comes to fruition in *the* incarnation of God in Jesus Christ. It derives its reality and creaturely independence from Jesus, the Son of God, who is also the model for creation's dependence upon God and the means for the cosmos to transcend its mortality (confirmed by the resurrection). Humanity is of highest significance within the created realm, because only it is the image of God reflected there. It represents and portrays God himself in the universe. No other creature, angel, or sphere is constituted as the form of God within his creation, nor was prepared to receive God into itself in the incarnation. The history of the universe is, in this incarnational perspective, "a prehistory to the coming of humanity." So "we humans can be called the goal of creation," particularly as that goal is realized in the incarnation. Humanity's destiny is not off in one corner. On the contrary, in them, "the destiny of all creation is at stake." All creation waits "for the manifestation of divine sonship in the human race," for only then will it find eternal life. Here, humanity represents God to the cosmos, and the cosmos to God.[262]

This understanding is not contradicted by science, which offers some coherent data in the anthropic principle and in its recognition of the holistic nature of socially embodied humanity. Pannenberg maintains that the Copernican principle and the possibility of extraterrestrials do not threaten human cosmic significance. The eschatologically mediated predestination of all things towards Christ allows the theologian to maintain that humanity is not an accident of history, but rather its goal and destiny. In incarnational perspective, the scientifically discernable anthropic conditions are coherent with this position, though science will be unable to arrive there on its own or supply its meaning. The creation as it culminates in humanity expresses this providential ordering towards Christ. The theologian can assert the *humanity* of the

---

262. Pannenberg, *Systematic Theology*, 2:73–74; *Anthropology*, 12.

cosmos, in the sense that cosmic history comes to focus and salvation in human beings. Because of God's intention to bring creation into his fellowship, the ordering of creation through time partially described by the anthropic principle can be seen as the way to make humanity possible (see chapter 6).[263] Thus, the universe has been designed to culminate not just in *conscious* being, but also in *human* being, and finally in God's being *in* humanity. As created, the universe is theocentric; in light of the incarnation it is also anthropocentric.

Pannenberg's realist approach to history and the resurrection gives rise to a theology that intrinsically entails human significance. The resurrection verifies the incarnation, the cosmic significance of Christ, and ultimately the cosmic significance of humanity. Even with the various flaws in Pannenberg's thought that might undermine human significance, his theology still supports it because it rests on the person and work of Jesus Christ. Insofar as Pannenberg represents realist Protestant theology, such theology will be inevitably anthropocentric. It must conclude that humanity occupies a place of central significance for the whole of the cosmos, representing or imaging God therein, realizing in Trinitarian fellowship the goal of creation, acting as the key upon which the fulfillment of the cosmos depends. This *critical anthropocentrism* is an inherent feature of Pannenberg's thought, woven into the entire structure of his theological program. It is an outworking of foundational Trinitarian and incarnational truths, part of the grammatical shape and the core constitution of Christianity itself, and enduring despite philosophical, methodological, or analytic flaws. Any attempt to remove this focus seems likely to require major distortions to Christianity's inherent structure.

---

263. Gunton, "Trinity," 115.

2

Karl Rahner

Human Evolutionary Transcendence and Its Incarnational Fulfillment

> Man is a personal subject from whose freedom as a subject the fate of the entire cosmos depends.
>
> —Karl Rahner[1]

Introduction to Rahner's Thought

KARL RAHNER, SJ (1904–1984), WAS PERHAPS THE MOST INFLUENTIAL German Roman Catholic theologian of the twentieth century. His theological agenda arose as a partial response to his contemporary philosophical milieu, and shows particular sensitivity to the theological issues that have arisen from the modern scientific endeavor.

Rahner's theological method has been described as embodying "a dialectic of the transcendental with the historical."[2] From its beginning, this theology is grounded upon a transcendent anthropology: a vision of humanity open to the possibility of God's own life. Humanity is his starting point: humanity defined in a specific way, centered on this concept of the transcendent. "Dogmatic theology today has to be theological anthropology . . . Such an anthropology must, of course, be a transcendental anthropology . . . [because] every theological question must also be considered from a transcendental point of view."[3] Rahner maintains that the human search for the transcendent is the foundation of all theological quests for truth. This search explains why humans are

---

1. Rahner, "Theology and Anthropology," 15.
2. Kelly, *Karl Rahner*, 33.
3. Rahner, "Theology and Anthropology," 1–3; Sheehan, *Karl Rahner*, 3.

never satisfied with any final and finite explanation for existence and reality. This is evidence of the orientation of the creation towards God, the infinite, expressed in humanity as a gift of grace,[4] so that God is the "foundational impulse behind every attraction to know truth and to love goodness."[5] Theological anthropology finds its warrant in the fact that all "transcendental awareness" exists, even as a possibility, in dependence upon and in reference to the absolute mystery.[6]

Tracing some of the philosophical and historical influences on Rahner will serve to introduce his thought, while at the same time illuminating this concept of transcendence. Thomas Sheehan identifies Aquinas as the philosopher from whom Rahner, by "reinterpretation" for the modern mind, derived his thought, particularly the "transcendental turn to the subject" as the basis for metaphysics. This metaphysic of subjective human cognition underlies Rahner's theological program.[7] George Vass identifies Kant, Maréchal, and Heidegger as other leading philosophical influences. Stephen Fields adds Hegel to the list. Rahner's overall philosophical approach is in its historical origins "a combination and continuation of Kant's criticism of human knowledge, Maréchal's correction of the same in the light of Thomistic analysis and Heidegger's presentation of the Kantian problem in ontological terms."[8] According to Karl Weger, Rahner has taken up Kant's theory regarding human transcendental knowledge, which questioned the validity of human knowing, emphasized its subjective aspects, and denied the possibility of true knowledge of the noumenal divine realm, and modified it by adding Joseph Maréchal's vertical extension of the transcendental to include the divine realm: for Rahner, there is the possibility of real knowledge of God.[9] Kant established the "Copernican turn" in his transcendental philosophy of human knowledge, restricting knowledge to the "objectivity of objects."[10] In Maréchal, human judgments of the affirmation of given concrete truths point to real knowledge of being; in turn the absolute character of these affirmations confirms the presence

---

4. Rahner, *Foundations*, 172.
5. Kelly, *Karl Rahner*, 37.
6. Rahner, *Theological Investigations*, 11:105.
7. Sheehan, *Karl Rahner*, 1–2.
8. Vass, *Theologian in Search of a Philosophy*, 24.
9. Weger, *Karl Rahner*, 23–24.
10. Losinger, *Anthropological Turn*, 7, 10.

of Absolute Being, which is a sign post pointing towards God.[11] Thus Rahner uses Maréchal's insight to modify the Kantian limitations on human knowledge and the Kantian definition of transcendence to include the possibility of the knowledge of God, based on this capacity of the human mind for the absolute and infinite.[12] Rahner takes this route because for him, "God is the presupposition, the 'condition of possibility' which Kant ultimately simply left unexplained."[13]

For Rahner, human transcendentality is its openness to mystery, to the divine. He makes use of Hegel's dialectic of Spirit, in which the perfection of reality is sought, and modifies it to allow a hierarchy of difference between "infinite and finite modes of being."[14] Absolute being is both the immanent cause of modes of becoming, as well as being distinct from them. Hegel is further evident in Rahner's doctrine of finite substances, which "entails the immanence of absolute Being."[15] He takes up Heidegger's question on the "Being of beings" and transforms it into a defining spiritual characteristic of humanity: humans are in search of Being because they are open to the source of Being who is God, and hence to the possibility of religious faith in God.[16] This existential openness to God forms part of the foundation of Rahner's "phenomenology of the experience of God."[17] At the same time, Rahner's turn to the subjective entails a rejection of the otherworldly "spiritual beyond," in favor of the world of the senses, while maintaining the possibility of a metaphysics of being. Human beings have an intuition of this infinite, a pull towards the absolute of God, which is never realized in the world, but is only approached asymptotically. This "projective anticipation" of the divine is what constitutes human "spirituality."[18] Michael Purcell locates the deeper significance of Rahner's transcendental theology here, in human existence as a "response to that mysterious other," which even supercedes being as we know it.[19] Human transcendentality is a key

---

11. Roberts, *Achievement of Karl Rahner*, 14.
12. Pasquini, *Atheism and Salvation*, 91.
13. Weger, *Karl Rahner*, 26.
14. Fields, *Being as Symbol*, 66–76.
15. Ibid., 75.
16. Vass, *Theologian in Search of a Philosophy*, 26–27.
17. Losinger, *Anthropological Turn*, 11.
18. Sheehan, *Karl Rahner*, 2–3.
19. Purcell, *Mystery and Method*, xxiv.

concept for Rahner's entire theological system, and will be examined in more detail on page 92.

The "unsurpassable climax of revelation" is, for Rahner, the incarnation of God in history in the person of Jesus Christ, when God's self-communication reaches its highest point.[20] It is here that God's love for the world is fully and finally revealed, and here can be found the true heart of Rahner's theology. If human yearning and uncertainty form the heart of his anthropology, then his theology is an outworking of God's loving answer to this situation. That answer can be summed up in Rahner's faith that God in Jesus Christ loves us: our journey "always ultimately ends in the arms of an eternally good, eternally powerful God."[21] This is revelation in the "absolute sense": God has declared himself decisively and finally *for* humanity as salvation, forgiveness, and love. In Christ, revelation is closed, because in him, "the definitive Reality which resolves history proper is already here." The incarnation is the final word of God, because in it, God and the world "have become one, forever without confusion, but forever undivided."[22] This closing of revelation is positive, not negative, because in this decisive event, all the plenitude of God is included for the world, and nothing of it is excluded. Prior to Christ, the utterances of God were an anticipatory shadow of the things to come. In Christ, the fullness of reality has arrived.

The closed nature of revelation in Christ does not preclude the possibility of new insight. Rahner's idea of human transcendentality as an orientation to the absolute explains why he is not satisfied with any purely dogmatic or authoritative statement of doctrine, because such would attempt to seal up and complete all that could be said theologically on a topic, thus limiting the potentially infinite by the finite. He supposes that human words alone cannot capture all that this transcendent yearning implies, so that human words and doctrines will always fall short of the truth they are intended to embody. While rejecting historical relativism by accepting that God has truly revealed himself in the acts recorded by Scripture, and most especially in the life of Christ, Rahner insists that these words remembering the events cannot capture *all* the truth the events contained, because human words are simply not able to capture all truth. This allows for the possibility of the develop-

20. Rahner, *Foundations*, 174.
21. Rahner, *I Remember*, 110–11.
22. Rahner, *Theological Investigations*, 1:49.

ment of doctrine and dogma over time, as further insight into the truths of a particular event are gained by people of different times, languages, and cultures.[23] Historical, cultural, and scientific developments are therefore important for uncovering the *fullness* of truth in any given event of God's action in the world, because they may reveal aspects of a doctrine previously unavailable.

This attitude towards the importance of history and culture in interpreting truth allows Rahner practical flexibility in his approach to revelation and dogma, while granting ultimate authority on what is orthodoxy to the church.[24] Though he has a high view Scripture as the "absolute norm" for the theologian,[25] maintaining that God has revealed himself in the "scripturally normed teaching authority" of the church,[26] his conceptual framework is largely built upon the philosophical worldview of his transcendental anthropology. This framework plays a key interpretative role in his program, sometimes seeming to eclipse the Scripture, though acknowledging that the end of the apostolic witness completes revelation in Christ.[27] Louis Roberts points to Rahner's use of the witness and theological technique of the early church as a model hermeneutic.[28] The apostles experienced the living reality of God in Christ, and struggled to adequately portray that reality in words. But they were not left with words alone: the Spirit was also given to them. By that Spirit they continued to wrestle with the mystery of God's love in Christ. So the church is ever dependent upon both Spirit and Word. As the gospel and the living reality of Christ continue to encounter new cultures and new philosophies, they have ever-new things to say, more of transcendent reality to illuminate. Thus a kind of evolution of truth takes place as history proceeds, which continues to explicate those past experiences of God's interaction with the world, as new insights are

23. Ibid., 43.

24. Ibid., 42.

25. Rahner, *Theological Investigations*, 11:110. Rahner says, "For theologians Scripture is indeed the absolute norm. But it is not because the revelation imparted by God takes place originally and for the first time in these human statements as such, but rather because in them the original experience of the Spirit and of its eschatological address to man in Jesus Christ has been objectified in a form which has abiding validity and with a purely normative force."

26. Marshall, *Trinity and Truth*, 63.

27. Ibid., 66.

28. Roberts, *Achievement of Karl Rahner*, 65.

added to old. Some of these might even eclipse older valued insights. Rahner does not use modern presuppositions or transcendental arguments to try to prove the tenets of Christian faith. Rather, he presupposes faith, and tries to show that it is sufficiently grounded in the depths of human transcendental experience to be credible to, and coherent in, the modern age.[29]

Sensitive to the theological challenges posed by the rise of science, Rahner has sought to interact creatively with these. In fact, he insists that modern theology "must engage consistently in direct dialogue with the modern natural and social sciences" to be heard in today's culture.[30] His use of evolutionary theory provides an example of both his general epistemological method and this interaction. He combines his Christology with an evolutionary worldview, supposing that all of history is a "divinely energized unfolding of . . . reality" moved along by God's transcendent causality. History is significant for the person of faith, and allows one to affirm Christ's role in the process of evolution, and Christ as end goal of that evolutionary process. God's creative Spirit transcendently directs the process in which the human spirit, "drawn to the divine Spirit, reaches toward and actually becomes itself the goal of historical development."[31] Evolution allows the created possibility of that communion between God and humanity that is realized in Christ. As such, evolution demonstrates how human existence takes place in unity with the rest of the cosmos, and individual histories take place within the history of Christ and humanity as a whole. Rahner's theological use of evolutionary theory will be examined later in the chapter. This approach to contemporary culture is typical of Rahner.

Rahner addresses the possibility of the existence of extraterrestrials and the related idea of multiple incarnations as possible implications of modern science that theology must take seriously. He is open to the possibility that an evolving and creatively fruitful universe might have given rise to other rational beings besides humans. He even finds a place for angels in such an evolutionary perspective. He is aware of the difficulties posed by modern science for an anthropocentric view of the universe. He addresses these issues with a method that seeks coherence

---

29. Marshall, *Trinity and Truth*, 66.
30. Rahner, *Theological Investigations*, 11:74.
31. Kelly, *Karl Rahner*, 54.

rather than absolute correspondence between science and theology. These issues will be examined later in the chapter.

This introduction to Rahner's thought has been necessarily brief and selective. His approach may be summarized as a christocentric theology engaged in transcendental anthropology. Significant features of his overall program have been set aside in the interest of the main anthropological theme. For instance, this analysis will largely bypass his devotional or mystical writings, his theology of the "anonymous Christian," and his engagement with eschatology and the church, among other things. Those issues germane to the subject will occupy the central focus, particularly Rahner's assessment of human nature and the incarnation, and his engagement with related issues from modern science.

The Uniqueness of Human Nature

The Definition of Human Nature

Rahner's defines human nature as that which is *indefinable*: humanity is "an indefinability come to consciousness of itself."[32] No "categorical definition" is sufficient to encompass the bounds of human nature, because that nature has no bounds[33]: its bounds could be limited only if there were a limit to what humans are concerned with, and to what is concerned with humans. But there is no such limit—human concerns are boundless and unlimited. Because even in relation to knowing itself human nature is not able to grasp this unlimited boundlessness, that nature is fundamentally a mystery. This mystery must be seen in the context of the wider horizon of the absolute mystery of God, because of human openness to God. "When we have said everything about ourselves that can be described and defined, we have still said nothing about ourselves, unless we have included or implied the fact that we are beings who are referred to the incomprehensible God." Rahner defines mystery as that which is ultimately incomprehensible, not merely that which is now unknown but one day to be revealed. Even to the beatific vision—the state of the fullness of knowing in which the knower will "know as he is known"—God will yet remain incomprehensible, more than can ever be grasped or understood.[34]

---

32. Rahner, *Theological Investigations*, 4:107.

33. Walsh, *Heart of Christ*, 69.

34. Rahner, *Theological Investigations*, 4:108. In this sense, "mystery" may be understood as a component of Rahner's mystical theology.

Rahner elaborates his definition of human nature in terms of transcendence, and begins to frame a background from which to perceive the place of humanity in the cosmos. "Human beings are bodily creatures who have a fundamentally unlimited transcendentality and unlimited openness to being as such in knowledge and freedom." Even though it may be possible to compare various features of general animal and human life (some animals may use rudimentary tools, some may have rudimentary speech, etc.), human beings are uniquely different from animals in theological perspective in that "human consciousness possesses that unlimited transcendentality in which there is present an openness, capable of legitimizing itself, to the absolute reality of God."[35] Rahner terms this openness and capacity for the life of God, which will ultimately take the form of a call to communion with God in Christ, the *supernatural existential*.[36] Human beings are the only creatures within the cosmos that possess this absolute openness to the reality of God distinct from the cosmos. Purcell identifies this as Rahner's essential theological orientation to "the Other."[37] Humans are unique in that they are constituted in such a way as to be able to hear God; they are able to receive the revelation of God's self because of their openness to the Absolute. In contrast to Barth, who maintained the complete dependence of human beings upon the grace of God for any perception of God whatsoever, Rahner's transcendental anthropology defines humanity as already oriented towards the open-ended infinite—already having the capacity and potential for this divine self-communication.[38] If this were not so, humanity would not have been the appropriate vessel for the incarnation. For if God becomes human, "there must be some characteristic of [human being] that enables him to be assumed by God as his own reality in the world."[39] At the same time, this *is* a grace-dependent situation, because it is God's grace that moves at every level of the development of the cosmos to move it closer to the place where it may engage in full communion with God.[40] Humanity is not

---

35. Rahner, *Theological Investigations*, 21:42–43; Purcell, *Mystery and Method*, xiii.
36. Rahner, *Theological Investigations*, 2:240.
37. Purcell, *Mystery and Method*, xiii.
38. Roberts, *Achievement of Karl Rahner*, 31, 39.
39. Walsh, *Heart of Christ*, 80.
40. Rahner, *Foundations*, 197–99; see also Carmody and Carmody, "Christology in Rahner," 196–97; Ludlow, *Universal Salvation*, 176–77.

the enemy of grace, but is utterly dependent upon grace for its very being and existence.

It is the potential for "immediacy to God" that characterizes human nature which requires theology to have an anthropological emphasis.[41] This transcendental anthropology, though theologically apprehended, finds warrant from certain objective features of human nature. Human beings are oriented towards the infinite, which is evident in religion, mathematics, and the human imagination. They are never satisfied with a merely instinctive life, nor with the given of their lot. They are always striving, even after "vanity" (Eccl 2:22–23). The theologian may assert that God "has set eternity in the hearts of humans" (Eccl 3:11), but this is universally visible as human *yearning*. All this natural world is and has to offer is not enough for the human, cannot answer the need of his deepest being. Thus, "man is a question to which there is no answer."[42] Perhaps for this reason, only humans wrestle with the specter of meaninglessness. The theological conception of the correspondence of the human being to God, revealed in the "relational-dynamic conception of the *imago dei*" in humanity, indicates that theology must have such an anthropocentric focus.[43]

The sense of being lost in the cosmos is, according to Rahner, an important signpost that marks human beings as unique. In retrospect, it is an inevitable result of being contingent creatures created in a finite universe by an infinite God. Formerly human beings might be able to fool themselves that their world was a relatively small place, and so they in perspective were relatively large and hence the center of things. But what natural science has done for us is show us in the physical analogy of the vast cosmos what we already knew theologically: in relation to the infinite God, human beings will always be and feel finite, contingent, lost. It is this "very *recognition* and *acceptance* of the fact of being lost in the cosmos [which] actually raises them above it and enables them to realize it as an expression and a mediation of that ultimate experience

---

41. Losinger, *Anthropological Turn*, 2; quoting Scheffczyk, *Einführung*, 99.

42. Rahner, *Christian at the Crossroads*, 1, 17.

43. Losinger, *Anthropological Turn*, 2, 9; quoting Scheffczyk, *Einführung*, 109. Losinger believes Rahner provides justification for the anthropocentric character of modern theology, in contrast to its medieval theocentric character, because all knowledge (including theological) is found in the [human] subject. This is *epistemic* anthropocentrism, and does not bear upon the validity of *critical* anthropocentrism.

of contingency which they, in virtue of their ancient faith, must perceive and accept before the infinite God as finite creatures."[44]

Rahner marks this sense of human awareness of, and displacement before, the vastness of the cosmos as an aspect of the spiritual component of human nature: it is a mirror of their cognition of themselves in relation to the infinite, and is manifest in the efforts of modern physics to measure the universe. These efforts demonstrate again the difference between matter and spirit, which is able to "reflect upon itself and its world, and then again place its world over against itself."[45] It is in human awareness of itself, and hence through humanity in nature's awareness of itself, that nature begins to be seen as being oriented towards humanity. "[If] Nature does become conscious of itself in him, then Nature is planned for him, since 'chance' is a word without any real meaning for the natural scientist who concludes from the result to a movement orientated towards it." Rahner makes this teleological conclusion of the "plannedness" of nature as a theological rather than scientific move—he is clear that he is making a statement of faith.[46] Yet he sees a coherence of the two views, because "theology sees man as the crown of God's creation, while evolutionary theory interprets hominization as the breakthrough to a new level of being." That new level is achieved because in humanity, nature attains to self-consciousness.[47] Keith Ward posits a similar anthropocentric focus in nature. Humanity possesses a special dignity and status in the cosmos, because in it the universe becomes aware of itself and because human reason brings to light truth; in it, "reason thrives and grows, and understands itself more fully by its own activity."[48]

Rahner maintains a unity of matter and spirit that is evident in the entire creation, and particularly in human nature. He opposes a platonic dualism that would rend asunder the spiritual (yet also physical) nature of humanity and the material essence of nature. He insists that the spirit must be regarded as a goal of nature. The human spirit in particular is the concrete manifestation of that goal. "Nature found herself in him, in spite of all the physical powerlessness of the individual man." A dualism

44. Rahner, *Theological Investigations*, 21:50.
45. Ibid., 50.
46. Rahner, *Theological Investigations*, 5:161.
47. Walsh, *Heart of Christ*, 72.
48. K. Ward, *In Defense of the Soul*, 155.

that separates the spiritual and material will lead to the unacceptable result of spirit being seen as the enemy of nature, as existing separately from nature, or of merely using "the material world as a kind of exterior stage." Even the spiritual consummation of human nature at the eschaton only takes place in the context of the redemption of the rest of the material cosmos—they are inextricably bound.[49]

Humanity in Relation to the Rest of Nature

Rahner raises the question of the human in relation to the animal kingdom, and asks whether we could even know if a similar ability to transcendence existed in the animals. His conclusion is that although there may be a degree of transcendence in the animals, the fact that this degree is surpassed by humanity means that we can be fairly treated in a separate category from animals by theology. Rahner is particularly concerned here to address the issue of the distinction of humanity raised by the theory of evolution. It is his answer to the attempt of the natural sciences to reduce human being to what is otherwise only accessible from that (natural science) realm. "Because of the transcendentality of human beings, they possess an element in their nature which forbids us simply to reduce them to that reality which otherwise appears in natural science and which limits its area."[50] Ward concurs that while evolutionary processes may physically describe the origin of humanity in a natural science sense, they cannot describe that origin in a religious or ultimate ontological sense. That is because such a level of origin is beyond the purview of the natural sciences.[51] Yet even taken from the physical evolutionary point of view, the process has climactically produced in humanity beings with rational souls. The idea of "soul" is contentious in the modern materialistic context, but Rahner's use of the term can be affirmed without going into the intricacies of that argument because he uses it to emphasize the rational and transcendent qualities of human beings. In Rahner's system, other beings in the cosmos may or may not have this same rational quality, but "the important point is that all rational souls do possess a special dignity and status" in the

---

49. Rahner, *Theological Investigations*, 5:161, 169.

50. Rahner, *Theological Investigation*, 21:44.

51. K. Ward, *In Defense of the Soul*, 52. His approach is similar to Polkinghorne's multi-level description of music.

entire evolutionary scheme.[52] This is because they are conscious toward the infinite.

It is because human beings are part spirit that they can never be completely identified with nature. Rahner believes this is affirmed by philosophy as well as theology. There is an "absolutely fundamentally legitimate development of the philosophical understanding of the human person, in which the latter gradually came to be seen, not so much as part of a cosmos, but as a transcendental subject with a world of his own which he projects in thought and action."[53] The mystery of human being is that it is both nature and spirit. The human spirit is that aspect of human nature that is oriented towards the infinite and transcendent, that is aware of "what is beyond the physical," yet in a way that is embedded in the natural world of sense experience.[54] Humans "cannot deny themselves and become merely a part of nature, an animal with technical sophistication; nor can they so act as if the spiritual center of the person in its autonomy and freedom were somehow elevated above, and free from, nature." Human beings are part of nature, and yet apart from it. As such they have a role "as the measure of all things." Yet they are not the answer to their own question; neither is there an answer to human transcendentality anywhere else within the purely natural realm. "Those who [have] attempted to ground themselves in themselves have fallen into an unfathomable abyss."[55] Only orientation towards God, only in God, is there any hope of a resolution of this unanswerable question. God, the infinite, the eternal, the transcendent, the incomprehensible and yet immanent in Christ, is that answer. He is the "answer to the question of meaning of man in his wholeness."[56]

Transcendentality and unlimited openness to God, the subjectivity of the human person, makes humanity the center of the cosmos. Leo O'Donovan comments that in light of the Christian belief that evolution has intentionally and actively culminated in the presence of the redeeming creator in the universe (Christ born of woman), and that humans can therefore now look forward to union with God, humanity cannot adequately be described by natural processes or "nature" alone.

52. Ibid., 56.
53. Rahner, *Theological Investigations*, 19:261.
54. Roberts, *Achievement of Karl Rahner*, 21.
55. Rahner, *Content of Faith*, 82, 120.
56. Rahner, *Theological Investigations*, 18:104.

"On the contrary, nature can only be fully understood with reference to humanity."[57] Humanity in its own nature and history provides the key to understanding the cosmos. Rahner elaborates on that significance: "A personal and free subjectivity oriented in unlimited transcendentality to being purely and simply (and consequently, to the ground of being which is God) is the center of the cosmos, even though this human subjectivity rests on a materiality which as such cannot be regarded as the center of all that is material, even if it made sense at all to speak of a material center of this material cosmos."[58] Such cosmic centrality is based upon humanity's unique (apparently, until such time as some other being is discovered with a similar property) mental orientation to the infinite. He dislocates the materiality of human subjectivity from that center as a response to the Copernican principle as well as to the possible dualism of mental vs. physical.[59] It is not the material substance or substrate of human beings that reveals their uniqueness, but the cognitive orientation towards the eternal that has arisen on that substrate.

Humanity would be doomed to be frustrated in its attempts to realize its transcendence, if it were not for the grace of God—the goal is "unattainable for the natural powers of man." Nevertheless, because of God's grace, "the Christian knows that this history of the cosmos as a whole will find its real consummation despite, in and through the freedom of man, and that its finality as a whole will also be its consummation."[60] Barth described this as God's covenant with humanity extending to embrace all of the cosmos. "It is man in covenant with God who reveals this plan. He does so representatively for the whole cosmos ... He alone sheds light on the cosmos. As he is light, the cosmos is also light. As God's covenant is disclosed, the cosmos is shown to be embraced by the same covenant."[61] The soteriological reality of the incarnation, and the eschatological hope provided by that reality, promise to humanity and to the cosmos a redemption of consummation, rather

---

57. O'Donovan, "Making Heaven and Earth," 296.

58. Rahner, *Theological Investigations*, 19:262.

59. This may be problematic, since Rahner is at pains elsewhere to correct this same dualism. This issue will be addressed later in the chapter. See Rahner, *Theological Investigations*, 5:169.

60. Ibid., 168.

61. Barth, *Church Dogmatics* III/2:18–19.

than annihilation. That future fulfillment of the cosmos is the point at which God, as the "absolute future," will be all in all.[62]

The Significance of the Incarnation

Rahner believes that in the incarnate Jesus, "God has uttered himself to man victoriously and unsurpassably" as the blessed and ultimate response to that question which humanity is in itself.[63] His approach to the incarnation significantly elevates human nature. He analyzes the relation between the Logos and human nature in the incarnation, asking whether human nature is simply "a mask assumed from without, from behind which the Logos hides to act things out in the world." His conclusion is that no, human nature "is the constitutive, real symbol of the Logos himself." The Logos is the Father's Word, and in the incarnation, it has emptied itself into the non-divine, but when this happens, "that precisely is born which we call human nature." Hence, "man is possible, because the exteriorization of the Logos is possible."[64]

Furthermore, the creation itself reaches a climax in the incarnation. "For the fact that God himself is man is both the unique summit and the ultimate basis of God's relationship to his creation, in which he and his creation grow in direct (and not in converse) proportion. This positive nature of creation, not merely measured in relation to nothingness but also in relation to God, reaches its qualitatively unique climax, therefore, in Christ."[65] In other words, creation and incarnation are not two separate and unrelated moves of God in relation to the cosmos, but are of one and the same initiative: the initiative of God's self-communication. The creation is a portion of the movement in which "God becomes world" in the event of the incarnation: God creating material reality because it will one day be "the environment of his own materiality."[66] Thus Jesus has not become human as if the incarnation were a divine afterthought to the fall. Rather, human being is what it is because it is predestined to be like Jesus, predestined to be conformed to his likeness, and prepared ahead of time *as* human being for this

---

62. Garaudy, "Meaning of Life and History," 68.
63. Rahner, *Theological Investigations*, 13:200.
64. Rahner, *Trinity*, 32–33.
65. Rahner, *Theological Investigations*, 3:43.
66. Rahner, *Foundations*, 197.

purpose. It can be formed into the image of God precisely because of that preparation. This and no other nature are ready to such union.

Braine agrees that from the beginning of creation God intended to become incarnate, and "in the very act of creation set what it would mean for a created being to be by adoption and grace a son of God."[67] The Scripture witnesses to this unified intention of creation towards incarnation and the saving work of Christ. Braine maintains that the incarnation is the only possible route to a real satisfying communion between God and his creatures. This is because without God taking upon himself creaturehood, the created realm can never transcend its finiteness, and so can never deeply and satisfyingly relate with its infinite Creator. Only in the sharing of the divine nature made possible by the incarnation does the finite being receive the gift of transcending its finiteness. Though humans are inherently beings of transcendentality, they cannot achieve the realization of this nature until they are in Christ, and even then, only in the Spirit as a sort of down payment on what will be fully realized in the eschatological future. The incarnation of the Son of God was planned first, and then suitable beings were created to make possible the incarnation; beings that by virtue of all that took placed in the incarnation would become capable of the type of infinite relationship that already exists among the persons of the godhead. This is the meaning of their adopted "sonship": that they are capable of and invited into infinite personal relationship with the infinite God, characterized by the love of the Father for the Son, and the Son for the Father, whose love together gives rise to the fruitfulness of the Spirit.[68]

Rahner believes creation can be considered christocentric because it is from its beginning made for the eventuality of incarnation. "The creation occurs in the Logos and the Logos has always been ordered toward the assumption of a material nature, a humanity, the concrete personality of Jesus of Nazareth."[69] Vass describes Rahner's centering of human salvation from creation as the "precondition" in grace of human partnership with God.[70] When God takes on human nature in Christ, the final consummation and goal of the cosmos comes to fruition. The

---

67. Braine, "Impossibility," 17.
68. Ibid., 16–17.
69. Carmody and Carmody, "Christology in Rahner," 205.
70. Vass, *Pattern of Christian Doctrines*, 24.

cosmos transcends itself and reaches its final consummation not just in the created spiritual creature humanity, but when it

> receives the ultimate self-communication of its ultimate ground itself, in that moment when this direct self-communication of God is given to the spiritual creature in what we call ... grace and glory. God does not merely create something other than himself—he also gives himself to this other.[71]

It is in a particular human nature, a single human person, that God displays "his own reality to the world."[72] This is the essence of the incarnation: God giving himself to humanity in the person of Jesus Christ. This may give cause for the "scandal of particularity," but is justified by the dogma of the Word become flesh.[73] The cosmos comes to fruition in him, and human nature is by this enfleshment of God given a unique honor and glory. "It is a fact of faith that when God desires to manifest himself, it is as a man that he does so," a man with a physical body, just like the rest of humanity. "If we want to know what man is, or what flesh means, then we must, so to speak, choose this theological definition of the statement 'And the Word became flesh,' saying: flesh, man as a bodily, concrete, historical being is just what comes into being when the Logos, issuing from himself, utters himself. Man is therefore God's self-utterance, out of himself into the empty nothingness of the creature."[74]

Rahner insists that God the immutable may be thought of as taking on the mutable nature of humanity. While God is immutable in himself, he may become mutable when he becomes something in another. The non-divine reality of the creaturely realm becomes the *"grammar of God's possible self-expression."*[75] God can express himself in the Logos as a creature; the possibility of that realization becomes the ground upon which creaturehood itself becomes possible. As Rahner puts it, "the possibility that there be men is grounded in the greater, more comprehensive and more radical possibility of God to express himself in the Logos which becomes a creature." He insists this is so,

---

71. Rahner, *Theological Investigations*, 5:171–72.

72. Walsh, *Heart of Christ*, 80.

73. Carmody and Carmody, "Christology in Rahner," 205. The scandal of particularity is that God only appears as incarnate in one particular historically-contingent individual.

74. Rahner, *Theological Investigations*, 17:74.

75. Rahner, *Foundations*, 223.

because otherwise, the humanity of God in the incarnation would be reduced to a kind of docetic disguise for the real God.[76] The humanity of Christ is not just a facade for God's appearance, as if his humanity were some kind of "vaporous and empty apparition" that has no value in comparison to the nature of God that it manifests. Rahner insists, "Since *God* himself 'goes out of' himself, this form of his existence has the most radical validity, force and reality."[77] In Trinitarian perspective, God as the giver becomes the same as God the gift in Jesus.[78] In him, the immutable Word of God, the eternal Logos *becomes* human.

Rahner rejects the tendency to monophysitism and docetism of much traditional Christology, which gave lip service to the hypostatic union, but ended up downplaying the humanity of Christ and overemphasizing his deity. He interprets the incarnation based on the hermeneutical principle of the Council of Chalcedon, which balanced the two natures of Christ, and insists that to be faithful to that principle, Christ must be seen as a real human being, with experiences that are essentially one with humanity in all ways, except for sin. Maintaining the balance between the two natures becomes possible only if human nature is already in its bodily essence fit for that union prior to the incarnation. That the Word could and did become human flesh (John 1:14) does not just elevate humanity, but reveals that human nature was already elevated and prepared: the correct nature in which God might appear. "The being of man is what comes into existence when God utters himself into the otherness of nothingness; and that means man, in so far as he is *sarx*."[79] The incarnation becomes possible because humanity as such is ready for it; God can take on human nature because it alone, unlike other creatures definable apart from transcendence, "can exist in total dispossession of itself, and comes therein to the fulfillment of its own incomprehensible meaning."[80]

In light of the incarnation, the creation itself must be regarded as christologically anthropocentric. Creation, as freely decreed by God and taking a christocentric form, is organized and aimed at the creation

---

76. Ibid., 224; *Theological Investigations*, 4:117–18.
77. Rahner, *Theological Investigations*, 4:117.
78. Vass, *Pattern of Christian Doctrines*, 26.
79. Walsh, *Heart of Christ*, 75, 80–81.
80. Rahner, *Theological Investigations*, 4:110.

of humanity.[81] This is so because it is created with the incarnation as its goal. For the incarnation is what happens when "God wills to become non-God."[82] The Logos is the abbreviated code word for God in the godless universe, whose form is human being: the human being who is the Son of Man, and humanity that exists in the final analysis because it was destined to be the vehicle of that incarnation. The cosmos was created with the goal of this ultimate self-revelation of God, which takes place in humanity, specifically in the Logos, the Son of Man. In Vass' words, "Jesus must be the highest realization of all creation."[83] For this reason, Rahner maintains that anthropology finds its beginning and ending in Christology. Anthropology must ultimately be theology if it is to capture the proper truth of human nature.

What Christ has accomplished exalts humanity further in God's grace. Barth observes that the incarnation of God exalts humanity, not to the status of deity, but rather in fellowship of life with God, to the "status of children."[84] No other beings in the cosmos, whether angels or animals, are given or expected to have this status. The incarnation is a manifestation of God's desire to enter into relationship with humanity. It is this desire that makes theology inherently anthropocentric, because God has willed it so, through his grace.[85] At the same time, humanity can only discover what it was meant to be when it surrenders itself to the worship of God, and transforms its anthropocentrism into theocentrism. As such, God is the actual meaning of human life.[86]

> [Man's] is a Christ-centered being, i.e., his being possesses an ontic and spiritual-personal capacity for communicating with Jesus Christ in whom God has forever made the countenance of man his own and has opened the reality of man, with an unsurpassable finality, in the direction of God; only thus was the real possibility of a direct communion of all men with God established with finality. Hence we can only speak ultimately of God by engaging even in the midst of all this [theology] in anthropology; and ultimately any information about anthropology,

81. Vass, *Pattern of Christian Doctrines*, 98.
82. Rahner, *Theological Investigations*, 4:116.
83. Vass, *Pattern of Christian Doctrines*, 99.
84. Barth, *Church Dogmatics* IV/:143.
85. Rahner, *Theological Investigations*, 17:55.
86. Rahner, *Theological Investigations*, 18:93.

about the nature and dignity of man, can be given only when we engage in theology about God and from God.[87]

Not only is man's meaning and destiny fulfilled in Christ, it can *only* be fulfilled in Christ.

One could imagine the situation if the Son of God had determined not to become incarnate, so that humanity remained, as it were, an experiment at a distance, an objective event among many events initiated by God. From such an imaginary point of view, humanity's theological status in the cosmos would seem to be indeterminate. But the incarnation confers a dignity and importance to humanity because it is precisely *for* them that the Word of God has become one of them—yet not only for them, but also through them for the whole of creation. God has stepped down from pure objectivity to become subjectively involved with his creatures, and so conferred upon them supreme nobility: he will always be one of them. He is only Christ in and for humanity; the meaning of his mission in his incarnation is only fulfilled as he suffers, dies, and is raised to life on behalf of human beings. The rest of creation receives the benefits: it will find its consummation in redeemed humanity. But it is on the salvation of the children of God that his mission is focused. Christ incarnate allows us to speak, with Barth, of the humanity of God.

Rahner's version of human nature prepared as the proper vehicle for incarnation leads to a more highly divinized version of the "children of God" than Barth's. These created beings receive an adopted sonship in that they receive this infinite capability for and relationship with God as a gift of grace, in contrast to Christ's native sonship. The union of divine and human nature becomes potentially almost equivalent to the hypostatic union in Jesus Christ, whenever a person accepts God's love in the body of Christ. This is because the "bestowal of the Spirit . . . works an 'assumption' of our human natures into the divine life that is at least analogous to the Logos' assumption of a human nature born of Mary."[88] The difference between human potential to realized divinity as children of God and the hypostatic union in Jesus of Nazareth is that his godhood is "perfect and irreversible," so that he both receives and

---

87. Ibid., 2:240–41.
88. Carmody and Carmody, "Christology in Rahner," 209.

offers God's gracious presence to the rest of humanity; we, on the other hand, only receive.[89]

Vass points out that despite the confusing nature of many of Rahner's statements on the subject, he nevertheless holds to an actual historical resurrection of Jesus Christ from the dead.[90] Rahner famously said, "Jesus has risen into the faith of his disciples,"[91] which can be read as a kind of psychological interpretation of the nature of the resurrection. But that is not all that Rahner meant by the resurrection. He posited that there were two necessary events: First, the historical event of the man conquering death, though not exactly historical in the sense of all other historical events, since it involves "rising into the inconceivability of God"—something not shared by other historical events.[92] Second, the event of the faith it inspired in his disciples. The resurrection is a necessary feature of his metaphysical system, in that it correlates with the already-present transcendentality of human nature. Human beings already have this (subconscious) drive or hope for eternal life, and finding it fulfilled in one particular person (Jesus Christ) is a natural extension of reality that matches this given interiority of the human situation.[93] Rahner's system of transcendental anthropology allows him to "expect" the resurrection in this sense. Thus his metaphysical system is not entirely dependent upon the scriptural account, though the biblical evidence remains for him part of fundamental theology. Rahner does not insist that historical investigation can prove the resurrection: "It can be said that by 'historical' we mean [sic] we would not reach the resurrection of Jesus, but only the conviction of his disciples that he is alive."[94] But our own transcendental expectations allow us to grasp that resurrection as a foretaste of our own, and so accept the witness of the Apostles.[95]

Rahner moves from the resurrection to comment on the implications of Christ's uniqueness, and describes the character of that infinite possibility of relationship as, among other things, being freed

89. Ibid., 209–10.
90. Vass, *Pattern of Christian Doctrines*, 134.
91. Rahner, *Foundations*, 268.
92. Rahner, *Theological Investigations*, 11:212.
93. Vass, *Pattern of Christian Doctrines*, 134.
94. Rahner, *Foundations*, 277.
95. Vass, *Pattern of Christian Doctrines*, 135–36.

from death. The resurrection is the sign of this freedom. Humanity is unique in creation in that it is the object of God's love in such a way that it already, if only in part, "stands beyond death's demarcation line, which distinguishes God from finite creation." That standing is a result of relationship with God in Christ. All this allows Christian orthodoxy to "start unabashedly with man, with his experience of himself, with his existence. And ... allow[s] us to end with man, too."[96]

Rahner's Response to Some Scientific Challenges

The typical view held by many in the name of natural science is that humanity is weak, hapless, and an accidental product of nature, and is doomed to be indifferently swallowed up by it.[97] Humanity has no purpose in the cosmos, "for the simple reason that the universe has no purpose."[98] In language reminiscent of Sagan regarding humanity's apparent insignificance in the cosmos, Rahner expresses the dilemma in which modern Christians find themselves:

> Nowadays the Christian has to live on a tiny planet in a solar system which in its turn is part of a galaxy of a hundred thousand light years with thirty billion stars and whereby this galaxy is estimated to be only one of a billion such galaxies in the universe. In such a universe it is certainly not easy for human beings to feel that they are the ones for whom this cosmos ultimately exists. In [such] a cosmos ... it is quite possible for human beings to feel that they are an accidental, marginal phenomenon, particularly when they know themselves to be the product of an evolution which itself has to work with numerous and improbable accidents.[99]

Such a perspective—Rahner's restatement of the Copernican principle—may easily give rise to an "existential dizziness," to being "lost in the cosmos."[100]

Yet Rahner does not conclude that the pessimism of this modern mindset is justified, or indeed even scientific. He describes this view of

---

96. Rahner, *Theological Investigations*, 17:63, 67.
97. Rahner, *Foundations*, 188.
98. S. Barr, "Anthropic Coincidences," 17.
99. Rahner, *Theological Investigation*, 21:49.
100. Rowan-Robinson, *Nine Numbers of the Cosmos*, 25; Pannenberg, *Systematic Theology*, 2:74.

humanity as a "marginal phenomenon," pre-scientific, pre-philosophical, and pre-theological. Though modern Western thought typically accepts this "Copernican anthropology," Rahner has already begun to show how actual human nature contradicts this view. He makes a strong case for recognition of human capacity that transcends the interpretive confines supposedly offered by chance and blind nature. It is not enough to judge the matter on the basis of the physical geographic of a tiny location in a small corner of the overall universe. This Copernican geographic fails to note the acutely scientific fact of human self-consciousness, of the directedness of natural processes that must be taken to make this possible, and of the human capacity that has developed in the history of the cosmos to begin directing those natural processes. It is because in humanity matter becomes conscious of itself, and by being self-conscious humanity begins to stand over and against matter, that natural science must recognize the unique and cosmically vital importance of humanity. Rahner concludes both science and theology must recognize that human beings have some unique characteristics that set them apart from all other creatures.[101]

The idea of human origins as a directed product of nature suggests teleology that is unwelcome to many scientists.[102] But Rahner argues that because humanity is recognized as a product of nature by natural science, and not as a being alien to those processes forced into the cosmos by some artificial transcendent cause, therefore human nature must be seen as the directed product of nature itself. Though this idea of directedness in a teleological sense is primarily a theological conclusion, it can be shown to be coherent with the scientific perspective.

Understanding Rahner's intention here yields an important insight into his overall method. In general, rather than using science to prove theological positions, Rahner is seeking to express the coherence of scientific and theological ideas. Faith and theology stand on their own as independent sources of the truth of reality. The methodological limits of science forbid it from making extensive statements beyond its naturalistic limits, since it is *a priori* seeking to describe reality within those limits. Theology transcends science epistemologically, because it can already show the limitations of scientific methodology in the human orientation towards the transcendent. Therefore Rahner is seeking

---

101. Rahner, *Foundations*, 188.
102. S. Barr, "Anthropic Coincidences," 20.

to demonstrate that some of the scientific data and its provisional conclusions can be taken as coherent with theological truth, though their method and limits are fundamentally different.

The idea of evolutionary directedness is a specific example of Rahner's method. Since the end result of natural processes is humanity, the scientist can "infer from the result at least a movement directed towards it."[103] Rahner's rejection of "meaningless chance" as a valid scientific explanation for this circumstance has already been highlighted.[104] Such explanations are rejected as a theological move, acknowledging that science is limited in what it can say on the matter. The concept of directedness in relation to evolutionary history deserves more careful analysis, especially as more elaborate scientific theories have been sought in recent years to explain the apparent directedness of the evolutionary process without appealing to God.

Theology and Evolutionary Theory

Rahner presupposes an evolutionary worldview, and seeks to make incarnation and Christology coherent and compatible with such a view. He does not force that compatibility, as if the incarnation could be regarded as a necessary product or goal of evolution. The incarnation must in a certain sense stand in "direct and simple contradiction" to human knowledge of evolution, because otherwise the theologian would be turning faith and revelation into philosophy and rationalism.[105] Rather, he wants to show that there is an affinity between the incarnation and an evolutionary worldview.

Rahner makes a case for an ontological interpretation of the scientific data, without too strongly binding himself to the technical details of that data of evolution. This is not to say that divine action could be discerned at the microscopic level at any particular stage of the process.[106] The divine process is describable on the ontological, rather than the scientific level. Rahner maintains that from the retrospective position offered by the incarnation of Christ, one must look back theologically

---

103. Rahner, *Foundations*, 188.
104. Rahner, *Theological Investigations*, 5:161
105. Rahner, *Foundations*, 179.
106. Rahner is not wrestling with the scientific data in any kind of technical sense such as that suggested by Intelligent Design (ID) theory (see Dembski, *Intelligent Design*). For more on this concept, see chapter 6, p. 265.

and say that God has been guiding the process to this incarnate end from the beginning.

Just as lower orders were the prelude to human transcendentality, so other successive self-transcendent moments in the evolutionary process had preceding lower orders. Human nature is the end result of evolutionary history, but is itself the prelude to the highest order of all in the incarnation. If evolution is regarded as the process of nature's "inward unfolding," taking place as a drive to self-consciousness on the part of matter, then human beings can be regarded as the summit of the process, in which self-consciousness has finally come to fruition. Human transcendentality is the conscious, "deliberate version of what all material existence strives after."[107] But if humanity is the actual "breakthrough point" of this evolutionary drive towards inwardness, "then in human nature one can find the cosmos 'disclosed' in a fundamental way," and "find a central revelation of what the evolutionary eons have been up to."[108] From the perspective of consciousness, human nature is a crowning achievement of the evolutionary process; however, it is more than this: it is the fulfillment of an inner dynamic of ever-increasing complexity and ever-increasing transcendence evident in the cosmos from the beginning of time. That human self-consciousness is a cause for wonder is not particularly contentious. But Rahner insists that it can be seen as the ultimate version of the drive to increased complexity evident in the entire evolutionary process. It should be regarded as the ultimate climax of the process because in humanity, self-awareness and transcendentality open material reality directly to conscious relationship with the Absolute. In theological terms, human beings have the highest capacity in creation for direct personal conscious relationship with God.

How is the evolutionary process able to result in beings that have become more than earlier beings? Rahner identifies this as the problem of becoming.[109] He describes this process, evident at each stage of evolution, as the process of self-transcendence. Self-transcendence is possible and explicable, according to Rahner, only by an empowering provided by the Absolutely Transcendent. Otherwise there is no source within the finite order that could "inspire" it to this self-transcendence.

107. Carmody and Carmody, "Christology in Rahner," 196.
108. Ibid., 197.
109. Stanley, "Transcendental Method of Karl Rahner," 200.

God is the "cause and primordial ground" of this process of self-transcendence, in the sense that it is God who actively upholds and enables the material cosmos to transcend itself in this way.[110] He enables the world to move in the direction of self-transcendence, having designed the cosmos to make that process possible.[111] Rahner emphasizes grace as the key to understanding God's relationship to the entire cosmos. God's grace enables the cosmic process from its beginning to its end in finite humanity's capacity to self-transcendence. At each stage of cosmic evolution, grace is the actively sustaining presence of God's love and self-communication enabling created matter to become more than itself. The human characteristic of transcendentality is likewise only made possible by grace, a grace finally illuminated and fulfilled when God's self-communication becomes complete in the incarnation.[112] There, the full grace of God is completely realized for the creation.[113]

Rahner does not believe this requires God to "meddle" with the process of evolution, interfering with it at given stages in some manner that might or might not be detectable to science.[114] Rather, the natural process unfolds freely and independently in a "basic cause-effect pattern," while being subject to transcendent causality, as God constantly upholds, enables, and directs the process towards the "emergence of free, transcendent persons." So Rahner posits God as the "ultimate environment" to which all of the changes that arise within the independent process of becoming must orient themselves, perhaps analogous to a magnetic field that orients iron filings. So he avoids the typical dichotomy between natural causes and causal acts of God.[115] Hans Urs von Balthasar agrees that the appearance "of humanity is written into nature

---

110. Ibid., 202.

111. This approach to transcendent causation "built into" the structure of creation has the advantage of being able to incorporate either direct or indirect divine causality, for instance in such concepts as ID theory's "irreducible complexity," or by Stuart Kauffman's "complexity theory." In either case, the ultimate theological explanation is divine grace. See ch. 7.

112. Carmody and Carmody, "Christology in Rahner," 197.

113. Stanley, "Transcendental Method," 203.

114. Rahner avoids the "God of the gaps" problem, in that God's transcendent causation is not the kind that disappears as science fills the gaps in a complete scientific explanation of the evolutionary process.

115. Stanley, "Transcendental Method," 202.

from the beginning."[116] Michael Schmaus says that though humanity might be the goal of cosmic processes, natural science could not be called upon to prove such a thesis.[117] Rahner's system has the advantage of giving God's causality a considerable degree of flexibility, so that science need not be called upon for justification of an ontological thesis. Oliver Rabut argues—with Teilhard de Chardin's phyletic principle—that whether or not all God's preparation of the process takes place in time or only from eternity, "nothing appears that has not been eternally in preparation."[118] Rahner's position is similar. It might incline towards deism, except that for Rahner the incarnation includes a decisive move by the transcendent God into the creation.

Rahner calls this gradual development of self-transcendence the history of the development of spirit out of matter. It is an evolutionary history of "matter discovering itself in spirit."[119] The culmination of this process is the full emergence of spirit in human nature. The unity of matter and spirit culminates in the transcendent capacity of human beings, such that when the incarnation finally takes place in the God-man, that evolutionary history of the development of spirit is complete. Human nature provides the backdrop for this development, containing the full realization of unified matter and spirit. Rahner rejects platonic spiritualism and naturalistic materialism as monocular, because each confuses its understanding of the parts of the world with the whole, a whole that is only comprehensible to holistically understood human nature.[120] He insists that dualisms that separate unified nature are particularly unacceptable to the modern mindset.[121] The "spiritual" aspect of reality is understandable in modernity in terms of transcendence. Human nature illuminates the inner structure of reality, and demonstrates that matter and spirit are not enemies or radically opposed to each other, but form a single unified world.

While Rahner's evolutionary Christology is not as strong as that of Teilhard, he does present a picture of the appearance of Christ in history that is akin to it. Christ is the culmination and crown of the

116. O'Donovan, "Making Heaven and Earth," 283.
117. Ibid., 284–85; quoting Schmaus, "Materie und Leben," 265.
118. Rabut, *Dialogue with Teilhard de Chardin*, 35.
119. Rahner, *Foundations*, 178–80.
120. Ibid., 182.
121. Carmody and Carmody, "Christology in Rahner," 196.

evolutionary process. Though attempting to distance himself from Teilhard's method, he is not averse to arriving at his conclusions. "If we really postulate a single history of the whole of reality ... it would have to be shown how even the very highest, although essentially new, can be understood as a variation of what existed previously." Rahner insists that the Logos of God has become present in the human nature of Jesus. He is the asymptotic goal of the evolutionary development of matter towards spirit. In Christ, the world in its graced development reaches out to God, and accepts the "self-bestowal of God," such that the limit of the asymptote is reached in the actual presence of God in human flesh. Rahner maintains that the hypostatic union is something "that must occur once and only once when the world begins to enter upon its final phase." It is the realization of the ultimate mystery of God in flesh, the initiation and "triumph of the movement of the world's self-transcendence into absolute closeness to the mystery of God." The incarnation is "the necessary and permanent beginning of the divinization of the world as a whole."[122]

John A. T. Robinson agrees, seeing in the Logos the "principle of the evolutionary process" fully realized in the incarnation.[123] It is a material process, but it culminates in "spirit" in humanity, and finally in Christ as the highest or fullest expression of spirit. Rahner's definition of spirit as transcendent rationality allows this. From within the immanent processes of evolution has emerged that which makes the transcendent destiny of humanity possible. Humanity is granted a share in that destiny through participation with Christ. The goal of the evolutionary process may therefore be described theologically in light of the incarnation as its divinization. In the event of the incarnation, "matter and matter's temporal saga come to a glorious term: union with their Creator." In this way, Rahner blends Christology and evolutionary theory, and presents a theology consistent with incarnation and evolution. Christ is the "absolute savior," the realization and guarantee in a person of the success of human history and of evolution; in him, God's self-communication is irreversible.[124] Creation and incarnation are part

---

122. Rahner, *Foundations*, 181, 186–87; *Theological Investigations*, 11:227.

123. Robinson, *Human Face of God*, 217.

124. Carmody and Carmody, "Christology in Rahner," 198, 202–4. They find in this aspect of Rahner's theology of grace a clear separation from process thought, since it offers a guarantee of both the meaning of the world's createdness and its fulfillment or

of one single act of God's self-giving and self-expression to the cosmos. Cosmic history proceeds through ever-fuller self-transcendence towards that moment when God's self-giving "can be and is accepted as such." Humanity is the being capable of receiving this incarnate self-giving of God.[125]

Angels and Extraterrestrials

That God has made a universe suitable for life leads Rahner to the possibility of extraterrestrials. While not committing to any view as to the likelihood of their existence, he believes that extraterrestrials are at least in principle possible. Since subjectivity and transcendence are the goals of the cosmos, it might be present elsewhere than in humanity. "If we imagine the cosmos as a world coming to be, and as oriented in its becoming to subjectivity, then it is really not to be taken for granted that this aim has been successful only at the tiny point [in the cosmos] we know as our earth."[126] He sees difficulties with the view that God might develop some other world to the point where intelligent life was possible, and then "arbitrarily break it off." Traditional angelology indicates a theological awareness that there are other personal beings besides humans in creation. Without committing to whether angels are an actual reality of the physical realm, or simply required by faith in revelation, Rahner is amenable to the possibility that they may be an ancient result of universal evolutionary processes. Thus the angelic activity recorded by Scripture and affirmed by the church magesterium could be that of beings that have emerged elsewhere in cosmic history. In other words, angels are in reality extraterrestrials.

Here Rahner diverges from Pannenberg. While Barth goes so far as to eliminate angels from consideration by removing them from the material to the spiritual "heavenly realm,"[127] Rahner locates them within material reality. He assumes that angels have an essential connection with the created material cosmos, and are more relevant to us than "possible 'human beings on other planets'" (sentient beings of matter and spirit). He grants that his understanding of angels presents a problem in

---

realization in the incarnation of the absolute savior. Process thought rejects a guaranteed successful future to evolution.

125. Rahner, *Foundations*, 197; *Theological Investigations*, 11:226.

126. Rahner, *Theological Investigations*, 19:262.

127. Barth, *Church Dogmatics* III/2:14.

light of the traditional and biblical understanding that the angels were present at the creation of the cosmos. To resolve this, he compares the function of angels to principles at the beginning of creation that have become in some fashion self-conscious, localized, or almost incarnate into the later cosmos. He also proposes that angels might be like the "unifying themes" apparent in different epochs of evolution on earth, or the principles of order and unity behind nations described in the book of Daniel as the angels of the nations.[128]

Evaluation of Rahner's Angelology

A critical assessment of Rahner's angelology prefaces the next issue, his wrestling with the implications of extraterrestrial intelligence. It is unclear whether his angelology is to be taken literally or metaphorically. He maintains his commitment to Catholic dogma, including the dogma of angelic reality, yet does not confine himself to the classical dogmatic picture of angels as transcendent spiritual beings. For example, redefining transcendent angels as principles present at the beginning of creation does not necessarily result in a clearer conception more acceptable to the modern mind. Are these principles the laws governing the unfolding of creation, such as those of basic physics or math? Are they divine attributes, since otherwise it is difficult to account for their pre-material existence without resorting to a transcendent heavenly domain? If so, positing such self-conscious localizations of divinity seems perilously close to attributing divinity to the cosmos itself. Does this mean a whole pantheon of divine attributes inhabits the universe?

Conceptions of angels as unifying themes of evolution or ordering principles of the nations also seem shaky. Are these themes also personal beings? Which themes in evolution are the unifying ones? Natural selection? Emergent complexity? Entropy? Are mathematics, gravity, and the anthropic conditions God's servants, angelic principles of divine rationality reflected in the cosmos? Are some of these "angelified" principles demonic? How do these themes fulfill the role of God's servants in the account of revelation? How did they speak to Abraham and Mary? Rahner's scheme offers an uneven fit with the scriptural data, which is by his own admission at the heart of the authoritative norm of the church's teaching office, and so the primary and most reli-

---

128. Rahner, *Theological Investigations*, 19:263, 270–72.

able source of information on angels.[129] For instance, Scripture offers an interpretive rule for the meaning of the symbolic animals as nations in Dan 7:16–17,[130] but these creatures are not the same as the personal beings that visit Daniel and war with each other.[131]

While Rahner admits theology has a greater grasp of reality than the materialistic naturalism of science,[132] he seems to be attempting a definition of angels from within that methodological limit. As a result, there is no clear and meaningful picture of their relationship to either material or transcendent reality.

There are parallels here with Rahner's Christology. Although it can be shown that his Christology is not simply "from below,"[133] it often overlooks the transcendent and pre-incarnate life of the Logos. Rahner admits the Son's divine life has a valid transcendent existence outside the immanent domain, but his theology has trouble thematically integrating that existence with the main data of revelation because of his methodological deferral to modern culture. He reduces the spiritual and material to a single unified domain to avoid dualism, but in effect this appears to cut off the transcendent realm. His angelology is restricted to the immanent universe in the same way that his Christology avoids that transcendent realm. Gunton calls this effort to escape from the scriptural worldview to accommodate the modern mind its own form of dualism.[134] Further analysis of this issue will follow later in the chapter.

Rahner's ideas on angels are creative theological speculation. He finds non-human intelligence easily imaginable in a vastly rich universe, and suggests that such might relate to us differently from our expectations of human communication. The biblical portrayal of angels and demons might describe from its contemporary cultural perspective what it looks like when these highly evolved servants or enemies of God

---

129. Marshall, *Trinity and Truth*, 63.

130. In fact, it is angels who deliver these internal rules of symbolic interpretation. John Collins believes these rules are loose, and the beasts could either represent nations, or rulers/kings of nations (Collins, *Daniel*, 312 n. 306; see also R. A. Anderson, *Daniel*, 88; Hartman and Di Lella, *Book of Daniel*, 204, 212).

131. These angels are conscious individuals, sometimes with personal names and roles to play in relation to the nations (Dan 10:5–6, 13).

132. Rahner, *Foundations*, 263.

133. Losinger, *Anthropological Turn*, 13–15.

134. Gunton, *Yesterday and Today*, 97–99.

move in human affairs. While the Scripture does not give a complete description of these beings, Rahner's redefinition to accommodate the modern worldview seems to stretch the concept far beyond the original scriptural meaning. In contrast to Rahner's immanent approach,[135] the biblical tradition seems to indicate that angels are from a transcendent realm, serving God in the cosmos.[136] However, if the only reliable data we have on the nature of angels—even in shadowy form—is in the teaching of the church, then an explanatory model that ignores much of that basic data might be seen as unwarranted.

The Possibility of Multiple Incarnations

Rahner believes that in light of our understanding of the immutability of God and the identity of the Word (the Logos) with God, that "it cannot be proved that a multiple incarnation in different histories of salvation is absolutely unthinkable."[137] Speculation on the existence of extraterrestrial intelligence (ETI) and the attendant possibility of multiple incarnations has had a long, if not very extensive, history in Western thought.[138] George Coyne observes that the possibilities inherent in the consideration of ETI are today some "of the most poignant topics on which scientific and religious thought interpenetrate."[139] Is it possible that Christ has visited other sentient worlds and there shed his human body to become incarnate, returning to some primal form of the Logos each time?[140] Peacocke insists that modern theology must be able to ad-

---

135. Rahner, *Theological Investigations Vol. 19*, 252–274.

136. For instance, the angelic appearances in Gen 28:10ff; Num 22:21ff and 13:3ff; 2 Kgs 6:16f; Dan 7–12; Matt 1:20; 28:2ff; Mark 16:5ff; Luke 1:11ff; 1:26ff; 24:4ff; Acts 5:19–20 and 12:7–9, and Revelations all suggest angels are transcendent beings present in the world as God's servants.

137. Rahner, *Theological Investigations*, 21:51.

138. Davis, "Search for Extraterrestrial Intelligence," 23–30; Dick, "Cosmotheology," 197–98. Democritus, Aristotle, and Thomas Aquinas considered the issue. Giordano Bruno was burned at the stake in the sixteenth century for, among other things, believing in infinitely many worlds. In the eighteenth century, Thomas Paine believed the existence of other worlds rendered Christianity obsolete (*Complete Writings*, 1:498–500). At the beginning of the nineteenth century, Thomas Chalmers wondered whether other beings on other possible worlds would also need other incarnations, but concluded not (Crowe, *Extraterrestrial Life Debate*, 186–87). More recently, but before SETI began in earnest, E. A. Milne, E. L. Mascall, and C. S. Lewis weighed in on the subject, Milne and Lewis rejecting the necessity of other incarnations, Mascall supporting.

139. Coyne, "Evolution of Intelligent Life," 178.

140. An episode of the original Star Trek television series suggested this possibility,

dress the prospect, since it is possible, in a universe constructed to make the emergence of life and consciousness likely, sentient beings will have arisen in other solar systems. "Would ET, Alpha-Arcturians, Martians, et al., need an incarnation and all it is supposed to accomplish, as much as *Homo sapiens* on planet Earth?"[141] Ernan McMullin wonders "how we can dare" to limit the ways the God who created such an immense universe might relate to such other creatures.[142]

Since the incarnation plays such a key role in establishing an anthropocentric cosmos, does human cosmic significance fade before a mélange of rational beings spread across the universe, each with its own incarnation of God?[143] This possibility will be evaluated by examining its coherence with Rahner's internal position on the cosmic significance of the incarnation. Are multiple incarnations coherent with Scripture? Does the idea make sense philosophically? Does the immutability of God really imply that the universe is open for multiple incarnations? Does the one known incarnation of God in Jesus Christ give sufficient information to rule out the likelihood of other incarnations?

Rahner takes the position that sentient beings on other planets are irrelevant to the human question. "At the present time it is not only unanswerable, but refers to living beings which at least up to now have not been incorporated in our own existential and theological sphere of life and thus existentially and theologically have no more relevance for us than any sort of 'dead' star anywhere in the universe."[144] Theologians will be able to say nothing more about such creatures, and must stick to affirming that the purpose of revelation in Christ gives them what they need for their own (human) salvation, and does not deal with questions that have no relevance to that purpose.[145] This approach appears to set the question aside, but it has the effect of decentralizing not only humanity, but the whole of theology in the cosmic scheme, since it sur-

---

as the crew visited a world with a history parallel to earth's history at the time of the Roman Empire. This episode portrayed the Son of God simply as a messenger of peace in a cruel and dark culture, not as a cosmic redeemer.

141. Peacocke, "Challenge and Stimulus," 103.

142. McMullin, "Life and Intelligence," 172.

143. The question only concerns other incarnations in *this* universe rather than in speculative alternate universes.

144. Rahner, *Theological Investigations*, 19:263.

145. Rahner, *Theological Investigations*, 21:52.

renders theology's right to infer from known revelation consequences beyond the human realm. Since by the advance of science and technology we are able to observe the universe billions of light years away, almost to the beginning of time, any theology that is unable to engage with reality with such cosmic scope will soon seem too parochial and antiquated to be credible.

Rahner considers multiple incarnations possible, even though he says theology need not engage the issue of ETI. But his internal doctrine of the incarnation supports a unique and cosmically singular event with significance for the history of the whole universe. It is Jesus Christ, "in whom *God has forever made the countenance of man his own.*"[146] The incarnation is the "unsurpassable climax of revelation," when God's self-communication reaches its highest point.[147] It is revelation in the absolute sense, so that in Christ revelation is closed because "the definitive Reality which resolves history proper is already here." Why would such a "definitive Reality" resolve only human history? For Rahner, the incarnation is the final word of God, because in it, God and the world "have become one, forever without confusion, but forever undivided," and in it, all the plenitude of God is included for the world, and nothing of it is excluded.[148] If there is nothing of God excluded for the world, and the world is part of a unified cosmic history of matter and spirit reaching its climax in Christ, in what sense can "more" of God be required for some other part of the cosmos? Rahner maintains that the incarnation we know in Jesus Christ "appears as the necessary and permanent beginning of the divinization of the world as a whole."[149] How could such a divinization be limited to the earth, since earth is part of the unified cosmos? By implication, this divinization must be for all material reality. Rahner believes that "man is a personal subject from whose freedom as a subject the fate of the entire cosmos depends."[150] Clearly he sees humanity as having pan-cosmic significance. Humanity in Christ already stands "beyond death's demarcation line,"[151] and in so doing represents the rest of creation. Why should another event be required to further

---

146. Rahner, *Theological Investigation*, 2:240–41. Emphasis added.
147. Rahner, *Foundations*, 174.
148. Rahner, *Theological Investigations*, 1:49.
149. Rahner, *Foundations*, 181.
150. Rahner, "Theology and Anthropology," 15.
151. Rahner, *Theological Investigations*, 5:168.

an already accomplished cosmic effect? Such a comprehensive and universal view of God's self-disclosure in the incarnate Christ seems to exclude the need for other incarnations. Thus speculative multiple incarnations are not coherent with Rahner's own internal view of the one verified incarnation.

There are other philosophical and scriptural problems with the notion. An incarnation of God in the universe requires, by definition, some kind of material and bodily existence. Braine draws attention to the distinction between an *incarnation* as God taking bodily form, and an *indwelling* as an occasion in which the spirit of God inhabits another separate (non-divine) bodily being. While an incarnation is unique and specific, an indwelling may occur in multiple times and places. The witness of the Scripture, the resurrection, and the church is that Christ came as God incarnate, not simply as an indwelling of God in a person similar to other persons. His incarnation is eternal: "he will reign over the house of Jacob forever, and of his kingdom there will be no end" (Luke 1:32-33). It is very specific in its human particularity—of such and such race, tribe and family. What becomes available to the rest of humanity at Pentecost as a result of Christ's work is an indwelling of God's presence, not a further incarnation.[152] Since there is only "one eternally begotten" Son of God (John 3:16), begotten before all worlds (the Nicene Creed), and his assumption of human form is eternal, his human incarnation precludes incarnations elsewhere in any other bodily form.

Johannes Brenz had observed this property of the incarnation as long ago as the sixteenth century, a consequence of the doctrine of the union of the divine and human nature. "Since deity and humanity are inseparably joined ... in one person of Christ, it is necessary that wherever the deity of Christ is there also is his humanity ... For if the deity of Christ is anywhere without his humanity, there are two persons, not one."[153] The doctrine of the resurrection proclaims that even in heaven, full human personhood entails a bodily existence, not some kind of disembodied spiritual state (1 Cor 15:42-44). Jesus' resurrection is notably human, not a return to some primal form of the Logos (John 20:27; Rev 5:6; see page 67). His resurrected body shows that even in eternity the Son of God is embodied as *human*, and subject to certain restrictions

152. Braine, "Impossibility," 1.

153. Jenson, *Systematic Theology*, 1:203 n. 40; quoting Brenz, *De personali unione*, 3-4.

of singular personal expression. If we accept the Son of God's unique begotten status, then a poly-incarnational existence is a logical impossibility, for the bodily nature of personhood requires that one person correspond to one body (otherwise a kind of bodily schizophrenia results if the singular Son of God exists in more than one body in the same time and place, destroying the meaning of personhood). This would not preclude the human Jesus from visiting other worlds, but this is slightly different from being incarnate *into* them.

Brenz also suggests that it is a basic confusion about the nature of heaven to suppose that it is simply another physical sphere related to the present one, to which Jesus goes to join God. We cannot attribute to Jesus' body an "extension or diffusion in space, but [must instead] elevate it beyond . . . all location."[154] If Jesus in the unity of his full divinity and humanity is thus elevated "beyond all location," he has from there the same relation to all reality that God the Father has: a relationship of "all in all." Robert Jenson, crediting Brenz, describes it thus: "Christ has risen to be in God's place. God, however, is *in* no place but *is* his own place; and over against God, the created universe is therefore just one other single place."[155] So Paul says Christ "is the same one who ascended far above all the heavens, so that he might fill" the whole universe (Eph 4:10). As he holds this eternal position, there is no reason to suppose such a move *from* God *to* the cosmos need occur more than once.

Christ as Cosmic Redeemer

The universal salvation offered in Christ also suggests the singularity of the human incarnation. This is explicit in several biblical passages. The ingathering of the redeemed is heavenly, not just earthly. "Then they will see 'the Son of Man coming in clouds' with great power and glory. Then he will send out the angels, and gather his elect from the four winds, from the ends of the earth to the ends of heaven." (Mark 13:26–27). The crucifixion binds the Son of God decisively to the doom of death that causes *all* creation to groan in frustration. His death—and by implication his resurrection—is not only for humanity, but also for the entire cosmos, declared "from the creation of the world" (Rev 13:8).

---

154. Ibid., 204 n. 44; quoting Brenz, *De personali unione*, 7.
155. Ibid., 203–4.

John Davis highlights Paul's cosmic Christology in Colossians[156]: "For in him all the fullness of God was pleased to dwell, and through him God was pleased to reconcile to himself all things, whether on earth or in heaven, by making peace through the blood of his cross" (Col 1:19–20). This cosmic reconciling and ingathering is accomplished only through Jesus, the Son of *Man*. Angels will worship the Son in human form (Heb 1:6), who is far superior to them, whose origins are from eternity, begotten not created.

The Scripture indicates that Jesus contains *all* the fullness of God, enabling the reconciliation of *all* things. God's presence in him is so vast, powerful, and all-embracing that it will reach out to include all things, whether in heaven or on earth, accomplishing God's purposes for the entire cosmos. The human arena set here in this tiny local time and space, seemingly a minor sideshow, is revealed as the center of the entire cosmic drama, not because of humanity *per se*, but because of the human incarnation. God need not repeat himself in multiple incarnations, because what has been done in Jesus Christ is enough for the whole creation. Cosmic fulfillment is revealed in its majesty at the end of the age, precisely in and through humanity:

> For the creation waits with eager longing for the revealing of the children of God ... [It] will be set free from its bondage to decay and will obtain the freedom of the glory of the children of God. We know that the *whole creation* has been groaning in labor pains until now. (Rom 8:19–22; emphasis added)

In the unified scriptural vision, the redemption of the entire cosmos is thus connected with the human redemption *at its heart*.[157] That redemption goes so far as to replace the existing laws of physics with new laws freed from death and suitable for eternal life, as human, divine, and cosmic history reach their unified fulfillment. Thus human cosmic redemption would seem to make other incarnations redundant.

George L. Murphy suggests cosmic Christology is evident in the idea—logically independent of Scripture though coherent with it—of the Logos as the universe's pattern maker. Jesus as the Logos cannot be just one aspect of the divine nature, one actualized pattern among many potential patterns, or he could not be regarded as the fullness of

---

156. Davis, "Search for Extraterrestrial Intelligence," 30–34.
157. Barth, *Church Dogmatics* III/2:4.

God incarnate. Similarly, his nature as fully incarnate Logos must be the foundation for the whole universe and for all other potential universes.[158] As the fullness of the cosmic pattern for this actualized universe, Christ is both its foundation and its conclusion. That is what it means to be the Logos of God. Therefore he can rightfully be called the Alpha and Omega. Since he is in himself the foundation and fulfillment of the whole cosmos, the need for multiple incarnations is eliminated.

Is there a scriptural counterfoil to such cosmic Christology? Hebrews is full of references to the universal salvific effect of Christ's finished work—a cosmic Christology encompassing the whole of creation (Heb 1:3; 2:5–9; 5: 8–10; 7:26–28; 9:25–26). He sustains "all things" by his powerful word; the world to come will be "placed under his feet"; he does not need to offer himself "again and again," but has appeared "once for all" at the end of the ages. Having suffered to learn obedience, he is "now made perfect." On the other hand, Scripture might hint at another possibility. Jesus says in John 10:16a, "I have other sheep that do not belong to this fold," which with a little imagination could be taken as a reference to extraterrestrial "sheep."[159] Hebrews emphasizes Jesus' human nature as necessary for his priesthood on humanity's behalf. He is only fit to be high priest because he is fully one of them (Heb 2:14–18; 4:15; 5:1–7). On its face, this seems to imply that he must share their humanity completely if his suffering, death, and resurrection are to count on their behalf. Gregory of Nazianzus' words might well have expressed this sentiment: "That which he has not assumed, he has not healed."[160] In order to accomplish salvation for extraterrestrials, would Christ necessarily need to become fully whatever they are, incarnate in their possible alternate form? Is there a dilemma here for either the incarnation or the fate of extraterrestrials?

---

158. Murphy, "Cosmology and Christology," 109–11. The Logos must be the pattern-making capacity of God for all potential universes. If he is only the pattern of this universe, then since this local pattern is only a subset of all possible patterns, the local logos is reduced to a subset or *part* of the whole Logos of God; in this case the fullness of God could not be said to be incarnate in Christ.

159. This is an unlikely meaning in context, and is probably a reference to the God-fearing Gentiles.

160. Gregory Nazianzus, "To Cledonius against Apollinaris," 218. In this context Gregory is defending Christ's full humanity and his ability to fully save humans, not making a case for his inability to save non-humans.

There are some solutions that avoid the need for multiple incarnations: (1) There are no other human-like creatures in the cosmos—no other material creatures that are made in the image of God but with non-human form. (2) If there are such creatures, they do not need or are incapable of such incarnate redemption (e.g., fallen angels). (3) If there are such creatures, they must be fully human already, somehow sufficiently like Jesus in his human divine creaturehood to be encompassed in his single terrestrial incarnation.

The third alternative is coherent with a picture of humanity created as the being that is based on the divine pattern of Christ. As Edmund J. Rybarczyk notes, "We do not *have* something(s) within us that constitutes the *imago Dei*; we *are* an image." He points out that in Eastern thought, it is not Adam who is the "great archetype after whom the rest of the human race was fashioned," but rather Jesus Christ himself.[161] Thunberg agrees, noting that in Christian tradition "the Logos is seen as the prototype, which God used in creating humans in his image, and Christ is seen as the archetype of what it is to be human."[162] If Christ the Logos is the cosmic pattern of God's image, then the material version of that image might well have the same *human* form everywhere in the cosmos.

If non-human creatures "of matter and spirit" were discovered, the definition of humanity might have to be broadened to include such new creatures, whether they are *Homo sapiens* or not. Davis defends this view, maintaining that Christ's death and resurrection is valid for the whole cosmos—all space and time—and so for sentient beings everywhere.[163] Braine suggests that if extraterrestrials are found, then the incarnation of Jesus Christ will be relevant to them in the same way that it was relevant to more than just the Jews. It had to be manifested in a particular time, place, and people such as the Jews, but is relevant to the entire human race. McMullin likewise supposes that if Christ's redemption is a unique event restoring the balance on a cosmic level, it can have a universal scope for creatures with or without a direct connection to Adam's sin.[164] In context, the passage sited in John reinforces a conclusion of a single and sufficient cosmic incarnation, for Jesus continues,

161. Rybarczyk, "What Are You, O Man?" 89.
162. Thunberg, "Human Person," 293.
163. Davis, "Search for Extraterrestrial Intelligence," 32.
164. McMullin, "Life and Intelligence," 173.

"I must bring them also, and they will listen to my voice. So there will be *one flock, one shepherd*" (John 10:16b; emphasis added). Though the human race may be the species in which the incarnation is manifest, its effects will be relevant to all beings everywhere in time and space, even to the angels.[165]

God's Immutability

Rahner believes the immutability of God lends itself to the possibility of multiple incarnations. Is this position sound? God in his immutability has taken on the mutable nature of humanity.[166] Having made an eternal decision regarding their creation and redemption, a decision anchored in cosmic plans encompassing the beginning and end of time, is it logical that God would require another and different program to further that redemption in some other part of the unified cosmos? Coyne observes that the universality of God's salvation is deeply embedded in Christian theology, appearing throughout the Scripture. The creation and redemption of the universe is grounded in the Logos. It is portrayed in Genesis and Revelation, in the Old Testament prophetic promises of the new creation, in the Johanine writings, Romans, I Corinthians, Colossians, and Hebrews. It is evident in the New Testament presupposition of the pre-incarnate divinity of the Son of God. While Coyne admits that God is completely free to choose his methods, and cannot be constrained by us, nevertheless we do know what he has *already* chosen to do: freely "send his Son to us."[167]

God has declared himself unchangeably *for* humanity in Jesus Christ. He has likewise declared himself unchangeably *for* the cosmos of which humans are a unified part. Human redemption can only be complete if it is in the context of the redemption of the rest of the cosmos, since otherwise redeemed humanity would be trapped in a cosmos that is condemned to death. If Christ's work ultimately destroys death, then there is no need for another such work elsewhere in the cosmos. Through him, "all things will be reconciled" to God (Col 1:20). Since Christ's cosmic salvation comes from the unity of his divine and human nature as the self-communication of God, another incarnation

---

165. Braine, "Impossibility," 11. Admittedly, some angels appear to be beyond salvation (e.g., Rev 20:10).

166. Rahner, *Foundations*, 223.

167. Coyne, "Evolution of Intelligent Life," 187.

elsewhere in space and time is no longer necessary. The human incarnation fulfills the yearning for transcendence of the entire universe. Since God has given himself *completely* to the cosmos in Christ, a single incarnation would appear to be most compatible with God's immutability. So if Barth is right in saying that in Jesus Christ "God does not exist without man,"[168] then God's immutability does not easily lend itself to the possibility of multiple incarnations.

Conclusion

On the basis of these arguments, it seems reasonable to maintain that despite our lack of knowledge and our inability to conclusively prove the singularity of the human incarnation, that there are some things that work against the need for multiple incarnations. There has been no ETI found yet. As shall be addressed in chapter 6, there is some scientific evidence to suggest that ETI will never be found. The philosophical (or logical) and scriptural arguments suggest the sufficiency of a single incarnation. Redemption in Jesus Christ is cosmic in scope, encompassing all beings "in heaven and on earth." The size of this small earthly stage is not relevant to the cosmic scope of Jesus' incarnate mission, which serves as a kind of cosmic moment of inertia for the consummation of the whole universe, including all possible ETI. In light of these arguments, there seems to be no need for multiple incarnations. Until concrete evidence emerges of ETI and alternate incarnations, it seems prudent to remain skeptical about the need for other incarnations, and prudent to resist wholesale changes to our theology based on speculation.

Some Relevant Problems in Rahner's Theology

Transcendentality, Rationality, and the Human Spirit

Rahner's conception of "spirit" can be somewhat confusing. According to Weger, the human dimension of transcendental experience is for Rahner the "supernatural, divine order of being."[169] The transcendent realm seems to be that of the traditional three-tiered universe. God is the eternal being beyond the material realm, and humanity's openness

---

168. Barth, *Humanity of God*, 50.
169. Weger, *Karl Rahner*, 142.

to God marks them as transcendent, as spiritual. Spirit is that which enables humans to engage in personal conscious relationships with others, both human and God. Humans are spiritual beings because they can relate to God, particularly to God in Jesus Christ.[170]

On the other hand, Rahner sometimes uses "spirit" simply to mean self-consciousness, as if human rationality actually constitutes the human spirit and separates it from the animals. Spirit is the "inner world of thought and action," primarily apprehended by reason. Humans are spiritual because "Nature does become conscious of itself in him."[171] Charles Stanley summarizes Rahner's position: the human unity of matter and spirit is a "moment of cognition."[172] This unity then seems identical with the "unity of mind and matter" that occurs in it, "with all its consequences: salvific importance of history as such, incarnation of the Logos, resurrection of the body, etc."[173] The union of matter and spirit in humanity points to the unity and commonality of matter and spirit in the entire cosmos.[174] Fields notes that for Rahner, "sublation can occur only in human reason, which Spirit constitutes as its own medium in order to bring itself dialectically to conscious realization."[175] This appears to make Rahner's understanding of spirit largely a Hegelian reduction of spirit to reason. So Purcell identifies the "convertibility between being and knowing" in Rahner, and a tendency to value "intellect over sense, spirit over world."[176] Appropriating another Hegelianism, history is for Rahner the immanent stage of preparation for the development of spirit.[177] "The peculiarity of the spirit in contrast to matter

---

170. Rahner, *Theological Investigations*, 2:239–41.
171. Ibid., 5:179.
172. Stanley, "Trancendental Method," 204.
173. Rahner, *Theological Investigations*, 19:261.
174. Roberts, *Achievement of Karl Rahner*, 161; Ian MacDonald, personal conversations. Some issues arise here about the meaning of spirit and its relationship to matter that are beyond the scope of this thesis. If spirit arises from matter, this would seem to destroy contingency, since the material has produced the immaterial (unless spirit is not defined as immaterial). Christian De Duve suggests we have been too focused on the study of matter from the side of physics and chemistry, and that even in a monistic worldview, the definition of matter must be enlarged "to include those properties that used to be attributed to spirit" (De Duve, "Lessons of Life," 10).
175. Fields, *Being as Symbol*, 66.
176. Purcell, *Mystery and Method*, 90, 119.
177. Rahner, *Foundations*, 177–78.

[is that it] can reflect upon itself and its world, and then again place its world over against itself."[178] Even though human transcendence is open to the realm of God's transcendence, the emphasis remains on human rational capacity. As Anne Carr phrases it, "supernatural transcendence is operative wherever one has achieved the conscious use of reason."[179]

Is this an adequate presentation of spirit in humanity? Certainly when God is spoken of as "spirit" in Christian context, it is in part a reference to his being distinct from the world, Creator not creature, not another material being alongside the material cosmos. Even in such process theologies as Peacocke's panentheism, in which the world is thought of as "God's body," God's being is still "distinct from that of the world."[180] In fact, God must in his being be independent for the contingent world to even exist, unless the world itself is divine. As Jenson observes, "God does *not* transcend creation, since he does not start from it."[181] It seems reasonable to suggest human nature would need some type of transcendent spiritual capacity in order to have real fellowship and communion with God. Belief in such an aspect does not require belief in the immortality of the soul or in the platonic superiority of spirit over body. But if human nature and spirituality are understood to be like the animals except for the extent of rational capacity, then it is difficult to discern how human "thinking animals" could reach beyond this realm of dust to be in relationship with the transcendent God. What is it that gives them their orientation to the transcendent? Is spirit for Rahner simply an end result of material processes in the form of rationality, without giving an adequate account of the human spirit or spirit as transcendence?

There is some debate on what relation Scripture intends between the human body and spirit. Joel Green and Ray Anderson argue that the dominant view of the New Testament is ontological monism, and believe Scripture does not support the concept of a disembodied spiritual component of human nature. Aubrey Johnson says that in the Old

---

178. Rahner, *Theological Investigation*, 21:50.

179. Carr, *Theological Method*, 202. Carr refers to Rahner's *Nature and Grace*, 180 n. 2.

180. Peacocke, "Challenge and Stimulus," 110. The analogy, which compares God's relationship to the cosmos with the human mind's relationship to the human body, breaks down, however, since Peacocke believes the human mind is an emergent property of the material universe, but not so God's mind.

181. Jenson, "Creator and Creature," 2.

Testament worldview, "man is conceived not so much in dual fashion as 'body' and 'soul,' but synthetically as a unit of vital power or (in current terminology) a psycho-physical organism."[182] Similarly, Pannenberg sees dualist notions as unbiblical remnants of Greek Platonic or Cartesian dualism.[183] Anderson insists human nature can only be understood holistically as a body-soul unity, and suggests the Christian doctrine of the resurrection shows there is no human existence apart from the body.[184]

On the other hand, James Barr argues that while there are evident strands of "totality thinking" in the Hebrew tradition, these are not the only ones. "God's creation of Adam as 'dust from the earth' and his 'breathing into his nostrils the breath of life' look ... in spite of all that is written ... awfully like two ingredients, of which Adam is a sort of compound." Barr also sees the preacher's use of *ruah* (spirit) in Eccl 12:7 for humans as highly significant: "for this word could not bear the highly physical components which people have attached to the 'totality' concept of *nephesh* [(soul)]. [The preacher] meant the *human spirit* which went in a different direction from the flesh which returned to dust." Barr suggests the paradigmatic opposition usually posited between Hebrew and Greek thought on this matter is "crude and questionable." Even the New Testament concept of the resurrection of the body is not as clearly monistic as some writers want to maintain.[185]

There are some Scriptures that support the idea of a non-corporeal aspect of human nature. Jesus explicitly warns, "Do not fear those who kill the body but cannot kill the soul; rather fear him who can destroy both soul and body in hell" (Matt 10:28). He is described as descending to the realm of the dead during the three days in the grave to preach to imprisoned spirits (1 Pet 3:18–20; the Apostle's Creed). James describes death as the separation of body and spirit (Jas 2:26), and Paul reports that to be "absent from the body" for a Christian is to be "present with the Lord" (2 Cor 5:8). He exhorts the Corinthians to pray with their minds as well as with their spirits in such a way as to draw a clear contrast between the two (1 Cor 14: 2, 14–15). Christ's words to the thief on the cross, "Today you will be with me in Paradise" (Luke 23:43), and his

---

182. Johnson, *Vitality of the Individual*, 88; Knibb, "Life and Death," 397–99.

183. J. B. Green, "'Bodies—Thas Is, Human Lives,'" 173; Anderson, "On Being Human," 182–86; Pannenberg, *Anthropology*, 523.

184. Anderson, "On Being Human," 182, 188–94.

185. J. Barr, *Garden of Eden*, 43–47.

statement that God is not the God of the dead but of the living—"for to him, all are alive" (Luke 20:38)—also suggest some mode of personal existence independent of the body.[186]

Whatever view one holds on the state of the person between death and the general resurrection, these passages seem to imply that there is an immaterial aspect of human nature, however attenuated, that exists apart from the body. Explanations that suggest the dead only exist as memories in the mind of God until the eschaton[187] hardly fit a vision of satisfying "presence to the Lord." This need not entail a simple form of platonic dualism, for it does not imply that human existence at its fullest is a purely spiritual phenomenon. As noted previously, embodiment is central to the Christian hope. Yet it would be a mistake to regard the doctrine of the resurrection as alone supporting a purely material body. Fraser Watts notes that mainstream Christian tradition has seen the bodily resurrection as a compliment to the survival of the soul, not as an alternative. He also reminds us that in science, "the jury is still out" on the issue of non-reductive physicalism.[188] Medical research into near-death experiences may even provide evidence of such an immaterial aspect to human nature (see page 232), so this idea cannot therefore be ruled scientifically invalid.

Eliminating a transcendent aspect of human nature seems to reduce the medium of human relationship to God to rationality. But humans need more than physical and intellectual sustenance; they require the life and love of God to be complete. Henri Nouwen notes that since Seneca defined humanity as the "reasoning animal" (*rationale animal est homo*) we have been tempted to think that what makes humans unique is our mind. Nouwen insists that it is primarily the *heart* that makes us human: "the center of our being where God comes to dwell with us and bring us the divine gifts of trust, hope, and love."[189]

The scriptural distinction between flesh (which may include rationality) and spirit also helps highlight this contrast between rationality per se and spirituality.[190] If the only effect of the Spirit's indwelling is

---

186. See also Eccl 12:7; Matt 17:3; Mark 9:4; Luke 16:20–22; John 20:22; Heb 4:12.
187. Pannenberg, "Resurrection," 257; Watts, "Multifaceted Nature," 183.
188. Watts, "Multifaceted Nature," 48.
189. Nouwen, *Finding My Way Home*, 55–71, 67–68.
190. Paul emphasizes that the work of the spirit is shown by the presence of divine power, not by even the wisest of words, so often taken as symbols of rationality (1 Cor

to change the believer's thinking pattern, then the regenerated person seems to be different from the unbeliever only in terms of their knowledge. Here, the spiritual man is the one who has somehow attained a secret knowledge, a superior rationality that may be judged on the same plain as fleshly rationality. This type of Gnosticism presents problems for salvation similar to those encountered in Pannenberg. Gunton points out that instead of guilt and the awareness of sin and separation from God underlying the human need for salvation, there is the need for a type of knowledge, for rational training, for a salvation that is ultimately mental and philosophical rather than material. Those who are saved will be those who are able to manage some kind of "God-consciousness." "Humanity is saved by a kind of christological triumphalism, by successful religiousness rather than by the 'failure' of the cross."[191] Yet the cross is central to Christian redemption, as Paul notes: "For the message of the cross is foolishness to those who are perishing, but to us who are being saved it is the power of God" (1 Cor 1:18). Rahner himself rejects such gnostic versions of "psychotherapeutic" salvation, wherein the absolutely transcendent mental spirit of God simply comes alongside the mental spirit in humanity without entering into the cosmos, insisting the Logos of God has truly entered the cosmos in Jesus Christ.[192]

A fuller definition of spirit seems to be implied in the idea of incarnation itself—else how can Jesus be anything but a mere man? From whence comes his connection to the transcendent if his nature, like ours, is entirely a product of the finite world? His *resurrection nature* must also be transcendent if it is to be thought of ultimately as anything more than resuscitation (1 Cor 15:35–49). If Jesus in his humanity has divine transcendentality, then native humanity would seem to require some reflection of it. Otherwise, we have an artificial joining of the natures in Christ—Rahner's objection based on the results of the modern exegetical enterprise—rather than a true hypostatic union.[193] We would have in Jesus a combination of physical and spiritual nature, a ghost

---

2:4–5; 12:7–8). The spirit stands for *power* and God's *presence*. Jesus is "declared to be Son of God with power according to the spirit of holiness by resurrection from the dead" (Rom 1:4). See also Luke 4:14; John 3:6; 4:24; 6:63; 20:22; Rom 8:1–4; Col 2:8; Phil 3:3.

191. Gunton, *Yesterday and Today*, 99.

192. Rahner, *Foundations*, 196.

193. Ibid., 195–96. The issue at the heart of Chalcedonian debates since the fifth century AD.

in the machine, while all the rest of humanity would be just physical, plain machines.[194] Rahner himself rejects such docetic Christology for compromising the humanity of Jesus.

Herbert Vorgrimler claims that Rahner offers a fuller and transcendent version of spirit as the drive for absolute being. Human beings are spiritual because they are metaphysically constituted so as to be open to transcendent revelation from God.[195] The Spirit of God "is the inner force of the spirit's self-movement."[196] While Rahner attempts to be coherent with the dominant monistic paradigm, perhaps there is room for a richer view of spirit as more than a purely mental and immanent phenomenon. He claims that our age is correctly more material than the Greek age, and that the Logos "establishes this corporeal part of the world as his own reality . . . in such a way that this very materiality expresses *him*, the Logos himself, and allows him to be present in his world."[197] By positing a materiality that *expresses* the Logos, he has tacitly admitted that the Logos is from outside that materiality. He has already presupposed the transcendent "spiritual" realm as the undergirding of his fundamental theology, even though he leaves much of it unspoken for the sake of emphasizing what will seem most coherent to the modern mind.

Difficulties in Rahner's Evolutionary Theology

There are some difficulties in Rahner's use of evolution, some from the perspective of science, others from theology. The typical view in evolutionary biology rejects any form of external guidance or directionality imposed upon evolution.[198] How then can Rahner maintain God's guiding presence in the process? This critique can be unpacked into a range of problems. Is God's part in the process redundant, so that it should simply be dropped by the principle of Ockham's razor? Can a christocentric pattern exist in the evolutionary process that can be scientifically discerned? Does even the theological proposal of such a pattern not

---

194. One alternative explanation: only humanity in Christ has such a (reborn) spirit. "The first man was from the earth, a man of dust; the second man is from heaven." (1 Cor 15:47).

195. Purcell, *Mystery and Method*, 24, 120; Rahner, *Hearers of the Word*, 16, 24, 89.

196. Vorgrimler, *Karl Rahner*, 62.

197. Rahner, *Foundations*, 196–97.

198. De Duve, "Lessons of Life," 7.

miss the fact that the human stage is transient; in the future, humanity will either "disappear or evolve" to something else?[199] Also, does not such a christocentric and anthropocentric pattern in evolution miss the value that other living creatures and the non-living cosmos must have for God?[200] Finally, can the apparently chaotic and often violent natural process of evolution be reconciled with a high view of God's love leading to his own presence in Christ at the end of the process? Does an evolutionary Christology give adequate recognition to the "absurdities and uncertainties" of life?[201]

Rahner admits that the incarnation stands in "direct and simple contradiction" to human knowledge of evolution, because otherwise the theologian would be turning faith and revelation into philosophy and rationalism.[202] He is clear that the incarnation is a statement of faith, not science. This is an important proviso in Rahner's approach. He is not trying to say that evolution must be perceived christocentrically, or that scientific details of the process will have a guaranteed theological meaning.[203] Rather, he is trying to show that incarnation and Christology are coherent even in an evolutionary worldview.[204] The presence of God enabling the process by grace to move in the directions it has taken, and to arrive at its ultimate destination of absolute grace, might or might not be scientifically discernable. Even if the current theory of evolution is superseded by some other scientific theory, theology will still be able to maintain grace as the divine backdrop upon which the cosmic processes unfold. It will be able to say that the transcendent is what emerges when grace interacts with matter. Theology will always need to look for new points of contact with culture, as worldviews change, in order to make the good news of God's love in Jesus Christ accessible. This missional purpose illuminates several problems in Rahner's thought.

---

199. Ibid., 10.

200. Peacocke, "Challenge and Stimulus," 95.

201. TeSelle, *Christ in Context*, 131. Stanley, "Transcendental Method," 204.

202. Rahner, *Foundations*, 179.

203. Faith need not capitulate to whatever is new in science just for newness sake. Otherwise, theology will have compromised its integrity by abandoning its moorings in revelation and grace, if it surrenders itself to the "tentative and provisional character of scientific theory" (Fowler, "Response to Fr. O'Donovan," 305).

204. Stanley, "Transcendental Method," 204.

The cosmic processes leading to *mind* open up potentially to the infinite in humanity, but actually achieve union with that infinite in the particular human being Jesus of Nazareth. In this sense a christological pattern can be said to be present in the evolutionary process; this pattern is the *horizon of the planned* within which the universal processes of chance and necessity leading to God's realization in the cosmos occur. While chapter 6 engages this question more fully, an overview of the perspective is appropriate here to justify Rahner's thought. Although the directedness of the process to the human end is a theological statement within this christological horizon of the planned, it may be coherent with the data of science. If *mind* is an emergent property of matter, its potential genesis must also be built into the laws of nature that science simply accepts as given. Since humankind is the one example of mind in the cosmos that is objectively verifiable, it is also coherent to maintain the ontological directedness of the process to mind realized in humanity. Even if *Homo sapiens* are regarded as utterly contingent and accidental in terms of local origin, they cannot therefore be regarded as ultimately accidental. From a theological perspective, human existence is the fulfillment of a requirement for incarnation that was in the divine plan from the beginning, and must be seen for that reason as providential. Therefore the question of human transience in the evolutionary stream becomes moot. In them, *mind* has already opened up to the infinite Absolute, and reached fulfillment through the incarnation. Cosmic destiny coalesces decisively in humanity.

Every moment in the entire evolutionary process is thus of importance and worth. If it all occurs within the *christological horizon*, then even if it reaches a climax and fulfillment in humanity, it is a fulfillment that promises to sweep up all within that horizon—the entire cosmos—into salvation. For this reason the human realization of God can be rightly described as a realization of *servanthood* on behalf of the entire cosmos. God enjoys humans, but according to the psalmist, he also cares for all his creatures, and satisfies them with good things (Ps 104). He defends the earth against, and ultimately judges, the wickedness of human beings: he will "destroy those who destroy the earth" (Rev 11:18). Yet God finally brings this creation he loves and serves over from death to life in *human* form. Rahner's evolutionary Christology contains an implicit ecological consciousness.

Is the sometimes vicious natural process compatible with this high view of God's love? Moltmann argues that Rahner's evolutionary Christology is simply too optimistic and positivistic, and ignores the reality of evil and the cross. If God as spirit is the world's "innermost life," how can this be reconciled with the "victims the process actually costs"? The modern destruction of the world that comes from reducing nature to material, evident in the ecological crisis and in global "atomic peril," makes Rahner's uncritical presupposition of the "evolutive world view" problematic.[205] Niels Gregersen's critique of religious Darwinist Henry Drummond's *Ascent of Man* (1894) might equally be applied to Rahner. According to Gregersen, Drummond failed to come to terms with theologically difficult aspects of evolutionary theory, such as "the wastefulness of nature, the neglect of the individual, the disappearance of love in the selection process, and most importantly, the absence of guarantees of an overall evolutionary progress."

> Drummond's position implies that God is not only omnipresent but also manifest everywhere. The Christian conviction of the ultimate good of salvation is conflated with inner-historical progress, eschatological hope with expectations for the immanent future to come.[206]

Moltmann suggests that an evolutionary Christology is incomplete if it focuses only upon Christ as pinnacle of human nature, and "not the humanity put to death on the cross." Christ's "self-transcendence through his active obedience (*potentia oboedientialis*)" needs to be replaced by "his rising from the dead." The problem is not just moral evil, but physical evil. Moltmann argues that Rahner's uncritical Christology, as "completion of nature's evolution," must be corrected by a focus on the new creation and the "raising of nature."[207]

Such a cross-conscious Christology seems more in accord with actual human and natural history. The often violent vicissitudes and vagaries of human history form the backdrop for the divine unfolding of grace in the history of Israel and Jesus of Nazareth. This is so even to the extent that crucifixion and death form the essential matrix from which redemption is wrought, the pit out of which resurrection triumphs.

---

205. Moltmann, *Way of Jesus Christ*, 297–301.
206. Gregersen, "Contextual Coherence Theory," 217.
207. Moltmann, *Way of Jesus Christ*, 300–301.

Since human history shows this type of parallelism with evolutionary history, theology should in principle find no problem maintaining that a redemptive Christology is coherent with a pattern of suffering in evolutionary history. It is love that pulls the creation on towards a redemptive, "happy," and victorious conclusion, even through suffering and what looks like defeat and death. It is for this reason that Christianity must have an eschatological doctrine of resurrection and redemption, not just a doctrine of gradual, ever-upward and continuous consummation and fulfillment, as if God need not join in with the death of the cosmos to bring it ultimate life. So it is reasonable to believe that God's love is present in "nature, red in tooth and claw."[208] This is a presence in the midst of suffering leading on to a future of glory, consistent with the fact that even the Son "learned obedience through what he suffered" (Hebrews 5:8).[209] So in light of the crucifixion and resurrection, creation can be declared "good" in its mortality, and even humanity "very good," but not in any ultimate sense. That is reserved for the eschaton, when all things will be made perfect in liberation from death.

Thus an evolutionary worldview may begin to be reconciled with a theological understanding of God's redemption of creation.[210] Though suffering in evolutionary history has a parallel in Christology, there is a certain sense in which Christian redemption moves in the opposite direction from evolutionary and human history. The redemption of the cross and resurrection breaks in upon the status quo, standing in stark contrast to all that the world expects and anticipates. Christian redemption is compatible in the sense of being coherent with evolution, but it is not something that science would likely arrive at of its own accord.

Can an evolutionary worldview be reconciled with a theological understanding of original sin and the fall? The traditional picture of Adam and Eve, the serpent, and the garden seems difficult to reconcile with modern science. Rahner suggests, along with Barth, that it is Christology and the cross that enable humanity to look within and understand its essential fallenness and brokenness. Barth insisted that

---

208. Alfred Lord Tennyson. See Peacocke, "Challenge and Stimulus," 97.

209. So Paul can write in 2 Cor 4:17, "For this slight momentary affliction is preparing us for an eternal weight of glory beyond all measure," and in Rom 8:18, "I consider that the sufferings of this present time are not worth comparing with the glory about to be revealed to us."

210. O'Donovan, "Making Heaven and Earth," 276.

the Christian doctrine of sin could not be arrived at apart from Christ.[211] It is possible for this reason to "decentralize traditional claims about Adam and Eve." The absolute redeemer highlights our own condition as mired in sin and death, a "bizarre antitype" to the life of God in Jesus Christ.[212] For Rahner, the story of the fall seems to be an archetypal story of the human moral situation in relation to God. If there was a day of moral dawning in the genesis of humanity—and even a purely naturalistic account would have to admit that there was—then humanity has refused to live up to the potential of that moral dawn. It is in rebellion against the love of God, and has been for its entire history since then. This may be only a partial solution to the problem, but suggests the categories of *fall* and *sin* remain valid in the contemporary context (see also page 167).

Christology from Below or Above?

Rahner's Christology has typically been represented as a theology "from below," starting with the humanity of Christ and his historical life and moving towards the divine.[213] While he refuses to reduce Christ to a product of evolution,[214] his reduction of spirit to rationality and his general method of avoiding the transcendent realm again lead to some difficulties. His approach tends to make the difference between Christ and other human beings one of degree rather than of kind. His insistence on the absolute solidarity of Jesus' nature with all humanity, so that Jesus as a man is not lost in the glory of Jesus as Son of God, is such that "degree Christology" seems inevitable.[215] If humans have transcendentality in their nature, Christ is the ultimate version of that transcendentality. If humans are capable of moral good, then Christ is the ultimate instantiation of that goodness. But if Jesus' divine significance really comes down to the unique degree to which he attains to certain human qualities, then this causes the divine transcendent to disappear. Christology becomes the achievement of a unique degree of

---

211. Barth, *Church Dogmatics* IV/3:369.

212. Marshall, *Trinity and Truth*, 152.

213. Lash, "Up and Down in Christology," 31–46. Lash objects to further "up" and "down" classifications in Christology as unhelpful to the ongoing theological dialogue.

214. Rahner, *Foundations*, 177–78.

215. Hick implies, somewhat approvingly, that all degree Christology is "Arian by definition" in his "Christology at the Cross Roads," 140.

humanity in Jesus. Christ's transcendence is accomplished by its rise in the immanent: he is still the culmination and crown of the immanent process of evolution, but in him we discover that which is ultimately transcendent.

If the incarnate Christ arises from this-worldly processes, then humanity is lifted to divinity by the proverbial bootstraps. If Christ is only different in degree from other humans, how can the true nature of God in this particular human be accounted for? Gregory of Nazianzus had already observed this problem in his opposition to Apollinaris. "For that which has a beginning or a progress or is made perfect is not God."[216] Rahner opposes a simplistic Teilhardian evolutionary Christology with Jesus as the physical end result of natural processes, the "next and final stage" in human evolution. But his leaning towards degree Christology seems to lead there.

If the process arrives at perfect God and perfect man in the incarnation, without adding something from the outside of nature, then another problem surfaces. If God is utterly transcendent, then how can an immanent evolutionary process, even one culminating in humanity oriented to transcendent mystery, produce his nature? If God is wholly transcendent, an immaterial being entirely disengaged from the material cosmos, then how can an immanent aspect of the cosmos properly reveal him as anything but a shadow or reflection? If God's presence in the person of Jesus arises in the universe as a result of independent natural processes, then either the universe or humanity itself must be divine. Otherwise there is no source for his divinity. In this system, Jesus is the perfect human, the one special example of the realization of a possibility potentially available to all human kind. If the divine nature of Christ is understood in this way purely immanently, then it is a short step to divinizing humanity without reference to Christ. Whether the cosmos or humanity is regarded as divine, the cosmos arrives at the presence of God without God's presence. This is a logical fallacy: the finite cannot produce the infinite, nor can the immaterial arise from the material as an emergent property without destroying contingency.[217]

Further, if the universe is divine, then there is no longer any basis for asserting that it must be rational or reasonable. When the universe ceases to be contingent and created, it also loses its intelligibility, since

---

216. Gregory Nazianzus, "To Cledonius against Apollinaris," 218.
217. Ian McDonald, personal conversations.

there is nothing beyond it to guarantee its rationality. Gunton argues that this returns us "to a pre-scientific view of the divinity of the cosmos." He insists, "unless the logic of the eternal is in some way distinct from the logic of the temporal, we can understand on their own terms neither the one nor the other."[218] However, it may be extreme to accuse Rahner of this position, since he emphasizes that the natural processes are embedded in God's transcendent grace, and that in the incarnation the universe attains to an infinite asymptote of that grace at which it could not have arrived on its own.

Rahner's degree Christology leaves open the question of whether Jesus has ceased to be human altogether. If Jesus is the crown of the evolutionary process, bringing to perfection the potentiality already present in humanity, then it might almost appear that he is a *new* species. Otherwise, there is no basis for claiming that he is a physical crown of evolution, or that he has something substantially different to offer humanity than it already has by virtue of its own place in the evolutionary scale or its own potentiality for divinity. If Christ is not one with humanity in his human nature, is the salvation he offers fully applicable to humans? How can his experience of life, suffering, and the cross serve in a priestly capacity on humanity's behalf? How can his resurrection be regarded as the resurrection of a human being, and therefore of primary significance for all human beings?

Rahner believes the bringer of salvation must have "absolute solidarity" with humanity, and they with him.[219] He also insists that the Scriptures as carefully examined by modern historical and exegetical study clearly demonstrates the full humanity of Christ. If Jesus *is* one with humanity in his biological nature, then his differentiation from them must be accounted for by other means. This is not a problem in classical Christology, because Jesus' differences are attributed to his transcendent deity—his preincarnate existence as Son of God. Gunton maintains that this can be portrayed adequately even to the modern mindset as the being in whom God and human are both fully present, neither destroying the other—the basic statement of Chalcedonian Christology. Rahner also tries to remain faithful to Chalcedon, while responding to the modern mindset in degree Christology to maintain Christ's essential humanity. But his presentation of the perfect man in

---

218. Gunton, *Yesterday and Today*, 126–27.
219. Rahner and Thüsing, *New Christology*, 6.

Jesus Christ seems to separate him from the rest of humanity.[220] This produces a Jesus who is so different from humanity (in his perfections of human potentiality) that he can hardly be regarded as human any more. He is too different to be one of us.

Murphy's insight on the pre-existent Logos, besides making multiple incarnations unlikely, also leads to the conclusion that the Logos must represent the transcendent realm, or else it cannot be the *whole* Logos. The issue is not simply the Logos' pre-existence before the birth of Christ, nor even the theophanies and cosmic Christology in Scripture, but his "activity in creating the pattern of the world." Since the Logos is identified as God's pattern-making capacity in general applied to all possible worlds, that capacity must pre-exist this world, both in terms of time and causality, or else this world cannot come into existence. Therefore, for the incarnation to be the Logos of God, it *must* be this pre-existent Logos.[221] Apart from this transcendent contact, there is no feature of the temporal order that could elevate it to eternity. Gunton believes Rahner's system bars the transcendent God from acting in the world, since the world is closed or self-sufficient.[222] The one locus of transcendence Rahner acknowledges is in the orientation of human nature. However, this orientation to the infinite does not mean the transcendent has breached the gap. Here the problem presents itself most acutely: in knowing Christ only "from below," and rejecting the numenal or any form of an upper/lower tiered universe, the eternal transcendent would have to be excluded even in the nature of Christ. Yet if the cosmos is mired in death, then there must be some contact with the eternal transcendent that is not already present in the cosmos, for instance as a potentiality for divinity in human nature, in order for death to be overcome.

While Rahner is accused of "from below" Christology, and often speaks from such a perspective, some of his writings suggest that in Christ, that gap between the transcendent and the immanent *has* been breached. The potential to human divinity is not the same as outright divinity. Humans do have capacity for the eternal and transcendent, which is a precondition for the coming of Christ. This is an improved anthropology that asserts the vital and unique role of humanity in the

---

220. Gunton, *Yesterday and Today*, 16–17, 160–62.
221. Murphy, "Cosmology and Christology," 109–11.
222. Gunton, *Yesterday and Today*, 97.

cosmos, but that role is only fulfilled *in Christ*. Humanity is tending towards the infinite, but that asymptote is only reached in Christ. Rahner insists Jesus is fully human and fully divine—fully human, but at the same time more than a mere man. Because he is human, Jesus does not know everything, but can grow in his knowledge—he can "tremble before the inconceivability of God." This must be so to avoid a monophysite Christology, to properly acknowledge the humanness of Jesus; it is not just a product of modern exegesis. But Christ is also fully divine, the full revelation of God in his life, self-awareness, death and resurrection. Jesus mission was/is not just a religious message about God: Christ himself *is* the message, and must have known himself to be so for the Easter event to have been meaningful to the early church. God's revelation in the life and resurrection of Jesus guarantee the reality of the incarnation, for with the resurrection one has reasonable grounds to hold that Jesus is the "absolute savior" of the world.[223]

Losinger insists Rahner never was entirely an immanentist, even in the foundations of his transcendental anthropology. "Because God Himself, by revealing Himself and at the same time graciously making possible the act of grasping Him, thus becomes the fixed point of the anthropological point of departure in theology, any question about the ambivalence of the starting points 'from above' and 'from below' ultimately becomes superfluous. Theology and anthropology have lost the appearance of being opposites."[224] Vass says that in Rahner's thought, the human Jesus is not just one among many human subjects, but must also be seen as an intimate aspect of the "life of the Triune God: God's self-utterance, his *Logos*."[225] Purcell says that for Rahner, human relationality is modeled after the relationality of God's being, "immanent within the Trinity."[226] Rahner explicitly acknowledges that in Christ, God has reached down into the world in a move from above, tacitly making room for transcendent reality.[227] From the beginning, he assumes the mystical and transcendent as the hidden foundation of all being and search for being. His apparent degree Christology may be a linguistic artifact of dialogue with the modern naturalistic mind.

223. Rahner, *Theological Investigations*, 11:189–99, 227; *Foundations*, 279.
224. Losinger, *Anthropological Turn*, 17.
225. Vass, *Pattern of Christian Doctrines*, 26–27.
226. Purcell, *Mystery and Method*, 293, 347.
227. Rahner, *Foundations*, 206–8, 262–63.

He respects the methodological limits of science, yet clearly sees these limits as an artificial restriction of all reality. The scientist may pursue his science using *a priori* naturalism, but he does not and cannot live his life by that method alone, since his existence and his moral choices already go beyond it.[228] So Rahner's theology is not purely immanent, though at times it appears to be so. Transcendent anthropology provides one approach to the human nature of Jesus Christ; but there is another and equally valid angle from above: a "descending" Christology that acknowledges the Logos of God.

Summary of Rahner's Contribution

Rahner's view of human cosmic significance can now be summarized, and some general theological conclusions drawn. Transcendentality and the incarnation give humanity a crucial status and importance in the cosmos. Human nature alone is ready and adoptable to become God in Christ, because it alone is indefinable without transcendence. Humanity is the one material creature (aside from speculative ETI) that transcends the material cosmos, and who can be regarded—as *the* material spiritual being—as the goal of nature, the culmination of evolutionary history. In them God has become incarnate once and for all time into his created universe. In them, properly located within the life of God given by the incarnation, the cosmos finds final consummation. In Christ, humanity alone already stands beyond "death's demarcation line." The ultimate freedom of humanity will be the consummation of the cosmos, for "the Christian knows that this history of the cosmos as a whole will find its real consummation despite, in and through the freedom of man, and that its finality as a whole will also be its consummation."[229] Clearly, humanity has cosmic significance in Rahner's systematic theology, despite qualifications.

Even with his somewhat speculative and controversial use of evolutionary Christology, Rahner nevertheless arrives at a cosmic and preeminent role for both humanity and the incarnation. He makes a serious effort to achieve a modern Christology that is still within the bounds of Chalcedonian Christology and his own Roman Catholic Church. Though with some problems and inconsistencies, Rahner has

---

228. Ibid., 263.
229. Rahner, *Theological Investigations*, 5:168.

interacted significantly with the issues of modernity in light of the unique events of Christian revelation. While his position is not always convincing (multiple incarnations, degree Christology), his overall thought shows to what extent Trinitarian and incarnational theology will be necessarily anthropocentric. A type of *critical anthropocentrism* is clearly present there, particularly as a result of his theological interaction with human nature and the reality of the incarnate Christ.

Rahner's interaction with science is humble enough not to venture very far in terms of scientific conclusions. Aware of science's limits, he points to the mutual coherence of theology and science, rather than using scientific data to prove theological statements. Faith and theology stand on their own as independent sources of the truth of reality. Theologically, the incarnation shows that ontologically, transcendent causality has guided the creation and evolutionary processes towards their human end from the very beginning. The scientist may not admit to this teleological and theological conclusion, but must admit the unique significance of the end result of the natural processes in the rational consciousness of humanity. At this interface, the scientific and theological views are coherent.

Even though Rahner believes theology has an epistemological position that transcends science, he is frequently at pains to make sense of theological data within the methodological confines of scientific naturalism. This is not always helpful to his theological structure, as in his extraterrestrial angelology or his degree Christology. This later seems indebted to his anthropology, and sometimes overemphasizes the immanent at the expense of the transcendent. These problems do not present a serious threat to a larger theological affirmation of humanity's vital role in the cosmos. Indeed, a critical analysis of Rahner's thought has shown that even taking into account possible objections, a high view of human significance remains an essential part of his incarnational theology.

Insofar as Rahner represents Roman Catholic theology after Vatican II, it is reasonable to conclude that branch of Christian theology remains deeply anthropocentric, maintaining humanity's key significance in the cosmos. The uniqueness of human nature and the fact of the incarnation as an aspect of the life of the triune God occurring in and for the cosmos confirm the theological conclusion that the universe can be described as *critically anthropocentric*.

3

John Zizioulas

The Correlation of Divine and Human Personhood

> It is in the human being that we must seek the link between God and the world, and it is precisely this that makes Man responsible, in a sense the only being responsible for the fate of creation ... Man is the glory of God.
>
> —John Zizioulas[1]

Introduction to Zizioulas' Thought

JOHN ZIZIOULAS (1931–) IS METROPOLITAN OF PERGAMON, IN THE Ecumenical Patriarchate of Constantinople. Born in Great Britain, Zizioulas was raised in the Greek Orthodox Church, and was a scholar and teacher at various divinity schools in London and Scotland. Zizioulas' body of writing is much smaller than either Pannenberg's or Rahner's, and the amount of secondary material on him also small in comparison. However, he does interact significantly with relevant issues in theology, anthropology, ecology, and science from the Greek Orthodox perspective, and provides an adequate base from which to engage various themes in this thesis.

Zizioulas bases his epistemology on his understanding and conviction that all Christian truth flows from Christology. This is particularly expressed as the eschatological reality of God's presence entering history *now* to fulfill it in a "communion-event." This event is both a reference to the Christian sacrament and an emphasis on the close interpersonal relationships thus made possible eucharistically in Christ. His theological program is dependent upon the concept of *personhood*,

---

1. Zizioulas, "Preserving God's Creation (2)," 45.

which shall be enlarged upon shortly. The truth of being can only be experienced through and in the event of communion, communion with the *Eikon*, or perfect image of God, who is Christ. The ultimate truth of being *is* this type of communion for Zizioulas: communion is truth.[2] In this sense, truth is not just cognitive or propositional in nature, though rationality is present. Rather, truth is ultimately personal and relational. Zizioulas founds his theology upon communion and the relational reality it expresses, particularly within the church. His theological reflections are primarily concerned with ecclesiology, and his discussion of the nature and status of the human person takes place in that context.

Zizioulas develops his theology in the context of what might be called a *sacramental* worldview. In some ways his thought attempts to traverse through the minefield of modernity by a return to the ancient view of the world as a "mysterious, sacred reality broader than the human mind can grasp or contain." At the same time, he wrestles with many significant issues of modernity, including theological issues raised by the natural sciences and the relationship between the human and non-human creation. He rejects the scientific naturalism that regards reality as closed off from the transcendent realm, and departs from the Enlightenment vision of the supremacy of human rationality, insisting that a sacramental worldview must acknowledge the supra-rational and supra-human dimensions of reality.[3] In this vein, he holds to such traditional doctrines as the literal virgin birth and the resurrection of Jesus.[4] He rejects the dichotomies between "nature and history, the sacred and the profane, reason and myth, art and philosophy" that have characterized so much of Western thought. He posits a "cosmic liturgy" like that of St. Maximus the Confessor, the seventh century Greek father, suggesting a sacramental aspect to reality, and a necessary sacramental approach if humans are to more fully comprehend reality.[5]

Zizioulas' theological anthropology is developed in the context of deeply Trinitarian themes, particularly the personhood of the Trinity, the doctrine of the incarnation, and ecclesiology. His cosmic Christology, expressed eucharistically through the ecclesiological priesthood of redeemed humanity, suggests a cosmos that has a Christ-centered as well

---

2. Zizioulas, *Being as Communion*, 100–101.
3. Zizioulas, "Preserving God's Creation (1)," 1–2.
4. Zizioulas, *Being as Communion*, 54–55.
5. Zizioulas, "Preserving God's Creation (1)," 1.

as a church-centered focus and destiny. His theological anthropology, his doctrine of creation and fall, and his incarnational and ecclesiological work on the relation between humanity and the cosmos provide some solutions to otherwise problematic issues in the dialogue between theology and the natural sciences. Several areas in that dialogue will receive special focus in this chapter, including human uniqueness, humanity's relation to the non-human world, original sin in evolutionary context, and the limitations of naturalism in theological perspective.

Finally, some potential weaknesses in Zizioulas' doctrine of the Trinity, in his emphasis upon divine and human personhood, and in his version of human cosmic priesthood will be explored. Several authors suggest that non-human and non-personal versions of the *imago Dei* should be preferred in the modern context, and their perspectives will be evaluated in light of his overall program. It will be suggested that the sweep of Zizioulas' theology is *critically anthropocentric*, and that engaging the natural sciences from the perspective of his thought provides further support for such an understanding of reality.

Human Significance in Trinitarian Context

Zizioulas' analysis of personhood and human nature in the church is based on his conviction that all authentic personhood comes from God's own personhood. He holds that the triune God's most fundamental and essential nature is that of personhood: the persons of God the Father, God the Son, and God the Spirit. It is their personhood, their being persons, which is the foundational substance of their divinity.

Zizioulas identifies *personhood* as the strand of modern thought, having its origins in ancient Christian theology, that most clearly demonstrates human uniqueness. The concept is derived from the Cappadocian church fathers' analysis of the persons of the Trinity. Cornelius Plantinga Jr. describes this patristic understanding of divine personhood as "a subject with distinct, non-parasitic life; with soul, mind, choosing, and willing."[6] Trinitarian personhood is what is reflected or *imaged* in created human beings. Thus the origin of personhood is God; to be a person is the very nature of God. Cause and freedom originate in

---

6. Plantinga, "Gregory of Nyssa," 340.

the persons of God, specifically in the person of the Father. As Zizioulas phrases it, "what causes God to be is the Person of the Father."[7]

Personhood as such is prior to and defines the general nature of God; it is not a secondary conception within all that is, but is the *primary mode* of existence for God, the very *essence* or *being* of God. Catherine LaCugna interpreting Zizioulas describes it thus: "*an ontology of God that treats divine substance apart from divine persons is a contradiction in terms.*"[8] Personhood is so essential to God that according to Zizioulas, not only can we say that God is a person, but also that *person is God*. In other words, to be a person is something that ultimately can be said only of God.[9] There is no general, somehow amorphous, divine nature that is subsequently expressed as the three persons of the Trinity. Rather, the personhood contained within the Trinity *is* the divine nature.

This personhood is only realizable and expressible within a community—in God's case, the community of the Trinity. Personhood is only possible in a corporate or communal context. Persons are who they are not individualistically, but only in relation to each other. This in the Trinity is the relation of *ek-stasis*—a relation of more than just "openness of being," but of actual communion "which leads to a transcendence of the boundaries of the 'self' and thus to *freedom*."[10] Zizioulas believes a key insight of Trinitarian theology is that the divine life is social; the life of God subsists in community.[11] Hall develops a similar concept in his relational interpretation of being: being means "*being-with*."[12] Cornelius Plantinga also points out this relational emphasis in the Cappadocians.[13] John O'Donnell concludes that the persons of God are relational realities, defined by intersubjectivity, shared consciousness, faithful relationships, and the mutual giving and receiving of love.[14] For Zizioulas, this ecstatic communal openness does not destroy the totality of the divine nature found in each person of the Trinity. The persons are each *hypo-*

---

7. Zizioulas, "Contribution of Cappadocia," 32. Gregory of Nyssa figures prominently in this discussion, in his *Against Eunomius*, bk. 1, 165–67.

8. LaCugna, *God for Us*, 246.

9. Volf, *After Our Likeness*, 78.

10. Zizioulas, "Human Capacity and Incapacity," 408.

11. Migliore, *Faith Seeking Understanding*, 69.

12. Hall, *Imaging God*, 116.

13. Plantinga, "Gregory of Nyssa," 351–52.

14. O'Donnell, *Mystery of the Triune God*, 109–11.

static—"the bearer of its nature in its totality." This is true for God and for humanity. Thus, while humans are made for communion, "in every human person we see not part but the totality of human nature"—in both the first Adam and in the last Adam, Christ. So also in each person of the Trinity is to be found the totality of the divine nature.

> *Ekstasis* and *hypostasis* represent two basic aspects of Personhood, and it is not to be regarded as an accident that both of these words have been historically applied to the notion of the Person. Thus the idea of Person affirms at once both that being cannot be "contained" or "divided," and that the mode of its existence, its *hypostasis*, is absolutely unique and unrepeatable. Without these two conditions being falls into an a-personal reality, defined and described like a mere "substance," i.e., it becomes an a-personal thing.[15]

Personhood and the Imago Dei

Human beings are unique within the created order in that they alone among all creatures are an image of this personhood of God. They have a general nature—a *fallen* nature, which is typified by individualism, mortality, sin, etc.—expressed specifically in each living human who lives and dies, and which falls short of reaching this communitarian personhood. But they also have another calling: to exist the way God exists, in personhood that is part of the community of God, made possible by the work of Christ. Zizioulas draws a distinction between the *individual* and the *person* as they occur in the human situation. Personhood is only realizable in communion with other persons, something that the individual may circumscribe from his existence. "True personhood arises not from one's individualistic isolation from others, but from love and relationship with others, from communion."[16] Benedict XVI picks up on this idea, agreeing that "to be the image of God implies relationality," and suggesting that this image is the source of the human capacity for relationship and for God.[17] Zizioulas identifies this as the calling to live as the *icon* (*eikona*) or image of God.

---

15. Zizioulas, "Human Capacity and Incapacity," 408 n. 3.
16. Zizioulas, "Contribution of Cappadocia," 37.
17. Benedict XVI (writing as Joseph Ratzinger), *In the Beginning*, 47.

Zizioulas insists that the word D*ei* in the expression *imago Dei* implies a Trinitarian and relational God, rather than the rational or mechanical God of deism.[18] He suggests the term *imago Trinitatis* is appropriate, because the nature of the image is relational and hence Trinitarian. The image of God in human beings includes this capacity for personhood, which is itself divine. This means that *human* personhood is not of this world, it is divine.[19] Walther Eichrodt agrees that for humans to be created in the image of God means that upon them, "personhood is bestowed as the definitive characteristic of [human] nature. He has a share in the personhood of God; and as a being capable of self-awareness and of self-determination he is open to the divine address and capable of responsible conduct. *Personhood* is that which comprises the essentially human, and distinguishes him from all other creatures."[20] Christ's prayer for the unity of his disciples (John 17:21–22) indicates that the type of relationship shared among the persons of the Trinity is potentially available to Jesus' disciples, his brothers and sisters, as children of God.[21] In all creation, humanity alone has this capacity, this element of the divine. Humanity's unique personal nature as the *icon* of God confers upon it an important role on behalf of the rest of the cosmos, which will be discussed shortly.

Zizioulas insists that Christian theology, through the Cappadocians, has contributed the unique concept of *personhood* to the prevailing modern understanding of human being as personal.[22] Humanity has a share in personhood because it is made in the image of God through the free love the persons of the Trinity have for one another. This allows humanity to rise above the necessity of the natural, biological, and instinctual order. Personhood, as it comes from God, "proves to be *in* this world—through man—but not *of* this world."[23] The key to human uniqueness and likeness in the image of God is its creativity, its freedom, and above all its personhood—realizable only within

---

18. Zizioulas, "Human Capacity and Incapacity," 446.
19. Volf, *After Our Likeness*, 85.
20. Eichrodt, *Theology of the Old Testament*, 2:126. Emphasis added.
21. Paul VI, "Pastoral Constitution on the Church in the Modern World," 223.
22. Zizioulas, "Contribution of Cappadocia," 23–37; *Being as Communion*, 35: "The Greek Fathers . . . gave history the concept of the person with an absoluteness which still moves modern man even though he has fundamentally abandoned their spirit."
23. Zizioulas, "Human Capacity and Incapacity," 420.

community. Zizioulas focuses upon general personhood rather than particular features of human existence such as rationality, intelligence, linguistic capability, psychological content, or morality. He believes all these other kinds of features are observable within the other animals, though in a lesser degree (see chapter 5).[24] Orthodox theologian Vladimir Lossky also stresses the importance of human freedom from nature. Personhood is only possible on the grounds of such freedom.[25] An emphasis on the corporate and communal nature of personhood is also evident in Moltmann. "Within the network of relationships, the person becomes the subject of giving and taking, hearing and doing, experiencing and touching, perceiving and responding ... The 'person' emerges through the call of God."[26]

For Zizioulas, there is no separate *nature* of either God or humanity's *being* apart from personhood. A representative passage is worth quoting at length:

> The *raison d'etre* ... of each one's being ... is not to be found in the *nature* of this being but in the *person,* in the identity created freely by love, not by the necessity of nature. As a person you exist as long as you love and you are loved. When you are treated as nature, as a thing, you die. And if your soul is immortal, what is the use? You will exist, but without a *personal* identity; you will be eternally suffering in the hell of anonymity, in the Hades of immortal souls. For nature in itself cannot give you existence and being in this unique and irreplaceable sense in which the person exists; the immortality therefore of one's soul, even if it implies existence, cannot imply truly *personal* being. Now that we know, thanks to the Patristic theology of personhood, how God exists, we know what it means truly to exist. As images of God we are persons—not natures: there can *never* be an image of the *nature* of God, nor would it be a welcome thing for humanity to be absorbed in divinity. Only when in this life we exist as persons can we hope to live eternally in the true, personal sense. But as is the case with God, so with us, too: personal identity emerges only from the exercise of love as freedom and of freedom as love.[27]

---

24. Ibid., 406.

25. Lossky, *Orthodox Theology,* 72–73; Laats, *Doctrines of the Trinity,* 117.

26. Brown, "Conclusion," 225; quoting Moltmann, "Christianity and the Values of Modernity."

27. Zizioulas, "Contribution of Cappadocia," 35.

Zizioulas proposes in this vision of the quintessentially *human* a type of freedom that is derivative from the freedom of God. God's freedom is expressed in the freely loving way the persons of the Trinity relate to each other. Similarly, fate or destiny does not bind humans. Nor are they destined to have their personality dissolve into non-being while retaining a soul or essence, which might reappear in some other time or place as another individual or even as an animal (as in reincarnation or the transmigration of souls). The transcendence of human personhood from this world towards the divine indicates that, to paraphrase Zizioulas, man does not exist for the world, but rather the world for man.[28]

The Eschatological Character of Human and Cosmic Destiny

Zizioulas describes human personhood and destiny as being essentially eschatological in character. The tragedy of human existence lies in the desire and drive to freely transcend the creation, coupled with the inability to do so. "Who am I?" is a question only a human being can ask. It is a question whose answer is wrapped up in the personhood of the human being, a question that no animal can ask. "It is thus the question *par excellence* that makes us human and shows personhood to be an exclusive quality of the human being in the animal world."[29] No animal is dissatisfied with its existence, strives to be something other than what it presently is, seeks to create its own world through whatever means so that it also changes in the process. Only the human being has the capacity—the freedom—to choose to go against the given necessity of nature, even so far as to engage in the destruction of the given.[30] Lossky also notes the importance of human freedom from nature, insisting this is what allows the human being to love "someone more than himself." This possibility for love also entails "the possibility of refusing and thus the freedom which makes the fall possible."[31] Zizioulas notes that freedom in human nature opens up to more than simply evil potentialities.

---

28. Zizioulas, "On Being a Person," 37. What Zizioulas actually says is intended to draw a contrast between the Christian vision of humanity and Classical Greek philosophy: "Classical tragedy enslaved its heroes—human *and* divine—in the destiny of natural or moral order and rationality. Man exists for the world, not the world for Man."

29. Ibid., 44.

30. Zizioulas, "Preserving God's Creation (2)," 45.

31. Lossky, *Orthodox Theology*, 72–73; Laats, *Doctrines of the Trinity*, 117.

This freedom may not be absolute, in that humanity is still bound by being part of what is given. But while the human being cannot reach this absolute freedom, yet it still strives to do so.

There is not yet a definitive present answer to the question "Who am I?" because the personhood of human beings is not yet fully realized, and will not be until the end of all things in Christ. This is why human personhood must be ultimately considered in its eschatological form. We are persons now—or perhaps the beginning of persons—but we will not be fully realized in unbroken relationship as the complete persons we are intended to be until "God is all in all." It is now in process, only in part. Then, it will be realized in full.[32] The eschatological character of human personhood is crucial for understanding the ambivalent position the church and baptized believers have in relation to the fulfillment of God's promises in and through them. They are the community of the "already but not yet." The full realization or proof of their hypostatic personhood can never be offered in this world or age, nor be accomplished using its tools and weapons. That fulfillment must wait for the end of the age, for the return of Christ.[33]

Humanity as the Priest of Creation

Some of the distinguishing features of authentic personhood are already present in humanity. The ability of human beings to relate with each other, to the world, and beyond the world to the ultimately transcendent—to God—in such a way that they rise above the ordinary pull of necessity, is one of the things that delineates them as superior to the rest of creation. This is not because of humanity's rationality, but because of its ability to be in relationship as persons.[34] The type of relationality possible to humans is unique in the material sphere, manifesting itself in personal relationship with God and other humans, and also with the rest of creation.[35] Gunton similarly suggests that creation "requires persons in order to be itself." It is unable to achieve its destiny, the praise of

---

32. 1 Cor 13:12: "Now we know in part; then we shall know fully, even as we are fully known" (my paraphrase).

33. Zizioulas, *Being as Communion*, 62.

34. This aptitude for the personal and the transcendent might even be regarded as *extra*-rational, in that it seeks to go beyond the bounds of the given natural world, beyond Nature's closed system of logic.

35. Zizioulas, "Human Capacity and Incapacity," 445.

its creator, because it is non-personal. "That is why it awaits with eager longing the revealing of the children of God (Rom 8:19)."[36] Vatican II also highlighted the idea of humanity as summary and summit of creation through which the creator is praised. "Through his bodily composition [man] gathers to himself the elements of the material world. Thus they reach their crown through him, and through him raise their voice in free praise of the Creator."[37] Humanity's ability to relate in this transcendent, eucharistic fashion is a type of priesthood on behalf of the rest of creation before God. There is thus interdependence between humanity and the creation, and the human being is not fulfilled until it becomes the "summing up of nature," as priest referring the world back to its Creator.[38] Moltmann expresses a similar thought with his idea of the *imago mundi* (image of the world): humanity as a microcosm represents the cosmos as macrocosm; humanity is the summing up of the cosmos in itself. As the image of the world, humanity represents the world to God as a "priestly creation and eucharistic being."[39]

Zizioulas is aware of the "ecological problem"—the imminent danger of environmental catastrophe at the hands of human beings. Ratzinger describes it as humans "sawing off the branch on which they sit."[40] Zizioulas suggests that humanity, in light of the destiny it has in Christ, is nevertheless still at the heart of the destiny of the cosmos. The fall of humans from their position as potential mediators between God and creation has had among its other consequences the selfish, thoughtless use and abuse of the world. At the same time, the ability to abuse and defy the given of its natural surroundings is one of the things that marks humanity as unique among created beings. One might not suppose that this commends humanity to a special place in the cosmos. Air is polluted, species are destroyed, and oil tankers spill as consequences of human action. Yet it is humans who have the capacity to do something about it, to clean up the mess and restore environmental harmony, to care even for an environment in which they have no personal stake. This is the flip side of human freedom that enables it to transcend nature. Only humanity has the ability not only to abuse its surroundings,

---

36. Gunton, "Trinity," 56.
37. Abbott and Gallagher, *Documents of Vatican II*, 212.
38. Zizioulas, "Preserving God's Creation (1)," 2.
39. Moltmann, *God in Creation*, 190.
40. Ratzinger, *In the Beginning*, 81.

but also to rise above itself, above necessity, above the given of nature for the good of the natural order, to exercise responsibility.

Zizioulas points to the Eastern Orthodox tradition's insistence that the image of God in human beings has spiritual and physical aspects; the *imago Dei* is not just to be found in the *mind*, but also in the *body*. He believes the West has fallen into an abusive posture towards the environment partly because of its overemphasis upon reason and rationality in the image. Humans are not simply rational spiritual beings in isolation from the world, destined to leave it behind and so ultimately unconcerned for earth's fate. Rather, the bodily dimension of the image of God emphasizes human continuity with the physical world and concern for the environment. Zizioulas sees the asceticism of the early church as breaking the selfish individualism behind the desire to dominate the external world.[41] He believes the redemption of not only the immediate world, but also the entire cosmos hinges upon humanity, as it brings God and the world into communion through itself. More will be said on these themes shortly.

The Significance of the Incarnation

How can humanity be the link between God and the cosmos if it has already failed, due to the abuse of its freedom, to unite them? The answer is in the person of Jesus Christ. Humanity is an organic part of the natural world, and this constitutes the necessary condition for it to represent the cosmos to God. At the same time it strives to transcend the given natural world. This striving towards transcendence is a feature of the *imago Dei* that qualifies humanity to represent God to the cosmos—not by itself, because it has fallen short of that transcendence, but in Jesus Christ. He is the human of all humans, the savior of the world, the ultimate priest, and the one upon whom the final fate of the cosmos rests. In Christ, and then in humanity in Christ, the universe is united in communion with its Creator, and freed from ultimate doom and death. Christ bestows upon the universe life and the infinity of possibilities that are open to God.[42]

The incarnation is particularly important for human identity and cosmic destiny in Orthodox thought. The human capacity for the pos-

---

41. Zizioulas, "Preserving God's Creation (1)," 1–5.
42. Zizioulas, "Preserving God's Creation (3)," 5.

sibility of personhood is God's plan, seemingly frustrated in the fall, but realized and fulfilled in Christ. Edmund Rybarczyk maintains that the West has tended to regard "the incarnation as a remedy for fallen humanity, but the East interprets the incarnation as God's eternally intended and perfect plan, and not a kind of accident (in the philosophical sense) due to sin."[43] Not only is the incarnate Son of God the original pattern after which humankind is fashioned, but the incarnation was God's eternal intention for the Son. Thunberg agrees, noting, "*Christ is always the true image of God* (both as identical with the creative Word, the Logos, and as incarnate in humanity), and actual human beings are only *according to* this image . . . The Logos is seen as the prototype, which God used in creating humans in his image, and Christ is seen as the archetype of what it is to be human."[44]

There is some scriptural support for this notion, as indicated by the discussions on the image in the New Testament and cosmic Christology (see pages 49, 120). God creates humanity as a preparatory component of a cosmos predestined for the "perfect paradigmatic figure" Jesus.[45] In this sense, incarnation and humanity as *imago Dei* are two sides of the same coin: the ultimate divine purpose for the destiny and fulfillment of the cosmos. Jesus Christ alone makes humanity able to rise above the ontological necessity of its biological, individual nature, and able to partake in free loving relationship with God as genuine communitarian persons.[46] In Christological perspective, only humanity has been so prepared by God so as to be assumed by his Son in the incarnation. This is the source of human capacity for personal, relational, and eternal existence. Miroslav Volf summarizes Zizioulas' position: "What gives us an identity that does not die is not our nature, but a personal relationship with God."[47] Christology illustrates on behalf of humanity and then guarantees to humanity as a whole its hypostatic destiny beyond what its general nature could otherwise have produced.[48] Christ is *the* human

---

43. Rybarczyk, "What Are You, O Man?" 89–90.
44. Thunberg, "Human Person," 293.
45. Rybarczyk, "What are You, O Man?" 89.
46. Zizioulas, *Being as Communion*, 56.
47. Volf, *After Our Likeness*, 36.
48. Zizioulas means by "hypostasis" a concrete and unique entity or identity that is not reducible to a general nature shared by all; the personhood of a particular being. See *Being as Communion*, 27–47.

being who, by restoring the communion of natures in and through his *personhood*, turns the cosmos into a realm where God is present rather than absent. "The world acquires thus its ecstatic catholicity as it is lifted up to communion with God through man."[49]

Zizioulas observes that the non-human cosmos is dependent upon the church for its future, in that only in and through the salvation of the church (the corporate christocentric humanity which comprises the church) will the salvation of the cosmos be effected. Since humanity has a full share in the material world, simultaneously transcending it through the freedom God has given them, humanity becomes, in the church, the priest of all creation. This is possible because the church is a corporate person with Christ as its head, and its priesthood is a share in the priesthood that Christ has as the incarnate Son, *the* priest of creation. Through the sacraments, the church brings all of creation—not just human beings—into relationship with God. "The church becomes in this way the very core and nucleus of the destiny of the world."[50]

The mystery of salvation hidden before all the ages is that humanity is to be incorporated into the eternal filial relationship that exists between the Father and the Son. It is only the church that holds this place of unity with Christ, and through him, with God the Father. This is a unity that is not yet fully realized—an eschatological unity—in which the church presently partakes as a kind of down payment on the future. In the church, humanity becomes the focal point of unity between God and creation in Christ.

The survival of the world is dependent upon its communion with God, but that communion takes place in and through humanity. Only human nature is able to contain the incarnation of Christ. Only human nature is able to open up towards God; only in humanity are "the creaturely conditions of space and time [able] to open up towards infinite capacity as they become bearers of the ekstasis of humanity in Christ."[51] Only this redeemed and in-Christ humanity, which has participated sacramentally in baptism with Christ in his death, is able to have communion with God; but through them the entire creation also participates in that communion. Thus humanity is fundamentally responsible for the survival of nature and of all creation.

49. Zizioulas, "Human Capacity and Incapacity," 447.
50. Zizioulas, "Mystery of the Church," 296.
51. Zizioulas, "Human Capacity and Incapacity," 438–39.

The Destiny of the Cosmos

It is clear that Zizioulas places great importance upon humanity in the cosmic scheme of things. It is not too much to say that in his thought, the cosmos has a human-centered destiny. The church is the vessel through which the incarnate work of God in Christ comes to fruition, not only for humanity, but also through humanity for the rest of the cosmos. The creation is subject to mortality, and doomed to frustration and death apart from this incarnate work. In this context, the fall of Adam represents a failure of potential to unite creature and Creator. That failure is anticipated, taken up, and ultimately redeemed in Jesus Christ. This redemption has both an earthly and cosmic scope as humanity in Christ represents and brings the entire created order to God.

The Mortality of the Cosmos

Zizioulas brings fruitful ideas from Orthodoxy on the doctrine of *creatio ex nihilo* to the analysis of humanity's relationship to the cosmos.[52] Christian teaching has generally held since the second century that the universe was created from nothing—that it had no progenitor of any kind, whether of eternal matter or immortal soul—and that God is alone responsible entirely by his own free will for the existence of what is. Some see a definite affinity between this doctrine and the scientific theory of the big bang (see chapter 6). Because the creation is from absolute nothing, there is no component of nature that is everlasting; otherwise, it would have qualities that only belong to God, making nature and God the same in a substantial way (Pannenberg has a similar idea in his belief that "God alone has unrestricted duration"[53]). If nature is not everlasting, then death for nature is inevitable—not only the death of all individual created entities, but the death of the entire cosmos itself. The cosmos is *mortal* by nature.

This mortality is entailed in the creation of the cosmos from nothing. Its mortality is not just a consequence of the human abuse of freedom; rather, that abuse frustrated the hope of uniting God with his creation and thus allowing the creation to transcend its mortality, until the advent of Christ. For Zizioulas, the significance of the fall does not lay in the introduction of death and frustration into what would have

---

52. Zizioulas, "Preserving God's Creation (3)," 2.
53. Pannenberg, *Systematic Theology*, 2:33.

otherwise been a forever-living realm, but rather in this tragic inability to unite an already mortal world with God, hardened into permanence by the abuse of human freedom. Humanity's fall does not represent a false dichotomy of freedom over against obedience to God, but rather the abuse or perversion of its given freedom.

Among other things, the universe's natural mortality suggests a partial solution to the theodicy problem of natural evil. David Fergusson puts the problem like this: how does one explain the presence of natural evil in a universe that God has declared both "good" and "very good" at creation?[54] Natural evil means the presence of death and destruction in the natural processes of the universe, apparently present even before humanity's creation. How can all the death, predatory violence, and extinction revealed by the fossil record, pre-dating humanity by millions to billions of years, exist in a "good" world? Rahner, Moltmann, Polkinghorne and others have proposed various related solutions to make room for evolutionary processes in the creation account.[55] Zizioulas' solution, based on *creatio ex nihilo*, is to suppose a naturally mortal, yet nevertheless good, universe. The creation is good, but this does not mean it is good in any final, unsurpassable sense. Levels of desirability are evident in the progress of creation. For instance, with the creation of humanity, the creation moves in God's judgment from "good" to "very good." The Orthodox insight is that even as "very good," neither creation nor humanity is perfect. If there was a potentiality, it was lost as humans failed to eat from the tree of life; instead, they have fallen into rebellion and corruption. The "very good" only gives way to the perfect in Christ, in whom mortality is decisively overcome.

Although the Genesis creation narrative hints at the possibility of immortality in the tree of life, the actual meaning of the tree is veiled. The promise of immortality is only realized in the incarnation, when the offer of life in Christ, the "true vine" (John 15:1), is renewed. If the tree of life symbolizes the life of God, and of choosing relationship with God and life over relationship with self and death, it is the later that is temporarily chosen in the Genesis narrative. Mortality is not overcome until Christ appears as "the way, the truth, and the life" (John 14:6), in whom all creation will be perfected and live.

---

54. Fergusson, *Cosmos and Creator*, 80. See Gen 1:4, 10, 12, 18, 21, 25, 31.

55. Rahner, *Hominisation*, 102–9; Moltmann, *God in Creation*, 190–92; Polkinghorne, *Reason and Reality*, 99; Fergusson, *Cosmos and Creator*, 80.

Rybarczyk notes that the Orthodox tend to define human beings as they were before the fall, and thus to have a more "positive view of human personhood" than the West. They do not view pre-fall human nature as perfect; instead, the Orthodox emphasize the need and potential for growth, present in both pre-fall humanity—but frustrated by their rebellion—and after the fall as humanity is united with Christ. This is illustrated by the Orthodox concept, held since the patristic era, of the difference between the *image* and *likeness* of God. "We have been created in God's image; it remains that we become like him."[56] Thunberg maintains that "*the very concept of image contains a dynamism. Image represents not only a status but also a potentiality, and this potentiality blossoms only when human beings are set free by Christ from enslavement to sin and are able to develop the potential capacities given at creation to their full maturity.*"[57] This human potential of becoming like God—the Orthodox concept of *theosis*—was subverted until Christ. Now humanity again has the opportunity of growth towards God as it is united with Christ, made possible by "deifying grace."[58] This union of life and growth means life for the whole creation.[59]

A cosmos that is intrinsically mortal is more easily reconciled with certain aspects of evolutionary theory, and resolves a number of scriptural motifs that do not fit neatly with a perfect and deathless pre-fall world. The command to "subdue the earth" (Gen 1:28) is stronger than dominion, suggestive of a world in need of subjection, filled with chaos.[60] The anti-mythical character of the creation account, in polemical opposition to pagan myths that divinize the world, portrays the world as neither alive nor divine on its own apart from God. God alone is the source of life.[61] The service of subduing is a uniquely human task,

---

56. Rybarczyk, "What Are You, O Man?" 92–95.

57. Thunberg, "Human Person," 298–99.

58. Meyendorff, *Gregory Palamas*, 161.

59. Thunberg, "Human Person," 299.

60. See Vawter, *On Genesis*, 59: "Man is not permitted to succumb to the cyclic routine of nature but is destined to make decisions"; Von Rad, *Genesis*, 60: Subduing is "surprisingly strong," suggestive of violence, conquering, a strong display of force; Eichrodt, *Theology of the Old Testament*, 2:151: Human dominion is shown to belong to the "special domain of God"s sovereignty."

61. Westermann, *Genesis 1–11*, 161; Vawter, *On Genesis*, 59. "Anti-mythical" refers to the absolute contrast between divine and creaturely realms in Genesis 1–3. The world is not divine, or intermixed with divinity.

a hint that the non-human creation can only be fulfilled or completed with humanity. The natural evils of the earth are not included as consequences of the fall in Genesis 3; these consequences are directed to people and the serpent.[62] Rom 8:20 describes the subjection of the cosmos to futility as being a result of God's *positive* will, rather than a negative result of human rebellion against God. The subjection to futility is part of the plan of God, established before the foundation of the universe, long before the first human beings appear in the created order. The will of God, not of Adam and Eve, subjects the creation to frustration; its groaning did not commence with the human fall into sin in Eden, but has been present from the beginning of creation. Entropy, mortality, and predatory death are in the essential created nature of the cosmos prior to the arrival of humanity, rather than being consequences of human rebellion against God.

The divine subjection of the cosmos to mortality transcends human history, including the Adamic fall, except insofar as humans are the context of the incarnation. Mortal from the beginning, the creation is predestined from its beginning towards the incarnation (Rom 8:29). Rybarczyk notes the Eastern Christian preference for this cosmic predestination towards incarnation, unlike much of Western theology, which has tended to see the incarnation as an emergency rescue measure.[63] It is the incarnation, planned before all ages, that leads to eternal life and the liberation of all things. Stephen Duffy agrees, noting that "the original plan for creation is not scrapped only to be replaced by a divine contingency plan that entails a Christ as its agent. There is but a single creative design, which intends the divine self-communication."[64] The universal process of the rise and interrelations of living beings is ultimately oriented to the incarnation, so that all created reality has an incarnational grounding.[65] The process is only partially complete with the arrival of not-yet-perfected humanity. All creation is longing eagerly for the revelation of the children of God, for only then will it be liberated from death and brought into freedom. Thus the drawing of the cosmos into communion with its Creator is part of a unified plan that includes creation, incarnation, and redemption. Robert Jenson notes that "God's

---

62. Clatworthy, "Let the Fall Down," 32.
63. Rybarczyk, "What Are You, O Man?" 89.
64. Duffy, "Our Hearts of Darkness," 619.
65. See also Pannenberg, *Systematic Theology*, 2:96–97.

overcoming of death is not, therefore, only his overcoming of something intruded into his creation. It is simultaneously his transformation of creature's natural temporal finitude, and just so his achieving of his original end for the creation in one of its defining aspects."[66]

This is why the creation of humanity is "very good." The only way to overcome the problem of mortality is to find a link between nature and God that at the same time does not erase the differences between Creator and created. Where can such a link be found? Zizioulas insists, "It is in the human being that we must seek the link between God and the world, and it is precisely this that makes Man responsible, in a sense the only being responsible for the fate of creation." This is humanity's responsibility and its mission. As a result of this cosmic responsibility, Zizioulas follows Irenaeus in declaring that with good reason, "Man is the glory of God."[67]

One implication of the mortality of the cosmos is that human personhood cannot be realized apart from a sharing in the divine life. There is no potentiality for this fullness of personhood inherent in human nature; it is only received as it enters into communion with Christ. As a result, there is no possibility for the authentic person to emerge gradually in the cosmos as a result of evolutionary processes, whether biologically via Darwinian means, or historically via Marxist means.[68] This is similar to Barth's position that humanity is not itself divine, nor does it have capacity for God in and of itself, but may only receive it by the act of God. It is not because of what it is or may do, "but because of what it has to suffer and receive—and at the hand of God," that human nature may receive into itself the incarnation of God.[69] Rybarczyk summarizes the Orthodox perspective: "the very mystical-personal experience of communion that the triune God enjoyed from eternity was the driving force behind why God created us after his image and likeness and why he became incarnate."[70] John Meyendorff notes this line of thought in the fourteenth-century Orthodox divine Gregory Palamas, who held that "communion with the living God" is "the only means of salvation for man, combating the conception of salvation as an extrin-

66. Jenson, *Systematic Theology*, 2:331.
67. Zizioulas, "Preserving God's Creation (2)," 45.
68. Zizioulas, *Being as Communion*, 59.
69. Barth, *Church Dogmatics* I/2:188–89.
70. Rybarczyk, "What Are You, O Man?" 96.

sic justification which leaves man free to live independently of God."[71] The development of authentic persons through the life of the church is made possible only through union with the authentic person of Christ. Authentic persons cannot arise anywhere in the natural universe without some move on God's part, some bestowing of the divine life. Zizioulas calls this "ecclesial hypostasis." Only when God is united with his creation does authentic personhood appear in the creaturely realm. This has begun to happen through Christ in the life of the church, in its communion with God. This ecclesial hypostasis will find its fulfillment in the future. Humanity appears in this church identity not as it is, but as it will be eschatologically.

The Cosmos' Human-Centered Destiny

For Zizioulas, cosmic redemption is human-centered, in the sense that the entire cosmos is brought to immortality through ecclesial humanity. The verification will be eschatological, but the essential Christian position is that in a naturally mortal cosmos, mortality will be the condition of *every* creature in the universe apart from the incarnate human work of God. In this sense, redeemed humanity is responsible for the fate of the cosmos. Only in the Messiah will creation be finally liberated from its mortality, when relations of life and peace will be established with God and between all creatures.

Thus a level of responsibility is established both at the beginning and end of the human story in regard to human relations with the cosmos. This is not a primacy for humanity at the cost of the cosmos, the world, or the animal kingdom, as if God were blessing human self-centeredness. Rather it is to the cosmos' benefit, calling the cosmos to something greater than it was before the arrival of the image of its creator, although the fulfillment of that calling is delayed until humanity's eschatological salvation and realization.

It is only when humanity is fully redeemed, when the priestly role of the church is realized in its eschatological fullness, that the new creation will arrive. Scripture describes this as "a new heaven and a new earth," in which "death will be no more; mourning and crying and pain will be no more, for the first things have passed away" (Rev 21:1-4). Christ in God is responsible for this redemption: "See, I am making all

---

71. Meyendorff, *Gregory Palamas*, 163.

things new ... I am the alpha and the omega' (vv. 5–6). This new heaven and earth, in which the city of God in bridal imagery recalls the church (vv. 9–10), is the place where God makes his home with humanity and lives among them, present in his fullness to creation and making all things new.

This is an ecclesiological fulfillment, because the city of God is built upon the foundation of Jesus Christ and the twelve apostles (21:14). This dual fulfillment, God with humanity, is at the heart of the new creation. There the wolf and the lamb will lie down together; the lion eat straw like the ox (Isa 11:6–9). There, death will be vanquished, suffering ended, eternal joy inaugurated. Since it is both a christological and an ecclesiological fulfillment, humanity is unified with God in establishing the new creation. Only when God and humanity are united, not merely in the incarnation of Jesus but in the fullness of redeemed humanity, will the new creation be realized. There is no wedding party without both bride and groom. This is what it means to say that the destiny of the cosmos is dependent upon the destiny of humanity.

This does not mean that humanity—even redeemed humanity—is an independent contributor to the salvation of the cosmos. As Barth observed, the anthropocentrism that takes humanity as its starting point without reference to God is dead. He insisted that the correct source of theology is not from humanity reaching upwards to find whatever might be god-like, but rather from the transcendent God reaching downwards to reveal himself to humanity in the incarnation.[72] So the children of God stand in their place of glory by grace because God has elected them. If there is an anthropocentric character to the cosmos and its fulfillment, it is only because God has willed it to be so, because the cosmos is centered on Christ in God.

Zizioulas does not pursue a theology of extraterrestrials in his short corpus of works. However, his thought suggests that even if extraterrestrials were found in the universe, they also would be disbarred from authentic *personhood* without an incarnational union with the Creator. This is because if such creatures were a normal result of the universe's evolutionary life, they also must have the same natural limitation of mortality. Zizioulas' view of the necessity of ecclesial hypostasis suggests that other incarnations of God will be unnecessary, since God has already decisively united with his creation

---

72. Barth, *Humanity of God*, 48–49.

in Christ. Every potential world in creation is already taken up in this redemptive work.

Prior to its eschatological fulfillment, humans are called *now* in Christ to be priests on behalf of the created order. As humans becoming—but not yet fully realized as—persons, they already have a measure of freedom in Christ to transcend mortal nature with its inevitable moral brokenness, to forgive and be forgiven, to die to the demands of sinful flesh, even to take responsibility for the non-human creation. Pannenberg observes that in Christ, God's kingdom is "already here," as "a power that shapes the future."[73] While creation continues to groan, and humanity along with it, it is human beings that have the "first fruits of the Spirit," the present seal of divine adoption (Rom 8:23). The results of forgiveness and divine-human reconciliation are already manifesting themselves in the life of the church. The Holy Spirit is actively bringing the kingdom of God among human beings and, to a certain extent, through humans to the non-human creation. Humans have the power to destroy nature, yet also to express now some of their future saving activity. They may in Christ renew the call of stewardship, shepherding and caring for creation. In this their efforts will only be partial, shadows of the fullness to come in the new creation, even as their own natures are now mere shadows of what they will one day be in glory.

Zizioulas highlights the Eastern Orthodox faith's approach to the hallowing of not just the sinner in the Eucharist, but also of the whole creation. The bread and the wine are to be recognized not just as the body and blood of Christ, but as elements and symbols of the non-human created order. The sacrament is a taking up of the whole creation into the worship of God.[74] As priests of Christ, humans may literally bring the creation to God in the midst of the service of Holy Communion, interceding for whatever aspect of brokenness in the created order needs redemption. Typically, Western theology has often limited this intercession to human sins and needs,[75] but the Orthodox perspective encompasses what is already true in principle: Christ's redemption is for all creation, not just for human beings. It is only human beings, as priests of Christ, who have this function. The praise of the Creator is taking place eucharistically through ecclesial humanity on

---

73. Pannenberg, *Systematic Theology*, 1:247.
74. Zizioulas, "Preserving God's Creation (1)," 4; also "Mystery of the Church," 296.
75. With some notable exceptions like Francis of Assisi.

behalf of all creation. H. Paul Santmire speaks of the "cosmic meaning of baptism and eucharist," pointing to these liturgical acts of praise as rooted in an eschatological awareness of completed creation, underlining the mighty acts of God in cosmic history.[76]

Zizioulas' conception of humanity's cosmic priesthood is not a simple return to Enlightenment hubris or its accompanying elevation of human rationality. The world is an event of history, not simply a self-explainable process, but its survival depends upon its referral back to God the creator in Christ. "It is at this point that the responsibility of Man as the one who refers the world back to the Creator arises and forms the basis of . . . his capacity to be the 'Priest of Creation.'"[77] There is no necessary conflict between a humanly activated (in Christ) cosmic redemption and an understanding of humanity *with* rather than set over and apart *from* the rest of creation.

The uniqueness of human personhood does not relegate the non-human cosmos to secondary and trivial status, because in incarnational perspective, human service and human-centered cosmic redemption actually elevate the status of the non-human creation. Zizioulas reintroduces a cosmos-centered rather than a "soul- or spirit-centered" worldview to sacramental theology.[78] His vision of cosmic redemption is human-centered in the sense of *agency* rather than ultimate *purpose*: humans are the agent for the redemption of the cosmos, not the sole purpose or beneficiary of its redemption. Thus, an end human goal of God's creative processes need not conflict with the worth of the non-human cosmos, as the former guarantees the ultimate life of the latter in Christ.

Issues in the Dialogue with the Natural Sciences

Zizioulas' thought suggests several areas of dialogue with the natural sciences. Many believe that theology ought to embrace as the whole picture of reality the naturalistic vision offered by science. Zizioulas suggests otherwise, with his mystical and sacramental view of the cosmos, with spiritual and transcendent aspects of creation manifest in such things as the nature of Christ, the virgin birth, and the power

---

76. Santmire, *Nature Reborn*, 85–87.
77. Zizioulas, "Preserving God's Creation (1)," 3.
78. Ibid.

of the Eucharist. Some insist there is more congruence than contrast between human and animal natures, a perspective to which Zizioulas is not altogether unsympathetic. He emphasizes certain aspects of human uniqueness such as freedom and creativity, yet couples this with a non-substantive approach to human significance, which is to be found in relationship to God rather than in particular substantive aspects of human nature. Some contend that the doctrine of original sin can no longer be maintained in an evolutionary context. Zizioulas' approach to creation helps integrate some otherwise disparate threads in the scriptural and scientific worldviews. These issues will be addressed here, with a more complete analysis given to some questions in the chapters that follow.

A Sacramental Worldview and the Limits of Enlightenment Rationality

Zizioulas sees in the rationality of the Enlightenment the culmination of a problem long brewing in Western thought: the elevation of rationalism to an idolatrous place in human knowledge.[79] Alvin Plantinga agrees that Enlightenment naturalistic rationalism has had profound and destructive consequences when taken over from science into theology.[80] A brief retrospective on the three theologians of this thesis shows that Pannenberg, Rahner, and Zizioulas all believe naturalism has limits. They believe God acts in the cosmos in both natural and miraculous ways, through nature's laws and in supernatural miraculous events like the resurrection of Jesus. Zizioulas in particular emphasizes the divine entering into the cosmos to bring redemption and liberation from death. Jesus' virgin birth, his human and divine nature, and his resurrection are all aspects of Zizioulas' sacramental vision of reality.

Whether Zizioulas is justified in abandoning the hegemony of Western rationalism for his sacramental vision of reality[81] will be addressed in chapter 4. A preliminary evaluation of the rationalities of both worldviews might help to establish some epistemological boundaries between science and theology, and mutual respect between the two disciplines.

79. Zizioulas, "Preserving God's Creation (1)," 1–3.
80. Plantinga, "Methodological Naturalism," 198–204.
81. Zizioulas, "Preserving God's Creation (1)," 1–2.

Human Uniqueness in the Animal Kingdom

Are human beings unique in the animal kingdom? Like many others, Zizioulas believes that the difference between humans and animals is a matter of degree rather than kind; that rationality, language, and morality are observable within the other animals, though in a lesser degree.[82] Yet he places heavy emphasis on the concept of the person as valid in light of the modern investigation of animal and non-human cognition. While various attempts have been made to redefine the concept of *person* to include many animals,[83] his non-substantive approach avoids the dilemma altogether. This approach allows him to avoid the natural sciences and substantive definitions of human nature, and focus instead upon the communal relationship to God as source and meaning of personhood. This human *being* comes uniquely into existence in the social and bodily context of freely given love.[84]

Jenson agrees that while there may be physical and neurological differences between humans and animals, the distinctive of the human image of God must be found in our relation to God. This approach is not necessarily at odds with actual substantive differences between human and non-human creatures. But highlighting the transcendent orientation of humans towards God shows the ontological distinction between humans and animals. We do not have the same hopes for ourselves as we do for the "beasts of the field."[85]

While modern science has closed some of the gap separating human beings from other creatures, it has also illuminated how wide and

---

82. Zizioulas, "Human Capacity and Incapacity," 406–7; Darwin, *Descent of Man*, 931; Peterson, "Are We Unique?," 177; Bekoff, "Considering Animals," 231.

83. E.g., Singer, *Practical Ethics*, 110–19.

84. Zizioulas, "Contribution of Cappadocia," 35. "Personal identity emerges only from the exercise of love as freedom and of freedom as love."

85. Jenson, *Systematic Theology*, 2:56–58. Jenson observes that treating "other animals like humans is also to treat humans like other animals... Anthropological nihilism [seems] relatively harmless in . . . the 'animal rights' movement, [but] has been tested in frightful adult practice," e.g., Nazi socialism, or modern anthropological nihilisms evident in abortion on demand, euthanasia, and infanticide. "As we destroy crippled horses, so we kill born and unborn children whose mothers for whatever reasons do not think they should raise them, or elders who have lost hope and burden the system or their families, or trauma victims in disheartening coma, or persons simply in pain they do not wish to endure or we do not wish to see them enduring. And there is no reason why we should not, if there is no ontological difference between humans and other animals."

fixed the gap remains. It may well be that some of the human distinctives observed by modern natural science ground Zizioulas' understanding of human personhood in creativity, freedom, and responsibility. Definitions of personhood that ignore these elements would seem to be inadequate. Theology need not rely solely on such substantive approaches, but the scientifically observable substantive differences do help underline the unique nature of human personhood. The emerging scientific portrait, far from undermining Zizioulas' larger position on the uniqueness of human personhood as *imago Dei*, actually strengthens it, since the capacities science recognizes as unique also serve to make human-divine personal communion in creativity and freedom possible. Chapter 5 wrestles directly with the scientific question of whether humans are different in kind or only in degree from other creatures.

Original Sin in an Evolutionary Context

With the rise of Darwinism, some thinkers have rejected the traditional Christian account of original sin and the fall. Patricia Williams says the Genesis fall story is a "Hebrew myth" that when misread as "human alienation" can become deeply misleading, since we are "of the earth."[86] Jonathan Clatworthy sees the fall myth as pitting humanity against nature, and contributing to the ecological crisis.[87] Peacocke insists that in evolutionary context,

> There is no sense in which we can talk of a "Fall" from a past perfection. There was no golden age, no perfect past, no individuals, and no Adam and Eve from whom all human beings have now descended and declined and who were perfect in their relationships and behavior. We appear to be rising beasts rather than fallen angels—rising from an amoral (and in that sense) innocent state to the capability of moral and immoral action.[88]

Can the scientific and biblical accounts of original sin be reconciled? Is there a necessary conflict between the two?

Perspectives on the Genesis narrative may vary without necessarily jeopardizing the meaning, unless one believes there is only one possible historical or factual meaning that must exactly coincide with

---

86. Williams, *Doing Without Adam and Eve*, 3–4.
87. Clatworthy, "Let the Fall Down," 33–34.
88. Peacocke, "Challenge and Stimulus," 97–98.

the symbolic or theological meaning. The question relates to the *purpose* of the text. Regarding the creation of humanity, Claus Westermann observes that "all exegetes from the church fathers to the present begin with the presupposition that the text is saying something about people, namely that people bear God's image... Scarcely one of the many studies of the text asks about the process that is going on... There can be no question that the text is describing an action, and not the nature of human beings."[89] Polkinghorne calls such stories mythic because their purpose is "to convey truth in narrative form," requiring story to portray the depth of meaning.[90] Whether an actual historical scene lies behind the text assumes lesser importance in that the archetypal reality continues to demonstrate itself to be true in every human life. The Darwinian rejection of the account is all too often based on artificial "process" readings of the text.

The doctrines of sin and fall do not necessarily depend upon the biblical account, and can be constructed apart from special creation. We have already seen this doctrine recentered upon Christology and the cross in Rahner and Barth.[91] Williams and Duffy agree that the doctrine is to be found "in the contradiction between what humans are and what they are called to become in Christ."[92] Alistair McFayden insists that we must retain the concept of original sin because it captures our human situation: "we have a fundamental solidarity in sin."[93] Piet Schoonenberg agrees, noting that the fall story is not about *a* man named Adam, but about *the* Adam, a "corporate personality" representing all humanity.[94] Alan Richardson notes, "God is eternally making man and holding him in being and seeing that his handiwork is good (Gen 1:31). And just as creation is an eternal activity, so the 'fall' is an ingredient of every moment of human life; man is at every moment 'falling,' putting himself in the center, rebelling against the will of God.

---

89. Westermann, *Genesis 1–11*, 155.

90. Polkinghorne, *Science and Theology*, 63–64.

91. Marshall, *Trinity and Truth*, 152; Barth, *Church Dogmatics* IV/3(1):369.

92. Duffy, "Our Hearts of Darkness," 618; Williams, *Doing Without Adam and Eve*, 3–4.

93. McFadyen, *Bound to Sin*, 17; "Child Killers, Sin & Forgiveness."

94. Schoonenberg, *God's World in the Making*, 101–4; *Man and Sin*, 124–26. Schoonenberg notes that various genealogies indicate Scripture holds to the historicity of Adam beyond the fall narrative.

Adam is Everyman." We are essentially broken before God and each other, and in solidarity with the Adam's sin (Rom 5:12). With or without a historical interpretation, the doctrine captures with "amazing insight ... the truth about human nature. Man desires to be as God."[95]

Sin is often rendered as selfishness or the survival instinct in evolutionary context—vestigial traces of our beastly nature. For instance, Williams, Peterson, Philip Hefner, and others see our sinfulness as resulting from our culturally and genetically inherited evolutionary propensity for selfishness.[96] In one sense, these approaches mesh with Zizioulas' view that human and cosmic mortality are together part of a continuum. There are, however, some limitations to such an evolutionary description of sin. Reinhold Niebuhr observes that sin is fundamentally theological: human "sin is defined as rebellion against God."[97] McFayden agrees, noting that "sin is an essentially relational language, speaking of pathology with an inbuilt and at least implicit reference to our relation to God."[98] Gordon Graham insists that morality is robbed of its content if the transcendent is stripped away, so that a truly *moral* choice implies God from the beginning. "Without the boundaries provided by the Absolute of God, there are no limits that are ultimately conceptually binding." All our moral choices imply such a divine background, otherwise words like "wrong," "evil," and "impure" lose their meaning. In Protagorean terms, "no boundaries can be enforced if man is the measure of all things that are and of all things that are not."[99]

Regarding sin as a vestige of animal ancestry may be a type of Wittgensteinian linguistic error.[100] Sociobiological descriptions of evolutionary selfishness and altruism may be utilitarian,[101] but they are not really talking about the category of sin,[102] since outside the theologi-

---

95. Richardson, "Adam, Man," 14–15.

96. Williams, *Doing Without Adam and Eve*, 151; Peterson, *Minding God*, 177; Hefner, *Human Factor*, 132–35.

97. Niebuhr, *Nature and Destiny of Man*, 17.

98. McFadyen, *Bound to Sin*, 4; "Child Killers, Sin & Forgiveness."

99. Graham, "Playing God."

100. See Leahy, *Against Liberation*, 3–7.

101. E.g., Wilson, *On Human Nature*. See his chapter on "Altruism," 149–67.

102. As Niebuhr puts it, "this evil cannot be regarded complacently as the inevitable consequence of [human] finiteness or the fruit of [human] involvement in the contingencies and necessities of nature ... Nor can [man], as in both rationalistic and mystic dualism, dismiss his sins as residing in that part of himself which is not his true self,

cal context, sin has no meaning, or at least not the meaning intended by a word that connotes a broken relationship between humans and God.[103] In this sense, no scientific evolutionary theory of social or biological motivation could adequately discuss such a condition, much less discover or repudiate it. Its linguistic models are made for something different. Personal responsible moral relationship between God and creature only comes into existence in human beings, because only they are *free to choose*. Animal survival instincts are not selfish in the way human God-rejecting moral choice is both sin and selfishness. Animals are amoral[104]; they cannot rebel against God. Attributing human sin to instinctual motivation is to construe the source of human evil as something other than moral. The evil of which humans are uniquely capable is only evil *because* it is freely chosen moral evil, in contrast to the natural violence of the instinct-driven predator, or of the hypothetical pre-moral hominid ancestor.

Part of the scientific dispute with the Genesis account is in the supposedly archaic forms of the fall narrative. Examining human origins is beyond the scope of this project, and is unnecessary for evaluation of original sin.[105] The question of interest here is, how could the first humans, in moving from innocence to guilt, have led to the condition and condemnation of the entire human race? We have already noted our solidarity in sin. In terms of our given nature, Peacocke describes the fall as "not only individual but also corporate and, in this sense, 'original,' i.e., consequent upon origins."[106] If our sinfulness has an evolutionary origin in "selfish" survival motivation, this makes it essentially corporate, written into humanity's very genes and blood. This reintroduces the idea of *corporate sin,* familiar to the Hebrew mentality, but frequently missed in the individualistic West. Zizioulas notes that recent scholarship has rediscovered this central biblical theme, which

---

that is, that part of himself which is involved in physical necessity" (*Nature and Destiny of Man*, 17).

103. McFadyen, *Bound to Sin*, 4; "Child Killers, Sin & Forgiveness."

104. Peacocke, "Challenge and Stimulus," 98.

105. So Teilhard de Chardin said, "at those depths of time when hominisation took place, the presence and the movements of a unique couple are positively ungraspable, unrevealable to our eyes at no matter what magnification . . . There is room *in this interval* for anything that a trans-experimental source of knowledge might demand" (*Phenomenon of Man*, 186 n. 1).

106. Peacocke, *Creation and the World*, 192.

applies to both Adam in sin, and Christ as "catholic" man.[107] If humans have capacities and propensities, including for sin, we share these in common with our ancestors, and are universally and corporately united in our slavery to sin.

Can one believe the first humans fell from some state of innocent immortal grace? Human free moral reasoning is arguably a universal characteristic that marks us as unique on earth (see chapter 5). However this free ethical and relational capacity originated, whether by special creation or by gradual evolution, it is only with its emergence that we have what Zizioulas defines as true *personhood*.[108] Hefner sees in the fall story a mythical representation of the move from amoral instinctual innocence to self-conscious freedom.[109] Watts agrees that the story may be taken as "roughly historical" in the sense of capturing in mythological form the truth about the acquisition of the knowledge of good and evil—moral capacity—that must have occurred as *Homo sapiens* evolved.[110]

The fall amounts to an abuse of that newfound freedom. Without God's own self within their nature to rightly direct this moral capacity, there is no reason to suppose humans will always choose the right thing. At some point they abuse their freedom in relationship to God—they fall. The moral capacity continues to be genetically inherited by their descendants, and continues to lack the inner life of God to animate and rightly direct it. This is the experience of every human. As continues to be the case in children today, innocence is the normal state of the moral disposition until choice is abused. The two trees in Eden can be seen as the objectification of this choice for or against God. The forbidden fruit is not "ethically arbitrary,"[111] but accurately represents what it means to reject God: an entry into "personal intimate acquaintance" with both good and evil, and knowledge of what existence is like *without* God. From this perspective, Christian theology must insist on the doctrine of the fall not only for our first moral ancestors, but also for each person

---

107. Zizioulas, "Human Capacity and Incapacity," 408 n. 3; refers to Robinson, *Corporate Personality*, 25–45; Johnson, *One and the Many*.

108. Zizioulas, "Human Capacity and Incapacity," 408 n. 3.

109. Hefner, *Human Factor*, 132.

110. Watts, "*Human Personhood*," 53.

111. Contrary to Barr's assertion in *Garden of Eden*, 12–14.

throughout history, as the authentic description of human brokenness and estrangement from God.

The fall is not the same as the entry of death into creation. Zizioulas' account of the cosmos created mortal from its beginnings[112] helps reconcile this part of the story with modern science, and is actually more faithful to the biblical text. There is no suggestion in the Genesis account that humans were created independently immortal. James Barr notes that the tree of life offers the potential for immortality, but that Adam and Eve never actually partook of it: they were not naturally immortal.[113] Thus human potential for immortality is extrinsic rather than intrinsic. There is no need to follow Augustine in his exaggeration of the consequences of the fall.[114] It is tragic because, according to Zizioulas, the potential ability to unite the world with God is lost by the abuse of human freedom. The divine-human relationship is broken, with the consequence of humanity being permanently unable to unite with God—of being excluded from the tree of life. There is no escape from mortality without a move from God towards humanity, a move in which God comes *into* human moral life to redeem and straighten it—to release it from its captivity to sin, evil, and death.[115] Thus incarnation is intrinsic to the creation of mortal humanity. For these reasons, Zizioulas insists there is no possibility for the authentic person to emerge gradually in the cosmos as a result of evolutionary processes.[116] He rejects the evolutionary hope that humans are gradually making their way upward towards God, the first animal to emerge into consciousness, and now gradually heading for union with the divine, because it provides no solution to the problem of death.[117]

---

112. Typical of Eastern Orthodox thought. See Rybarczyk, "What are You, O Man?" 89–90.

113. Barr, *Garden of Eden*, 4–11. Some of Barr's interpretation is controversial, but this much is clear from the text.

114. See Williams, *Doing Without Adam & Eve*, 40–47.

115. The New Testament describes this, among many metaphors, as "being born from above" (John 3:3–7). Zizioulas calls it *ecclesial hypostasis*, an "already and not yet" process that will be completed in the eschaton (*Being as Communion*, 59).

116. Zizioulas, *Being as Communion*, 59.

117. Peacocke, "Challenge and Stimulus," 89–90. Peacocke's "Genesis for the Third Mil-lennium" (the "evolutionary epic") presents such a gradual dawning of spiritual aware-ness.

Zizioulas' Eastern Orthodox concept of the mortality of the cosmos provides a context that enables evolutionary thought to be coherent with biblical discourse. Sin is broken divine-human relationship and failed human potentiality, manifesting itself individually and corporately, though sin will be visible to natural science largely in terms of secondary lateral effects (e.g., selfishness, inordinate desire). The tension between the moral relational capacity of humans for God and the possibility of a morally right choice without the inner life of God is resolved by the predestination of the cosmos, including *all* of human history, towards the incarnation and the promised indwelling of the Holy Spirit. The possibility to transcend mortality appears in humanity, but is only finally realized in the incarnation of Christ, and through him in ecclesial humanity. In them, the universe receives a communion of unity with its Creator that results in eternal life.[118] Thus a doctrine of original sin remains coherent with, though different from, evolutionary discourse about human nature.

Relevant Problems in Zizioulas' Theology

Zizioulas' Doctrine of the Trinity

Zizioulas' interpretation of the Trinity may have some weaknesses. His communal doctrine of personhood flows from his Trinitarian theology, in which he stresses the personal nature of God while ignoring many of the other metaphors and analogies for God. This may lead to an overemphasis on the divine nature as purely and ultimately personal without an adequate backing, whether scriptural or philosophical. Daniel Migliore points out that the classical objection to *tritheism*—the idea that there are really three gods in the Trinity—is that the Father, Son, and Holy Spirit "are not three gods but distinct personal expressions of the one yet differentiated love of God."[119] This might lend itself to a different emphasis on the ultimate nature of God—not of personhood, but of *love*. While these may not be incompatible, in the sense that Zizioulas' concept of personhood includes communion and love, it does suggest some vulnerability in his approach to the Trinity.

---

118. Zizioulas, "Preserving God's Creation (3)," 5.
119. Migliore, *Faith*, 61.

Zizioulas follows the Cappadocian fathers in positing the person of the Father as the cause of the Son and Spirit. Alan Torrance wonders if this emphasis actually undermines Zizioulas' overall attempt to make *communal personhood* central to the doctrine of God. If God is primarily personal, and personhood automatically entails corporate interpersonal communion, then how can a person such as *Father* exist in some form that enables prior causation when there are no other persons to whom he may relate? Since personhood has no meaning apart from its corporate and communal context, it becomes problematic to speak of God as personhood while using the language of causation in inter-Trinitarian relations. A. J. Torrance is glad to have personhood properly emphasized in Western Trinitarian theology, but suspects that if the Father is the source of the Trinity, this must make his personhood quite different from that of the Son and Spirit, who are "derivative and contingent." He believes "this has the effect of reducing the unity of the Godhead to the personal singularity of the Father."[120] Once the nature of personhood becomes fluid in this apparently individualistic way, does the idea of personhood itself become too fluid? How could God be defined as person, his essence defined as communal personhood, in such a situation?

Can God the Father be understood as a person if ontologically he is prior to other persons of the Trinity, and personhood is fundamentally a communion of *ekstasis* between persons?[121] Zizioulas does not require that all the individual members of communally related persons must be absolutely identical in every way (though identical in character). In this sense, differences in personhood between the members of the Trinity are not problematic. If various personal roles are possible in human communal relations—father-mother-son-daughter, brother-sister, husband-wife—without endangering personhood, neither should it be completely alien if found in God. Zizioulas can hold such a view since communal personhood as the chief aspect of the *imago Dei* in human beings is not merely metaphorical of God's nature, but *is* God's nature. The key point is that personhood is realized corporately and communally, but need not imply sameness among the members of the community.

120. Torrance, *Trinitarian Description*, 290–92.
121. A. J. Torrance, *Persons in Communion*, 293; Zizioulas, "Human Capacity and Incapacity," 408.

However, it might be suggested that God was not *Father* "before" he caused the Son and Spirit, since causation entails priority and contingency. Then what was God's essence prior to this ontological causation? T. F. Torrance notices this flaw in the Cappadocian fathers, arguing that the derivative quality of the Son and Spirit destroys the unity of the Godhead.[122] Zizioulas could even be taken as supportive of a type of non-Trinitarian monotheism, since he explicitly claims, "God = the Father in the Bible." This suggests he really believes there is only one monad God, God the Father, so that when he speaks of God, he is really speaking only of the Father, or at least of an over-subordination of relationships within the Trinity.[123] This seems to depersonalize God and further endanger the primacy of personhood in the divinity, which is problematic given Zizioulas' insistence on that primacy.

Some theologians have suggested that a sole focus on personhood as constitutive of the Trinity overlooks other aspects of the nature of God. For instance, Sarah Coakley has attempted to show that the emphasis on the personal nature of the Trinity is not as critical to the thought of Gregory of Nyssa, an inspiration for social Trinitarianism in Eastern Orthodoxy and Zizioulas, as first appears. She suggests that this is one analogy among many used by Gregory for understanding the Trinity.[124] In answer, LaCugna argues that relationality must be more than merely the face of God, as God appears to us; it must be the essence of God's inner being, or we are left with a unitarian God incompatible with what is known of God's complete giving of himself to us in the cross.[125] A Trinitarian understanding of God, especially as revealed in Christ, is a God who is definitively *for us*, whereas a unitarian version of God, such as might be suggested by Zizioulas' emphasis on the Father, with Christ as a kind of appendage or reflection, may or may not be for us; such a God might ultimately be only for himself. Without the proper emphasis on personhood, some other characteristic of the Godhead becomes primary, e.g., power, will, or love.

Yet the divine love is not contrary to personhood. This seems to be what LaCugna sees in Zizioulas when she claims, "love causes God to be who God is." For her, "love is constitutive of God's being as a predicate

122. Torrance, *Trinitarian Faith*, 238–39.
123. Zizioulas, "Mystery of the Church," 95; "Contribution of Cappadocia," 3.
124. Coakley, "'Persons.'"
125. LaCugna, "Baptismal Formula, 243 n. 169.

of *person*, not substance" (emphasis added). God's personhood is what it is because "God is towards another," hence the intra-communitarian nature of God's personhood.[126] It is the Father's love which gives rise to the Son and the Spirit, hence to the Trinity itself, which in turn extends love to the world and humanity. Thus Zizioulas claims, "what causes God to be is the person of the Father."[127] T. F. Torrance suggests that this Cappadocian thought needs to be corrected by rejecting causal relations and incorporating Cyril of Alexandria's idea of the "coinherence in the one identical being of God, according to which the Father, Son and Holy Spirit mutually indwell and contain one another while remaining what they are." What God is inherently, indivisibly and eternally in the "consubstantial Trinity," he is toward us in the incarnation of his Son Jesus Christ and in the Spirit. Thus God's being is not isolated in the Father, but is one in nature and being, activity and will, sovereignty and power, perfectly expressed in "each divine person . . . of the Consubstantial Trinity."[128] A. J. Torrance agrees, believing this would re-center God's rule ("Monarchia") on the Trinity as it relates to the creation and humanity, rather than upon internal Trinitarian relations.[129] This seems prudent since, as Migliore reminds us, any ontology of divinity must be necessarily speculative.[130] The problem may be that humans can only think of causation in material terms, but that such terms are inadequate to describe what happens within the Trinity (T. F. Torrance observes awareness of this in Gregory of Nazianzus[131]). The twin notions of the Son's "begottenness" and the Spirit's "procession" are metaphorically rich, but it would be inadequate to read what we know of these notions directly onto inter-Trinitarian relations.

A. J. Torrance sees a further problem for anthropology in Zizioulas' distinction between human biological and ecclesial personhood (hypostasis). He wonders whether this gives an adequate account of those whose personhood is undeveloped or damaged, such as the very young and the mentally handicapped or infirm. He is also concerned

---

126. LaCugna, *God for Us*, 260–61.
127. Zizioulas, "Contribution of Cappadocia," 32.
128. T. F. Torrance, *Trinitarian Faith*, 338–40.
129. Torrance, *Persons in Communion*, 294–95.
130. Migliore, *Faith*, 61.
131. Torrance, *Trinitarian Faith*, 239.

that Zizioulas' brand of salvation is limited to the church.[132] However, it would be a mistake to take Zizioulas' description of the move from biological to ecclesial hypostasis as quite as dependent upon cognitive categories as this. The Eastern Orthodox Church believes in infant baptism, which sacrament is the sign for Zizioulas of entry into the Eucharistic ecclesial life of God. Further, the Christian hope of redemption draws a clear contrast between this corruptible mortal nature and the incorruptible nature of the resurrection (1 Cor 15:35–50). Short of that fulfillment, every human is fraught with the infirmities of mortality, some more than others, but all equally pale in comparison to the glory to be revealed in the children of God.[133] Cognitive limitations are therefore not ultimately relevant to human fulfillment in the kingdom of God.[134] Further, Zizioulas' theology of eschatological hope is not an isolationist salvation. Since even non-human creatures find salvation in the Eucharistic redemption, there is no reason to believe it excludes those persons whose cognitive capacity is impaired through either ignorance or infirmity. Zizioulas' Eucharistic ingathering sweeps the entire creation up into God's life, yet takes seriously the doom of those who actively reject that communion.

Personhood and Competing Non-human Versions of the Imago Dei

Several competing non-human versions of the *imago Dei* have been offered in recent years that attempt to answer various critiques of traditional theology, and might be a foil to Zizioulas' emphasis on personhood. Lucy Larkin attempts to define the image of God simply as relational capacity, so that various relations in the animal kingdom might represent the image.[135] Peacocke and Sally McFague suggest a move from a human-centered to a creation-centered version of the image: "the world is to God . . . as our bodies are to us as personal

---

132. Torrance, *Persons in Communion*, 301–2.

133. "So it is with the resurrection of the dead. What is sown is perishable, what is raised is imperishable. It is sown in dishonor, it is raised in glory. It is sown in weakness, it is raised in power. It is sown a physical body, it is raised a spiritual body" (1 Cor 15:42–44).

134. Recall Matt 18:3: "Unless you change and become like children, you will never enter the kingdom of heaven."

135. Larkin, "Douglas John Hall," 19.

agents."[136] While God's ontology is distinct from the world, the symbolism is of God as the *Mind* of the universe. Langdon Gilkey argues that the whole creation, rather than just human beings, should be viewed as the image of God.[137] Peterson agrees, noting the advantage of such a perspective is that it acknowledges "not only our relation to God but our relation to the rest of creation." He goes further, suggesting that consciousness and cognition is key to the image of God. "It would be better to say *not* that nature is in the image of God, but that nature is in the process of imaging God and in humans that imaging is, though not exclusive, most manifest."[138] Celia Deane-Drummond wonders if the image can really be confined to humans, since every creature of creation has "the imprint of the trinity."[139] Others offer differing Trinitarian and non-Trinitarian alternatives to Father-Son-Spirit that may be non-personal. To put the problem a bit crudely, if God is "the Rock," do rocks image God wherever they are found? Perhaps the image is unknowable to us. We may infer *mind* in the cosmos by the universe's intelligibility, the apparent rationality of law-like regularity in nature, perhaps even by the information rich environment of the biosphere. But is it our own human minds that we see thus reflected, since only by analogy with our own inner nature do these facets of the universe come into focus?[140]

Previous discussions in chapter 1 (see also chapter 5) have shown some of the problems with ascribing God's image solely to *relationality, creativity, nature,* or *mind*. The image of God is much richer in meaning, and such functionalistic approaches are not enough to capture the scriptural picture of either human or divine nature. While Noreen Herzfeld argues that the biblical material is too scant to found a robust doctrine of the image,[141] we have already seen how the New Testament in particular gives a full-bodied depiction, fully illuminated in the person of Jesus (see chapter 1). The heart of the issue is what Jesus himself, as the being who is God incarnate, reveals about God's nature and be-

---

136. Peacocke "Challenge and Stimulus," 110; McFague, *Body of God*, 13–22.

137. Gilkey, *Nature, Reality, and the Sacred*, 175–92.

138. Peterson, "Are We Unique?," 159, 177; *Minding God*, 147–50; "Nature as the Image of God," 489–505; "Evolution of Consciousness," 300–304.

139. Deane-Drummond, "Navigating the Maze." She refers to the "incarnation," rather than "the image."

140. Roush, "Copernicus, Kant," 30–32.

141. Herzfeld, *In Our Image*, 11–14.

ing. Lossky agrees, noting that because of the fall, the image of God is covered in humanity. For this reason we must start with Christology, and then move to human being in order to understand the *imago Dei*.[142] The incarnation means the *imago Dei* is inseparable from humanity. The relational, sovereign, bodily, and moral dimensions of the image in Jesus Christ and in the church highlight the uniquely human quality of the *imago Dei*. Neither inanimate nature nor any other living material creature is capable of exercising freedom and love in relationship, moral judgment, or dominion.[143] Contrary to Gilkey's contention, we might end up with a very different picture of God if the created cosmos "red in tooth in claw," subject to natural imperatives, mortal and mired in death, were taken as normative of the image. The essential *humanness* of the *imago Dei* is not invalidated by its brokenness in mortal and fallen humanity, because its reality and perfection are only revealed for what they are meant to be in Jesus Christ.

Some object that God's fatherhood may be overstated in classical Christianity.[144] Its eclipse would seem to imply a change in status for *personhood* as well. But many insist both are indispensable, since they are in Jesus the highest revelation of God.[145] This is not to say "Father" is the only name of the first person of the Trinity, but that it does remain essential. Pannenberg insists the church may not surrender language about God *the Father* as a mere image among other images. Rather, it is *the name*—the highest personal name—whereby Jesus addressed God, whether in prayer, or in expressions of his mission, or as the God of the kingdom of his preaching. "In its function as a name, the name of God in Jesus' own teaching and prayer, the word 'Father' cannot be replaced by another one. It would no longer be the God of Jesus to whom we

---

142. Laats, *Doctrines of the Trinity*, 118.

143. Chapter 5 will examine the extension of "person" status to animals, and deny the claim that personhood can be extended in this way beyond human nature without losing its meaning. *Creaturehood* is not enough to capture the image of God.

144. Soskice, "Can a Feminist Call God Father?," 15–29; E. Johnson, "Redeeming the Name of Christ," 120–23; LaCugna, "God in Communion," 100–108.

145. Zizioulas, like Barth, insists that only a real virgin birth could allow Christ to overcome the "hypostasis of biological existence," and transcend the necessity of nature, by moving his reference of origin beyond this world to the Holy Trinity. Hence Jesus' naming of God as father is of direct ontological significance. Zizioulas, *Being as Communion*, 54–55; Barth, "The Miracle of Christmas," in *Church Dogmatics* I/2:177–79.

relate, if we were to exclude the name Jesus himself used."[146] Jesus himself, in his life and teaching, is the most significant revelation of God's fatherhood and nature—"whoever has seen me has seen the father" (John 14:9). He shows that the fatherhood of God is deeply personal, relational, and sacrificial. The biblical description of divine father encompasses Ian McFarland's concept of surrender, support, and love, as in the father in the prodigal son story, and in Christ's sacrificial love of the church.[147] Moltmann insists we must see the brokenness of the cross as "*the pain of God . . . the divine co-suffering*" of compassion. Through Christ's "surrender God seeks out the lost beings he has created, and enters into their forsakenness, bringing them his fellowship, which can never be lost."[148] T. F. Torrance concurs:

> By revealing himself in the Lord Jesus Christ as *his* dear Son, God reveals that Fatherhood belongs to his eternal Being, and in giving his Son to be the Savior of the world, he reveals that he loves us to the uttermost with an eternal fatherly love.[149]

He and others suggest that the problem is not in God's fatherhood, but in its pale and broken reflection manifested in human fatherhood.[150] Jesus shows that God's fatherhood does not mean isolation, patriarchal abuse, and distance, but rather the opposite. He gives of himself out of love, rescuing his lost children, providing for, caring for, and disciplining them so that they might become all they are meant to be.

It seems that Zizioulas derives his view of God's personhood largely from his Christology and anthropology: the Son of God could become a human being, and human beings made in God's image are personal. It is not clear that the fullness of a reality can be grasped by analogy with its image, nor that a full description of the nature of the Son of God may be obtained from the data that he was incarnate as a

---

146. Wainwright, "Pannenberg's Ecumenism," 212. Wainwright sites Pannenberg as the origin of the "thoroughly Trinitarian" statement in the World Council of Churches' text of the apostolic faith in *Faith and Order Paper 140*.

147. McFarland, *Listening to the Least*, 132.

148. Moltmann, *Way of Jesus Christ*, 178.

149. Torrance, *Christian Doctrine of God*, 55.

150. Ibid., 57. T. F. Torrance notes this is the reason for Paul's insistence that the source of "all fatherhood in heaven and earth" is "the Father of our Lord Jesus Christ" (Eph 3:15). So Eun-Chul Kim wonders if bad images of human fatherhood underlie some feminists' rejection of God's fatherhood ("Honor Be to God," 5).

human being. Simply put, there is probably a lot more to God than we can see in ourselves or even in Christ. We are not sure what parts of the divine nature Christ put off in becoming incarnate besides his power and glory, but we do know he "emptied himself, taking the form of a servant" (Phil 2:7).

On the other hand, the fact of the incarnation does seem to indicate something fundamental and inescapable about God's personal nature. The Son of God has become incarnate as a human being, and chosen to retain this human nature—albeit transformed in the resurrection—for all of eternity. Jesus' revelation of the personal nature and name of God casts into doubt efforts to re-characterize God, abandon the traditional Trinitarian formulation, or exchange personhood in the *imago Dei* for some other central motif. Substantial or functional understandings of God's name and image, based on his activities and characteristics in such names as Creator, Mind, Ground of Being, Rock, Sustainer, or even Parent are simply inadequate as holistic terms for God.[151] Christ reveals that both human and divine natures are best understood in terms of *personhood*, rather than substance or function. When theologians de-emphasize God's personal names and personhood, such as in the redefinition of the *imago Dei* to non-personal terms, or the feminist rejection of God's fatherhood, important features of revelation are lost.[152]

Jesus reveals that God is not primarily some*thing*, nor some *action*, but some*one*.[153] Indeed Athanasius, in his dispute with the Arians, noted that when Philip asked Jesus to "Show us the Father," "He said not, 'Behold the creation,' but, '*He that hath seen Me, hath seen the Father.*'"[154] Zizioulas' contentions that *personhood* is fundamental to the nature of God, and that his image is revealed clearly in creation in human beings, are credible in light of the incarnation. The incarnate divine person Jesus Christ establishes an irrevocable bond between human person-

---

151. A "rock" is a thing. "Parent" is too generic and non-particular, too impersonal. I am not simply my son's or daughter's "parent." I am their father!

152. LaCugna, "Baptismal Formula," 243. She observes, "While it is true that the Bible sometimes assigns . . . certain functions to one of the divine persons (e.g., Christ is called Savior [e.g., Acts 5:31], and the Spirit is called Counselor and Teacher [e.g., John 14:26]), more often than not a variety of actions is mentioned in connection with each name (e.g., sometimes Christ is called Savior, and at other times God is called Savior) [e.g., Luke 1:47; John 4:42; Acts 5:31; John 4:14])."

153. Migliore, *Faith*, 66.

154. Athanasius, "Four Discourses against the Arians," 197.

hood and God's personhood. Human personhood is therefore of infinite worth. People are not *things* (cf. Rev 18:13).

The Limits of Human Cosmic Priesthood

Several authors note problems with the type of human cosmic priesthood proposed by Zizioulas, suggesting the idea is exaggerated. Stephen Clark suggests the priestly model is flawed because it exaggerates human power over nature. The notion of cosmic redemption is not implicit in nature, nor is it to be expected apart from divine revelation. Apart from the "good will" of God, there is no reason to believe that life, including human life, will "win" out in cosmic history, nor any reason to believe "our works will last" or the victory of life will be in a form that humans hope for.[155] It is just as likely that we humans will bring about our own destruction, as well as that of the ecosystems in which we live.[156] Given the realities of primordial mass extinctions, and the present human capacity for total self-destruction as possibly the medium of its own future fiery judgment (in either a nuclear or scriptural apocalypse, or both), the priestly model offered by Zizioulas, Andrew Linzey, and others exaggerates human capacity to affect and save creation as a whole. The Orthodox picture of the cosmos encompassed in the Eucharist may show our bodily solidarity with creation in the bread and wine, but at the most it can be symbolic of the salvation we hope for eschatologically in Christ, not our own capacity to affect that salvation.

This has the net effect of underscoring the proper theocentric focus of theology. Only God can redeem the cosmos. John Cobb agrees that the salvation of *all things* in the cosmos comes in Christ, not simply in humans. The highest natural efforts of humans to save the endangered and abused animal kingdom still end in death. Only in Christ are all creatures truly and forever reconciled and redeemed—"slaughtered and slaughterer, tortured and torturer—to one another and to God."[157] The chief anthropocentrism here lies in the fact that God's salvation is *in Christ*. Here, the claim that the animal kingdom is dependent upon humanity for its salvation can only be substantiated tangentially. While it is God's plan of redemption to bring *all* creation to glory with the

---

155. Clark, *Biology and Christian Ethics*, 269, 319.
156. Clark, *Animals and their Moral Standing*, 8.
157. Cobb, "All Things in Christ?," 179.

children of God, it is God, in the human Jesus Christ, who is the primary actor, *not* the bulk of the human race. With the rest of creation, we *also* groan while waiting. Humans are as dependent upon God for salvation—perhaps more so for their willful sin—as the rest of creation. Zizioulas' concept of human cosmic priesthood exaggerates the responsibility of the human race, including the redeemed church, although this criticism does not affect the status of the incarnate Jesus Christ.

Zizioulas might well answer that Clark and Cobb have failed to understand the mystical power, responsibility, and destiny of the body of Christ, the church. It is precisely because it is *Christ's body in the world* that the church continues to have a priestly role in creation. So Paul says God's intent was that "through the church the wisdom of God in its rich variety might now be made known to the rulers and authorities in the heavenly places. This was in accordance with the eternal purpose that he has carried out in Christ Jesus our Lord" (Eph 3:10–11). To forget this role may be a failure to understand the true nature of the church. The idea of human cosmic priesthood will be revisited in chapter 7.

Summary of Zizioulas' Perspective

Zizioulas' theology highlights human significance in several important ways. Humanity is unique in all creation in that it is the *imago Dei*—more precisely the *imago Trinitatis*. Humans alone of all creatures in the cosmos are created as *persons* with *personhood*, capable of *theosis*—potentially being made into the likeness of God in Christ. They alone are capable of transcending the given nature of the cosmos in freedom, creativity, and love. Because of the person and work of Jesus Christ, they are offered a share in divine personhood, to be fulfilled eschatologically. The cosmos is prepared from its foundations for the incarnation of the Son of God, which takes place in creaturely and hypostatic humanity. Thus humanity is the fulcrum that unites the nature of God with the cosmos. Christ, in whom the communion of the divine and human natures is restored, turns the cosmos into a realm where God is present rather than absent. His divine life is extended through the redeemed humanity of the church, his corporate body, so that "the church becomes . . . the very core and nucleus of the destiny of the world."[158]

---

158. Zizioulas, "Mystery of the Church," 296.

This elevated view of humanity is not at the expense of the nonhuman creation, for ecclesial humanity is priest in Christ *for* the creation, able to represent the cosmos to God, and God to the cosmos. It brings the cosmos into communion with its Creator. The church is thus the focus of unity between God and the creation. This finding is not compromised even if the priestly responsibility of humanity is exaggerated in Zizioulas. Only in humanity, and specifically the humanity of the church, does the creation unite with its Creator, and so transcend its mortality and find eternal life. The fate of the entire universe rests upon humanity in this sense: in them it will be released from death and renewed with immortality. Thus humanity is the hope of the whole creation. Only in and through them does God finally unite with his creation and the new heaven and earth appear. Thus "man . . . is the only being responsible for the fate of creation."[159]

In conclusion, it is evident that Zizioulas' theology is deeply and intrinsically anthropocentric. This Trinitarian and incarnational perspective places humanity at the heart of cosmic destiny in Christ. Though embedded in an explicitly sacramental worldview, his theology is neither irrational nor unable to interact with modernity. Insofar as Zizioulas represents the Orthodox Christian tradition, it would seem that stream of Christianity contains a high view of human significance, correlating divine and human personhood at the center of universal history.

---

159. Zizioulas, "Preserving God's Creation (3)," 3; "Preserving God's Creation (2)," 45.

PART TWO

Human Significance in the Natural Sciences

4

Some Boundary Issues between Science and Theology

> The "supernatural" can only designate the reality essentially distinct from the creature, the divine life itself.
>
> —Gregory Palamas[1]

Introduction

BEFORE MOVING INTO THE DISCUSSION OF WHAT SCIENCE SAYS ABOUT human significance, it is appropriate to establish some basic boundaries for dialogue. This is necessary in order to protect the integrity of what each discipline claims to be *true* in its own domain, and to discover what the boundaries of those domains are. The particular problem relevant to this thesis is that many have attempted to isolate theology in a realm of *meaning* and *value*, and give science, through the doctrine of materialistic naturalism, *carte blanche* for describing the full content of reality. Is this a fair move?

Methodological naturalism serves as a fairly standard boundary of the scientific enterprise. There are many who would extend this boundary to include theology, moving in the positivist direction of denying the possibility of miracles, access to the transcendent, and knowledge of God. This is evident in scientific polemicists like Sagan, Richard Dawkins, or Daniel C. Dennett, and also in those engaged in the science/theology dialogue, such as in Willem Drees' "naturalist account,"[2] Page's

---

1. Meyendorff, *Gregory Palamas*, 163.
2. Drees, *Religion, Science, and Naturalism*, 268. Drees' naturalism is particularly unsatisfying. To such basic metaphysical questions as "Why is there anything?," "Why is there order?," or "Why is the universe fine-tuned?" his answer is, "Reality is assumed, rather than explained. This applies also to my naturalist account."

"sub-deism,"[3] or Peacocke's non-interventionist version of "emergentist monism."[4] This naturalistic program is held by some to undermine incarnational theology, to reduce the status of Christian revelation to irrelevance, and thus to refute the inherent anthropocentrism of Christian theology. If naturalism holds as the ultimate boundary description of reality, there could not be a real incarnation, a real resurrection, or indeed any kind of objective divine revelation. Therefore it is important to assess the claims of naturalism if theology is to maintain belief in supernatural or miraculous Christian claims. The critical anthropocentrism evident in Zizioulas, Pannenberg, and Rahner seems in each case to be dependent upon such transcendent claims, so this assessment is necessary to establish the coherence of Christian anthropocentrism in modern context beyond purely metaphorical uses.

Pannenberg, Rahner, and Zizioulas all believe naturalism has limits. They believe God acts in the cosmos in both natural and miraculous ways, through nature's laws and in supernatural miraculous events like the resurrection of Jesus and the eschatological redemption of the cosmos. Pannenberg emphasizes the resurrection, and Rahner emphasizes human openness towards transcendence, while Zizioulas emphasizes the divine entering into the cosmos to bring redemption and liberation from death (Jesus' virgin birth, human and divine nature, and resurrection). Zizioulas sees in the rationality of the Enlightenment the culmination of a problem long brewing in Western thought: the elevation of rationalism to an idolatrous place in human knowledge.[5] Alvin Plantinga insists that Enlightenment naturalism has profound consequences if taken over from science into theology.[6]

Naturalism is an aspect or product of Enlightenment foundationalism (EF). The scientific enterprise and worldview that so dominates modern culture has been deeply naturalistic since its rise in EF philosophy. From Hume and Spinoza to Sagan and Dawkins, many influential thinkers have believed in Enlightenment naturalism. There has been a

---

3. The term is used by Palmer, review of *God and the Web of Creation*, 750. See chapter 7 for an extended critique.

4. Peacocke, "Challenge and Stimulus," 89–93. Peacocke supposes life, neurology, and personhood emerge at successive levels of reality, free from interference by God. God's job: to "let Other be. And let it have the capacity to become what it might be." Jesus' resurrection, as in Page, seems to be an exception.

5. Zizioulas, "Preserving God's Creation (1)," 1–3.

6. Plantinga, "Methodological Naturalism," 198–204.

growing critique of EF in recent philosophy.⁷ Many philosophers hold that Enlightenment and modern foundationalism has collapsed.⁸ A brief evaluation of their arguments is in order. If they are right, then EF's contingent naturalism is also suspect, and remains so even in the nonfoundationalist postmodern setting. This has wide-ranging implications for theology—especially for protecting the objectivity of events like the incarnation and resurrection and for defending the rationality of God's ongoing relationship with the cosmos—even while naturalism continues to be useful in science.

Definition and Basis of Enlightenment Foundationalism

EF naturalists hold that just as science seeks to understand reality without reference to a supernatural or transcendent realm, so all approaches to reality, including theology, must operate within those same limits. If there is a God, he does not or cannot intervene in the chain of secondary causation. Miraculous and supernatural events are ruled out of bounds *a priori*. Rudolf Bultmann summarizes the perspective neatly: reality is a "closed continuum . . . that cannot be rent by the interference of supernatural, transcendent powers."⁹ Thus miraculous events like the resurrection are seen as inherently impossible, to be given nonrealist interpretations as symbolic, metaphorical, or mythological in meaning or value.

The "Properly Basic"

EF is primarily an empirical belief structure. It accepts as foundational only beliefs that are empirical: those that are "*intrinsically credible or self-evidencing.*"¹⁰ A properly basic belief (x) in this structure is one that:

---

7. McGrath, *Foundations of Dialogue*, 11–13.

8. Wolterstorff, *Reason within the Bounds of Religion*; A. Plantinga, "Reason and Belief in God," 48–63; Lindbeck, *Nature of Doctrine*; Grube, "Religious Experience after Foundationalism," 37–52; Philips, *Faith after Foundationalism*; Williams, *Problems of Knowledge*.

9. Bultmann, *Existence and Faith*, 291–92.

10. Williams, *Problems of Knowledge*, 83.

refers "solely to the content of a single experience,"[11] and must be self-evident, incorrigible (indisputably related to one's own sense-experience), or evident to the senses.[12]

Enlightenment foundationalists are skeptical about beliefs built outside this basis. As Enlightenment science flowered, the world came to be seen as autonomous, self-sustaining, and without the need of transcendent properties or orientation.[13] The emerging naturalism claimed that the miraculous and supernatural were neither examples of nor derivable from empirical grounds. The boundary of experience came to be seen as *a priori* excluding the miraculous and the supernatural. In this way, religious belief in miracles and the supernatural came to be seen as irrational.

The Collapse of Enlightenment Foundationalism

Philosophers suggest that EF has collapsed for three reasons: (1) it is self-referentially incoherent, 2) its empirically based system is local and cultural rather than universal, and (3) it provides the wrong analytical technique for supernatural events or experience.

Self-referential Incoherence

EF claims its belief structure is rational *all the way down* to the ground of incontestable empirical experience: what is properly basic (x), as defined above. Its claim to ultimate rationality is thus contingent upon the validity of this notion of a properly basic belief. However, there is no way to prove that this understanding of x is itself properly basic to knowledge. The intuition that this is the final ground of knowledge seems to require a defense of reasons. But, as Shults points out, once such a defense is offered, then the intuition itself is no longer foundational; rather, the reasons then become foundational. Then these reasons must be justified, and so on *ad infinitum*.[14] Furthermore, as Plantinga demonstrates, the *basis* is logically incoherent. EF's notion of the "properly basic" cannot be shown to be "self-evident, incorrigible, or evident to

---

11. Ayer, *Language, Truth, and Logic*, 10.

12. McGrath, *Foundations of Dialogue*, 12; see also Williams, *Problems of Knowledge*, 84.

13. G. Ward, *Postmodern God*, xx.

14. Shults, *Postfoundationalist Task*, 32–33.

the senses." It is not self-evident or evident to the senses that the only things that may be rationally believed as foundational are those that are self-evident or evident to the senses. Since EF's "properly basic" is not itself properly basic, therefore EF's foundations are self-referentially incoherent: "the modern foundationalist violates . . . the condition of proper basicality he himself lays down."[15] EF is thus a circular belief system, rather than being rational all the way down, and can make no claim to *ultimate* rationality.

Culturally Local, Not Universal

Besides its self-referential incoherence, EF's claim for the universal rationality of its perceptual orientation cannot be justified. This is due to the inherent limitations of human empirical perceptions. While the Enlightenment wanted to claim some kind of direct link between human perception and reality, in fact every act of perception is wrapped up in a host of cultural and linguistic assumptions.[16] Van Huyssteen says that "because we relate to our world epistemically only through the mediation of interpreted experience, the observer . . . is always in a relationship to what is known, and thus always limited in perspective, in focus, and in experiential scope." Beliefs interpret experience, and experience shapes belief. "Our interpreted experience thus becomes the matrix within which meaning and knowledge arise." This is true for the religious believer as well as the scientific researcher.[17] Denying this, Enlightenment foundationalism suffers from what Wilfred Sellars pejoratively calls "the Myth of the Given."[18]

Cultural anthropology has shown that what one culture and time take as common sense, another culture and time may regard as nonsense. "What is 'obviously true' seems to many to depend on the inherited assumptions concerning evidence and warranty on the part of the thinker, including a cluster of beliefs that may not be consciously articulated."[19] Clifford Geertz points out that the process of enculturation leads to the selective evaluation of experiences based on deeply

---

15. A. Plantinga, *Warranted Christian Belief*, 94–95.
16. Williams, *Problems of Knowledge*, 94–104.
17. Van Huyssteen, *Essays*, 19–20.
18. Sellars, "Empiricism," 253–359.
19. McGrath, *Foundations of Dialogue*, 13.

and often subconsciously held cultural expectations. The perceptual filtering process is part of the template for understanding reality formed during the enculturation of the individual. Human "notions, however implicit, of the 'really real' and the dispositions these notions induce in them, color their sense of the reasonable, the practical, the humane, and the moral."[20] Reality simply cannot be known outside the limitations of cultural perceptual capacity: absolute perceptual objectivity is a myth. Terry Winograd and Fernando Flores note that concealing the commitments of a given person situated in their given worldview leads to an "illusion of objectivity." The result, however, is not real knowledge, but blindness.[21] So Margaret Archer notes that cultural pressure applied to protecting the consensus rather than finding the truth is evident even in science and academia.[22] The Enlightenment belief that the experiential bounds of naturalism are universal and objective is therefore an illusion. Scientific worldviews, including that of naturalism, are necessarily limited, prone to revision, and even to radical paradigm shift with the accumulation of anomalies.[23]

Plantinga, Gunton, and Richard Rorty all notice the limitation of EF's perceptual claims.[24] It is fatally dependent upon human sense experience, granting absolute authority and confidence to the human ability to know reality. This is fatal, not just because it is a poor kind of anthropocentrism, but because it shows that a disguised form of naïve realism is hidden at the roots of the Enlightenment vision, elevating human perceptual capacity to absolute godlike status. William Alston calls this "epistemic imperialism."[25] It is absurd to claim that any particular human culture is able to know all there is to know about reality.

While there have been continuing eyewitness experiences of miracles in EF culture, these have been regarded as untrustworthy, since they seem contrary to the EF version of common sense and do not seem to be

---

20. Geertz, *Interpretation of Cultures*, 124.

21. Winograd and Flores, *Understanding Computers and Cognition*, 156. They point out the false confidence in computer projections as "objective" based on similar rationalistic reasoning.

22. Archer, *Culture and Agency*, 225.

23. Cantor, "Does Religion Impede the Progress of Science?"

24. A. Plantinga, "Reason and Belief in God," 57; Gunton, *Yesterday and Today*, 144; Rorty, *Philosophy and Nature*, 38–41.

25. Alston, *Perceiving God*, 249.

happening at all times and all places.[26] The continuing Roman Catholic practice of confirming sainthood by the occurrence of miracles in the name of a deceased believer, miraculous healings at religious shrines such as at Lourdes, France, or "enthusiast" experiences at religious revivals such as in the Wesleyan holiness movement[27] have usually been dismissed without serious investigation.[28] Only naturalistic evidence is admitted. Evidence for the miraculous and supernatural is ruled out of bounds *tout court*, even where it claims empirical justification.

While naturalism is supposed to be objective, it is in fact no more rational and objective than supernaturalism. So Pannenberg insists, "the so-called methodological atheism of modern science is far from pure innocence."[29] In light of cultural limitations, it can no longer be taken for granted that the evidence of the transcendent is really absent. Many modern cultures, including subcultures in the Western world, continue to include perception of the supernatural and miraculous in their experience of reality, like Cone's insistence on the present experience of Jesus Christ in the black American church,[30] or the fact that many modern religious believers continue to report that some kind of answer to prayer or miraculous healing or intervention is part of their religious experience. Just because adherents of naturalism disregard these experiences does not automatically invalidate them or render them less rational than naturalism; such rejection is to be expected given naturalism's filtering template.

Wrong Analytical Technique for Evaluating Religion

Alston observes that just because transcendent experiences do not have the type of universal repeatability and predictability as those observable by the natural sciences does not make them irrational.[31] Since naturalism's analytical techniques are all geared to accommodate its own

26. Nichols, "Miracles in Science and Theology," 706–7.

27. E.g., Wesley, *Complete Works*, 1:191, 267, 269, 405, 570–71. Wesley was careful for what he allowed to happen in his revivals (344). For a modern example of an "enthusiast revival" complete with supernatural healings, see the Toronto Airport Christian Fellowship, online: http://www.tacf.org.

28. Nichols, "Miracles in Science and Theology," 706–7.

29. Pannenberg, *Toward a Theology of Nature*, 16.

30. Cone, *God of the Oppressed*, 121–22.

31. Alston, *Perceiving God*, 249.

worldview, it may not offer the best technique for evaluating past or present events with transcendent elements. As Michael Williams puts it, "procedures are reliable only given a range of circumstances in which they are *supposed to operate*, which is something for us to determine in the light of our needs and interests."[32] Alston concludes that it is unwarranted to take features of the checking and prediction systems typical of scientific perception "as the norm for all perceptual belief forming practices."[33] Holwerda adds that history as the realm of the particular is likewise outside the investigative system of universals-seeking science.[34] If with Palamas the *supernatural* is taken to be the reality distinct from the material creation, then a study of the regularities of the creaturely world (science) will not necessarily even see supernatural reality.[35]

For example, one reason for naturalism's rejection of miracles is that they are not a part of everyday experience. This checking system misses an important feature of scriptural miracles in the traditionalist worldview: they serve as signs that point to an unusual revelation of God. While some cultural supernatural claims, such as those for magic, manna, or similar animistic constructs, might be candidates for scientific assessment because they allege observable relations of law-like regularity in the world, *miracles*, in contrast, require a backdrop of natural law regularity against which they become apparent; they cannot be everyday affairs, or they would not qualify as unusual enough to draw attention to a unique message from God. Science cannot evaluate them even in principle, because miracles are neither repeatable scientific events, nor an expected outcome of the normal flow of nature. Thus Michael Polanyi observes, "It is illogical to attempt the proof of the supernatural by natural tests, for these can only establish the natural aspects of an event and can never represent it as supernatural."[36]

The incommensurability of religious with other verification systems is particularly evident in Christianity's faith claims. Christianity claims its version of faith comes from a transcendent source, as a gift from God (Eph 2:8). For those following Pannenberg's approach, Jesus' authority is confirmed by an inherently supernatural event: the resur-

---

32. Williams, *Problems of Knowledge*, 174.
33. Alston, *Perceiving God*, 249.
34. Holwerda, "Faith, Reason, and the Resurrection," 289.
35. Meyendorff, *Gregory Palamas*, 163.
36. Polanyi, *Personal Knowledge*, 284.

rection.[37] Though making propositional and historical truth claims, Christianity maintains that its ultimate foundation is a person: Jesus Christ (1 Cor 3:11). Testing Jesus' veracity requires both personal *believing* commitment (not so different from Polanyi's claim for the scientist's personal commitment) and *action*. Jesus said, "If you *continue in my word* . . . you will know the truth" and "Anyone who resolves to *do the will of God* will know whether [my] teaching is from God."[38] These are matters that can only be investigated from the "inside," promising confirmation to those who are willing to abide in Christianity's verification system. It is therefore unwarranted to expect that the revelation of religion—the Christian religion in particular—will be reducible to or understandable in terms of the naturalistic method of science.

D. Z. Philips calls the prevailing dominance of naturalism a philosophical scandal: "we are asked to accept as the only appropriate philosophical method for establishing the rationality of religious belief, a method which actually distorts the character of religious belief." He sees part of the problem as being linguistic, after Wittgenstein: using the language of science to describe religious knowledge confuses the independent character of these epistemic and linguistic domains.[39] These domains are cultural constructs based on "the conventions of the community" that use them, but have themselves no deeper rational foundation.[40] Naturalism is a local linguistic construct that is particularly useful to the scientific community to describe the material dimension of reality, but it is not a facet of universal reason nor does it necessarily provide the fullest apprehension of reality. To rely on it as such is to fall into the trap that Mikael Stenmark pejoratively calls "scientism": making the scientific claim to discover things about the general nature and features of the world into an authoritarian decree that *only* what science can discover about the world is real.[41] Neither can the problem be reduced to the community linguistics of the Dilthey-Gadamer dichotomy, with science as "explanation" versus religion as "understanding."[42]

---

37. So those who continue to adhere to naturalism will be unconvinced by events such as resurrections. E.g., Buss, "Meaning of History," 150–51.

38. John 8:31–32; 7:17. Emphasis added.

39. Philips, *Faith after Foundationalism*, 12, 115–17.

40. N. Murphy, "Introduction," 15.

41. Stenmark, *Scientism*, 21.

42. Barr summarizes the dichotomy in his *Holy Scripture*, 112.

That dichotomy depends upon the EF model of rationality. The ultimate irrationality of naturalism means that religion's account of *experience* cannot be confined to a "meaning" role; religion may have things to disclose about objective reality that move between explanation and understanding. As van Huyssteen observes, "both the scope and content of theological explanations may set them apart from explanations in other areas." The collapse of foundationalism "dispels the common myth that science is about reason and theology is about faith."[43]

The EF naturalist has been guilty of using what Alston calls a "double standard," accusing the traditionalist of having a circular belief system, which is exactly true for naturalism.[44] Descartes' excessive faith in human reason and perception, Spinoza's cultural aesthetic preference for a self-contained cosmos, and Hume's forced delineation of the problem in terms of unbreakable natural laws[45] resulted in a cultural blindness to other options, other possibilities that were equally rational. Interestingly, the Enlightenment scientific paradigm of a closed, mechanistic, and eternal universe of Euclidean regularity has given away to a contemporary paradigm of quantum indeterminacy, relativity, energy-for-matter, and multi-level explanation. The laws of modern physics have changed dramatically from those upon which EF naturalism was built.[46]

Implicit Naturalism in Postmodern Thought

Many philosophers recognize the collapse of EF.[47] But the tacit view of much modern theology has been to continue to assume that naturalism is still valid; this is so even where EF is explicitly seen as passé, as in much postmodern and nonfoundationalist theology. Ernest Gellner observes, "the hermeneutic relativists do not *really* treat all cultural visions as equally valid. Their accounts of alien systems of meanings as they present them are still, deeply and inevitably, located within a natural milieu conceived in terms of current Western science."[48]

43. Van Huyssteen, *Essays*, 231–32; Shults, *Postfoundationalist Task*, 68–72.

44. Alston, *Perceiving God*, 249. Alston evaluates the rationality and reality of Christian mystical experience.

45. Keith Ward attacks Hume's construct in his "Believing in Miracles," 741–50.

46. Pannenberg, *Systematic Theology*, 2:49–72, 106–7; "Resurrection," 259.

47. See note 72.

48. Gellner, *Postmodernism, Reason and Religion*, 85.

For instance, the collaborative effort *The Postmodern Bible: The Bible and Culture Collective* explicitly acknowledges the fall of historical criticism to postmodern critique, along with the Enlightenment illusion of "dispassionate objectivity and psychological distance," but is completely blind to its own continued adherence to foundationalist naturalism.[49] In fact, as R. W. L. Moberly observes, the writers of *The Postmodern Bible* are not even interested in the question of God, much less God's potentially real activity in history.[50] The same situation is evident in other works, where the postmodern worldview supposedly "does not dictate one perspective and approach," and yet naturalism is the tacit exception.[51]

The postmodern enterprise is sometimes seen as built on the "ontology of absence,"[52] not least of the absences being that of the transcendent. But this analysis shows that a belief in the absence of transcendence is itself a form of cloaked foundationalism. It is *naturalism itself*, as the hidden element of foundationalism, that must be set aside as the dictating worldview, and which postmodernity must recognize as a limited and non-binding cultural construct. Further, absolute relativism is no longer tenable once the realm of the transcendent is admitted back into epistemology. With the transcendent comes the theoretical plumb line of absolute truth. Whether or how humans access this theoretical transcendent truth is a different question from admitting its possible existence. The fact that science operates by at least tacitly admitting this plumb line (e.g., in assuming the intelligibility and regularity of the cosmos) shows the hidden poverty of an ontology of absence.

While some will attempt to recast naturalism in nonfoundational terms, this does not suddenly revive its claim to universal rationality. The burden of proof will be upon them to show what nonfoundational system gives warrant for belief in naturalism beyond its boundary function in science. Coherentist systems alone will not do the job, as naturalism cannot be shown to be anything more than part of an exclusively "belief-by-belief" structure, based upon internal relations rather than

---

49. Aichele, *Postmodern Bible*, 1–2, 4, 44.

50. Moberly, *Bible, Theology, and Faith*, 34.

51. Jobling et al., *Postmodern Bible Reader*, 1–30; McKnight, *Postmodern Use of the Bible*, 150, 196.

52. Kendall, "Intratextual Theology," 106.

an empirical relation to the world.[53] Almost by definition, "postmodern" systems are unable to ground naturalism as universal, and are not justified uncritically assuming its truth.

Critical Realism in Science and Theology

The collapse of EF is really about the limitations of human epistemology. It does not imply that there is no objective reality, or that there is no relationship between aspects of human knowledge and that reality. The EF adherent will point to the technological successes of the natural sciences as an indication of their validity. Their mastery of nature seems to transcend cultural boundaries and capture part of reality as it is. Thus natural scientists often disdain the postmodern position as irrelevant.[54] The postfoundationalist insight is to deny that there are universally rational foundations for *human* knowledge. But Rom Harré and Michael Krausz insist that Rorty and the relativists have not shown "that a progressivist, world driven conception of the improvement of knowledge is not viable."[55] The increasing success of science surely indicates, according to Harré, that the references of scientific discourse are "about something other than one's own states": they are about reality, hence the position of scientific realism.[56] W. H. Newton-Smith agrees that the progress of science is best understood as the improving approach to verisimilitude: it captures more and "more truth about the world."[57]

The success of science, while real enough, is also epistemologically restricted. Scientific theories never perfectly and fully explain or describe reality. There are always new anomalies that accumulate, with the possibility, as Kuhn observed, of new paradigms replacing older ones.[58] Further, Stewart notes the social limitations and elasticity of the "scientific horizon" of research: individuals and groups "can be actually

---

53. "Coherentist" approaches to reality have their own problems (see Williams, *Problems of Knowledge*, 118–20). As representative of alternative rationalities, they will not work to ground naturalism as universal; it could have in them no more binding status than the proverbial "made-up" fairy tale.

54. E.g., after the Alan Sokel parody. See Koertge, *House Built on Sand*.

55. Harré and Krausz, *Varieties of Relativism*, 202.

56. Harré, *Varieties of Realism*, 145.

57. Newton-Smith, *Rationality of Science*, 208.

58. Kuhn, *Structure of Scientific Revolutions*.

concerned with only a small part" of that horizon.[59] Newton-Smith observes that while iterations of the scientific process bring improvements in verisimilitude, modern science has moved away from the "necessary truths" and deterministic assurance of Newtonian physics, and been forced to accept the "probabilistic character" of uncertainty and quantum indeterminacy. Such modern worldviews preclude absolute determinist understandings of reality. The scientist is also often reliant upon his own judgment without explicit grounds—he cannot even produce those grounds, as they are rooted in his perceptions, his intuitions, and in his aesthetic sensibilities. Even what scientists consider valuable and appropriate to the theoretical description of reality evolves over time. "This means that a rational representation of science should consist not of a single model but of an evolving series of models . . . [each based] by reference to the model which articulates the beliefs of the scientists of the time concerning what makes a good theory a good one."[60] Hence most modern scientists believe an objective reality exists (realism), but also admit that our human ability to fully apprehend this reality is limited, provisional, and in need of constant correction (it is *critical*).[61]

Harré and Krausz note that modern scientific realism does not entail an exact correspondence of theories with reality. But it does posit that the models of reality science constructs can be compared with the world as it is, and become more adequate as the mapping from one to the other is refined. Hence, "we can leave the logicist myths behind us without adopting post-modernist anarchism."[62] Scientific knowledge is provisional, not absolute, and most practicing scientists accept a position of *critical realism*.

Van Huyssteen points out that critical realism is not a "theory about truth," but rather "a theory about the epistemic values that shape scientific rationality." A *theological* critical realism, though different from the scientific version in that the objects of its interest are different, is similar in that it acknowledges human limitations while maintaining the existence of objective reality. Religious language is not just a "useful system of symbols" for guiding action and giving meaning to

---

59. Stewart, *Reconstructing Science and Theology*, 106.

60. Newton-Smith, *Rationality of Science*, 222, 232–35, 245.

61. E.g., McGrath, *Foundations of Dialogue*, 154–64; Polkinghorne, *Science and Theology*, 16–17.

62. Harré and Krausz, *Varieties of Relativism*, 205–6.

the believer, but can be about an objective reality that is independent of our linguistic models, experienced on different terms than that described by scientific rationality. Theological critical realism admits to provisionality, and like much of scientific rationality, also claims the possibility of making "reliable cognitive claims about domains of reality that lie beyond our experience, but to which interpreted experience is our only epistemic access."[63] Under the condition of such limited access, the language of simile and metaphor is the natural mode for both science and theology.[64] Theology can accept the transcendent realm as a given of faith, or with Aquinas take as basic that the existence of God is self-evident,[65] while admitting the ultimate mystery of God is beyond finite human grasp. Our openness to transcendence does not entail our complete comprehension of it. Thus its own form of *critical realism* is appropriate to theology.

The success of science has sometimes blinded culture to its epistemological limitations. This is probably nowhere more evident than in various anti-theist polemics that ignore the indebtedness of science to metaphysics.[66] In these, science's normal methodological reductionism is inflated into claims for ontological reductionism. Yet science's success is ontologically unrelated to the possibility of a transcendent realm or supernatural events. Naturalistic science is simply the wrong medium for investigating those aspects of reality, which are perceivable in a worldview alien to and incomprehensible in naturalistic terms. They are beyond the domain of natural science to either confirm or disconfirm.[67] When the mutual humility of critical realism is combined with the awareness that some religious claims will be unavailable for evaluation by science, this leaves room for the two disciplines to exist separately, but with mutual respect. Theology will have its own things to say about reality, even in a critically realist mode, that may not be challenged or falsified by simple appeals to scientific truth. Science may have things to say about reality that may or may not correspond to theological data. Since the belief structure

---

63. Van Huyssteen, *Essays*, 41–44.
64. Harré, *Varieties of Realism*, 7; Van Huyssteen, *Essays*, 44.
65. Thomas Aquinas *Summa Theologica* I.2.1.
66. See Chapter 6. E.g., Sagan, *Cosmos*, 4; Dawkins, *Blind Watchmaker*; Atkins, *Creation Revisited*, 23.
67. Berry, "Divine Action," 725.

of naturalism is neither rationally compulsory nor universal, a fair approach to topics transcending that boundary will be openminded, rather than disregarding some options on *a priori* bases.

General Conclusions

It may be suggested that the critique of naturalism cuts both ways, and demonstrates that religious claims to foundational truth are also ultimately irrational, at least in foundationalist terms. The critical realist position has no trouble admitting this; it acknowledges the general limitations of all human knowledge. But the injustice of philosophy has been to allow the knife to cut only in the direction of transcendence, rather than admitting that it cuts equally in the direction of naturalism. To this degree, the most reasonable conclusion is to admit what Van Huyssteen and Shults call the "fiduciary rootedness" of all knowledge.[68] This position realizes that a scientific or theological dismissal of the supernatural is a type of fideism: a pre-committed faith position unrelated to rationality. It serves as an EF filter or mirror that views reality in its own anti-supernaturalist image. This may be an appropriate filter for examining the regular behavior of the material world, but it is not suited for noticing aspects of reality that transcend those bounds. It cannot claim its naturalistic conclusions about scriptural miracles and transcendent reality are a result of scientific or historical investigation.[69] Contrary to long-held notions of naturalism's ultimate rationality and superiority, belief in the transcendent realm and miracles is *just as rational and perhaps more so* as belief in materialistic naturalism.

In light of the discussion, Pannenberg, Rahner, and Zizioulas all have grounds for accepting the openness of full reality to the transcendent.[70] This type of realist respect of the transcendent protects the epistemic rationality and objectivity of the incarnation, the resurrection, and other significant aspects of theology. This analysis of EF naturalism shows the equal rationality of such transcendent or sacramental epistemologies.

---

68. Van Huyssteen, *Essays*, 44; Shults, *Postfoundationalist Task*, 81.

69. Alston, *Perceiving God*, 244–45.

70. Pannenberg, *Jesus*, 98; "Concept of Miracle," 762; Rahner, *Theological Investigations*, 21:44; Zizioulas, "Preserving God's Creation (1)," 1–2.

There are real boundaries between science and theology, and these are not necessarily reducible to "explanation" vs. "understanding." Theology may have things to say about both physical and transcendent reality (e.g., miracles) that are unobservable to science. Theology does not have to bow to the ultimacy of science, but is independent and authoritative in its own right. If one accepts the rootedness of science in metaphysics in such things as the intelligibility and regularity of the universe, there may even be grounds, as Pannenberg observes,[71] for claiming that science is indebted to theology. On the other hand, science is a domain with its own legitimacy on the material level. Though bounded by methodological naturalism,[72] it may legitimately claim to be discovering things about the natural world that theology cannot simply ignore. Theology may seek to be coherent with the findings of science at an appropriate level, even while being aware that (1) these findings are provisional and subject to correction, (2) they are limited by the artificial (for theology) boundary of naturalism, and (3) they are unable to see the transcendent dimensions of reality available to religion.[73]

Given the mutual respect that science and theology ought therefore to exercise with regard to each other, it is time to turn to the natural sciences. In the chapters that follow, contemporary natural science is taken seriously, and an effort is made to discover what it says about human significance, and whether this is coherent with incarnational theology.

---

71. Hefner, "Role of Science," 273.

72. Stewart, *Reconstructing Science and Theology*, 11, 51.

73. Given these limitations, it may not even be too much to claim that theology is in an epistemologically superior position to science, since it can encompass science in its purview, but the reverse is not true. Pursuing this line of thought is beyond the scope of this thesis.

5

Human Uniqueness in the Natural Sciences

> The walls of human uniqueness are in pretty good shape after more than a century of Darwinian battering.
>
> —Robert Foley[1]

Introduction

ARE HUMAN BEINGS REALLY UNIQUE, AND IF SO, IN WHAT SENSE? These are the first questions for the natural sciences. Pannenberg, Rahner, and Zizioulas all emphasize the uniqueness of human nature and personhood, albeit in different ways. Can this emphasis be maintained in light of what contemporary science reveals about human distinctives. Darwin himself insisted his theory implied the continuity of animals with humans: he was sure the differences between them were a matter of *degree*, not of *kind*.[2] There are many similarities between humans and animals, such as physical features, possible common ancestry, and possession of a type of reason, emotion, and even relationships. Perhaps these indicate a closer link between humanity and the animals than Christianity's *imago Dei* doctrine has room for. Perhaps personhood is not only for humans and God. Humans share almost 99 percent of their DNA with apes and chimpanzees.[3] Many species of animals live in communities and have relationships with each other that bear striking similarities to human relationships. Whales and dolphins have strong kinship bonds and what may well be friendships with one another, including elements of communication and commitment. Recent studies seem to indicate

---

1. Foley, *Another Unique Species*, 1.
2. Darwin, *Descent of Man*, 931.
3. Gribbin and Cherfas, *First Chimpanzee*, 5.

that even sheep develop friendships and have cognitive recognition capabilities.[4] Some animals display aspects of friendship towards human beings, so that the loyalty and faithfulness of dogs is proverbial. Do we extend Christ's words, "No one has greater love than this, to lay down one's life for one's friends" (John 15:13), to the dog that dies defending its master, or to the animal mother that fights to the death defending her offspring? Do similarities to human qualities in animals mean they must be accorded human dignity?

Some, like Zizioulas or Hall, prefer a relational approach to the *imago*, perhaps to avoid altogether the substantive issues. Larkin goes so far as to ask whether relational capacity images God wherever it occurs.[5] Kevin Laland, following Darwin, argues that the difference between human and animal intelligence is one of degree rather than of kind, "since rudimentary forms of that which has traditionally been regarded as exclusively human are consistently found in animal populations."[6] Peterson agrees, believing modern theology would be better served by viewing the whole creation as the image of God, rather than confining that honor to humanity.[7] Peter Singer, with ethical rather than theological interest, wants to redefine personhood to include the animals. He argues that limited rationality, self-consciousness, and communication in many non-human creatures should lead us to treat them equally as "persons."[8]

Human Uniqueness in the Animal Kingdom

Animal Intelligence

How reasonable are these claims about the boundary between humans and animals? Are the substantive differences so small that the traditional uniqueness of the *imago* effectively disappears? These differences will be evaluated in terms of communication, intelligence, culture and ethics, summed up in the concept of the *human mind*. It is clear that many animals—not just the primates—have some type of inter-indi-

---

4. Kendrick et al., "Sheep don't forget a face," 165–66; see also Connor, "Sheep cannot be accused," 1.
5. Larkin, "Douglas John Hall," 19.
6. Laland, "Evolution of Culture," 433.
7. Peterson, "Are We Unique?," 177; "Evolution of Consciousness," 300–304.
8. Singer, *Practical Ethics*, 110–19.

vidual communication. E. Sue Savage-Rumbaugh insists that studies of apes, "dolphins, parrots, sea lions, elephants, and wolves" undermine the human notion of separateness. Since the closest approximation to human language and intelligence has been unveiled by primate research, this study will focus on that field.

Savage-Rumbaugh claims that captive ape language studies bring down "the boundary wall" between humans and apes.[9] She and Duane M. Rumbaugh taught a now-famous bonobo chimpanzee named Kanzi a repertoire of several hundred signs, which the bonobo was even able to manipulate in simple (two-word) sentences. Kanzi was tested at the age of eight against a one and a half-year old human child, Alia, and found to exceed her capabilities in many aspects of language.[10] Rumbaugh was so confident about primate language capacity that he declared, "the chimpanzee language projects allow us to state that neither the public production of language nor the cognitive prerequisites for this production are uniquely human. For a completely unique trait, we shall have to look elsewhere."[11] Kanzi's teachers were so optimistic that they suggested language was "the inevitable outcome of the social interaction of intelligent creatures."[12]

What are the implications of Kanzi's abilities? He has shown aptitude for certain aspects of language, such as symbol mastery and simple two-word sentence construction,[13] but this is not really what we mean and achieve with human language. His symbol mastery is close to that of a two-year old human, but, as the research of Jean Piaget and others on human cognitive development shows, the potential for moral development and other cognitive capacities present in two-year old human brain and intelligence is simply absent in other primates.[14] Kanzi surpassed one-and-a-half-year-old human Alia at some aspects of

---

9. Savage-Rumbaugh and Lewin, *Kanzi*, 253, 280.

10. Savage-Rumbaugh and Rumbaugh, "Ape-Language Research," 404; "Emergence of Language," 92–99; Peterson, "Evolution of Consciousness," 297.

11. Rumbaugh, *Language Learning*, 305.

12. Savage-Rumbaugh and Rumbaugh, "Eemergence of Language," 106; Savage-Rumbaugh and Lewin, *Kanzi*.

13. Peterson, "Evolution of Consciousness," 296–97.

14. Piaget, *Moral Judgment of the Child*; see also Smith et al., *Understanding Children's Development*, 218.

language,[15] but Alia rapidly eclipsed Kanzi's language skills—without the aid of artificial enhancements (keyboards and voice simulators)—and developed cognitively and morally in a way that is impossible for Kanzi. Even this comparison is misleading, because as Noble and Davidson note, human brain development is still ongoing at this early age, and so we should not expect a young child's abilities to match those of more mature humans, even while containing their potential. "Humans, of all primates, have the longest period of brain growth outside the mother. In consequence, human infants are dependent on caregivers for a higher proportion of their infancy, and much brain development takes place during this critical period."[16] Gordon Gallup Jr. and Steven Platek note that children only learn to recognize themselves and begin to show evidence of "prosocial and altruistic behavior" after eighteen months of age, commensurate with brain development underlying self- (and hence other-) recognition.[17] Peter Smith et al. note that *premoral judgment* is present in human children up to the age of four or five.[18] While by age eight, Kanzi did indeed have over one hundred fifty vocabulary symbols, and could string them together in two-word sentences, Steven Mithen observes:

> By the age of three a child frequently strings ten words together by the use of complex grammatical rules. By the age of six a child will have a vocabulary of about 13,000 words. Young children are constant commentators on the world around them and on what others say. Almost the entire sample of Kanzi's utterances is demands for things; his comments on the world are extremely rare.[19]

So Savage-Rumbaugh et al. admit that "near the completion of [their] test, Alia began to produce complex multiword utterances, and, across the next 6 months, her productive capacity leapt dramatically ahead of that of Kanzi, who failed to improve noticeably."[20] Terrence Deacon comments that despite years of such intense primate language research,

---

15. Savage-Rumbaugh and Rumbaugh, "Emergence of Language," 92–99; "Ape-Language Research," 404; Peterson, "Evolution of Consciousness," 297.
16. Noble and Davidson, *Human Evolution*, 213.
17. Gallup and Platek, "Cognitive Empathy," 36.
18. Smith et al., *Understanding Children's Development*.
19. Mithen, *Prehistory of the Mind*, 87.
20. Savage-Rumbaugh et al., *Language Comprehension*, 98.

neither Kanzi nor any other animal or species has shown more than a human toddler's grasp of symbolic communication.[21]

Savage-Rumbaugh and Rumbaugh want us to note that apes are capable of some aspects of language, but they are aware this is not fully developed language as humans have.[22] This slippery re-imagining of the meaning of language may be a sliding-definition ruse, since real language in humans involves a suite of features, all of which are present in human beings, including speech, "vocabulary, grammar, reference, representation, and syntax."[23] William Noble and Iain Davidson list the linguistic capacities of various non-human primates, including Kanzi, in terms of the design features of language outlined by Charles Hockett and Stuart Altmann, summarized in table 1 below. They suggest the key differences between human and non-human primates are the lack in the later of "four sets of features: (1) semanticity and arbitrariness; (2) discreteness, productivity, and duality of patterning; (3) displacement; and (4) (probably) traditional transmission."[24] If some of these features are absent or severely truncated in all primates, can claims for sharing language with them really be maintained?

Savage-Rumbaugh admits that apes are unable to speak because they lack the proper vocal anatomy.[25] Primate communication does not allow vocal instruction, discussion of previous experience, or future planning, as human language does.[26] Other animals have forms of communication, but the differences between language and all those other forms are vast. Chimpanzee vocalizations are emotive rather than cognitive, being controlled by the limbic system and brain stem rather than by the higher brain centers. While empathic responses have been observed in many types of animals,[27] these responses are in humans "extensively under cognitive control."[28] Animal communication is not

---

21. Deacon, *Symbolic Species*, 254–25.
22. Savage-Rumbaugh and Rumbaugh, "Ape-Language Research," 398–404.
23. Ibid., 398.
24. Noble and Davidson, *Human Evolution*, 46–47.
25. Savage-Rumbaugh and Lewin, *Kanzi*, 278; Savage-Rumbaugh et al., *Apes, Language*, 74.
26. Ronen, "Domestic Fire as Evidence," 444.
27. Preston and de Waal, "Empathy," 1–20.
28. Bandura, "Reflexive Empathy," 24.

just a different kind of language, as in *Dr. Dolittle*; it is different *from* language, closer to human non-verbal communication.

	Vervet	Gibbons	Orang-utan	Gorilla	Wild chimp-anzee	Wild bonobo	Kanzi	Human
Vocal-auditory	Y	Y	Y	Y	Y	Y	Y/?	Y
Broadcast/directional	Y	Y	Y	Y	Y	Y	Y	Y
Rapid Fading	Y	Y	Y	Y	Y	Y	Y	Y
Inter-Changeable	Y	?	?	?	?	?	?	Y
Total Feedback	Y	Y	Y	Y	Y	Y	N	Y
Specialized	Y	Y	Y	Y	Y	Y	Y	Y
Semanticity	?	Y/?	N	N	N	N	Y	Y
Arbitrariness	?	Y/?	N	N	N	?	?	Y
Discreteness	Y	Y	?	N	N	?	Y	Y
Displacement	N	N	N	N	N	N	?	Y
Productivity	N	N	N	N	N	?	?	Y
Traditional Transmission	Y	?	?	?	N/?	?	Y	Y
Duality of Patterning	?	N/?	N	N	N	N	?	Y

TABLE 1: Vocal utterances of some primates classified by design features of language.[29]

Ian Tattersall concludes that, contrary to the hopes of the most dedicated researchers involved in the most successful ape language ex-

29. Noble and Davidson, *Human Evolution, Language and Mind*, 47 (Used by permission. Adapted). Explanation of categories: *Vocal*—"vocal auditory channel"; *Broadcast/directional*—transmissions are broadcast with "directional reception"; *Rapid Fading*—speech sounds do not "hover in the air"; *Interchangeability*—members of "speech community" are interchangeably transmitters and receivers of linguistic sig-

periments, apes do not have even a rudimentary form of language as we know it, nor the "cognitive abilities that could be called prelinguistic." They "show no ability to comprehend grammar or syntax, can master no more than a handful of signs, and have no linguistic learning curve—or rather one which rapidly trails off to nothing. In sum, they do not have language, as we know it."[30] Barbour agrees, noting that chimps have "remarkable communicative abilities, but they fall far short of human symbolic language."[31] Tattersall concludes, "Human beings are truly unique in having language and in possessing the apparatus that permits them to acquire and express it ... [Our linguistic ability] with all the mental apparatuses of abstraction and association that involves, does appear to represent a quantum leap away from any other system of communication we can observe in the living world."[32] Deacon also insists linguistic capacity is a difference in *kind* of communication from that which takes place in all other creatures, not merely one of degree. Language is an "evolutionary anomaly, not merely an evolutionary extreme."[33]

---

nals; *Feedback*—"speaker hears everything relevant of what he says"; *Specialization*—"direct-energetic consequences of linguistic signals are biologically unimportant; only the triggering consequences are important"; *Semanticity*—associations "'between signal elements and features in the world' allow language signs to 'function to correlate and organize the life of the community'"; *Arbitrariness*—the meaning and symbol are independent—there is no "physical or geometrical resemblance between the two"; *Discreteness*—"possible messages in any language constitute a discrete repertoire rather than a continuous one"; *Displacement*—language can refer to things "remote in time, space, or both"; *Productivity*—"new linguistic messages are coined freely and easily, and, in context, are usually understood"; *Traditional transmission*—language is "passed down by teaching and learning," not biologically; *Duality of patterning*—patterning in language takes place in "arbitrary but stable meaningless signal-elements" and also in a "minimum meaningful arrangement of those elements." For category definitions, see Hockett and Altmann, "A Note on Design Features," 63–64. Table sources: Cheney and Seyfarth, *How Monkeys See the World*; Fossey, "Vocalizations of the mountain gorilla"; Hocket, "The origin of speech"; Hocket and Ascher, "The Human Revolution"; Hopkins and Savage-Rumbaugh, "Vocal communication in Pan paniscus"; Kano, "Study on the ecology of Pygmy Chimpanzees"; MacKinnon, "The behavior and ecology of wild orang-utans"; Marler, "Social organization, communication and signals in chimpanzee and gorilla"; Mitani, "Comparative studies of African ape vocal behavior"; Mitani, "Singing behavior of male gibbons"; Tuttle, *Apes of the World*.

30. Tattersall, *Becoming Human*, 32, 48, 60–68.
31. Barbour, *Nature, Human Nature, and God*, 44.
32. Tattersall, *Becoming Human*, 66–68.
33. Deacon, *Symbolic Species*, 13–33, 254–55.

Humans can only have language because of their unique vocal tract and their anomalously large brain.[34] The human cerebrum is larger in proportion to body size in humans than in any other animal, and the cerebellum is larger than that of most other animals.[35] Noble and Davidson note that while analogs to human communication centers are present in other primate brains, specific and unique areas of the human brain are "specially related to speech production and perception" (e.g., Broca's area).[36] Paul Mellars notes that "there is no doubt that modern human brains are significantly more complex, highly structured, efficient and intelligent than those of even the most intelligent great ape."[37] Deacon comments, "human brains are not just large ape brains, they are ape brains with some rather significant alterations of proportions and relationships between the parts." These alterations reflect an adaptation to the heavy cognitive demands of symbolic and representational learning. Language and the human brain are uniquely fitted to each other—they appear to be "coevolved." Humans are automatically adapted to learn language in a social environment, and language is developed by the brain, but conditions the brain to develop in particular ways. While there may be an unbroken continuity of evolutionary brain development from other animals to human beings, there is a "singular discontinuity between human and non-human minds." Human mental experience is qualitatively different from animal experience because only language opens the door of the symbolic and representational "virtual world."[38]

These qualitative differences are discontinuous with previous existent animal behaviors, possibly as a result of *emergence*. Harold Morowitz notes that unpredictable novelty seems to be generated throughout nature through processes of "emergent complexity," which "lead to a whole that is different from the sum of the parts," with otherwise unknowable system properties. Language and the human mind may well be an example of such emergence. If so, then its unique differences from animal mentality should not be surprising, even given physical evolutionary continuity, because such discontinuities have occurred throughout the history of nature, unpredictable and unknowable until they arrive on

34. Ibid., 13–33.
35. Penrose, *Emperor's New Mind*, 483–84.
36. Noble and Davidson, *Human Evolution*, 16.
37. Mellars, *Neanderthal Legacy*, 366.
38. Deacon, *Symbolic Species*, 22, 109, 254–55.

the scene.³⁹ Peacocke comments, "the concepts needed to describe and understand each emerging level in the hierarchy of complexity are specific to and distinctive of these levels."⁴⁰

Mary Midgley rightly points out that language cannot be "the only source of conceptual order," or else all other animals "would live in a totally disordered world."⁴¹ Animals are certainly intelligent, and likely have some type of self-consciousness or self-awareness, as evidenced by survival and self-defense reactions and more famously in mirror experiments, red-spot recognition by dolphins and chimpanzees, and animal self-grooming practices. Some primates deceive one another for survival, and some researchers even believe apes might show partial awareness of other's mental patterns.⁴² Do animals—particularly apes—recognize other's minds, or understand another's mental state? Do they have a "theory of mind"?

This is a key question. While it is difficult, as Thomas Nagel observed, to "get inside the minds" of other species to discover exactly how they experience reality,⁴³ observation suggests that animals generally lack a theory of mind. Dorothy Cheney and Robert Seyfarth note that even in chimpanzees, "there is very little evidence that [they] recognize a discrepancy between their own states of mind and the states of mind of others ... They show little empathy for each other, and they do not explicitly teach each other." Chimpanzees grieve at the loss of close friends, and have their own mental states, but do not seem able to empathize or be aware of others with similar mental states. "Monkeys and apes do occasionally act as if they recognize that other individuals have beliefs, but even the most compelling examples can usually be explained in terms of learned behavioral contingencies, without recourse to higher-order intentionality." Monkeys see the world in terms of action, not thinking and feeling.

> Although they are acutely sensitive to other animal's behavior, they know little about the knowledge or motives that cause animals to do what they do. In a monkey's world, the knowledge

39. Morowitz, *Emergence of Everything*, 14, 23, 159–62.
40. Peacocke, "Biology and a Theology of Evolution," 699.
41. Midgley, "Animals and Why They Matter," 56.
42. Bekoff, "Considering Animals," 229–45; Tattersall, *Becoming Human*, 47–48, 64–66.
43. Nagel, "What Is It Like to Be a Bat?," 165–80.

possessed by an individual exists in a kind of vacuum: the individual does not know what he knows and cannot recognize knowledge (or lack of it) in others."[44]

Rumbaugh also admits that "the so-called learning set skills of apes and monkeys are remarkably brittle ... something one would not expect if there were really a knowledge base of a human type underlying the mastery manifested by the animals ... Animals are not humans. Their cognitions, if extant, are surely both different and more circumscribed than in humans."[45] Daniel Povinelli et al. have found no "evidence that chimpanzees reason about intentions as internal states." In cooperation experiments, even trained chimpanzees, "when trained with ignorant partners ... do not respond by demonstrating the needed actions, or even by directing their ignorant partners behavior to the relevant features of the task—perhaps because they do not conceive of knowledge and ignorance to begin with." Povinelli et al. conclude that great apes and chimpanzees lack reasoning about other's internal mentality. They can solve very many problems, but "low-level models that envision chimpanzees as intelligent empirical generalists have consistently generated more accurate predictions about their behavior than have high-level models that envision them as making inferences about unobservable mental states."[46]

The development of a theory of mind and higher-order intentionality has long been recognized as a "watershed in children's cognitive development."[47] Michael Tomasello argues that human mental life uniquely involves understanding social intentionality and physical causality, both of which contribute to cultural cognition and social learning. He sees this social nature of human cognition, more than anything else, as unique to the human mind. Human enculterated learning is based on the ability to understand behavior as intentional. Children learn to use artifacts, tools, "symbols and other cognitive amplifiers of their culture by attempting to reproduce adults' intentional relations to them" or to the world. Children by age one are engaging in "all kinds of joint attentional interactions with others."

---

44. Cheney and Seyfarth, *How Monkeys See*, 252–55, 300–302.
45. Rumbaugh, "Animal Thinking," 35.
46. Povinelli et al., "Towards a Science of Other Minds," 531.
47. Cheney and Seyfarth, *How Monkeys See*, 252–55.

Because other primates do not understand conspecifics intentionally, they do not engage in cultural learning of this type, and, as a consequence, their societies do not follow the trajectory of human cultures in which the cognitive achievements of individuals accumulate and become embodied in artifacts over time—so that *developing children are able to participate in the whole cognitive history of their species.*[48]

Povinelli et al. conclude that "Darwin's view of psychological continuity" has severely limited our perceptions in analyzing non-human primate psychology, and held theories hostage to a theoretical framework that does not allow the animals to show both their similarities *and differences* from humans. This has resulted in models of cognitive development in which new mental abilities are "tacked on to the end of the developmental sequences of ancestral species ... ultimately leading to the [false] idea that chimpanzees" have achieved the psychological development of two- or three-year-old children. While there is continuity at some levels of human-animal psychology, Darwin "was wrong in assuming that introspection could reveal the nature of this similarity." Evolution of the ability to interpret behavior in mental "terms (our so-called theory of mind) may simply turn out to be a specialization" of the uniquely human hominid line. Humans and chimpanzees thus understand "nearly identical behaviors in radically different ways." The evolution of second-order intentional reasoning "allowed humans to re-interpret existing, extremely complicated social behaviors that evolved long before we did." Once this new mental representation "was in place, there may well have been cascading effects on larger aspects of the system—in this case, material and social culture including pedagogy and ethics, to name but a few."[49]

Language plays an enormous role in the structuring of the human mind. Noble and Davidson agree, noting that symbolic-linguistic behavior is responsible for the social construct of the modern human mind.[50] Dennett also agrees, and notes that we should not expect the other animals to have minds that are similarly structured. Since they lack language and have no need for language, their consciousness will be very different from ours: they will have no "Center of Narrative

---

48. Tomasello, "Primate Cognition," 357. Emphasis added.
49. Povinelli et al., "Towards a Science of Other Minds," 533, 535–36.
50. Noble and Davidson, *Human Evolution*, 84–87, 212–27.

Gravity," no regrets, no nostalgic reminiscences, no complex yearnings, no self-reflection on what it is like to be themselves.[51] In fact, language so structures the human perception of reality that in a real sense, "*nothing exists except through language*." This is not to advocate a type of "linguistic solipsism that denies our embedding in a world outside of our speaking." Rather, it acknowledges the unique language-shaped qualities of the domain of human interaction and commitment.[52] Merlin Donald notes that "our genes may be largely identical to those of a chimp or gorilla, but our cognitive architecture is not."[53]

Even the basic level of symbol mastery achieved by Kanzi only takes place in the context of an intensely human social environment.[54] Andrew Lock and Michael Colombo argue that ape intelligence may not just be revealed as "upgraded" by these various experiments; instead it may be the case that their intelligence is "scaffolded" on the support structure of human culture.[55] The fact that no kind of symbolic representation or linguistic mastery ever arises in other animals' natural condition,[56] is difficult at best to inculcate even for immature primates (when learning is apparently most easily accomplished[57]), and never reaches the level sufficient for moral reasoning, is indicative of the deep gulf between human and non-human intelligence. Tattersall insists that human intelligence is unique: we are not just more intelligent—we are *differently* intelligent, in a manner that allows us to view ourselves, but also to manipulate the environment around us, in a *qualitatively* different way from other creatures. Peterson admits that human intelligence *is* different. "It is not only the case that chimpanzees are less intelligent or less self-conscious than we are but also that they are *differently* intelligent, with their own drives, abilities, and emotional repertoire."[58] Tattersall concludes that while the "perceived cognitive gulf" between

---

51. Dennett, *Consciousness Explained*, 447–48.
52. Winograd and Flores, *Understanding Computers*, 68–69.
53. Donald, *Origins of the Modern Mind*, 382; *Mind So Rare*, 139–48.
54. Noble and Davidson, *Human Evolution*, 46.
55. Lock and Colombo, "Cognitive Abilities," 632.
56. Noble and Davidson, *Human Evolution*, 49–50.
57. Deacon, *Symbolic Species*, 125–27.
58. Peterson, *Minding God*, 136.

primates and humans has narrowed, it "is far from closed, and obviously never will be."⁵⁹

Neanderthal Intelligence

Did Neanderthals, who appear to have been our closest relative in the hominid family tree, have language, as we know it? Avraham Ronen argues for three distinct capacities evident in the paleontological-archaeological record that mark the uniqueness of humans: the presence of controlled fire, the elaborateness of burial customs, and the presence of symbolic representation, such as in art and burial objects. Controlled fire is "strictly and uniquely human," and Ronen concludes that it must have required language because of the level of social group cooperation, recognition of opposites (the beneficial hidden in the dangerous), and mathematical abstraction required for its maintenance.⁶⁰ Noble and Davidson agree, noting that "general control of production of fire" is unlikely prior to the modern human.⁶¹ Mellars attributes the extinction of Neanderthals at least in part to their inability to fully harness fire. When human population pressures where already marginalizing the Neanderthal, a period of sharply colder climate at approximately 33,000 years ago was overwhelming to the remnant Neanderthal population.⁶²

Tattersall notes that while Neanderthal brains were as big as ours, they were shaped differently, particularly in the area where much of our own thinking is done. Their skeletal remains bear witness to short and difficult lives, and the cultural traces they have left behind show little sign of symbolic representational thinking. While modern humans show rich symbolic thinking in cave paintings over 28,000 years old, as well as elaborate burial practices and grave goods indicative of belief in an afterlife, no such "represented symbolic activity [beyond] the simple expression of grief and loss" is evident at Neanderthal sites.⁶³ They appear to be foragers rather than collectors, with an absence or lesser expression of forward planning such as that displayed by modern humans.

59. Tattersall, *Becoming Human*, 48, 64–66.
60. Ronen, "Domestic Fire as Evidence," 439–47.
61. Noble and Davidson, *Human Evolution*, 207.
62. Mellars, "Impact of Climatic Changes," 501–3.
63. Tattersall, *Becoming Human*, 162, 178; see also Ronen, "Domestic Fire as Evidence," 441.

Jeffrey Laitman, Raymond Heimbuch, and Edmund Crelin have reconstructed the vocal tracts of various extinct and extant hominids and primates, and believe that Neanderthal vocal tracts were incapable of the vocal range available to modern humans. While which particular sounds Neanderthals could make is conjectural, they "probably had a different, narrower, range of vocalization available to them than do modern humans."[64] Tattersall concurs, noting their fossils generally show the wrong type of laryngeal descent for the complexity of adult human linguistic articulation.[65] Noble and Davidson argue that while limited physical linguistic potential might or might not have been present in Neanderthals, the real indicator of its absence is the lack of symbolic cultural remnants at Neanderthal sites.[66] Mellars and Tattersall agree that this is the most telling indication of all.[67] Tattersall notes that they have left no trace of such artifacts, found in modern human sites already at 30,000 years and indicative of the kind of grasp of "art, symbol, music, notation, language, feelings of mystery, mastery of diverse materials, and sheer cleverness" demonstrated by modern humans. He concludes:

> Symbolism lies at the very heart of what it means to be human ... if there is one single thing that distinguishes us from all other life forms, living or extinct, it is the capacity for symbolic thought: the ability to generate complex mental symbols and to manipulate them into new imaginative and creative combinations.[68]

Mithen notes the distinctive evidence in the archaeological record that marks the first manifestation of the modern human mind is the explosion of culture, what he calls the "big bang" of human mental capacity evidenced by symbolic artifactual remains. Evidence for something like the human mind is absent from Neanderthal sites, and is one of the reasons that it is much more difficult to imagine what it was like to be a Neanderthal (like Nagel's proverbial bat) than to be like the earliest modern humans.[69]

64. Laitman et al., "Basicranium of Fossil Hominids," 31.
65. Tattersall, *Last Neanderthal*, 171–72.
66. Noble and Davidson, *Human Evolution*, 212.
67. Mellars, *Neanderthal Legacy*, 366–91; Tattersall, *Becoming Human*, 177.
68. Tattersall, *Becoming Human*, 177.
69. Mithen, *Prehistory of the Mind*, 150.

Some have argued for a multi-regional model of human evolution, theorizing that Neanderthals were a related but different "population within a single evolving species," having contributed to the gene pool of modern humans. Such models propose a close evolutionary link between Cro-Magnon and Neanderthal, suggesting their coexistence in many times and places lead to crossbreeding and a significant Neanderthal contribution to the modern human species. But new research into the mtDNA of Cro-Magnon (23,000–25,000 years ago) and Neanderthal (29,000–42,000 years ago) by Giorgio Bertorelle and colleagues shows such sharp differences in the two species that crossbreeding is highly unlikely. Cro-Magnon DNA is almost indistinguishable from modern human DNA, while the genetic differences between modern humans and Neanderthals are noticeable and abrupt. While the multi-regional model predicts no major discontinuity if modern humans and Neanderthals are a single population observed at different times, the actual data and analysis of the DNA is inconsistent with such a theory. Bertorelle and his colleagues conclude:

> These results are at odds with the view whereby Neanderthals were genetically related with the anatomically modern ancestors of current Europeans or contributed to the present day human gene pool.... The sharp differentiation among them represents a problem for any model regarding the transition from archaic to modern humans as a process taking place within a single evolving human lineage.[70]

These findings are significant in that they demonstrate the real genetic distance between modern humans and Neanderthals, even during a time when they co-existed (Cro-Magnon—Middle/Upper Paleolithic). If interbreeding had been present, at least some mtDNA lineage relationship should be apparent, but it is not. The findings also give weight to the single out-of-Africa model for anatomically modern humans,[71] and undermine the contention that Neanderthal nature and intelligence is a closely evolved or intertwined cousin in the modern *Homo sapiens* lineage.

It appears from these findings that popular images of Neanderthals as our "close cousins"[72] are perhaps misleading, conveying a closer

---

70. Bertorelle et al., "Evidence for a Genetic Discontinuity," 6593–97.
71. Ibid., 6596.
72. E.g., in *X2: X-Men United* (2003) the mutant character "Storm" (played by Halle

sense of genetic, natural, and intellectual kinship with modern humans than is actually present. It seems from the paleontological record that Neanderthals did not have language or culture, as we know them, did not contribute to the human family tree, and likely did not relate to one another in the mode made possible by the symbolically structured human mind.

Human Ethical Capacity and Responsibility

One key aspect of human intelligence is ethical capacity or moral reasoning. George Gaylord Simpson called humans the "moral animal," arguing that humans represent not only a new phase of evolution, but also a new kind of evolution, possessing social, spiritual and intellectual capacities to an "incomparable degree." He claimed that human distinction is an "absolute difference of kind and not only a relative difference of degree."[73] Yet some argue that ethics are not uniquely human. Singer sees a type of ethics in certain primate behaviors, such as helping behavior or dominance structure.[74] Frans de Waal sees a kind of precursor to morality in "chimpanzee justice": behaviors of reciprocity and retribution that seem to suggest chimpanzees are "governed by the same sense of moral rightness and justice" as in humans.[75] Is morality really shared by other animals?

While recent research reveals the common ground shared by humans and primates, it also confirms human moral uniqueness. Christopher Boehm notes that human conceptual capacity is not present even in our closest living primate relatives, the chimpanzees, who appear to lack "an implicit conceptualization of death...and of killing as the immediate cause of death." Chimpanzees have no "morally induced positive and negative social incentive system that motivates individuals." Their "prey animals are killed incidentally in the process of being consumed," and strangers that are "savagely attacked are abandoned wounded."[76] Jane Goodall noted the extreme gap between chimpanzee and human emotional capacity. "I cannot conceive of chimpanzees

---

Berry) teaches children at the Museum of Natural History (NYC) that Neanderthals and early humans interbred to produce modern humans.

73. Simpson, *Meaning of Evolution*, 284, 293–95.
74. Singer, *Ethics*, 6–7.
75. Waal, "Chimpanzee Justice," 67–69.
76. Boehm, "Segmentary 'Warfare,'" 165.

developing emotions, one for another, comparable in any way to the tenderness, the protectiveness, tolerance, and spiritual exhilaration that are the hallmarks of human love in its truest and deepest sense. Chimpanzees usually show a lack of consideration for each other's feelings which in some ways may represent the deepest part of the gulf between them and us."[77]

Sociobiologists and evolutionary philosophers like Dawkins, Dennett, and Edward Wilson maintain that human moral behavior is an instinct or illusion—for Dennett, the very *self* is an illusion—a product of physical systems, natural laws, or the quest for genetic survival.[78] Others like Elliot Sober, David Wilson, and Holmes Rolston point out the diversity of motivations that are apparent in human behavior, some of which include self-interest, others altruism. It is too simplistic to regard such action as subconsciously motivated by survival or procreation; it simply does not fit the reality of Mother Theresas, self-sacrificing soldiers, and the practice of hospitality to strangers.[79] Rolston points out the category confusion in even attributing moral qualities like selfishness or altruism to non-human life forms that have no moral power to choose. Human moral capacity may be the product of natural selection, but once present, it is independent of the genes and endows humans with real freedom of choice.[80] So Watts notes the difficulty Dawkins has justifying or explaining altruism in his reductionist system.[81] Further, Leon Eisenberg insists that "theories that human behavior is based on instincts violate the findings of developmental biopsychology." Human intelligence "permits the conscious choice of goals and so differentiates [humans] from the rest of animate existence."[82]

Michael Leahy agrees that animal communication and related rational activities take place within a wholly determined instinctual limit.[83] Philip Hefner says, "the creatures who precede *Homo sapiens* ... live almost entirely on the basis of preprogrammed genetic information,"

77. Goodall, *In the Shadow of Man*, 194.
78. Dawkins, *Selfish Gene*, 2; Dennett, *Consciousness Explained*, 38–42, 95–98, 416; E. Wilson, *On Human Nature*, 4.
79. Sober and Wilson, *Unto Others*, 273, 324.
80. Rolston, *Genes, Genesis, and God*, 212 n. 1, 277–78.
81. Watts, "Multifaceted Nature," 54–55.
82. Eisenberg, "*Human* Nature of Human Nature," 123, 126.
83. Leahy, *Against Liberation*, 3–7.

relating "to the basic rhythms and requirements of their nature." As "the decisively cultural animal," humans remember their own rootedness in the age of predetermined instinct, and so have a sense of longing for that simple past, but are freed from necessity by their neo-cortically mediated mind and culture.[84] Peterson admits humans have a type of freedom shared by no other creature: only humans have the ability to override "what would in other species by inviolable biological drives."[85] Only human beings are capable of this type of free moral choice and action independent of instinctual imperative, and are thus able to engage in genuine open-ended interpersonal relationship. There is no such ability to choose available to the animals, whose behavior is largely determined by instinctual limitations.

The type of freedom humans possess is grounded in our unique capacity for symbolic reasoning, which makes possible a "new level of self determination" in the exploration of alternative futures and self-representation.[86] Morowitz suggests the capacity for such mental and linguistic mapping is also an emergent feature of the human mind, rooted in cellular and neurobiology.[87] Ayala notes the implications for ethics: ethical behavior is dependent upon human linguistic capacity, including abstract thinking and self-awareness, and "is not causally related to the social behavior of animals, including kin and reciprocal 'altruism.'" He notes three sufficient and necessary conditions for moral reasoning: (1) the ability to anticipate the consequences of one's own actions, (2) the ability to make value judgements, and (3) the ability to choose between alternative courses of action. Being able to anticipate one's actions requires the ability to connect means and ends, to anticipate imaginary potential futures. Being able to make value judgements requires the capacity for abstraction, "the capacity to perceive actions or objects as members of general classes." Being able to explore and choose between alternatives requires being released from instinctual imperatives, and understanding both the capacity for and consequences of our choices. Rudimentary forms of anticipation are present in earlier hominid toolmaking, but our ability to mentally explore complex future

---

84. Hefner, *Human Factor*, 132.

85. Peterson, *Minding God*, 175.

86. Barbour, *Nature, Human Nature, and God*, 44–45; referring to Deacon, *Symbolic Species*, 340.

87. Morowitz, *Emergence of Everything*, 161, 170–74.

alternatives and to compare classes at the moral level is contingent upon abstract symbolic intelligence. Our moral free will is dependent upon our well-developed intelligence and the capacity to explore multiple paths of possible action.[88] De Waal agrees that human ethical capacity depends upon its linguistic ability, and concludes that proto-moral behaviors are not moral in the sense of the deliberate, free, cognitive choices normative in human ethics. "Members of some species may reach tacit consensus about what kind of behavior to tolerate or inhibit in their midst, but without language the principles behind such decisions cannot be conceptualized, let alone debated."[89]

Rolston suggests that "chimpanzee justice" is at best "preethical," as there is "no sense of holding chimpanzees morally culpable or praiseworthy." He concludes that only humans are capable of ethics, of moral reasoning. Moral considerability (or worth) is not the same as moral capacity, which is present only in human beings.[90] So Deane-Drummond insists that it is a category mistake to ascribe moral reasoning to animals, "because they do not have a deliberative capacity. They do not participate in reason and so cannot have moral virtues."[91] Animals may be morally considerable, but only to humans, not to themselves. Leahy notes we sometimes attribute to animals purely human characteristics, leading to confusion about their capacities. Dogs are said to look guilty or sycophantic, foxes sly, owls wise, and apes cheeky. This is Wittgensteinian linguistic fuzziness, which leads to wrong conclusions about the subjects of discussion. In reality the ability to choose or defy a natural path on a moral basis, to engage in self-referential mental subterfuge, or to externally defy internal standards of behavior is simply not present in any creature except human beings.[92] Animals often display survival and predatory characteristics that could be interpreted as natural evil, yet these actions have no moral content, and so cannot be regarded as morally evil in the sense that is applied to human behavior. Animals uniformly act within a framework dictated by and consistent with their nature, in contrast to the human being, who alone

---

88. Ayala, "Human Nature," 41–45; Tattersall, *Becoming Human*, 65–68.
89. Waal, *Good Natured*, 209.
90. Rolston, *Genes, Genesis, and God*, 212 n. 1, 223.
91. Deane-Drummond, "Navigating the Maze."
92. Leahy, *Against Liberation*, 3–7.

seems capable of willful evil, of willfully violating its own nature and nature around it.

The moral and rational freedom of humans is a difference not merely of quantity, but of *quality* from the animals. This quality is what enables humans to have the highest form of relationship with each other and with God. They can be in free I-Thou relationship, rather than live out their lives in perpetually predetermined instinctual limits. This capacity for socially mediated symbolic representation, ethical freedom in relationship, and self-determination not only marks humans as unique, but also fundamentally underlies the essence of their *personhood*. Symbolic and representational thinking and communication are a prerequisite for moral reasoning, for meaningful choice and freedom in relation to the other, and for openness to the full reality of the other, including the transcendent God. Only a severe contraction of the concepts of personhood and morality will allow us to follow Singer. Although Zizioulas cautions us to beware of substantive definitions of personhood, it seems reasonable to suggest that at least in part, it is these substantive capacities that underlie what makes human beings *persons*, rather than simply animals or things. We are the symbolic species and the moral species, and this is why we can relate to each other and to God in the unique way that we do. This is what we mean by calling ourselves *persons*.

Human moral freedom and symbolic reasoning enables the exercise of *responsibility*. Emil Brunner highlighted this uniquely human capacity, believing it differentiates humans from both the animal kingdom and God. Humans are capable of responsibility because they have freedom, a limited freedom that flows from their creation in the image of God, who has ultimate freedom.[93] Only humans have the capacity for responsibility, and are therefore capable of receiving a charge to care for the world. Only they have the potential capacity to exercise responsibility beyond themselves, and to call the creation to more than itself. Leahy maintains that Singer has emasculated the concept of personhood because he has failed to incorporate this notion of responsibility. Though Singer wants to grant equal "human" rights at least to the class of animals that are minimally self-conscious and rational, he stops short of attributing to them responsibility, "because this would allow them to be punished for *wrongdoing* . . . of which all are agreed they can have no conception." By lowering the criteria for what we mean by personhood

---

93. Brunner, *Christian Doctrine*, 56.

to incorporate animals, Singer's concept "forfeits profitable comparisons with the treatment of human persons."[94]

The capacity for responsibility is thus a hallmark not only of the biblical picture of the *imago Dei*, but also of the scientific portrait of human uniqueness. Humans are free in relation to the world and can transcend it, be creative within it, master it, and be responsible for it. To follow Larkin in maintaining that the capacity for relationship might image God "wherever it occurs," is to conflate the radically different types of relationships that are possible between and among humans, animals, and God. Such an understanding of relationship does not take into account the unique realities of human personal, mental, and social life. It would be better to say that relationship is *part* of, rather than *being*, the image of God.

Conclusion

While modern science has closed some of the gap separating human beings from other creatures, it has also illuminated how wide and fixed the gap remains. Rolston insists that we "may welcome any continuity with animal life, while resisting reductions and rejoicing in the distinctively novel phenomena when humans arrive. Quantitative differences add into qualitative differences" that exceed previous evolutionary achievements.[95] Tattersall insists that the argument that *Homo sapiens* only did what its ancestors had done, only a little better or a little differently, is simply not true. Modern humans are a new kind of hominid, "qualitatively distinct in highly significant, if limited respects."[96] Donald concludes that "having reached a critical point in our cognitive evolution, we are symbol-making, networked creatures, unlike any that went before us ... This much is not speculation: humans are utterly different. Our minds function on several phylogenetically new representational planes, none of which are available to animals."[97] Ayala summarizes humanity's uniqueness as "embodied in a suite of features" that includes religious beliefs, ethical behavior, and enhanced intelligence.[98] Christian

---

94. Leahy, *Against Liberation*, 25.
95. Rolston, *Genes, Genesis, and God*, 141–42.
96. Tattersall, *Becoming Human*, 188.
97. Donald, *Origins of the Modern Mind*, 382.
98. Ayala, "Human Nature," 48.

De Duve concludes "one must be either deranged or dishonest not to view as immensely important and significant" humanity's unique creativity, rationality, and spirituality.[99] Thus these aspects of human uniqueness appear to be coherent with scientific data.

The common conviction that the difference between human and animal intelligence is one of degree rather than of kind overlooks the unique features of human symbolic, referential, social, and moral intelligence. While levels of communication, rationality, and consciousness are present in the animal kingdom, the human linguistic, social, and moral mind is unique, opening humans to freedom, responsibility, and a hitherto impossible depth of interpersonal relationship. Human symbolic reasoning, language, and moral capacity are not even potentially present in the rest of the animal kingdom. The further orientation of the human mind towards the transcendent, evident in worship, in wonder, in religion, and perhaps in mathematics, also appears to be absent in other material creatures. If it exists, it leaves no trace or observable symbolic artifact of itself. So Braine observes, "the order exhibited by human knowledge and understanding seems to exceed any of the kinds of order which materially precede it."[100] It is precisely because the human mind cannot be nailed down and predicted that it continues to elude scientific explanations. It is not one object among other objects, nor does it behave as essentially every other object does.[101] No other material creature discloses this indication of transcendence. Humans are not just different in *degree* from the animals. They are a different *kind* of creature.

Artificial Intelligence and Human Nature

Another modern challenge to human uniqueness and significance has arisen with the development of computer science, and particularly with the quest to create artificial intelligence (AI). Barbour remarked that Darwin threatened human dignity by leveling us with animals, and now at least in the minds of some, "human uniqueness seems to be threatened

---

99. De Duve, "Constraints," 532.
100. Braine, "Impossibility," 6.
101. Ian MacDonald, personal conversations with author at New College, Edinburgh, 2002.

by our resemblance to computers."[102] Zizioulas specifically questions the "substance" approach to human uniqueness because of the "growing prospect" of the creation of AI.[103] Will AI equal or surpass human intelligence? Some scientists argue that human intelligence is a result of complex organic brain circuitry that will eventually be mimicked and surpassed by the evolution of computers. They regard humans as "very sophisticated computers, [whose] self-conscious selves [are] a sort of sophisticated software that runs on the advanced neural circuitry of our brains."[104] Minds and brains are regarded as complicated machines, "composed of smaller things that cannot think at all."[105] The triumph of advanced IBM computer Deep Blue over Gary Kasparov in a game of chess in 1996 was widely hailed as a precursor to the AI future.[106] The 2001 Stephen Spielberg (and Stanley Kubrick) movie *A.I.* (2001) dramatized such a future, in which humanly designed AI beings eventually evolved and replaced humans as the highest life forms from the Earth. The movie concluded with these AI beings searching a frozen, dead Earth for clues about their now extinct creators. In a related twist on the "cosmic anthropocentrism" theme, Tom Stonier suggests that *"the cosmic function of Humanity is to act as the evolutionary interface between Life and Intelligence."*[107]

Noreen Herzfeld notes that the goal of much AI research is to create an *"imago hominis*, a machine that is in some way created in the image of the human person." That image is "more or less loosely defined" with various aspects of human nature, particularly *intelligence*. Herzfeld notes two questions at the center of the pursuit of AI. First, what is human intelligence? Second, how would we know if something sufficiently like it were present in a machine? She notes three different approaches to solving this problem. (1) *Symbolic*: construction to achieve the capacity for reason and rationality. (2) *Functional*: in which certain (not all) human tasks are successfully emulated by machines; successful single function emulation is said to represent *weak* AI, while a full production

---

102. Barbour, *Ethics in an Age of Technology*, 168.

103. Zizioulas, "Human Capacity and Incapacity," 407.

104. Peterson, "Are We Unique?" 5. Peterson gives Marvin Minsky and Douglas R. Hofstadter as examples; see Hofstadter, *Gödel, Escher, Bach*.

105. Minsky, *Society of Mind*, 322.

106. Peterson, *Minding God*, 3.

107. Stonier, *Beyond Information*, 214.

of human nature would be *strong* AI, after John Searle's nomenclature. (3) *Relational*: in which the machine is able to successfully produce the features involved in human relationships. The goal of each is to discover what it would take to ascribe to a machine the *imago hominis*, to create a machine capable of being a true friend to human beings.[108]

The Symbolic *Approach*

The *symbolic* approach has produced computers capable of some kinds of rational activity that have already surpassed human capacity. Complex mathematical calculations and proofs and Deep Blue's chess-playing ability are examples. However, as computer science has developed, the divergence between computer intelligence and human intelligence has become ever clearer. Peterson points out that while computers are excellent at algorithmic functions, following established sets of rules and logic to accomplish tasks, it is clear that their capacities "are quite modest when compared to human capabilities."[109] Initial hopes of surpassing this aspect of human intelligence, such as Marvin Minsky's prediction in 1970 that soon there would be "a machine with the general intelligence of an average human being,"[110] have given way to pessimism. The symbolic reasoning research has shown itself to be subject to the law of diminishing returns, giving ever less than its initial promise. The problems have included the difficulty inherent in encoding a huge general background database, in making gigantic visual and sensory input streams digestible, and perhaps even in the nature of human rationality itself.

Winograd, Flores, and Hubert Dreyfus argue that human intelligence is not just "a process of symbol manipulation," but includes bodily experience of the world and intuition not reducible to "symbolic manipulation."[111] The rationalistic mistake has been to view language purely as the vehicle for the transmission of data and information, and to overlook its deeply social role, including its central place in the structure and capacity for commitment. "To be human is to be the kind of being that generates commitments, through speaking and listening . . .

---

108. Herzfeld, *In Our Image: AI*, 33, 35–49.
109. Peterson, *Minding God*, 141.
110. Darrach, "Meet Shaky," 58D. See also Herzfeld, *In Our Image*, 37.
111. Herzfeld, *In Our Image*, 40–41.

We treat other people not as merely 'rational beings' but as 'responsible beings.'" Computers built on the rationalistic model are good as *tools* of language, "but they are incapable of making commitments and cannot themselves enter into language."[112] They conclude that it is unlikely the symbolic approach will produce "full, human-like intelligence."[113]

T. F. Torrance believes it is absurd to suppose AI can replicate the human mind because it is an attempt to replicate in machine structure a "mathematically impossible idea ... that logical-deductive systems can be consistent and complete ... [since] they are open to verification only beyond themselves."[114] Douglas Hofstadter, himself expecting to overcome this problem, traces the idea to J. R. Lucas, who insists that a machine must be subject to Gödel's incompleteness theorem, because a machine is by definition a "concrete instantiation of a formal system." Because of this limitation, "no machine can be a complete or adequate model of the mind ... minds are essentially different from machines."[115] Andy Clark argues that we must abandon the Cartesian notion of "the mental as a realm distinct from the body," and capture the essential embodiedness of human nature and intelligence—"spread ... across brain, body, world, and artifact"—if true artificial intelligence is to be achieved.[116] The modern understanding of the human person as a holistic embodied entity shows that the isolated creation of abstract mind will not be the equivalent of human nature. Our tendency to glorify *mind* has tempted us to dumb down human nature and complexity, and even to misunderstand the nature of mind itself. Herzfeld reminds us that our minds are fundamentally social and communal. "Rationality or Intelligence, by itself, is not the defining characteristic of being human. It [(being human)] cannot, in fact, be captured as an isolated quality."[117]

---

112. Winograd and Flores, *Understanding Computers*, 76, 106.

113. Dreyfus and Dreyfus, *Mind over Machine*.

114. Torrance, "Ultimate and Penultimate," 161. Refers to work done by Pascal, Cantor, Gödel and Turing on the inherent incompleteness of formal mathematics. Torrance critiques positivism, which "discounts the fundamental relationship between thought and being ... understanding and reality ... which any science precisely as science must presuppose."

115. Lucas, "Minds, Machines, and Gödel," 44; Hofstadter, *Gödel, Escher, Bach*, 577.

116. Clark, *Being There*, xi–xiii, 218, 220.

117. Herzfeld, *In Our Image*, 52.

The Functional Approach

The *functional* approach has also produced limited success, such as in industrial robots, in Deep Blue's chess playing capacity, or in the ability to compose music. David Cope created a computer program that emulated the musical style of famous classical composers, using principles of deconstruction, commonality ("retain that which signifies style"), and recombinancy ("recombine into new works"). Cope notes that "the works have delighted, angered, provoked, and terrified those who have heard them."[118] The music so created is convincing enough to fool even professionals.[119] Today's parallel processing machines are said to "learn," to be programmable as "expert systems," and are used to encode vast amounts of information to provide analysis and solutions in specialized fields.

But does the capability to mimic certain human roles make a machine artificially intelligent? The claim for *weak* AI is successful, since a narrow and specific human function is effectively replicated. However, the claim for *strong* AI has not been met. John McCarthy points out those expert systems are only expert in a very limited domain of expertise. Outside this narrow domain they are "brittle": they crack and break down.[120] The creators of Deep Blue insist its capacity is not artificial intelligence, since its parallel processing and standard programming do not in any way imitate real human thought.[121] As David Stork notes, "chess is far easier than innumerable tasks performed by an infant, such as understanding a simple story, recognizing objects and their relationships, understanding speech, and so forth. For these and nearly all realistic AI problems, the brute force methods in Deep Blue are hopelessly inadequate."[122] Others such as Barbour, Herzfeld, Winograd, and Flores insist that human intelligence is essentially embodied, social, and cultural, and cannot be realized in AI without such dimensions.[123] Rodney Brooks insists that now "human-level intelligence is too complex and too little understood to be correctly decomposed into the right

---

118. Cope, "One Approach," 21–25.
119. Peterson, *Minding God*, 144.
120. McCarthy, "Some Expert Systems," 129–35.
121. Herzfeld, *In Our Image*, 43.
122. Stork, "End of an Era."
123. Herzfeld, *In Our Image*, 47; Barbour, *Nature, Human Nature, and God*, 87; Winograd and Flores, *Understanding Computers*, 6–68.

subpieces," or to delineate the proper relationship between subpieces.[124] What looks at first like AI, such as Cope's musician's mimic, turns out to be a complex but limited program rather than true intelligence. Despite his program's success, Cope believes the computer is ultimately "just a tool with which we extend our minds." [125] As extensions, they are not independent competing minds. Indicative of the change in attitude towards *strong* AI's likelihood, McCarthy notes that formerly optimistic timelines projecting success in 50 years have changed to 500-year projections.[126]

The Relational Approach

The *relational* approach has likewise met with limited success. Initial optimism suggested computers could be taught to successfully imitate humans in conversational relationship. Alan Turing proposed the "imitation test" (the so-called "Turing Test"): if a human judge in blind conversation with a computer could be fooled into believing it was a person, the computer was deemed to be thinking.[127] To accomplish this task, algorithms for conversation emulation have been thoroughly, though not altogether successfully, programmed into computers. But is this really what we mean by "intelligence"?

The nature of human *consciousness* is central to the issue. Anne Foerst, working with the MIT robot COG (which has both embodied and social learning aspects in its assemblage), notes that many AI researchers consider consciousness to be illusory, and so adopt a functionalist view of both human and robot capacities.[128] Dennett, for instance, believes all human thought, from self-consciousness to decision-making, is ultimately computational and reproducible.[129] However, Foerst also notes that the AI research model of intelligence is not a comprehensive model, and does not take into account typically theological elements of human nature such as intuition, emotion, and spirit.[130] While some re-

124. Brooks, "Intelligence without Representation," 395.
125. Cope, "Experiments in Musical Intelligence," para. 8.
126. Herzfeld, *In Our Image*, 41, quoting McCarthy in a public lecture at Stanford University, March 10, 1999.
127. Turing, "Computing Machinery and Intelligence," 433–35.
128. Foerst, "COG, a Humanoid Robot," 104.
129. Dennett, *Consciousness Explained*.
130. Foerst, "COG, a Humanoid Robot," 108.

searchers insist cognition and emotion can be separated, and analogues to emotion programmed into machine software (e.g., fear and anger as self-defense programming), others point to the holistic nature of human consciousness that includes thought, emotion, and intuition rising in interrelated unity within the socially embodied person.[131] Nicholas Humphrey similarly suggests that human intelligence is incomprehensible without these fundamental aspects of sensation, emotion, and intuition. He is among those pessimistic about AI research pursued on purely symbolic grounds.[132]

Further, it is unclear that computer learning is the same as human learning, even when embodiedness is incorporated and relational aspects simulated. Searle argues that this is not truly human intelligence, because it confuses semantic understanding and intentionality with simple grammatical and syntactical competence, and simulation with duplication.[133] The machine is doing a programmed task without knowing it is doing it. Syntactical and grammatical competence may increase, but the machine does not "know that it knows" that it is learning; it is not truly *self*-conscious. As Rosalind Piccard notes, "biological processes may be simulated in a computer and we may construct computational mechanisms that function like human feelings, but this is not the same as duplicating them."[134]

Some Deeper Issues in the Quest for AI

Peterson believes the real question, beyond the form AI might take, is whether it is even possible, in particular because the nature of human consciousness is still not understood.[135] Even material reductionist Francis Crick admits, "what may be difficult or impossible to establish is the details of the subjective nature of consciousness, since this may depend upon the exact symbolism employed by each conscious organism."[136] Nagel agrees that the problem of subjectivity is central

---

131. Barbour, *Nature, Human Nature, and God*, 87–88.
132. Humphrey, "Private World of Consciousness," 23–24.
133. Searle, "Minds, Brains, and Programs," 417–24.
134. Picard, *Affective Computing*, 136.
135. Peterson, *Minding God*, 143.
136. Crick, *Astonishing Hypothesis*, 252.

to the mind-body question.[137] This question is at the heart of the AI quest. A successfully *strong* AI machine would have to at least have symbolic, functional, and relational capacities equivalent to human nature, including real subjectivity. But Piccard concludes that because human consciousness is still not understood, we simply cannot yet tell if it can be duplicated, rather than simply imitated in a computer. Perhaps our biology is "uniquely able to generate" human subjective feelings.[138] "Scientists have not yet foreseen any means of bridging the deep chasm between what machines can do and the kind of experience, emotional or not, we as humans have continuously."[139] Barbour suspects that human consciousness "requires forms of organized complexity or properties of neural cells and networks that have no parallels in silicon-based systems" and therefore computer consciousness is an empirical (though not metaphysical) impossibility. He leaves the question open on the grounds of our current ignorance.[140]

The dominant paradigm in modern natural sciences is that human nature is entirely a product of the physical world. *Mind* is understood as essentially a phenomenon of brain states, an emergent property of a complex physical system, although various levels of complexity and relatedness between the mind, brain, and body are recognized.[141] For instance, Crick openly declares, "You're nothing but a pack of neurons," after rejecting body-soul dualism in favor of materialistic reductionism.[142] Owen Flanagan opts for a non-reductive materialist model as the best explanation of the human mind.[143] Both models are monistic in holding to a purely physical description of human nature. However, there is no guarantee that the monistic view is correct. As both De Duve and Peterson observe, the mind-brain problem has yet to be solved. Human consciousness still has "only a phenomenological account but no objective explanation."[144]

137. Nagel, "What Is It Like to Be a Bat?," 165–67.
138. Piccard, *Affective Computing*, 136.
139. Picard and Klein, "Computers That Recognize," 162.
140. Barbour, *Nature, Human Nature, and God*, 89.
141. De Duve, "Lessons of Life," 8–9; see also Barbour, *Nature, Human Nature, and God*, 90–100.
142. Crick, *Astonishing Hypothesis*, 3.
143. Flanagan, *Consciousness Reconsidered*, 220–22.
144. De Duve, "Lessons of Life," 9; Peterson, *Minding God*, 49.

If human intelligence is just an emergent property of a sufficiently complex neural network, linguistically expressed by a suitably embodied social and cultural apparatus, then it may well be possible that in x years, scientific advances will replicate the necessary conditions for self-aware AI in a machine of some type, perhaps on an organic rather than a silicon substrate. If such were to happen, Barbour suggests that AI beings would have to be included in our sphere of moral concern, just as are animals at their level of intelligence. Human dignity would nevertheless not be fundamentally jeopardized, because AI status would be based on its *similarity to us*.[145] Then humans might look on themselves, as Stonier suggested, as the cosmic *Adam* of intelligent beings, their original ancestor and creator. Peterson agrees with Barbour that the Christian doctrine of the *imago Dei* has caused us to emphasize our uniqueness rather than our similarity with other creatures, and the creation of such AI would offer occasion for a debate like that surrounding the moral status of animals.[146] Foerst suggests that the success of AI, while keeping us humble, need not be taken as negative or threatening to human dignity, because AI is "yet another story about humanity," about our created nature and our own creativity, and can help us understand ourselves without challenging our status as *imago Dei*. For Foerst, the image of God is not the same as the *imago hominis*. The *imago Dei* is not something that marks us as qualitatively different from other creatures, including potential AI. It is not to be found in unique skills and abilities, but is rather *performative*, found in the promise of a relationship between God and humans.[147]

There remains the real possibility that human consciousness and intelligence are more than physical constructs, more even than emergent properties of non-reductively understood natural systems. Because the consciousness problem has not been solved, the possibility of an immaterial or "spiritual" dimension to human nature cannot be eliminated. There may be some evidence of a more complex relationship between the mind/body/brain/spirit than that offered by the monistic materialist view, in medical research into near-death experiences (NDE). People who have had NDE report many phenomena suggestive of some type of non-corporeal aspect to human nature. These reports include out-

---

145. Barbour, *Nature, Human Nature, and God*, 89.
146. Peterson, *Minding God*, 148.
147. Foerst, "COG, a Humanoid Robot," 104–9.

of-body experiences, meeting deceased persons, moving through a tunnel, communication with light, observation of colors, observation of a celestial landscape,[148] and observing objects or people (often medical personnel) in their surroundings that they should not have been aware of in their unconscious or "dead" state.[149] Dr. Pim van Lommel, in a famous thirteen-year study of NDEs at various hospitals in Holland, comments:

> How could a clear consciousness outside one's body be experienced at the moment that the brain no longer functions during a period of clinical death with flat EEG? Also, in cardiac arrest the EEG usually becomes flat in most cases within about 10 s from onset of syncope. Furthermore, blind people have described veridical perception during out-of-body experiences at the time of this experience. NDE pushes at the limits of medical ideas about the range of human consciousness and the mind-brain relation.[150]

Van Lommel is not alone, as many medical researchers report similar findings.[151]

Some suggest that consciousness is a quantum mechanical phenomenon, after Roger Penrose's idea, and may continue to exist in the quantum sphere for a time after death, independent of the body.[152] While Penrose's suggestion is controversial and speculative, it does point to the real issue. Susan Blackmore says the crux of the argument is whether NDEs are a result of the dying brain or are indicative of the afterlife or a non-corporeal aspect to human nature. While Blackmore attributes these experiences to the dying brain, her position is not the majority position among NDE researchers even by her own admission. Interestingly, in her own out-of-body experience ("inspired" by drugs), Blackmore reported seeing her disembodied self connected to her physical body by a silver cord (see Eccl 12:6.).[153] Others, like neurolo-

148. Lommel et al., "Near-death Experience," 2039–45.
149. *BBC News*, "Life after near death."
150. Lommel et al., "Near-death Experience."
151. E.g., Clute and Levy, "Electroencephalographic Changes," 821–25; Aminoff et al., "Electrocerebral Accompaniments," 791–96; Ring and Cooper, *Mindsight*; van Lommel refers to Sabom, *Recollections of Death*, 37–52. See also Morey, *Death and the Afterlife*; Cooper, *Body, Soul and Life*.
152. BBC2, "The Day I Died"; Penrose, *Emporer's New Mind*, 483–578, esp. 552.
153. Blackmore, *Beyond the Body*, 225–52; *Dying to Live*, 260–64.

gist Bruce Greyson of the University of Virginia, suspect there is more to it than brain states. As Paul Badham puts it, "people who report near death experiences sometimes 'see' things that it would be impossible for them to see if they had been unconscious on an operating table."[154]

It would be foolish to claim too much for NDEs. As Elizabeth Hillstrom observes, NDErs from variant religious backgrounds seem to have experiences of the afterlife that reflect their own expectations. This suggests that at least some NDE content "may tell us more about the NDEr's cultural and religious expectations than about the afterlife."[155] But NDEs are at least suggestive of a component of human nature that transcends modern physicalist and non-reductive materialist interpretations.[156] This evidence at the frontiers of medical research is even more compelling given the failure of current paradigms to solve the consciousness problem.

There are other good reasons to believe that monistic naturalist approaches to the world and human nature are inadequate, despite their dominance. Watts notes, "the scientific tradition is actually more confused on these matters than attention to neuroscience alone would suggest."[157] At least some, like Penrose and Polkinghorne, suggest that our human perceptions of mathematical truth indicate a connection to a non-material "noetic" realm of reality.[158] Penrose believes modern physics has not progressed far enough to even understand this consciousness of "the Platonic world of mathematical forms."[159] Peter Dodwell notes that "old-fashioned materialism is the way things are in cognitive science." It still subscribes "to a view of the material basis of the world . . . that was abandoned by physics no later than the 1920s." Dodwell believes this older view may provide "too severe a constraint on the possible ways of understanding mind."[160] This may help to explain the lack of success in solving the mind-body problem and in reconciling a host of theological and scientific perspectives on various related issues,

---

154. *BBC News*, "Life after near death," quoting Paul Badham of Lampeter University.

155. Hillstrom, *Testing the Spirits*, 91.

156. Sabom, *Recollections of Death*, 245–55.

157. Watts, "Multifaceted Nature," 49.

158. Polkinghorne, *Science and Creation*, 75–77.

159. Penrose, *Shadows of the Mind*, 406–420.

160. Dodwell, *Brave New Mind*, 9, 169.

since expectations can blind perceivers to actual and viable alternatives. Super-string theory in astrophysics, if true, suggests that there are multiple dimensions to reality beyond the four (three spatial + time) normally perceived dimensions of human experience. With perhaps even as many as ten dimensions needed to reconcile quantum physics with relativity,[161] theoretical physics intimates the limitations of basic human experience for accessing a complete understanding of reality.

The transcendent aspect of human nature suggested by NDE might indicate that no purely materialistic AI project could be completely successful. De Duve's insistence that our view of material reality must be enlarged to encompass what was formerly called "spirit" might be instructive in this regard.[162] The current paradigm seems likely to be too limited to explicate the human mind. If the human spirit is *nonmaterial*, then it is a category error to suppose it could be empirically evident to or reproducible by the natural sciences. That this appears to be a form of dualism does not automatically invalidate it.[163] Picard notes that while the belief in "something in humans beyond duplicatable mechanisms—something akin to an élan vital—is derided by many of today's philosophers, their derision is not based in science. It is a valid possibility that there may exist some aspect of humanity that we cannot duplicate, short of procreation."[164] Then the best AI might be expected to achieve would be the reproduction of something perhaps analogous to animal intelligence[165]: *weak* AI.

Conclusion

Current AI research cannot produce a machine or robot that is self-conscious, emotive, intuitive, willful, capable of personal bodily relationship, moral choice, or personal responsibility, and seems unlikely

---

161. Greene, *Elegant Universe*.

162. De Duve, "Lessons of Life," 10.

163. This need not imply the theological rejection of a holistic embodied view of human completion, which is entailed in the Christian doctrine of the resurrection (see §3.5.1).

164. Picard, *Affective Computing*, 136.

165. Assuming animals lack the equivalent of the human spirit. Paul Badham sees three possible reasons to suspect this is so: "the experience of separation from the body near the point of death, the experience of reflective rational thought, and the experience of divine human encounter in ways that transcend the physical ("Do Animals Have Immortal Souls?," 189).

to do so in the near future. Since science is still far from solving the mind-body-brain problem, there is a real element of the unknown that may prove to be forever insurmountable. In theological perspective, if AI were to be truly an *imago hominis*—*strong* AI—there would need to be a true "I" within the machine capable of moral responsibility, of I-Thou relationships with humans, perhaps even possibly with God. Even given the success of a *strong* AI project, human status may still not be jeopardized, since it would be AI only by virtue of human genesis and genius.

Finally, a theological appraisal of both *weak* and *strong* AI will be aware of the differences in the scientific and theological perspectives on reality. Even if science succeeded in creating what it deemed to be *strong* AI, it might, as Foerst notes, still be far from a theological understanding of human nature as the *imago Dei*. "If one could reduce human personality and subjectivity to computational and mechanistic processes, one would interpret humans . . . *as objects*."[166] In this sense, the *imago hominis* is not the same as the *imago Dei*; the two should not be confused. Barbour agrees that AI "is not a threat to human dignity unless we start to think of ourselves as only information processors and symbol manipulators."[167] This is the advantage of Zizioulas' insistence that human nature must be understood in terms of *personhood*, not substance. Such an understanding moves us beyond issues of "capacity and incapacity."[168]

Scripture is essentially silent on the issue of artificial intelligence, outside of one intriguing passage in Revelation 13:14–18 that may just refer to something like AI. There, the "image of the beast" is given breath so that it "could even speak and cause those who would not worship the image of the beast to be killed." This is placed in the same context as the "mark of the beast," which is given to the inhabitants of the Earth who cannot buy or sell without it. This image has been a popular apocalyptic icon in our computer-saturated market culture.[169] Does the "mark" represent computer labeling? Does the "breath" and "power to speak" represent some type of artificial intelligence? Whatever this may mean

---

166. Foerst, "Artificial Intelligence," 681–93. Emphasis added.

167. Barbour, *Ethics in an Age of Technology*, 175.

168. Zizioulas, "Human Capacity and Incapacity," 407.

169. Various modern apocalyptic writers use the image as a sign that our age is already preparing for such a "beastly" day.

about the future possibility of AI, the passage does point to humanity's idolatrous temptation to self-worship, to know themselves as other than *persons* made in God's image. It also points to theology's responsibility to call all human quests for knowledge to account before God, for the beast *is* the beast precisely because it utterly rejects God and puts humanity in the place of God.

Human Uniqueness and Extraterrestrial Intelligence

While data on animal, hominid, and artificial intelligence is readily available from the natural sciences, the same cannot be said of evidence concerning extraterrestrial intelligence (ETI). For this reason, most of the discussion on the subject is speculative and philosophical, dealing with probabilities, theories, and potentialities, rather than concrete facts. There are some scientific data that are relevant to the discussion, particularly related to the Earth's suitability for life, which may shed light on the probability of ETI. After reviewing the speculative and philosophical views, this data will be investigated for its implications, and conclusions drawn on the probability of ETI and the significance of human existence from a strictly natural science perspective.

Extraterrestrial Life—the Unanswered Question

A review of the ETI perspectives already uncovered in the three ecumenical theologians illustrates the diverse conclusions also present in the natural sciences. Pannenberg notes the basic facts concerning the current scientific data on ETI, which may be summarized succinctly: there are none. With no hard data available to decide the case, there is no agreement as to whether non-terrestrial life and intelligence will ever be found, some researchers supporting, others refuting the possibility.[170] Rahner is more open to the possibility of ETI due to his incorporation of evolutionary processes in the center of his theological program, and he is ready to downgrade human cosmic uniqueness to the point of speculating on multiple incarnations. He is also ready to include the biblical angels in the ETI category, since he believes angels might be creatures that have arisen in the earlier history of the universe's evolutionary processes. Some of the problems in these views have already been examined, including their internal inconsistency and lack of sup-

---

170. Pannenberg, *Systematic Theology*, 2:75–76.

porting evidence. Without repeating those arguments, angels will be set aside from ETI consideration as currently inaccessible to the natural sciences. Zizioulas is essentially silent on the topic of ETI, although a neutral but human-centered position may be inferred from his emphasis on cosmic Christology.

Without any concrete data from SETI or other sources on the existence of ETI, some believe objective science is best served by remaining open-minded—unconvinced without hard data but open to the possibility. Others insist that ETI will be ubiquitous in a universe governed by laws of emergent complexity, and that we are justified in putting our faith in their existence. Still others are skeptical, insisting evolution is a series of strung-together lucky chances, unlikely in the first place, and unlikely to be repeated elsewhere. A divide is apparent, which will now be examined more closely.

The Theoretical Probability of ETI

A sample of perspectives in the natural sciences on the question of ETI, particularly as it is supposed to be a result of evolutionary processes, is sufficient to show the divide in the debate.

Jacques Monod thinks life's rise on the Earth was by chance, a freak accident that has never happened again.[171] Ernst Mayr concludes that "an evolutionist is impressed by the incredible improbability of intelligent life ever to have evolved."[172] Stephen Jay Gould agrees, noting the improbability and contingency of all evolution, including human.[173] Rolston points out that while intelligence in general may be favored by evolution, the type of intelligence in "self-conscious personality sufficient to build cumulative transmissible cultures" has only appeared once in Earth's evolutionary history. This is so despite the fact that there are "five to ten million species" alive today, and "five to ten billion species that have come and gone over evolutionary time."[174] In a similar vein, Deacon notes that we tend to think that given enough time, the Earth will inevitably have *Planet of the Apes* scenarios: something like language is prefigured into evolution. We expect the same thing of the

---

171. Monod, *Chance and Necessity*, 43–44, 145–46.
172. Mayr, *Toward a New Philosophy*, 69.
173. Gould, *Wonderful Life*, 292, 323.
174. Rolston, *Genes, Genesis, and God*, 113.

rest of the universe, hence the enthusiasm in SETI. However, he believes this is a subconscious kind of teleology. Once the concept of design is eliminated as a subconscious reading of evolution, then in fact only the budding of evolution into unfilled niches makes any sense, and the niche representing massive brain function is "near the extreme of the distribution." He maintains that "there is no evidence in living species that some inevitable progressive trend leads to us." Humans are not the trend, but the exception.[175]

Dawkins offers something of a bridge perspective: "The essence of life is statistical improbability on a colossal scale. Whatever is the explanation for life, therefore, it cannot be chance." He suggests that single step cumulative selection, by "slow and gradual degrees," has driven the evolutionary process toward inexorable diversity.[176]

De Duve and others take neural evolution as likely because a "more effective brain" is a survival advantage. They point to the gradual increase over time of brain size in animals, and particularly in hominid fossils, as evidence of this contention. De Duve holds that "the emergence of humankind or, at least, of conscious, intelligent beings, appears as much less improbable than many maintain. Contrary to what Monod stated, the biosphere *was* pregnant with man."[177] Peacocke is hopeful that in light of laws of emergent complexity, life and higher life forms are an essential part of the universe's potential. Since in his view no part of life is a result of special creation, but rather is everywhere a result of purely natural processes, ETI is likely given the inbuilt potentiality of the universe.[178] Simon Conway Morris agrees that evolution inevitably moves towards increased complexity, believing the wonderful proliferation of life in the world suggests a process rich with potentiality and possibility. Mathematically bounded complexity in seashells and other creatures, and convergent evolution in divergent species towards eyes, limbs, brains, and other organs, suggests to Conway Morris inevitability in the process.[179]

While Deacon sees the question as essentially dysteleological, De Duve takes an opposite position, ready to see the divine hand behind

---

175. Deacon, *Symbolic Species*, 30.
176. Dawkins, *Blind Watchmaker*, 317.
177. De Duve, "Lessons of Life," 8; "Constraints," 525–31.
178. Peacocke, "Challenge and Stimulus," 103.
179. Conway Morris, *Crucible of Creation*, 199–206.

the evolutionary scheme. If Deacon is right, then his observations highlight human uniqueness in a strictly reductionistic scientific sense, even without teleological considerations. If De Duve is right, this seems to place humanity in a richly spiritual context that gives meaning and significance to human existence based on this relationship to the divine, even without human uniqueness.

However, the problem with both views is that they remain philosophical and speculative on the ETI question. They are representative of the wider philosophical divide as to whether evolution is a quirky chance process of dumb luck, or an inevitable outcome of universal laws. Life is either unique to Earth or present everywhere. The universe demonstrates teleology or it doesn't. ETI must exist, or cannot exist. The divide seems immense. Is there some objective means for deciding which view is correct?

The Rare Earth Hypothesis

Perhaps a middle way between the two extremes may be found that takes account of physical data and might allow for a more fully supported answer to the SETI question. The natural sciences are aware of the *anthropic* conditions that are necessary for the universe to develop conscious life. But these initial conditions are not the only conditions needed for life. There are ongoing, very specific and contingent conditions needed to explain the rise of intelligent life locally, on planet Earth—conditions that might or might not be the inevitable results of cosmic processes. These are what might be called "local fine-tuning" features, which are as necessary and important for the development and existence of life specifically on Earth as those anthropic conditions are for the general rise of life in the whole universe.

Peter Ward and Donald Brownlee examine and catalog some of these conditions, formulating their so-called *rare Earth* hypothesis as a conclusion.[180] A representative sample gives a general feel for the type of unique boundaries Earth's biosystem requires. Among these are:

1. The nature and location in the galaxy of Earth's star Sol: too close to the center of the galaxy, and there is too much radiation; too far from the center, and there aren't enough heavy elements.

---

180. Ward and Brownlee, *Rare Earth*, xxiv, 275.

2. The age and location of our galaxy in the whole cosmos. If our galaxy is too young and metal poor, there are not enough of the elements needed for life; too old, and the galaxy's shape may be disastrous.

3. The presence and circular orbits of the gas giants Jupiter and Saturn. Without such "sweepers" in perfect orbit, catastrophic, life-terminating asteroids would hit the Earth at too frequent intervals, and life would never have gotten off the ground; if their orbits were too elliptical, the gas giants would tear Earth apart by tidal forces.

4. The location, dimensions, and content of Earth and its moon. Earth is the optimal distance from the sun for carbon-based life forms, has its own internal heat source, is large enough to retain an appropriate atmosphere, and has tidal forces that are essential to make an appropriate life environment, but not so strong as to tear the Earth apart.

5. Various mass extinction events have formed contingent boundaries for significant changes in the history of life on Earth. Evolution took some far from predictable turnings—so far as to put human intelligence at the extreme outside of any curve of evolutionary probability—at least in part due to these extinction events.[181]

Ward and Brownlee have combined the work of others to draw their conclusions. For instance, George Wetherill and Ray Jawawardhana observe the special role Jupiter plays for life on Earth, and its rarity in the universe.[182] Andrew Fortes and others have noted the importance of Earth's magnetic field in supporting and protecting life from destructive solar and interstellar radiation. Planets without a circulating iron core like Earth's do not generate such fields. This may be one reason why Mars has no full atmosphere and no unambiguous evidence of life: smaller than Earth, its molten core, the source of its ancient magnetic field, has solidified long ago. Without magnetic protection, the solar wind has long since ripped away much of the atmosphere (referred to as "scavenging"), including large amounts of oxygen and nitrogen and

---

181. Ibid.; Ross, "Design Evidences."
182. Wetherill, "How Special Is Jupiter?," 470; Jawawardhana, "No Alien Jupiters," 1527.

much of the water, and killed most potential for life the planet may once have had.[183]

There are a host of similar conditions that have bounded the development of life on Earth. Taken separately, each condition might be distributed throughout the universe. Taken together—the requirements for life on Earth—they may converge extremely rarely. It is also clear that evolutionary complexity is contingent upon local time-bound conditions. Life's history on Earth shows vast periods of evolutionary stasis: for three billion of the last three and one-half billion years, most life has been limited to the simplest of single-celled organisms. Evolution does *not* have to give rise to just any outcome or other, including higher life forms. Rapidly advancing evolution is therefore by no means a foregone conclusion. Carter suggests an *anthropic* reason for believing sentient evolution is far from inevitable. In our case, it only happened half way through the typical life of a stable hydrogen-burning star, and there are many reasons to believe the "*typical* time taken for biological evolution is *much greater* than stellar ages."[184] Conway Morris notes the rarity of habitable Earth, and agrees sentience may be equally rare, even if evolution progresses inevitably once started.[185] A unique constellation of life-supporting features has come together in this corner of the galaxy, in this solar system, and on this planet Earth, that may well never have happened anywhere else in the cosmos. Earth is at the least very rare and possibly unique in its suitability for the development of life, as we know it.

Conclusions

We are now in a position to tentatively apply this data to the question of ETI. Based on the evidence, Ward and Brownlee conclude that while lower life forms might be common in the universe if laws of complexity hold, higher life forms are probably much rarer, and suggest that sophisticated intelligence like humanity's may be so rare that it has only had time to happen once in cosmic history. While universal laws of evolutionary development might readily move matter from states of lower

---

183. Fortes, "Magnetic Fields of the Planets" and "Magnetic Fields at Mars"; Acuna et al., "Magnetic Field and Plasma Observation"; Ross, "Design Evidences."

184. Carter, "Anthropic Principle," 290.

185. Conway Morris, *Crucible of Creation*, 223–24 n. 1; see also his *Life's Solution*.

to higher complexity, including into actual forms of life elsewhere in the universe, this is no indication or guarantee that ETI equivalent to human intelligence has ever developed or could ever develop without a host of contingent and together highly unlikely conditions. Conway Morris concludes that while the richness of the process of evolution on Earth makes the appearance of something like humans inevitable, it seems that Earth-type planets may be vary rare in the universe—"much rarer than hoped." Although the laws of the universe are "tailor-made" to enable the development of such living complexity, they operate only in suitable conditions, conditions possibly unique to Earth or likely to be found only rarely in the universe. "Inevitable humans, yes, but in a lonely Universe."[186]

From the preceding discussion, it seems that there may be scientific grounds to believe that ETI either does not exist at all, or is vanishingly rare in the cosmos, such that we may expect never to find it. From such a perspective, until concrete evidence emerges of higher life in other solar systems, it seems prudent to remain skeptical about its existence.

Conclusion

In conclusion, the modern natural sciences have converged to recognize those aspects of human nature that are unique not only on the Earth, but also very likely in the universe. Human intelligence, linguistic capacity, moral and relational freedom, spiritual nature and awareness, and social and cultural creativity are unique in the world, and—as far as we know—in the material cosmos. There is no creature in the animal kingdom with comparable capacities and potential. Artificial intelligence is unlikely to copy human nature anytime soon. In fact, it may well be impossible practically and theoretically to establish true humanlike self-consciousness and volition in a machine. Extraterrestrial intelligence also appears unlikely to challenge human uniqueness. Although it may not be theoretically impossible—depending on one's position on evolutionary inevitability—ETI may be statistically improbable, especially in light of Earth's uniqueness.

As the one creature in the cosmos made in the image of the Creator, this is not a surprise to theology. Christianity has long recognized the divide between humans and other creatures that is now apparent in

---

186. Ibid.

certain aspects of science. So Barbour concludes that the picture of human uniqueness emerging from "our knowledge of evolutionary history" is consistent with the Scripture that draws "*an absolute line* between humans and all other creatures."[187] Ingrid Shafer observes that human linguistic uniqueness "has been intuitively grasped since ancient times," preserved "in Judeo-Christian tradition . . . in such images or stories as God revealed/concealed in the four letters of the Tetragrammaton, as Adam naming the inhabitants of Eden, as the importance of the Holy Scrolls in Judaism . . . and in the definition of Christ as the divine Logos, the Word of God."[188] Since language and symbolic reasoning form an essential part of relational personhood, it is revealing that the person of God the Son incarnate is described as the Logos, God's *word*. Linguistically mediated personhood appears to be in the nature of God's own personhood.

The uniqueness of human symbolic reasoning and second-order intentionality enables us to relate to each other face to face in I-Thou relationship, to open up to not only imaginary worlds, but to the transcendent realm, and ultimately to have the capacity to relate to God, all underlined in the biblical distinction given to humans made in the image of God.[189] The emerging scientific portrait of human uniqueness, far from undermining a Christian insistence on human personhood as *imago Dei*, actually strengthens it, since the capacities science recognizes as distinctive also serve to make human-divine personal communion in creativity and freedom possible. This does not require us to rely upon purely substantive approaches to human nature in theology, but the scientifically observable substantive differences do help to underline the unique nature of human personhood, and undergird the non-substantive approaches taken by some theologians. We *are* unique—the most complex life form in the cosmos—which is summarized theologically in the concept of the *imago Dei* but also noticed by the natural sciences in terms of the free, symbolic, social, ethical, and transcendent nature that makes personhood possible. What is

---

187. Barbour, *Nature, Human Nature, and God*, 50. Barbour also reminds us of the scriptural emphasis on human community with the rest of creation, and human finiteness before its Creator.

188. Shafer, "What does It Mean to Be Human?" 133–34.

189. Buber, *I and Thou*, 56, 80, 180–81.

meaningful in this context is the coherence of the two disciplines in their understanding of human being.

6

Cosmic Evolution and Human Existence
Providence in Science and Theology

> The more I examine the universe and study the details of its architecture, the more evidence I find that the universe in some sense must have known we were coming.
> —Freeman Dyson[1]

Introduction

THE THEOLOGICAL CONTENTION OF THIS THESIS IS THAT HUMAN EXistence is a divine goal in the creation of the universe, and that the cosmos' ultimate fate depends upon humanity in Jesus Christ. Is this in any way coherent with scientific discourse? The stereotypical view is that science teaches humanity is not central to the universal order of things. For instance, P. Davies observes, "The revolution begun by Copernicus and finished by Darwin had the effect of marginalizing, even trivializing, human beings."[2] Other prominent scientific voices insist there is no meaning or purpose to existence, human or otherwise. Sagan declares, "the Cosmos is all that is or ever was or ever will be."[3] Dawkins insists that despite appearances to the contrary, there is no evidence of divine design in life or human existence.[4] Peter Atkins proclaims, "everything is driven by motiveless, purposeless decay."[5] Must one conclude this from the scientific data? Do modern science, Darwinism, and the processes

---

1. Dyson, *Disturbing the Universe*, 250.
2. P. Davies, *Mind of God*, 20.
3. Sagan, *Cosmos*, 4.
4. Dawkins, *Blind Watchmaker*, 5, 317–18.
5. Atkins, *Creation Revisited*, 23.

of "cosmic evolution"[6] prove that human existence is a cosmic accident with no purpose or ultimate meaning?

This chapter will attempt to answer this question by revisiting the cosmological argument and the argument from design. Here, the intention is to "defeat the defeaters" (to use Alvin Plantinga's terms) of a teleological view of human existence rather than give any single knockdown proof of it. An overview of the scientific data of cosmic evolution will be coupled with metaphysical analysis of its meaning with reference to human existence, teleology, and providence. This will require sensitivity to the boundary of science with theology. While metaphysics is native territory for theologians, it is not the natural domain of science.[7] It is therefore important to discern and test the metaphysical character of (anti-) teleological statements claiming to be the automatic result of science. It will be argued here that the highly metaphysical and anti-teleological views of Sagan, Dawkins, Atkins, and others, are not contained in the scientific data.[8] Recognizing the partial separateness of science and theology (chapter 4), what is sought is a level of coherence between the two perspectives on reality.

It might just be worth asking, by way of connecting the medieval view to the present, whether our geographical position in the universe has any bearing on human existence. The Hubble space telescope reveals a "universe that looks the same whichever direction we look." Stephen Hawking notes that "it might seem that if we observe all other galaxies to be moving away from us, then we must be at the center of the universe ... There is, however an alternate explanation: the universe might look the same in every direction as seen from any other galaxy too ... We have no scientific evidence for, or against, this assumption. We believe it only on grounds of modesty: it would be most remarkable if the universe looked the same in every direction around us, but not around other points in the universe!"[9] While it is a legitimate possibility

---

6. Here "cosmic evolution" refers to all processes that move the universe from states of lower to higher complexity, including those in the big bang, in atomic, molecular, galaxy, star, and planet formation, and in the development of life on Earth culminating in human beings.

7. Jeffrey Wicken wryly observes that scientists "officially eschew" metaphysics, but "love it dearly and practice it ... whenever they get the chance" ("Toward an Evolutionary Ecology of Meaning," 162).

8. Polkinghorne, *Faith of a Physicist*, 9.

9. Hawking, *Brief History of Time*, 45, 130–31.

that the reason we see uniformity in every direction is because *we are at the center of the universe*, this is unverifiable. In particular, if everything came from a central big bang, then in one sense, all parts will register the same ultimate age and initial location. A geographically central location is, in this perspective, meaningless.[10]

On the other hand, there may be non-geographical ways of assessing human centrality and cosmic significance. The *anthropic principle* stands at the heart of this discussion, since it somehow seems to tie human existence to the essence of reality. In it, the cosmological argument shades into the teleological argument, suggesting to some evidence not only for the existence of God, but also for cosmic design. The principle represents significant scientific discovery and insight, cataloging the requirements for life and consciousness, as we know it, illuminating the connection between the small- and large-scale structures of the universe, and noting the unusual cosmic position of human consciousness. Humans are frequently spoken of as the being in whom the universe has "become aware of itself,"[11] possessing in the human brain "the most complex object in the known universe."[12] Some versions of the principle even suggest that consciousness *had* to come into existence—though it might not have been in *human* form.[13] Since we could not exist without

---

10. Given the age of the universe and the speed of light, the size of the universe in light years is $\lambda = ct_u$, where c is the speed of light and t_u is the age of the universe. If the universe is about seventeen billion years old (plus or minus three billion years), and we observe seventeen billion light years distance to stars and galaxies in any particular direction, then we are half way between the farthest ends of the universe. Does this place us at the center of the sphere whose radius is seventeen billion light years? Maybe. Malcolm S. Longair indicates that "all observers note, correctly, that they are at the 'center of the Universe' and, when the expansion is extrapolated back to the origin, they were all present at a single point at the very beginning of the expansion" (*Our Evolving Universe*, 108). Our observations are based on the temporal light cone—the further away in distance, the further back in time we are observing. Since every other point in space will have likewise originated at t=0, it too will see its past-light cone in a fashion similar to earth's (ibid., 17–18, 133–34). See also Barrow and Tipler, *Anthropic Cosmological Principle*, 384.

11. Polkinghorne, *Faith of a Physicist*, 12.

12. Polkinghorne, *Science and Theology*, 49; Peterson, *Minding God*, 20.

13. This is the *strong* version of the principle. The scientific rationale is that intelligent life *must* evolve in order for the universe (or quantum effects) to be observed. This is a bit like the riddle about the tree falling in the forest: if no one hears it fall, can a sound be said to exist? If there are no observers, can the universe be said to exist, or be known to exist? See Barrow and Tipler, *Anthropic Cosmological Principle*, 15–23; Ellis, "Theology of the Anthropic Principle," 374.

anthropic fine-tuning, perhaps the universe is tailor-made for human existence, and humans are the "goal of creation."[14] This last statement is especially contentious. Some believe the principle supports the idea, while others vigorously deny it.[15] What is a reasonable conclusion?

A brief review of the anthropic principle is in order before considering whether it can be thought of in teleological terms, or what bearing it has on human existence. The general consensus in contemporary science is that the big bang marked the beginning of the universe as we know it. The anthropic principle observes that the initial conditions and laws that have governed all matter in the universe since the big bang are exactly right for the production of intelligent life.[16] These parameters have been catalogued to some extent, as this small sample list illustrates.[17]

1. The Smoothness Problem: Large regions coming out of a big bang could be expected to have erratic differences in density, but instead it is remarkably smooth. The density of matter would have had to be tuned to within 1 in 10^{60} of its present value at the Planck time (10^{-43} seconds) following the start of the big bang to achieve such smoothness.[18]

2. The Inflation Problem: If an initial inflation after the big bang gave rise to the present general homogeneity of the universe, the initial conditions of inflation would have to be tuned to within 1 in 10^{123} of the present cosmological constant to drive such expansion. A change in the force of either gravity or the nuclear weak force of 1 in 10^{100} would end the effectiveness of this constant.

3. The Flatness Problem: The expansion of the early universe would have to be fine-tuned to within 1 in 10^{55} in order to arrive at the remarkably flat space of our universe. In the absence of such flatness, or regularity in the curvature of space, the spatial structure

---

14. Pannenberg, *Systematic Theology*, 2:75.

15. P. Davies, *Mind of God*, 200.

16. Or exactly right for the privilege of being observed. Carter, "Large Number Coincidences," 291–98.

17. Leslie, *Universes*, 3–6; Barrow and Tipler, *Anthropic Cosmological Principle*, 408–12; Ross, "Design Evidences."

18. Some account for the smoothness by "inflation theory," but see the next condition. Ellis and Stoeger, "Introduction to General Relativity," 197.

of the universe would be vastly different, possibly collapsing all matter within a short time of the big bang.

4. The Expansion Problem: A speed decrease of 1 in 10^6 when the big bang was a second old would have produced a re-collapse of the universe before the universe's average temperature fell below 10,000 degrees.[19]

5. The nuclear strong force must be within 1 percent of its present value, or carbon would not be formed within stars.

There are a host of such parameters, with more being discovered each year. So far, these observations are merely descriptive. Even at a descriptive level they are fascinating, since without something very nearly exactly like these initial parameters, neither galaxies, stars, planets, oceans, atmospheres, organic compounds, nor life as we know it would have been possible. However, the questions of interest to theologians arising from this data are metaphysical: Can one extrapolate directly from the big bang to a design principle? Why was the big bang so "loaded" towards life? Does the big bang correspond in any meaningful sense with the Judeo-Christian idea of *creatio ex-nihilo*? Is life in the universe inevitable or highly unlikely? Is it unique to earth or ubiquitous? Chapter 5 assessed the likelihood of ETI in light of "rare earth" conditions, but does human "cosmic loneliness" equate to human significance? Are human beings included in the *why* of the universe, or are they simply a contingent accident? Is human existence providential and part of a teleological "cosmic plan," or is it an unintentional throwaway?

In order to evaluate the metaphysical questions, several related areas in the science-theology dialogue will be explored in order to build a sequentially persuasive argument. (1) The cosmological argument will be revisited in light of the big bang and the anthropic principle. (2) The anthropic principle will be examined for considerations in the range from cosmology to teleology. (3) The relationship between the anthropic principle and human existence will be explored. (4) The scientific portrait of the process leading to human existence will be evaluated in terms of providence. The key question to be answered: is it fair for the theologian to assert, with reference to the evidence from science, that

---

19. Leslie, *Universes*, 3, 29; Bradley, "'Just So' Universe," 75.

providence has guided cosmic evolution to its human end? This must be a summative overview of the material, rather than an exhaustive review, sufficient to support the argument.

The Cosmological Argument Revisited

The cosmological argument for the existence of God has reemerged in the last few decades because of two previously non-existent conditions in the natural sciences. The first involves Edwin Hubble's research into the motion of distant stars and galaxies in the 1920s, which has lead to the wide acceptance of an initial big bang at the beginning of the universe. The second condition involves the theoretical and technological advances that have made possible the observation of the anthropic conditions. Until general relativity, quantum mechanics, atom smashers, and high-powered telescopes came on the scene, it was not practical to research many of these ultra fine, life-enabling tolerances.

Many in the science-theology dialogue believe that God is the best explanation for the existence of the anthropic universe. Peacocke, Polkinghorne, and others believe the coincidences are too unlikely to have happened by chance, and attribute the existence of the universe including its potentiality for life to God.[20] Others, like Stephen Hawking and Willem Drees, suggest these data can be explained without reference to God. For them, teleology and providence appear to be out of the question. A brief look at the cosmological argument in light of contemporary science will ground further discussion.

Steady State vs. Big Bang

Prior to Hubble, the widely accepted scientific view was that the cosmos was in a steady state—neither expanding nor contracting. The status quo in astrophysics was that matter was immutable, nothing being able to come from nothing, and therefore matter was necessarily eternal.[21] The universe was believed to be infinitely old, with laws and governing principles or constants that were a given of the system. Albert Einstein even adjusted his relativity equations in order to fit a steady

---

20. Peacocke, "Challenge and Stimulus," 89; Polkinghorne, "Friendliness of Science and Religion"; *Science and Creation*, 27–31, 38.

21. Pius XII, "Theology and Modern Science," 165; referring to Svante Arrhenius and Plate.

state universe, because the alternative of an absolute beginning of space and time seemed too metaphysically non-scientific.[22] Hubble's findings were so traumatic for the dominant paradigm that some, like Fred Hoyle, even suggested the universe was forever replenishing itself from within: a continual creation of matter in the empty stretches of space could account for the observed motion of galaxies.[23] Prior to Hubble, theologians could avoid metaphysical problems with the static universe by claiming that the important thing was not that God had done something at a particular time, "but rather that at all times he keeps the world in being."[24] This ontological approach was not satisfying to everyone, and steady-state theory was used by some as grounds for dismissing the notion of divine involvement altogether.[25]

Hubble's data revealed that the universe is expanding.[26] He observed that almost all stars and galaxies show a characteristic red shift in their light spectra, as a result of the speed at which they are receding from us.[27] Their velocity is directly proportional to their distance from us; the further away, the faster they are receding.[28] The implication of this expansion is shown by theoretically running the universe's clock backwards, which reveals the universe contracting to a point—called a singularity—at its beginning, a point at which all matter was compacted into an area of incredibly small size and nearly infinite density. Such events are called singularities because at such size and density all the known laws of physics break down. Penrose and Hawking gave theoretical weight to this finding by proving mathematically that a universe with the amount of matter that we observe must have an origin at a huge explosive singularity, given the laws of general relativity and the condition that gravity continues to hold its attractive power under the initial conditions of the universe.[29] Further confirmation came from

22. Weinberg, *Dreams of a Final Theory*, 178.
23. Ibid., 26; Barrow and Tipler, *Anthropic Cosmological Principle*, 601.
24. Polkinghorne, *Science and Creation*, 54.
25. Hawking, *Brief History of Time*, 49.
26. P. Davies, *Mind of God*, 51.
27. Analogous to the Doppler effect in sound waves. If the galaxies were moving towards us, they would be characterized by a blue-shift in their light spectra. The galactic red-shift could also be due to a stretching of space, rather than the stretching of light waves.
28. Hawking, *Brief History of Time*, 41.
29. Ibid., 53.

observation of the microwave background radiation left over from the explosion by Arno Penzias and Robert Wilson in 1965, and from data collected by the COBE satellite in 1992.[30] These findings also put to rest modern steady-state theories like Hoyle's.[31] The initial explosion of all matter out of a singularity—popularly called the big bang, and now widely accepted as the best physical description of cosmic genesis—has resulted in the universe in which we live.

Big Bang, Quantum Cosmologies, and Metaphysical Problems

For many, the something-from-nothing nature of the big bang seems to be compatible with the cosmological argument for God's existence. For others, such metaphysical solutions are inherently non-scientific and unsatisfactory. Some suggest a quantum fluctuation at the beginning could account for the appearance of something from nothing, since matter and energy must be conserved, and a quantum fluctuation would balance potential and kinetic energies with matter to maintain the laws of conservation.[32] This is supposed to do away with the need for an interfering hand of God to account for initial energy input. Others, like Hawking and James Hartle, propose quantum models that seek to eliminate an initial moment (t=0) in an effort to get around a beginning, which Hawking says "smacks of [the] divine." He claims that while time is limited in the past, there is neither a precise boundary nor a singularity that requires abandoning the laws of physics and "hopelessly giving up" in the face of the something-from-nothing problem. "The universe would be completely self-contained and not affected by anything outside itself. It would neither be created nor destroyed. It would just BE," with "no edge of space-time at which one would have to appeal to God."[33] This is clearly a metaphysical claim despite protestations of disinterest about metaphysical questions, and is Hawking's attempt to get around a divine beginning.

---

30. Barrow and Tipler, *Anthropic Cosmological Principle*, 368; Hawking, *Brief History of Time*, 44.

31. Weinberg, *Dreams of a Final Theory*, 26–27; Hawking, *Brief History of Time*, 49–51.

32. P. Davies, *Mind of God*, 62.

33. Hartle and Hawking, "Wave Function of the Universe," 2960–75; Hawking, *Brief History of Time*, 49, 141, 144; Russell et al., *Quantum Cosmology*, 10.

However, such quantum models, when carefully examined, have some serious metaphysical flaws.[34] For one thing, it not clear that quantum models are appropriate for singular events, since they are by definition designed for probabilities of ensembles of particles.[35] Further, Hawking admits that quantum cosmology is speculative, and incomplete in any real sense. In fact, general relativity and quantum mechanics are as yet mutually incompatible, and cannot both be applied to the same system.[36] Scientists speculate that they are part of a greater theory that unites them—a quantum gravity theory. Preliminary suggestions have been proposed, such as string or super-string theory, but no complete unifying theory yet exists.[37] Polkinghorne maintains that any such theory will have to be conjecture, because the very high energies present at the big bang are "beyond our certain knowledge."[38] Hawking says he takes an instrumentalist view of the kind of theory he and Hartle are devising in their quantum cosmology: it "is just a mathematical model we make to describe our observations." He takes "the positivist viewpoint that a physical theory is just a mathematical model and that it is meaningless to ask whether it corresponds to reality. All that one can ask is that its predictions should be in agreement with observation."[39] On an instrumentalist basis it need not correspond to reality at all except to make testable predictions, and so the actual beginning has not been eliminated. Such a description might be explanation at one level, but it does not claim to be full ontological explanation. Whether any kind of metaphysical conclusions could or should be drawn from partial or instrumentalist quantum cosmologies is therefore debatable.

Even if such problems are ignored, quantum cosmologies as divine substitute do not really give something from nothing. John Leslie says of the Hartle-Hawking model, "a zero volume with *three-dimensional geometry and sufficiently subject to the laws of quantum physics to allow*

---

34. P. Davies, *Mind of God*, 61.

35. Isham, "Quantum Theories of the Creation," 56, 79–80.

36. Rees, *Our Universe*, 29.

37. Superstring theory posits that basic particles are neither waves nor points but behave as if they were loops or strings. Hawking, *Brief History of Time*, 63, 138, 173–75; Isham, "Quantum Theories of the Creation," 77.

38. Polkinghorne, *Science and Theology*, 35.

39. Hawking, *Brief History of Time*, 141, 144; Hawking and Penrose, *Nature of Space and Time*, 4.

for talk of 'tunneling' from it can look interestingly different from pure nothingness."[40] Polkinghorne agrees, pointing out that the quantum vacuum out of which the universe originated "is not an empty nothingness but an active medium full of fluctuating energy."[41] Other quantum origination theories, such as those of Andre Linde or Alex Vilenkin, also assume the presence of this mathematical superspace.[42] Perhaps without realizing the ontological predicament in which it will place his theory, Hawking innocently admits that "in order to predict how the universe should have started off, one needs laws that hold at the beginning of time."[43] Eliminating the first temporal moment leaves unanswered the question, from whence came the basic forces, the unlimited laws, the "highly ordered mathematical domain"?[44] Even in models that supposedly begin with absolutely nothing, this overarching governance of pure mathematics is still in play. In other words, something has not really come from nothing; there is no "free lunch" for cosmological physicists. The explanatory problem is simply moved back a causative generation: where did these laws and foundational mathematics come from? Therefore, it is clear that physical theories of the Hawking-Hartle variety have not eliminated the need for a deeper explanation to reality.

The Anthropic Principle and Multiple Universes

The current scientific understanding suggests that the universe's particular anthropic form is astronomically improbable—effectively impossible.[45] The *weak* form of the anthropic principle states that this should not be surprising, because if it were not so, we would not be here to observe the universe. While some use this line of reasoning to dismiss the need for God, this approach does not really account for the order that exists. Even if there are no observers such as ourselves in the universe, the orderly arrangement of laws and matter that make life possible de-

---

40. Leslie, *Universes*, 81
41. Polkinghorne, *Science and Theology*, 35.
42. Isham, "Quantum Theories," 68–71.
43. Hawking, *Brief History of Time*, 138.
44. K Ward, *Religion and Creation*, 295.
45. One estimate of the odds of cosmic matter emerging in its present arrangement by chance from the Big Bang is given by Barrow and Tipler as only one in ten to the 10^{30} power (*Anthropic Cosmological Principle*, 448); cf. Bartholomew, *God of Chance*, 37–39.

mands a philosophical explanation.[46] As Richard Swinburne observes, "the fact that this peculiar order is a necessary condition of the [order] being perceived at all makes what is perceived no less extraordinary and in need of explanation."[47]

Another theory that claims to eliminate the need for God as creator is the idea that this universe is just one of a huge collection of universes—perhaps even an infinite number—a *multiverse*. There are various versions of this theory, from quantum branching, to innumerable inflationary bubbles, to infinite "breathings" of a big-bang/big-crunch cycle.[48] Whether in serial, parallel, or contiguous form, the main argument simply suggests the eternal existence of an "ensemble" of worlds. According to Barrow and Tipler, this ensemble involves "either hypothetical other possible universes possessing different sets of fundamental constants or different initial conditions."[49] One among this vast ensemble of universes just happens to have the right conditions for carbon-based life.

Does the *multiverse* solution eliminate the need for God? Perhaps more to the point, is it a valid scientific explanation for the anthropic principle? The crucial issue is the need for a real ensemble of choices from which the one living anthropic universe might have been selected. To use an illustration inspired by Leslie, if we have won the lottery, we might not be surprised, since someone had to win sooner or later. But if gunmen rush into the room just before the draw shouting, "You are dead if your ticket isn't drawn!" we might be very surprised indeed to find ourselves alive a few minutes later. We would want an explanation. Two possibilities present themselves: either someone is on our side, or else gunmen rushed into every other ticket holder's home with the same threat and we are the only ones left standing. In order for the later possibility to be real—for our universe to have been selected by process of elimination as an observer-rich universe—there must be other universes that could have been materially chosen from. If there

---

46. B. Davies, *Introduction*, 117.

47. Swinburne, *Existence of God*, 138.

48. Everett, "'Relative State,'" 454–62; Hawking, *Brief History of Time*, 137–38. Hawking disproved the inflationary bubbles model in a theoretical paper, and points out that it does not agree with the empirical finding of the microwave background radiation.

49. Barrow and Tipler, *Anthropic Cosmological Principle*, 255.

are infinitely many universes, then perhaps ours just happens to be the one with the otherwise statistically impossible array of anthropic conditions. But in order for any multiple-worlds theory to work, there must be actual other universes that could have been selected, or the selection effect cannot operate. Given a billion tickets and a billion contestants, if lottery tickets are given to all contestants, someone *must* be a winner. Given a billion tickets and one contestant, since the contestant receives only one ticket, there will probably be *no* winner. As Leslie puts it, "No Observational Selection Effect without Actual Things from Which to Select!"[50]

The postulate that there are other universes is unverifiable by science, and as such is inherently metaphysical.[51] There is no empirical evidence for their existence; they are by definition unobservable. This is perhaps the most devastating critique of the multiverse theory—it is a *metaphysical* rather than a *scientific* explanation. The choice between infinitely many universes, one of which is bound to produce intelligent beings like us, or one universe, extremely fine-tuned by the will of God, may ultimately be a matter of faith. The multiverse theory at least has the same handicaps as the metaphysical assumption of God, and perhaps even a few more. Polkinghorne argues that since there are no observable ways to test related phenomena such as might be done in principle for the religious alternative, the multiverse option is inferior.[52] God's existence can theoretically be verified using religious experience, answered prayer, the historical investigation of faith claims such as the resurrection, or other metaphysical or philosophical considerations.[53] Alternate universes are completely inaccessible except to the imagination. Finally, even where multiple universes are posited, these are not

50. Leslie, *Universes*, 14, 12–24.
51. Polkinghorne, *Science and Theology*, 38.
52. Polkinghorne, "Friendliness"; *Science and Creation*, 27–31, 38.
53. See Alston, *Perceiving God*; Pannenberg, "Gott der Geschichte," 87. E.g., experiments to study the power of prayer, such as the prayer and cardiac recovery study conducted by St. Luke's Hospital in Kansas City, Missouri, under the direction of William Harris, PhD. The study concluded that a type of prayer known as intercessory prayer might make a real difference, concluding "prayer may be an effective adjunct to standard medical care." The exact meaning of this particular study may be debatable, but the case illustrates the possibility that religious claims are, in principle, open to investigation. Harris et al., "Randomized, Controlled Trial," 2273–78; Rauch, "Probing the power of prayer."

in necessary conflict with the existence of God, since the ontological aspect of their existence remains a problem: the question remains why there is something—a multiverse—rather than nothing. God remains as a satisfying and metaphysically coherent explanation.

Ontology, Causation, and Creatio Ex-nihilo

Some refuse to ask the *why* question altogether,[54] claiming such questions are beyond the bounds of science and need not be pursued. But this tactic is either arbitrary or self-referentially incoherent if a *full* account of reality is sought. For instance, the multiverse theory is generally seen as the only robust competitor to the idea of God as an account for the anthropic universe. But the multiverse is itself a purely metaphysical answer to the *why* problem, and so is an incoherent option for the "avoider of whys." Others like Willem Drees take the anthropic universe as a brute fact—"reality is assumed, rather than explained."[55] But this is arbitrary, since explanation and connection is sought at every other level of reality. As Paul Davies observes, "you don't explain something by simply declaring it has always been there."[56] The theological account of reality, moving as it does between explanation and understanding, is fuller *because* it wrestles with the *why*, at least attempting to make the existence and structure of the universe intelligible.

Polkinghorne and others believe the ontological aspect of creation is a key theological insight. Just as the existence of a multiverse would still require an explanation for its being, so the general existence of *something* rather than *nothing* requires a cause.[57] Davies recognizes the ontological problem when he admits, "the fact that the universe might have no origin in time does not explain its existence, or why it has the form it does."[58] Efforts to discover a "theory of everything" that would make all features of the universe inevitable products of basic underlying laws, even if successful, would still not render the universe-as-accident or brute-fact solution satisfying. The existence of the laws and the intel-

---

54. B. Davies, *Introduction*, 118.
55. Drees, *Religion, Science and Naturalism*, 268.
56. P. Davies, *Fifth Miracle*, 232.
57. Polkinghorne, *Science and Christian Belief*, 73; Russell, "Finite Creation," 294–300.
58. P. Davies, *Mind of God*, 56.

ligibility of the universe would still require explanation. Does such a cause have to be God?

There are traditionally two types of causation: *natural* and *intentional*. While *natural* causation works to explain some levels of reality, a *final* explanation for laws that govern cosmic processes must automatically exclude natural or material explanations, since these would by definition be themselves natural, and thus in need of further explanation. Intentional causes, on the other hand, have the advantage of being free from logical necessity, and thus offering an order of causation that is outside such necessity. Aquinas gives the argument to *intentionality* or personal agency as follows: "Now whatever lacks intelligence cannot move towards an end, unless it be directed by some being endowed with knowledge and intelligence; as the arrow is shot to its mark by the archer. Therefore some intelligent being exists by whom all natural things are directed to their end; and this being we call God."[59] Brian Davies notes that if we allow that the vast temporal regularity "is not explicable scientifically, we could account for it in terms of something analogous to decision." So it is reasonable to believe in intelligent agency when confronted with non-logically necessary order, unless good reason is given to dismiss it.[60] Neither natural laws nor a "mathematical superspace" suggest logical necessity, so it is reasonable to believe an intentional, intelligent agent—God—is responsible for their existence.

Perhaps another mysterious means of causation exists which is simply beyond our thought and experience, which could account for the origin of temporal and spatial order. Let us call this third means "Mystery," since we seem unable to know what it is. Then we have in fact returned for explanation to God, who is, in Rahner's words, the "absolute mystery."[61] It is appropriate to admit that comparing original or ontological causation to human intentional causation has its limits. If the source of the universe were some kind of hypothesis that could be completely known, verified, and delineated by our finite and limited science, then that source would not be worthy of being called God, who must as infinite Mystery transcend the finite realm of human experi-

---

59. Thomas Aquinas, *Summa Theologica* I.2.3.
60. B. Davies, *Introduction*, 118.
61. Rahner, *Theological Investigation*, 11:105.

ence.[62] Such a perspective is coherent with the "provisional and fallible" nature of human knowledge.[63]

Some take an ontological perspective, accepting that God is responsible for everything and holds creation together from beginning to end, not just at one particular finite moment in space and time called the big bang. So Polkinghorne says, "theology is concerned with ontological origin and not with temporal beginning. The idea of creation had no special stake in a datable start to the universe."[64] Here, the initial instant fades in importance, since God's role is to sustain the cosmos in being at all times, not just to act once in the beginning. The doctrine of *creatio ex-nihilo* then stands for the existence of something—a universe—by divine fiat where the existence of nothing was also a logical option. Others regard the initial moment of history as critical to a theological understanding. Pope Pius XII saw the big bang as so friendly to faith that he said it confirmed the universe's contingency and the "epoch when the cosmos came forth from the Hands of the Creator."[65] Peters insists the doctrine of creation is disappearing when God's providential and preservational roles are recast as "continuing creation." He believes the big bang singularity is consonant with a theological position based on revelation and is equivalent to *creatio ex nihilo*.[66]

Perhaps a middle way is more helpful. Robert Russell argues for subsuming the temporal explanation within the broader ontological one.[67] On the one hand, the pure ontologists seem indifferent to the implications of big bang cosmology, and are too eager to establish a dichotomy between ontological and empirical, perhaps because in the past pinning one's theological colors to then-current scientific theories has been disastrous. Likewise, the temporalists may be in danger of one day losing their empirical base, for instance if quantum cosmologies such as the Hartle-Hawking model are accepted. Their position might be in danger of reducing theism to deism, and may not account for all the ways in which God might act in the cosmos.[68] Yet the temporalists

62. Rev. Raymond Santos, personal conversation, Edinburgh, 2003.
63. Fuller, *Atoms and Icons*, 31.
64. Polkinghorne, *Science and Christian Belief*, 73.
65. Pius XII, "Theology and Modern Science," 146, 165.
66. Peters, "On Creating the Cosmos," 291.
67. Russell, "Finite Creation," 300–325.
68. K. Ward, *Religion and Creation*, 296.

can claim to be extrapolating from empirical rather than purely theoretical bases. The directness of correspondence between the big bang and the theological idea of *creatio ex-nihilo* is attractive partly because it is simple and empirical, not merely philosophical. In either case, God appears as the best current explanation for both the causal and ontological aspects of the big bang, and for the anthropic fine-tuning of the universe.

Teleology and Cosmic Evolution

The Meaning and Scope of Teleological Explanations

What is meant by a teleological explanation? According to the *Compact Oxford English Dictionary*, teleology in philosophy is explanation of phenomena "with reference to the purpose they serve." The traditional arguments have posited that the best explanation for the structure and order of the universe is intention or intelligence. The idea is that the universe appears to be designed at various levels, from its law-bounded beginnings to its culmination in living systems, and that this design needs explanation. B. Davies offers two versions of a design argument: the argument from purpose and the argument from regularity. In each case, aspects of the world are suggested to be as they are—designed as purposeful or regular—because of the existence of an intentional immaterial agent—the minimum qualifications for God.[69]

William Paley's example of a watch found "in crossing a heath" illustrates the idea of design. It is known to be purposive because it is composed of parts that operate together to accomplish a goal. It is orderly and regular. Showing such purpose and order, we are bound to attribute its creation to an intelligent agent, unlike the apparently purposeless stone lying randomly next to it. Paley calls such goal-directed or purposive objects "teleological systems." They are teleological because they have a purpose—in the case of the watch, the goal of telling time.[70] Paley's thesis is that such goal directedness is observable in living systems, for instance in the eye, the heart, or the muscles, each of which is built appropriately for, respectively, the goal of seeing, pumping blood, or moving a body. He argues that such goal-directed objects

---

69. B. Davies, *Introduction*, 94, 109, 114.
70. Paley, *Natural theology*, 1.

or processes must be more than accidental. Since the only other known purposive objects or processes are created intentionally by human beings, some type of intentional intelligent being must also be responsible for living teleological systems. Aspects of this argument will be examined later, since some believe that non-intentional causation is sufficient to explain life.

The purpose of this section is not simply to revisit the classic teleological debate, but rather to examine the relationship between the anthropic universe and the teleological argument. The case for divine design at the basic level of governing universal laws behind the big bang and anthropic fine-tuning has already been made. In the anthropic principle, the cosmological argument shades into the teleological argument; this may be stated thus: *God has designed the universe to make life and consciousness possible.* This also implies *purpose*: it is a divine purpose for the universe to produce life and consciousness. Notice that this initial apprehension of design is independent of anthropocentric bias, in that conditions are defined in terms of fitness for life rather than fitness for *human* life.[71] There may be other purposes, but the apparent anthropic design suggests that the production of conscious life is at least one such purpose.[72] The anthropic principle is therefore coherent with a teleological view of reality. The question is whether or not design exists at other levels in the universe, ordering its unfolding at atomic, stellar, galactic, planetary, molecular, living, and ultimately neuronal levels. In short, is there evidence of teleology in those levels of cosmic evolution most closely associated with human existence? Is such "further up" teleology coherent with the scientific evidence, and metaphysically sound?

At one level, the answer seems obvious, since it is clear that universal anthropic laws and conditions are in operation at every level, enabling the increasing complexity that leads from the simplest subatomic structure to the most complex object in the universe, the human brain. But not everyone agrees the logic can be thus extended. Two problematic aspects of cosmic evolution will be examined for possible evidence of design: (1) the unique boundary conditions for life on earth, and (2) the local evolution of life. Can a reasonable case be made for a

---

71. See Manson, "Anthropocentrism and the Design Argument," 175.

72. Keith Ward says, "Every new scientific demonstration of the precision of the mathematical structure needed to produce conscious life is evidence of design." Even the process of entropy has "a very clear purpose." *God, Chance & Necessity*, 52.

teleological reading of all natural processes, including those leading to human existence? It will be argued that such a position is reasonable, that human existence cannot be regarded as accidental or arbitrary in the ultimate sense, and that "scientific" claims to the contrary are metaphysical rather than scientific. This is not an effort to redo something like Teilhard's evolutionary Christology, but is rather less ambitious: to examine whether the scientific evidence is consistent with a teleological view of reality.

Teleology and the Rare Earth Hypothesis

How far up in cosmic processes does design extend? Classically, the anthropic principle has focused on the initial conditions of the universe necessary for the rise of conscious life. The initial conditions are not the only necessary conditions, as the *rare Earth* hypothesis investigated in chapter 5 makes clear. Ward and Brownlee, Conway Morris, Martin Rees and others note that without those special rare earth conditions, higher life could never have evolved on earth, or, for that matter, anywhere else.[73] These local conditions might or might not be the inevitable results of cosmic processes.

Do the rare earth conditions have any teleological meaning? While it is logical to conclude that God designed the universe's global fine-tuning, this is not necessarily true of earth's fine-tuning. Taken in isolation, the local situation might be the result of a cosmic dice game, since there are billions of galaxies, and within each, billions of stars. In Leslie's terms, there may be a sufficiently large selection pool for the selection of a "rare earth" to be attributed to chance.

There are some who argue for a goal-directed process as the best explanation for earth's success in producing rational beings. For instance, Keith Ward believes natural selection could not accomplish the goal by itself. "A continuing causal activity of God seems the best explanation of the progress towards greater consciousness and intentionality that one sees in the actual course of evolution of life on earth."[74] Rolston

---

73. Ward and Brownlee, *Rare Earth*; Conway Morris, *Life's Solution*; Rees, *Our Universe*, 9; Gribbin and Rees, *Cosmic Coincidences*, 289–91.

74. K. Ward, *God, Chance & Necessity*, 76–78.

agrees, believing earth's situation and living complexity is powerfully suggestive of a special focus of divine inspiration.[75]

Christopher Southgate et al. argues that there is no parallel possible between local and universal fine-tuning, and that Ward has "overestimated our knowledge of the probability," as well as misunderstood it. "Evolution had to give rise to some outcome or other," and since the experiment has only run once that we know of, we cannot make further extrapolations about local divine activity.[76] While Southgate is dubious about what can be learned from the "one experiment," the local constraints illuminate many boundaries that must apply for life to exist anywhere in the cosmos. These include sufficient gravity, atmosphere, chemical composition, molten iron core, magnetic field, lunar tidal forces, solar radiation, orbital regularity, planetary companions, intergalactic location, etc. It is debatable in light of these data that the evolution of life will even begin in most parts of the universe, much less proceed very far beyond beginning. Further, the contention that evolution must "give rise to some outcome or other" is also debatable, especially since most of the almost four billion years of life's history on earth have shown stasis in evolution in the form of simple bacteria. This does not disprove the one-in-a-billion-billion prize-draw approach to earth's success at the game, but neither does it disprove Ward's position.

The nature of God's ongoing causative role in cosmic evolution is part of the issue. While many consider that God must have built both chance and natural law into the cosmos to allow it the type of freedom and creativity needed for life to arise, perspectives on God's further causative role vary.[77] Peacocke, Page, Rudolf Brun, and others believe God gives possibility and freedom to cosmic evolution, but is not otherwise involved beyond holding it in being.[78] Earth's situation is a fortuitous outcome of closed cosmic processes, and the particular

---

75. Rolston, *Genes, Genesis, and God*, 368.

76. Southgate et al., *God, Humanity, and the Cosmos*, 278; Southgate, "God and Evolutionary Evil," 808.

77. Polkinghorne, *Faith of a Physicist*, 76–77; Southgate, "God and Evolutionary Evil," 804; Peacocke, "End of All Our Exploring."

78. Peacocke, "End of All Our Exploring"; Page, "Animal Kingdom," 2, 6 (her argument will be examined in chapter 7); Brun, "Cosmology," 182.

form human beings have taken is so highly contingent that they could have turned out any number of ways.[79]

Others oppose this view of "creation as *abandonment*," to borrow a phrase from Simone Weil.[80] Ratzinger insists, "a mere 'first cause,' which is effective only in nature and never reveals itself to humans, which abandons humans—has to abandon them—to a realm completely beyond its own sphere of influence, such a first cause is no longer God but a scientific hypothesis."[81] Rolston and K. Ward think the billion-billions-odd chances against human life make local inspiration more likely. These thinkers generally suppose that while God has limited his interference out of love, this would not be contrary to some types of divine intervention. Polkinghorne, who seems ambivalent but not unfavorable to the idea of local divine intervention, observes that it might be in ways that "would be scientifically indiscernible."[82] Rolston agrees that detecting or limiting God's causative influence upon the universe is beyond the capacity of science: "chance is an effective mask for the divine action." Thus if the rare earth conditions involve a more direct form of divine guidance, there is no reason to expect such guidance will be evident scientifically.[83] From a theological perspective, beyond creation, God's intervention in the history of Israel and Jesus Christ give precedent for his intervention at other points in the process. Ward and Rolston's contention is therefore reasonable and coherent with the current scientific data, though empirically unverifiable.

For purposes of teleology, do we need to choose sides on this question of causation? What if the local conditions *are* a purely contingent outcome of the universal conditions and earth has won the cosmic lottery? Does God's hand have to be actively involved in the local conditions for these to be understood as teleological? Even if chance is operating from one perspective, it cannot be said to operate from the ultimate perspective. Pannenberg's observation on the connection between the large- and small-scale structures of the universe is illuminating.[84] There

---

79. Their position on this does not seem entirely coherent, since all three profess belief in the resurrection, which clearly represents profound intervention by God.
80. Weil, *La Connaissance Surnaturelle*, 49.
81. Benedict XVI (writing as Joseph Ratzinger), *In the Beginning*, 85.
82. Polkinghorne, *Faith of a Physicist*, 78; see also Polkinghorne, *Work of Love*.
83. Rolston, *Genes, Genesis, and God*, 368.
84. Pannenberg, *Systematic Theology*, 2:74–75.

is every reason to see a correlation between the universal and local contingencies of nature required for life and particularly human life to have emerged. The universal and local cannot be isolated from each other, since the former conditions the latter. At the very least, earth's conditions are the particular expression of the general potentiality of the universe. Put another way, *the structure of the universe is evident both universally and locally.* That matter can move from sequentially lower to higher levels of complexity, from subatomic organization ultimately to the most complex object in the universe, is possible because of the same universal laws that govern the entire set. From a teleological perspective, it is artificial to separate the two domains. If God is responsible for the cosmos' general structure and fine-tuning, then he is responsible for that structure at all levels.

Teleology in the Evolution of Life on Earth

There are divergent views on the theoretical probability and meaning of evolution, as discussed in the previous chapter. Some, like Monod and Mayr, see life and intelligence on earth as incredibly improbable accidents.[85] Monod is convinced there is no God overseeing the process. Rolston and Deacon suspect that humans with their unusual intelligence, having appeared only once among the billions of species in the evolutionary history of the earth, are not the trend but the exception.[86] Deacon believes only mistaken teleology makes human existence look inevitable, while Rolston perceives divine inspiration in the process. De Duve takes evolution toward human-like complexity as likely given our current knowledge ("the biosphere *was* pregnant with man") and is ready to see the divine in the evolutionary scheme even without intervention.[87]

Paley's design argument provides a useful reference point for a teleological assessment of evolution in light of these divergent interpretations. According to Paley, living systems show an orderly, purposeful complexity that can only be explained by intelligent agency. Dawkins insists that non-intentional Darwinian processes can account for living, purpose-manifesting systems. Like Monod, who insisted an essential

---

85. Monod, *Chance and Necessity*, 145–46; Mayr, *Toward a New Philosophy*, 69.
86. Rolston, *Genes, Genesis, and God*, 113; Deacon, *Symbolic Species*, 30.
87. De Duve, "Lessons of Life," 6–8; "Constraints," 531.

quality of living beings was their *endowment with a purpose or project*,[88] Dawkins does not dispute the appearance of design in the systems—they do function with limited goals bounded by evolutionary and environmental constraints—but insists that purely natural forces—random mutation and natural selection—have worked together over vast amounts of time to produce these purposive systems. Since he thinks he has shown that living systems appear purposive, but not intentionally so, he claims that there is no ultimate *divine* design or purpose behind their appearance, and hence no need for God.[89]

Dawkins also claims that a truly intentional and intelligent designer would have done things differently in the history of life, appealing to aesthetics. These arguments are less convincing because they are too open to subjectivist charges. Southgate notes that a reaction of horror before the spectacle of animal activities such as parasitism and infanticide is "a negative aesthetic response in us," but doubts whether this is a greater burden to theodicies than the general presence of pain and death in the world. Our aesthetic perspectives are by nature particular and limited. "Horror is part of some human beings' reaction to the process but is not part of the process itself."[90] Michael Behe also notes that what appears to some to be dysteleology or poor engineering may turn out on closer examination to be engineering for higher-level efficiency or a solution to an unrecognized or generalist problem (fingers are suited for many general problems, though perhaps not ideally suited for every particular problem—cutting paper, for instance).[91] Behe observes that the dismissal of so-called junk DNA as non-functional and redundant may really be premature, based on an inadequate understanding of the natural processes. One example: recent research by Shinji Hirotsune et al. has shown a previously unknown function for genes formerly labeled "pseudogenes." "The peril of negative arguments is that they may rest on our lack of knowledge, rather than on positive results. The contention that unintelligent processes can account for complex biological functions should, to the extent possible, be supported by positive results, rather than by intuitions of what no designer would do. Hirotsune et al's

---

88. Monod, *Chance and Necessity*, 9. Monod calls this property *teleonomy*.
89. Dawkins, *Blind Watchmaker*, 5, 21, 317–18.
90. Southgate, "God and Evolutionary Evil," 804.
91. See chapter 7, page 281 for the connection to the theodicy problem.

work ... has forcefully shown that our intuitions about what is functionless in biology are not to be trusted."[92]

Even without emotional, aesthetic, or intuitive judgments on the suitability of particular designs, the heart of Dawkins argument remains. He claims natural processes imitate intentionality in the production of purpose in living systems. Eyes are made to see, and muscles are made to move by the interaction of chance and relentless natural laws. Like Dawkins, both Dennett and E. O. Wilson believe the evolutionary rise of life is a result of "mindless, motiveless mechanicity."[93] Natural laws represent, according to Dennett, mindless activity "all the way down" in cosmic processes. Do such natural explanations effectively eliminate the need for God?

The question may be phrased in terms of the problem of information. Monod noted that living structures "represent a considerable quantity of information whose source has still to be identified: for all expressed—and hence received—information presupposes a source."[94] The mystery is to explain the increase of information, not only in the fine-tuning of the universe, but also in the entire process of evolution. The development of life on earth represents information's vast and continual increase, particularly evident in the increasing complexity of DNA in species over geological time. Some suppose that information can increase based on the interplay of chance and natural law. Others believe only intelligent agents can account for information.

Stuart Kaufmann suggests that laws of emergent complexity are responsible for the presence and vast increase of information. He speculates that these laws, analogous to those governing crystal formation or water flow, are responsible for the ways in which DNA has mutated into new species patterns during the course of evolution. Chaos theory already hints at a type of order that arises in the midst of apparently chaotic systems. Perhaps the chaos of genetic mutation is also bounded by such order, leading to the emergent complexity of speciation.[95] Such

92. Behe, "Functional Pseudogene?"; Hirotsune et al, "An expressed pseudogene," 91–96.

93. Dennett, *Darwin's Dangerous Idea*, 63, 73–83; Wilson, *On Human Nature*, 1; *Diversity of Life*, 77–80, 329.

94. Monod, *Chance and Necessity*, 12.

95. Kauffman, *At Home in the Universe*, 19–25.

laws are thought to obviate the necessity of God—shades of Dawkins, Dennett, and Wilson.

The increase of information suggests to others the *presence of mind* rather than mindless chaos. Freeman Dyson believes that "the peculiar harmony between the structure of the universe and the needs of life and intelligence is a . . . manifestation of the importance of mind in the scheme of things."[96] Evolutionary information seems to Rolston to be as "plausibly . . . mindlike as mindless mechanicity." He believes earth may represent a special focus of mind: "An 'information explosion' on our earth, rare in the universe, might be a clue that 'inspiration' is taking place."[97] Proponents of *intelligent design* (ID) theory like Behe and William Dembski suggest that it is precisely from the existence of so much information on earth that we can infer an intelligent designer. In ID theory, "specified" or "irreducible" complexity is given a formal and technical definition based on information theory. DNA, like letters, words, and language, is a repository of information, and often produces results that are irreducibly complex (e.g., blood-clotting, cellular molecular machines).[98] Such information is found to increase in the rest of the world only with reference to intelligent intentional agents, so its presence and increase in living systems suggests to ID theorists the analogous influence of intelligence.[99]

A third option combines both perspectives. De Duve, Peacocke, and others suppose that laws of emergent complexity are in play, but the existence of these laws is coherent with the idea of divine design.[100] Their position points to the key issue for teleology, which is not whether the causal intermediary step of natural Darwinian laws can explain teleological systems, but whether the natural laws themselves can be explained without reference to intelligence. While the results of Darwinian processes may or may not evade the need for intelligent cau-

---

96. Dyson, *Disturbing the Universe*, 252.

97. Rolston, *Genes, Genesis, and God*, 365, 368.

98. Take away any one part, and the machine will cease to function. Dawkins attacks this notion in *The Blind Watchmaker*, supposing gradual accumulation of parts can accomplish the end goal. ID theorists disagree.

99. Behe, *Darwin's Black Box*; Dembski, *Intelligent Design*. ID theorists do not specify that the intelligent designer must be God. For instance, intelligent aliens may be responsible for apparent design in life. But this begs the question of the source of the *alien* intelligence.

100. De Duve, "Lessons of Life," 12–13; Peacocke, "Challenge and Stimulus," 89–93.

sation, the laws governing those processes do not. Swinburne puts it like this: the world may be a "machine-making machine," but its ultimate machine-constructing capacity must have a non-machine explanation.[101] So Anthony Kenny observes that if the argument from design in living systems works at all, it is not refuted by the Darwinian claims. "The ultimate explanation of such adaptation must be found in intelligence; and if the argument is correct, then any Darwinian success merely inserts an extra step between the phenomena to be explained and their ultimate explanations."[102] Penrose agrees that there may be teleology behind phenomena like consciousness, but discussion of these "in terms merely of the ideas of natural selection would miss this purpose completely."[103]

In other words, this is the same problem encountered with metaphysical explanations for the anthropic principle: *Why is there order in the universe?* Kaufmann's laws of emergent complexity return us to these same arguments for the divine designer, since such order also requires ontological explanation. The level at which that order is found extends from the big bang and the anthropic fine-tuning all the way through cosmic evolution to the human mind. Atkins sees in the laws of entropy only "purposeless decay."[104] But K. Ward notes that entropy is actually necessary to the temporal order of nature, and "enables local concentrations of energy to form the vastly complex and intricate structures needed to enable consciousness to emerge."[105] Dawkins sees only natural laws at work, and Dennett claims that the operation of these laws represents mindless activity "all the way down" in cosmic processes.[106] But it is the orderliness itself that demands explanation, and which these non-theistic accounts are unable to provide. Unless one is content with "assuming its existence,"[107] the order of the universe evident "all the way up" in cosmic processes is unintelligible without reference to

---

101. Swinburne, *Existence of God*, 135–36.

102. Kenny, *Five Ways*, 118. He is uncommitted to the design argument, believing this must wait for analysis of whether adaptation of means to ends can be said to exist "over and above" a systems' being "regularly adaptable for the benefit of the system in question," as sign of intelligence.

103. Penrose, *Emperor's New Mind*, 524.

104. Atkins, *Creation Revisited*, 23.

105. K. Ward, *God, Chance & Necessity*, 52.

106. Dennett, *Darwin's Dangerous Idea*, 63.

107. Drees, *Religion, Science and Naturalism*, 268.

transcendence. As K. Ward observes, "the whole history of evolution seems superbly well designed to lead to the existence of consciousness. It is designed, in other words, to lead to levels of explanation and reality beyond itself."[108] Conway Morris agrees, noting that phenomena like convergent evolution show "that life 'navigates' to inevitable solutions through a hyper-dimensional landscape [of functional morphospace] that in itself determines the available routes." Consistent with a creation, he thinks convergence indicates the final outcome is "in some sense preordained."[109] It seems the evolution of life on earth, however it has taken place, is goal directed, and this is coherent with mind, intention, and divine design. Such design warrants a teleological reading of the process.

Conclusion

Brun suggests the term *teleomorphic* to describe a cosmos created with properties that evolve naturally towards ever-greater complexity. The process is subject to chance and contingency and free to become what it will, but the form of the process is the synthesis of ever-greater complexity. This idea of chance and necessity as the driving interplay of increasing complexity is fairly common. Peacocke calls this the "potentiality" of the cosmos, which results in it having the property of "emergent complexity." Brun supposes the "teleomorphy" is in the universal engineering towards complexity, towards "sequential synthesis," rather than in any specific details or interference. The evolutionary processes show that "there is an inherent drive towards complexity (*not progress!*) in nature" (emphasis added). Both he and Peacocke believe the universe is not predetermined towards a specific outcome (so Brun claims it is not teleological), but is given freedom to develop towards ever-greater complexity, finally sufficient to support reciprocal relationship with the Creator.[110]

Brun suggests that God's saving activity in Christ occurs in the midst of the free and contingent cosmos, though there are some inconsistencies in his model. It is a paradox that the freely evolving universe enters a phase of history in Jesus Christ in which, despite the world's

---

108. K. Ward, *God, Chance & Necessity*, 148.
109. Conway Morris, "Paradoxes of Evolution," 8.
110. Brun, "Cosmology," 182, 187; Peacocke, "Challenge and Stimulus," 89.

freedom from God's interference, God's plan for the universe's salvation is exactly fulfilled. The political and religious leaders execute the Son of God according to their own free will, and at the same time fulfill God's greater will for the universe by enabling Jesus' sacrificial death and triumphant resurrection, which promises to redeem the cosmos from death (Acts 4:28; they "did whatever your hand and your plan had predestined to take place"). The same paradoxical perspective can be applied to the entire history of the cosmos. The free "teleomorphic" history of the universe actually unfolds according to God's perfect will, throughout the development of stars, galaxies, planets, life, conscious life, humanity, human history, and climactically in the person and work of Jesus Christ.[111] This reading of the world's freedom is problematic: the resurrection looks like something very different from "freedom from God's interference." The leaders may *enable* the resurrection by killing Jesus, but they certainly do not *cause* the resurrection.

Further, Brun's *teleomorphy* really is a form of *teleology*. If the universe is given potential for emergent complexity and has an in-built drive towards sequential synthesis, such that an end goal of reciprocal relationship with the Creator is eventually likely or even possible, then the process is clearly a goal-oriented process. It is difficult to see how the fulfillment of a drive towards complexity in such a system is *not* progress. By definition, if the design or "teleomorphy" of the system is sequential synthesis, then the successful appearance of increasing complexity *is* progress. The appearance of beings capable of reciprocal relationship with God can hardly be thought of as a happy accident, an unexpected but fortuitous outcome for an otherwise indifferent Creator. It seems unlikely that God, having designed the universe to make life and consciousness possible, perhaps by a combination of chance and necessity or in teleomorphic form, was then pleasantly surprised to find it developing beings that are capable of relationship with him. The local accidental occurs within the horizon of the planned, and so is not finally accidental.

The teleomorphic form of the universe, even conceived in these deistic terms, looks very much like a driving order. Giving a system potential and placing within it a drive for something is the equivalent of engineering and design. It evidences both purpose (increasing complexity; support reciprocal relations with the creator), and regularity

111. Brun, "Cosmology," 187.

(necessity; the interplay of chance and necessity, e.g., chaos theory): this is teleological in the fullest sense. Deism has its own problems both theologically[112] and scientifically,[113] but a teleological conclusion is warranted whether God has simply enabled the universal process of sequential complexity, or has specifically engineered and/or intervened in the local conditions and systems to make human life possible. This need not imply that emergent consciousness and something like human existence is the *only* goal or purpose of the creation, but it does imply that it is *a* goal of the creation.

The argument has tried to show that the best ontological explanation for the origin, existence, and fine-tuning of the universe, and for its consequent development in the direction of organized complexity, is divine design. Further, purpose and teleology can be discerned from some perspectives on the universal processes of cosmic evolution. For these reasons, naturalistic accounts of local and cosmic evolution fail to defeat the argument from design. This is so whether one prefers ID theory, laws of emergent or sequential complexity, or some other as-yet-unnamed theory of life's genesis. The exact method whereby causation or "inspiration" might be occurring is less important theologically than the realization that God is ultimately responsible. Sagan, Dawkins, and Atkins have made ideological and metaphysical claims that are not warranted by the evidence, rather than scientific claims. Once the structure of the anthropic universe is understood as designed, then even if the rise of life has a local contingent and accidental character, it cannot be regarded as ultimately accidental, since it is an expression of God's will for the increasing complexity of the cosmos. A theological analysis may well conclude more, but a reasonable metaphysical analysis could not conclude less.

---

112. See chapter 7, page 282. Scheffczyk notes that deism is prone to "turn the automatic universe into something absolute, to conclude from its admirable order that the universe is a god." If divine, its creaturehood and contingency are destroyed. He believes the deistic approach eviscerates the doctrine of providence. Scheffczyk, *Creation and Providence*, 203.

113. See chapter 1, page 56, and chapter 7, page 282; e.g., its close association with Newtonian cosmology.

Providence and Human Existence

Those who observe the amazing correlation between the order and intelligibility of the universe and the order and rationality of human consciousness would appear to be seeing not just a coincidence, but a possibility intrinsic to cosmic evolution, a potentiality that theology can coherently hold was conceived by the Creator. So T. F. Torrance sees in the "astonishingly improbable but effective laws" that make life possible in the cosmos "the hallmarks of a *personal Author*." He supposes that human personhood that comprehends the intelligibility of the cosmos is reflective of the personal God whose authorship is stamped upon nature.[114] Pannenberg insists the scientific analysis leaves room for the truth revealed by the incarnation, that humans are the goal of creation.[115]

That science "leaves room" does not mean such inherently theological data as the incarnation are scientific. It does suggest, however, coherence between the two domains. Science points to the metaphysical "blank spaces" in its own perspective, for which theology may give fuller ontological explanation.[116] As Freeman Dyson puts it:

> Being a scientist, trained in the habits of thought and language of the twentieth century rather than the eighteenth, I do not claim that the architecture of the universe proves the existence of God. I claim only that [it] is consistent with the hypothesis that *mind* plays an essential role in its functioning.[117]

Science observes the boundary conditions of human existence and leaves considerable room for theology to interpret these without violating the scientific data. Scientific review could not evaluate the meaning of human existence, or prove that the universe was designed for specifically human life. Nor does the evidence prove that human life is a cosmic accident, or that the universe was *not* designed with specifically human life in mind. As Peacocke observes, science cannot explain *why*

---

114. Torrance, "Transcendental Role of Wisdom," 142–44; Gunton, "Trinity," 115.

115. Pannenberg, *Systematic Theology*, 2:75.

116. Since science must "bracket off" ontological considerations, it should not be expected to describe the whole of reality thus illuminated by theology. See Stewart, *Reconstructing Science and Theology*, 11, 51.

117. Dyson, *Disturbing the Universe*, 251. Emphasis added.

there are cosmic laws, or anything else for that matter.[118] The fact that science is unable to decide whether biogenesis and human existence are incredibly improbable or inevitable may point to such a "blank space." Only metaphysical or theological explanations can give coherence to the existence and intelligibility of reality, and explain the place of human beings within it.

As a *teleological* statement, the verification of an anthropocentric universe is a metaphysical task, but on that level, the data offered by science is suggestive. The anthropic principle and processes of cosmic evolution show the whole universe structured to engender increasing levels of complexity. The highest known level of such complexity is human being. The theological analysis suggests that the best explanation for universal order and complexity is the divine economy at work: *God's providence* guiding the cosmos towards the minimally apparent goals of *complexification*[119] and consciousness.[120] So De Duve maintains that the "emergence of life and mind are such extraordinary manifestations that their existence can only be a telling revelation of ultimate reality." The human mind can, for the first time in at least this earth's evolutionary history, see beyond the veil "to the reality behind appearances"; it can perceive there not only the laws and structure of matter, but also beauty, goodness, truth, and love. That ultimate reality is what "many give the name of God."[121]

One can maintain this providential care regardless of one's position on God's ongoing causative relationship to creation. The history of creation leads to the fulfillment of God's will. This is so even when some of that will is accomplished through the medium of other processes (teleomorphic ones) and persons (the leaders who crucify Christ). In theological perspective, the human climax of *complexification* is capable of a unique type of relationship with God, so that in the human being Jesus Christ, God himself enters into and unites the cosmos with himself. The process thus shows the divine economy at work through the whole creation to bring forth the incarnation of the Logos.[122]

---

118. Peacocke, "End of All Our Exploring."

119. Brun, "Cosmology," 181.

120. These goals do not exclude the possibility of other goals, e.g., God's enjoyment of the process and its various non-human creatures.

121. De Duve, "Lessons of Life," 12–13.

122. Gunton, "Trinity," 115.

Conclusion

The scientific data of the big bang, the anthropic principle, and cosmic evolution are coherent with the cosmological and teleological arguments for the existence of God. While it is not the task of science to find evidence of teleology, it does in its own indirect way confirm the findings of theology. The development of the cosmos from its beginnings to the present has manifested remarkable order, the propensity to develop in the direction of sequential complexity, and the potentiality for and actualization of life. These features of the cosmos are strongly suggestive of teleology. Science by its methods might be unable to detect God's activity at a certain level, but could not circumscribe ultimate divine causation, including such causation or inspiration on earth. Debate on the nature of God's involvement may continue on other grounds, but the scientific data does not exclude it as a possibility, and might indirectly witness evidence of it in the universal and local anthropic conditions and in the tendency towards sequential complexity. Theology may go further and describe these data as the natural residual evidence of God's providence. What science describes as the processes of cosmic evolution may in theological perspective be aspects of God's care and guidance of the cosmos.

The concept of sequential complexity suggests a place of convergence between theology and science. Science notices the end result of the sequential processes of cosmic evolution in the transcendentally oriented intelligence of human beings, who are oriented towards unbounded possibilities and capable of a unique degree of freedom. Theology observes that this species, as the pinnacle of complexity in the known universe, appears to be capable of a unique degree of conscious relationship with the Creator: they open up towards the infinite in their thoughts, their yearning, their experience, and in their responsible worship. If specially created by God, humans can think of themselves in teleological terms. But even if human existence is an emergent result of non-predetermined natural processes, these processes are also in theological perspective ultimately teleological. In this case, human existence could be regarded as accidental only in a limited sense. Its providential appearance would be an outcome of possibilities built into the cosmos by God the creator, and therefore ultimately intentional and thus teleological. The doctrine of providence can encompass either interpretation. If extraterrestrial intelligent life were ever found, this conclusion would still hold, but God's providential preparations would be shown to have wider-ranging scope than is currently evident.

Whether or not the universe has been designed to culminate simply in a *conscious* being or in *human* being, it is in humans that the universe is finally prepared to relate to and receive *God's* being. It is a theological datum of faith that the universe has been designed to culminate in the incarnation, but the idea that humanity might be thus a goal of creation is coherent with scientific discourse. Contemporary science observes the process and result of sequential complexity in human nature. This observation is coherent with and perhaps even indirectly confirms a theological faith position on the providential nature of human existence.

7

Critical Anthropocentrism and Ecological Concerns

> *His eye is on the sparrow, and I know He watches me.*
> —Civilla D. Martin[1]

Introduction

DOES CRITICAL ANTHROPOCENTRISM GIVE AN ADEQUATE ACCOUNT OF nature and the animal kingdom? Does an emphasis on the uniqueness and significance of human beings relegate the non-human cosmos to secondary and almost trivial status? To many, it has seemed that the kind of anthropocentrism represented in this thesis must automatically lead to the disregard of animals and the non-human creation, the rape of nature, and ecological catastrophe (see chapter 1, pages 37–38). While Judeo-Christian tradition insists the world is not divine, opinions differ on whether this desacralizes the world. Hall insists the world is still sacred in Christian faith because it is God's creation.[2] But others insist Christianity turns the world into an object, a "back-drop for the human play," a view they believe is no longer tenable in an era of ecological awareness.[3] Others argue that sensitivity to the modern natural sciences and a more penetrating examination of Christian theology and tradition ought to lead us away from any anthropocentric conclusions and elevate our regard for the non-human world.

This chapter seeks to provide a fuller engagement with the general critique of anthropocentrism by those who are sensitive to some of the

---

1. Martin, "His Eye Is on the Sparrow."
2. Hall, *Imaging God*, 48.
3. Buller, *Unity of Nature and History*, 151; McHarg, "Place of Nature," 174.

contemporary ecological and ethical issues in the relationship between the human and non-human creation. Ruth Page and Andrew Linzey provide a focal point for the analysis, as they present some substantial objections to any anthropocentric account of God's relationship with creation. Page insists that all of creation, not just humanity, praises its Creator.[4] She also believes humans are not necessary for communion between other creatures and their Creator.[5] She regards the claim for human cosmic priesthood as anthropocentric arrogance. Linzey rejects anthropocentric theologies for their tendency to promote instrumentalist views of animals. He attempts to rescue Christian theology from such views and find alternatives within the tradition that provide a basis for an ecologically sensitive ethics.[6] While others have argued along similar lines, Page and Linzey provide enough material to demonstrate that ecological and world-centered concerns do not necessarily defeat the claims of *critical anthropocentrism*. Despite their assurances to the contrary, a type of anthropocentrism is still evident either between the lines of their ideological program, or above and beyond their individual critique. This analysis will suggest that *critical anthropocentrism* can interact with and remain sensitive to ecological issues without surrendering its objective claims.

Ruth Page and the Cosmos' Independence from Humanity

Overview of Page's Position

If there is an anthropocentric reality at the heart of Christianity, is it inimical to the good of the rest of creation? Page seems to believe this is the case. She has rightly pointed out that the non-human creation already praises God without the help of humanity.[7] This is evident in numerous passages of Scripture, from Psalm 19 "the heavens are telling the glory of God"; to Isa 55:12, "the trees of the field shall clap their hand"; to Rev 5:13, "Then I heard every creature in heaven and on earth and under the earth and in the sea, and all that is in them, singing

---

4. Page, "Fellowship of All Creation," 5–6.
5. Page, "Animal Kingdom," 2.
6. Linzey, "Animal Theology," 23–25.
7. Page, "Fellowship of All Creation," 5–6.

[praise to God]." Russell Stannard agrees, pointing out that the universe may have been created for other reasons—for God's simple enjoyment, for instance—rather than simply to produce human beings. God may have created humans in order to have someone with whom to share his sense of joy at creation; "however, the angels could equally well fit such a description of persons with whom to share creation, and Scripture even testifies somewhere that they rejoiced together when God created."[8] If praise is not unique to humanity, in what sense might the rest of creation actually depend upon humans for its worship? Humanity cannot simply be affirmed at the expense of the other creatures, nor can anthropocentrism be affirmed by denying God.[9]

On the other hand, God's relationship to humanity in grace through Jesus Christ occasions an increase of that praise. This relationship is such that even "angels long to look" into it (1 Pet 1:12). A tremendous change will take place in the non-human creation's praise in consequence of its relationship to humanity. The fact that the non-human creation praises, and is important to and loved by, God does nothing to change this. The rest of the creation praises, but is subjected to frustration (Rom 8:20), groaning until the children of God are revealed. It is in humanity that the frustration of all creation is satisfied and fulfilled. To isolate the non-human creation's praise thus seems an unrealistic assessment of the quality of its relationship to God apart from humanity.

Page also suggests that humanity should be demoted from its position of cosmic priesthood. We are "humans-come-lately" on the evolutionary scheme, and God had a relationship with creatures prior to our arrival. Further, God and the animals were interrelated without us, and therefore humanity is not a necessary part of their communion with God. Hence humans should not consider themselves to be priests of creation, and it is false to hold that only humans can connect animals with God.[10] Anthropocentrism should be abandoned because we ought to celebrate the natural world's independence from humanity under God, and express "a fellow-feeling (rather than a management-feeling) for our fellow creatures, since we are all part of the one creation."[11] Southgate also wonders whether a theological focus upon the end result of cre-

---

8. Stannard, *God Experiment*, 195.
9. Abbott and Gallagher, *Documents of Vatican II*, 216.
10. Page, "Animal Kingdom," 2.
11. Page, "Theology and the Ecological Crisis," 111.

ation in "conscious reciprocal relationship with God" can ultimately portray the other living creatures as anything more than "means to the divine end."[12] Richard Bauckham agrees with Page that the non-human creation has value independently of human beings.[13] Peacocke concurs, insisting that we must "escape our anthropocentric myopia and affirm that God as Creator takes...delight in the rich variety and individuality of other organisms *for their own sake*."[14] The non-human creation cannot be regarded simply as an appendage to human existence.

In order to provide a context for making sense of the non-human creation's relationship to God, Page lays out a cosmology that circumscribes God's relationship with creation. She holds that God has withdrawn from the evolutionary flow of the history of life to enable possibility and freedom to the creation. God (1) creates by granting possibility and freedom, (2) accompanies all creation, not just humanity, and (3) God's presence is inherently salvific, not just for humanity, but for all creation. This cosmology is thought to provide further ammunition against the anthropocentrism "so often criticized in traditional doctrine." She believes evolutionary theory demonstrates that God had nothing to do with the rise of living creatures and ultimately humanity. She cannot accept that God would use a billions-of-years process of continuously divinely directed evolution to create life, nor that as a loving God he would allow mass extinctions such as occurred to the dinosaurs. She insists God does nothing but set it going in the beginning with the capacity for freedom and possibility.[15]

Critique

There are a number of problems in this cosmology. Page insists dinosaur extinction refutes the active hand of a loving God, and as a natural evil poses too large a problem for God's intervention in the world (theodicy). Page appears to be assigning an arbitrarily high value to the dinosaurs (or other non-human creatures), and by maintaining an equality of dinosaur and human worth has assumed what she is trying to prove (that dinosaur's or any other fairly advanced creature's death

---

12. Southgate, "God and Evolutionary Evil," 808.
13. Bauckham, *God and the Crisis of Freedom*, 172.
14. Peacocke, "Challenge and Stimulus," 95.
15. Page, "Animal Kingdom," 6.

is as evil as human death). She also interprets physical death to be final and morally insurmountable, in contradistinction to much Christian teaching on the greater importance of spiritual or eternal death. Jesus makes clear that it is not this world's physical death we are to fear, but rather God, "who is able to destroy both body and soul in hell" (Luke 12:5); eternal damnation or spiritual death is what is to be dreaded.

For Page, physical suffering such as that experienced by the dinosaurs is supposed to disprove that God's hand was actively involved in evolutionary processes, or could be intentionally leading to the creation of humanity. But Mark Wynn points out that such views of natural evil—fairly common in scientific polemics against the existence of God (e.g., Hume, Darwin, Gould, Crick)—fail to take into account the necessity of decay, predation, and pain as preconditions for various forms of flourishing. Such negative and contestable human aesthetic value judgments on natural processes are examples of "epistemic anthropocentrism." What is bad for humans may not be bad for the ecosystem as a whole. An ecosystemic perspective undermines the belief that natural evil is clumsy, cruel, or the same as moral evil. A Christian account that combines an ecosystemic perspective with the doctrine of the fall and a cross-centered redemption can answer this type of theodicy,[16] by drawing a clear distinction between human moral and culpable evil and natural amoral processes, and by offering a Creator who redeems his creation by entering into its suffering and death on the cross and giving it life through the resurrection.

Page wants to distance herself from deism by the use of her concept of "concurrence": God's *withness* or *Mitsein* with creation, a type of ongoing mutual relationship between God and the cosmos.[17] But if anything, God's transcendence and otherness from the creation are so emphasized in her view that God is effectively isolated from its physical creatures. Clare Palmer calls this "subdeism."[18] God is essentially a spectator rather than an active participant in relationship to any part of the universe, since otherwise he would be interfering with its freedom. This type of isolationist deism is fairly common in the science-theology dialogue. For instance, Brun insists God cannot interfere in the process, even at the beginning, lest he interfere with freedom and become

---

16. Wynn, *God and Goodness*, 104–15; Moltmann, *Way of Jesus Christ*, 297–301.
17. Page, *God and the Web of Creation*, 7, 58–62.
18. Palmer, review of *God and the Web of Creation*, 750.

responsible for evil.[19] Peacocke talks about God's role as "letting other be," and granting existence, "freedom and possibility" to creation, but otherwise not interfering (and so also not disappearing in the "God of the gaps" problem).[20] Polkinghorne calls this the "free-process defense": God allows freedom to the world to *be*, and supports it with love; he accords natural processes respect in the same way he allows humans free will (Polkinghorne does make room for miracles).[21]

Whether or not this free process defense really works is debatable. Leo Scheffczyk notes that the deist view of creation ultimately means that humanity "is left to itself in a world left to itself."[22] At least as it appears in Page's position, this translates to an essential problem for divine-creature relations. Southgate wonders how Page can talk of God's encouragement and companionship with creation at the same time that God is isolated from the cosmos.[23] What does God's "salvific presence" with creation mean when he has completely withdrawn from the process and cannot interfere for freedom's sake? How could creatures in her version of history have any real type of communion with their absent Creator? Freedom is key in Page's model, but Gregersen wonders, what benefit is freedom for non-human creatures that have no ability to accept or reject relationship with God?[24] Further, Southgate notes that Page's primary concern is to relieve the burden of theodicy, but even when only the initiator, "God is still responsible for the ontological aspect of the problem—for the existence of the world in which ... suffering takes place."[25]

Page's use of freedom appears to conflate the type of intentional and moral freedom available to human beings with the contingent freedom of natural and biological processes. While freedom of natural processes means *indeterminism*, Palmyre Oomen points out that human freedom means *self-determination*: choice bound by one's own commitment. "That is why [human] freedom ... clearly does not simply coincide with

---

19. Linzey, "Animal Theology," 23–25.
20. Peacocke, "End of All Our Exploring"; "Challenge and Stimulus," 89, 94.
21. Polkinghorne, *Science and Providence*, 66–67, 45–58.
22. Scheffczyk, *Creation and Providence*, 204.
23. Southgate, "God and Evolutionary Evil," 821 n. 9.
24. Gregersen, "Autopoiesis," 133.
25. Southgate, "God and Evolutionary Evil," 811.

unpredictability."[26] A rock crystal's growth or a DNA strand's mutation has no component of intentional or relational freedom, no element of moral responsibility. To call contingency in natural processes "freedom," and then to judge this by the same standards applied to human moral and relational capacity (or to impute that judgment to God) is to use a sliding definition of freedom. God's respect of natural processes working inside of contingent parameters is different from respect of human moral freedom in the same way that my respect of a roulette wheel is different from my respect of my neighbor's personal boundaries. One is indeterminate, non-personal, and amoral; the other is a matter of intentional freedom and personal responsibility. God may or may not "respect" indeterminism. But to argue he must do so on the basis of *moral* equivalency is a non sequitur.

Page believes that God shows no "partiality either to humans or to animals, but rather is equally open to all, at all times."[27] She also seems to assume the type of communion between God and the animals in the past is static and can never be surpassed in the future. It is true that humanity was not a necessary part of their past relationship with the Creator, whatever that was. However, it is not clear that *communion* is the appropriate word to describe her non-participatory God's relationship with any part of creation. In Christian eschatological perspective, God's past and present relationship with creation is a shadow of what it will be in the resurrection, and human beings are a necessary part of any future communion with the Creator. The wolf does not now lie down with the lamb, but one day it will through the medium of human incarnate redemption. To be sure, this is eschatological humanity, completed in Christ. But as such, humans are priests in the highest sense of the word: making the difference between life and death for the rest of creation. Thus we are not simply fellow creatures. Not only are we of much more worth than the sparrows (Matt 10:31), we can take responsibility for the sparrows and their brethren, while they cannot. The non-human cosmos is subjected to frustration, groaning until the children of God are revealed. The liberation of the creation from its bondage to decay only takes place through human and incarnate agency: through Jesus Christ. To deny this aspect of human destiny is to be blind to what exactly we are in the Christian God's economy of salvation.

26. Oomen, "On Brain, Soul, Self, and Freedom," 384–86.
27. Page, "Animal Kingdom," 2.

Further, Page wants to look to Jesus as some kind of divine revelation, and even talks of the resurrection. But how, if he exceeds other forms of God's self-revealing, is there not a human aspect to God's universal salvific work? Further, Jesus is for Page the incarnation of God "because in his words and actions (his concurrence)" God's *Mitsein* became visible and effective. Yet she insists that there is "no special divine aspect" to his being.[28] This is the type of degree Christology critiqued by Gunton and others that approaches Jesus only from below.[29] One wonders from where Jesus got his amazing power (e.g., to heal, deliver, confront) and righteousness, and how he was even able to rise from the dead, without God acting in the cosmos—and in some very special ways—both in and for Jesus. Page, Brun, and Peacocke all have God interfering in the cosmos in the life of Jesus, at least in his resurrection, while insisting God cannot interfere with the cosmos for freedom's sake.[30]

While Page claims her cosmology downgrades human significance, in fact her isolation of God from creation makes the need for a local representative of God in creation all the more poignant. Humanity is the ideal candidate for a materially present image of the Creator, with both transcendent and immanent capacities. This is what Zizioulas, Moltmann, and others indicate is part of the meaning of the *imago Dei*. There is no sharing on the part of the non-human creation in God's mode of love or knowledge, or in God's mode of life, until humanity in the incarnation bridges the gap. Without that bridge, the distance between Creator and creation remains infinite in a way that Braine describes as "incompatible with friendship or any kind of companionship."[31] This is not to say that a level of relationship is not present between God and animals, or between humans and animals. It is to acknowledge that a new depth or level of friendship and companionship become possible with human beings. For this reason Adam finds "no suitable companion" among all the rest of the animal kingdom in creation (Gen 2:20). Hall says, "in this creature the inarticulate (though never silent) creation

---

28. Page, *God and the Web of Creation*, 61.

29. Feenstra and Plantinga., *Trinity, Incarnation, and Atonement*, 9.

30. Page, *God and the Web of Creation*, 61–62; Brun, "Cosmology," 185; Peacocke, "Challenge and Stimulus," 89–93.

31. Braine, "Impossibility," 15.

becomes articulate."[32] This rings true not only of the interpersonal human situation, emphasizing the unique quality of human relationships, but also of the human-divine situation, especially as illuminated in the life of Jesus and his followers.[33] Personhood and personal relations only appear on the scene fully in human beings. At both the human level and the God-human/God-creation level, relationships are stunted until the incarnation and redemption. The history of the cosmos reveals stages of preparation in God's relationship to the cosmos, leading up to the appearance of the Son in human flesh. Humanity's arrival in the cosmic drama is at "just the right time" in God's plans (Rom 5:6), so that finally in Christ, communion with the whole creation becomes possible.

Zizioulas notes the type of freedom shared by the persons of God is shared in measure by humanity, and thus in them by the rest of creation.[34] This freedom and independence is modeled upon the type of freedom the divine persons have in relationship to each other in their unity. The incarnation decisively ties and extends this freedom to the creation, as the Creator becomes creature. Page would like to give to the creation a similar freedom in the name of the freedoms of nature supposedly guaranteed by modern physics. However, her version of God's interaction with natural law cannot maintain this freedom. If the laws of physics are self-sustaining apart from God, and God's sole function is to preserve or uphold the laws, then freedom must ultimately disappear, because the cosmos has no possible real referent or connection to God's infinite life. Without that life, the cosmos is doomed to finiteness rather than ultimate freedom. It cannot transcend its mortality. *Death* is what finally undoes Page's argument, for death is everywhere clearly present and reigning in the cosmos, and death is what ends the communion of the non-personal creation until salvation comes in human form. Southgate thus wonders why Page's distant deistic God "should be the object of worship or the recipient of prayer," and maintains that her view is "not a basis for a Christian theology of creation and involvement with the cosmos."[35]

32. Hall, *Imaging God*, 204.

33. Page is ready to admit "human specialness and difference from the rest of creation" in light of the New Testament focus on the God-human relationship. "Theology and the Ecological Crisis," 109.

34. Zizioulas, "On Being a Person," 37.

35. Southgate, "God and Evolutionary Evil," 811.

Conclusion

In conclusion, there are significant problems in Page's cosmology. While making what appears to be a deistic move to solve the problem of evil in the non-human creation, God remains responsible for the ontological aspect of what Page believes is a naturally evil world. God is supposed to be with the creation in companionship, but the value of that companionship is questionable without any type of real personal relationship or interaction between creature and Creator. She conflates moral freedom with natural process indeterminism and contingency, and judges the two separate concepts as if they are one and the same. In her thought, God's interaction with the cosmos is inconsistent, since God is supposed to be unable to interfere with his creation, but does so decisively in the person and work of Jesus Christ. Finally, and especially since she posits Christ as God's revelation, she has failed to show that human beings do not have a central role in fulfilling the non-human creation and in offering it real, life-filled communion in Christ that has eternal dimensions.

Andrew Linzey in Defense of Animal Rights

Overview of Linzey's position

Andrew Linzey critiques aspects of Judeo-Christian tradition for its "instrumentalist" view of animals. He and Dan Cohn-Sherbok note that those in the West have been too inclined to treat animals purely as objects for human use, and to disregard their moral status. Scripture and religious tradition condoned the use of animals for food, for ritual sacrifice, and for hard labor.[36] Humans are prioritized ahead of the animals, and animal well-being is subservient to human well-being. While the killing of animals is allowed in Scripture, the murder of humans is forbidden and punishable by death, because "in his own image God made humankind" (Gen 9:6). Even though death is inevitable after the human rebellion, God clothes the first humans with animal skins, the first sacrifice of an animal's life to cover the effects of human sin (Gen 3:21).[37] Though prior to the fall animals are not for food, after the fall

---

36. Linzey and Cohn-Sherbok, *After Noah*, 2–13.

37. Jamieson et al. *Commentary, Old Testament, Vol. 1: Genesis-Psalms*, 16; Clarke, *Commentary*, 1:70.

they are accepted as sacrificial substitutes and later as food "destined to perish with use" (Able—Gen 4:4; Noah—Gen 8:20; Col 2:22). Jesus encourages his disciples, "Do not be afraid; you are of more value than many sparrows" (Matt 10:31; Luke 12:7).

Linzey and Cohn-Sherbok also maintain that philosophers and theologians such as Aristotle and Descartes, Augustine, Aquinas, Luther, and Calvin demarcated characteristics of "non-rationality, non-community and intellectual inferiority" in the animals, and gradually defined them "out of the moral picture." Animals have been regarded as machines without true sentience, moral capacity, soul, or ultimate worth, and as undeserving of moral status. Their sufferings were irrelevant and they were to be used and experimented on without pity.[38]

Yet Linzey suggests that many Scriptures show that the animal kingdom does have real value to God. From commands for animal compassion in the Torah (Lev 24:18, 21), to proverbs on the proper treatment of animals (Prov 12:10), to God's concern for the cattle of Nineveh (Jonah 4:11), to his warning that the sacrifice of animals will be regarded as just as reprehensible as the murder of a human (Isa 66:3), it is clear that God loves the non-human creatures of his creation. In the eschaton, the lion and lamb lie down together, and little children will play with deadly serpents (Isa 11:6–8). Too often, God's care for humans has eclipsed the basic truth that "his eye is [also] on the sparrow."[39]

Linzey insists the creation is endowed with what he calls *theos-rights*, borrowing a concept from Dietrich Bonhoeffer intended solely for human affairs. Linzey says these rights are given intrinsically to all creatures independent of animal relations to human beings, because God is *for* his creation, and the creation is *for* God. By reverencing creation, we are reverencing God because of "*God's own rights* in creation": true worship of God entails respect for all of God's creatures.[40] He insists that we must "abandon our sharp, sometimes arrogant, separation of humankind from nature." Christ is Lord not just of and for human beings, but of and for all creation.[41] On the other hand, humans are the priestly mediators of this divine prerogative. Linzey and Cohn-Sherbok believe the positive strands in the religious tradition, uplifting the status

---

38. Linzey and Cohn-Sherbok, *After Noah*, 2–13.
39. Martin, "His Eye is On the Sparrow."
40. Linzey, *Animal Theology*, 23ff.
41. Ibid., 9–10.

of animals and emphasizing their value and, for Linzey, implicitly joining them within the Eucharistic redemption of all things, even hint at the possibility of their ultimate fellowship. The paradoxical scriptural perspectives are unified in the redemption, when there will be life and peace between all creatures in heaven and earth. Death comes to all creatures this side of the eschaton, but death's reign over *all* creatures is likewise doomed in Christ.[42] As a result of this reassessment of animal status in theology, Linzey would like to do away with all instrumental use and mistreatment of animals, or at least of mammals, including their use as food and for experimentation.[43]

Critique

Deane-Drummond believes Linzey's logic is insufficiently rigorous, and maintains his reading of both Aquinas and Descartes is simplistic and sometimes false.[44] As a caricature, it serves the critique of human abuse of animals, but it is factually inaccurate. Leahy notes some problems in Linzey's thought, of which Linzey is himself aware. (1) There seems to be a clear "psychic hierarchy" in the Old Testament. (2) In the natural world, animals kill and eat each other regularly for survival, so that Linzey notes "to posit notions of animal rights in a creation that hardly admits of them is theological fantasy." (3) In the New Testament, Christ probably ate meat (e.g., paschal lambs), and certainly ate fish,[45] even in his resurrected body (Luke 24:42). Linzey later attempts a more robust defense of rights language, arguing "the Christian tradition has historically inspired, if not pioneered, some kinds of rights language."[46] Bauckham agrees that Jesus in his teaching and action valued animals, but "in principle . . . human beings are of more value." Jesus elevates the worth of animals in many of his stories and parables, but elevates humans even further.[47] His diet and his use of the foal on Palm Sunday as a beast of burden demonstrate that non-human animals also have

---

42. Linzey and Cohn-Sherbok, *After Noah*, 94–104.

43. Deane-Drummond, "Navigating the Maze."

44. Ibid.

45. Leahy, *Against Liberation*, 211–12; Linzey, "Reverence, Responsibility and Rights," 43.

46. Linzey, *Animal Theology*, 26.

47. Bauckham, "Jesus and Animals," 37–45, 48.

divinely ordained servant roles in creation, which may include service to humans.

Perhaps the most severe criticism can be leveled at Linzey's idea of human priestly responsibility on behalf of non-human creatures (see chapter 3 on similar issues in Zizioulas). Bauckham critiques this as "top-down" and "anthropocentric." He insists that there is not a trace of such arrogance in the Scriptures, and rejects the idea that "the rest of creation can only be itself in relation to God" through "human mediation." He insists the "anthropocentricity that treats humanity as the summit and goal of all things rose not from the traditional Christian worldview, but from the Renaissance exaltation of humanity above the angels and the Enlightenment rejection of both angels and God." He insists that humans only praise God together with the other creatures, and do *not* somehow enable their praise.[48] Bauckham's case may be overstated, as the theological analysis has shown. Scripture clearly elevates humanity, especially in the incarnation (e.g., Gen 1:28; Pss 8:5; 139:13–14; Matt 10:31).

Deane-Drummond agrees that the top-down view is condescending. Animals are together with humans in their mutual submission to God's natural law, so that some type of theocentric focus must be maintained. Bauckham even suggests that the best thing humans could do is to leave parts of nature alone, as "wildernesses." "Creation praises God very well without us," and it is to be valued by us as God values it for the way it glorifies God in itself.[49] Rolston agrees, noting the need for wilderness zones, not just rural and urban zones. He believes it is morally naïve and obsolete to continue "living in a reference frame where one species takes itself as absolute and values everything else relative to its utility."[50] With Gruen, we can agree there is no need to defend such "pernicious anthropocentrism."[51]

We have already seen Cobb's and S. R. L. Clark's critiques of the exaggeration of human priestly responsibility in Zizioulas, which highlights the properly theocentric focus of theology.[52] Theology must

---

48. Bauckham, "Joining Creation's Praise," 48–50, 59; see also his *God and the Crisis of Freedom*, 140.

49. Bauckham, "Joining Creation's Praise," 51.

50. Rolston, *Environmental Ethics*, 153–54, 159, 326–27.

51. Gruen, "Revaluing Nature," 369.

52. Cobb, "All Things in Christ?," 179; Clark, *Biology and Christian Ethics*, 269, 319; *Animals and their Moral Standing*, 8.

recognize that God in Jesus Christ is the principal actor in salvation, not the rest of the human race. As Isaiah prophesies, "I looked, but there was no helper; I stared, but there was no one to sustain me; so my own arm brought me victory" (63:5). The place of humans in this scheme is grateful receptivity, not exaggerated claims of self-importance.

A Middle Way

A middle position may be more reasonable than either excessive or abdicatory claims for human cosmic priesthood. Michael Northcott notes that Judeo-Christian faith does not focus on *rights* one way or the other, but upon duties and responsibilities, including those of humans to their fellow creatures.[53] On a mundane level, Linzey's focus on *theos-rights* to effect a better treatment of non-human creatures highlights the inevitably anthropocentric aspect of any effective ecological policy. Katherine Kortenkamp and Colleen Moore note that on a practical level, anthropocentric ethics are as likely as ecocentric ethics to promote pro-environmental responses in the ecologically sensitive.[54] Tony Lunch and David Wells believe "the 'non-anthropocentric' stream of environmental ethics" is unable to provide moral motivation, because it disintegrates the foundation of moral choice by removing the human distinctive. Assigning equal moral worth to all creatures leads to an ethical impasse, because it does not take human moral capacity seriously. Such a leveling ethical principle is "ecopathy," because it has destroyed its own moral underpinnings. Whether or not this leads to the charge of "human chauvinism" is irrelevant, because it is humanity itself that is the "fundamental modality of moral concern." Rejection of moral justification on the basis of "special relationship" (e.g., a human rescuing a fellow human from an attacking predator) is a *refusal of the moral*, "rather than a demand for its purification." Lunch and Wells suggest "aesthetic reverence" is a more stable platform upon which to defend the environment than such anti-anthropocentric ethics.[55]

---

53. Northcott, *Environment and Christian Ethics*, 184–85.

54. Kortenkamp and Moore, "Ecocentrism and Anthropocentrism," 260, 269.

55. Lynch and Wells, "Non-Anthropocentrism?," 151–63. The following anecdote provides the practical ethical quandary that exposes "ecopathy": As you are walking through the jungle, you suddenly come upon a large animal violently attacking a fellow human being. You have a loaded gun, and "have no doubt you can hit what you aim for." What do you do?

Since the ascription of significant moral status and value to animals is only meaningful to and for humans, the attempt to evade "anthropocentric condescension" ends up highlighting uniquely human capacities and responsibilities. Page agrees, noting "those who plead for animal rights are appealing precisely to the moral conscience and the intelligence of human beings concerning animals who lack these superior features."[56] Ariansen concurs that even among the animal rights activists, all "positions agree that only humans can take on moral responsibility and that inter-animal action does not trigger morality at all."[57] As Deane-Drummond notes, recognizing that all rights come from God does not diminish human responsibility, because only humans have the rational power to understand and obey God's commands, to discuss and implement law for nature, rather than just be subject to it.[58]

While humans are incapable of ultimately saving the cosmos, and may even contribute to earth's destruction, nevertheless, they alone are capable of consciously cooperating in the at least partial mediation of God's love and care for the earth. Cosmic priesthood may find its actual realization and fulfillment only in Jesus Christ, but the church is his body on the earth, and shares that priesthood in some measure as it calls people everywhere to repentance and responsibility.

Conclusion

In theological perspective, humans must beware of exaggerating their own place in creation, or of valuing nature only relative to themselves, rather than to God. Creation's praise of God is independent of humans. Indeed, some of God's greatest "human" praise is only passively expressed: God's glory is revealed in them because they are the *recipients* of his gracious love.

Yet efforts to eliminate anthropocentrism from practical solutions to the ecological crisis and evaluations of the worth of the non-human creation seem to ignore some fundamental realities of the human situation in relation to the world. The non-human creation's moral status is fundamentally an anthropocentric reality, ascribed *by* humans, though

---

56. Page, *God and the Web of Creation*, 106.
57. Ariansen, "Anthropocentrism with a Human Face," 154.
58. Deane-Drummond, "Navigating the Maze."

this is not incompatible with the more basic theological reality that all worth comes from God.

It might seem that Pannenberg, Rahner, and Zizioulas' treatment of human nature and personhood gives inadequate moral status to animals. However, their incarnational perspective on human service to God and creation, and their similar approach to cosmic redemption actually provides a fuller foundation upon which the insights on positive animal status may be grounded. Pannenberg highlights stewardship as a feature of God-given human dominion in creation, properly imaged in the life and ministry of Jesus Christ. For Rahner, the human realization of God in Christ is a realization of *servanthood* on behalf of the entire cosmos. Stewardship is the natural conclusion. Similarly, in Zizioulas' vision, humans are the *agent* for the redemption of the cosmos in the person of Christ and in the corporate church, not the sole *purpose* for its redemption.

Not every aspect of their theological approach can be fully substantiated—e.g., exaggerated claims for human cosmic priesthood beyond the reality of the incarnation. Yet there need be no necessary conflict between one goal of God's creative processes being something like human beings, and the independent worth of the non-human creation. While humans have a call to mediate God's will towards the earth in more elaborate fashion than other creatures (we are not just to "be fruitful and multiply" but are to "have dominion" and "subdue the earth"; Gen 1:22, 28), theology's essential anthropocentric claim in regard to the environment is the incarnation, since in Christ humanity guarantees the ultimate life of the rest of creation. Only because Jesus is human, and the agent of God's cosmic salvation, can the theologian insist a measure of anthropocentrism is appropriate in light of final ecological concerns and issues. In the meantime, theology can highlight humanity's ongoing responsibility before God for the animals, the earth and its ecosystems.

Conclusion

The Anthropocentric Cosmos

> What are human beings that you are mindful of them, mortals that you care for them? Yet you have made them a little lower than God, and crowned them with glory and honor.
>
> —Psalm 8:4–5

Restatement of Thesis

THIS THESIS HAS PROPOSED THAT HUMAN BEINGS ARE OF VITAL SIGnificance in the cosmos, and that this significance is visible to both theology and science, in respectively different though coherent ways. While modern science is supposed to have made the medieval worldview of humanity at the center of the universe obsolete, a modern variation of that medieval perspective is in fact still valid. While not every form of anthropocentrism is defensible, such as those centered on human perspective, arrogance, prejudice, or prioritization, *critical anthropocentrism* can be defended. This position avoids the scientific naiveté of the pre-Copernican vision and certain other excesses and errors, but concludes that humans *are* of key cosmic significance. The theological investigation shows that contemporary Trinitarian and ecumenical theology, as represented by Pannenberg, Rahner, and Zizioulas, continues to be deeply and irrevocably anthropocentric. This commitment emerges from the doctrines of the *imago Dei* and the *incarnation*. The natural sciences agree that humans are unique and cosmically significant, especially as the unique human mind is seen to be a result of cosmic evolution. Ecological concerns do not destroy the viability of the position and can be encompassed within it. With provisos, *critical anthropocentrism* is valid both theologically and scientifically. Human beings are cosmically significant as part of God's holistic plan in Christ for the salvation of the cosmos, and this is coherent with contemporary scientific thought.

The Theological Perspective

Recall the theological problems posed at the beginning. Is the Sabbath better understood as the crown of creation rather than humanity? Is the image of God to be found elsewhere than in unified human nature, perhaps in the human mind or in nature? Is the revelation of God in Christ just about our local human needs, or does it have larger scope? Could extraterrestrial sentient creatures also image God, and be in need of their own incarnation for salvation? Does the contemporary setting of theology and science really destroy *teleology*? Is humanity just an artifact of nature, or is there evidence of providence in its existence?

This study has shown that Pannenberg, Rahner, and Zizioulas each wrestles with the subject of human nature in Trinitarian and incarnational perspective, and each is sensitive to related issues in the natural sciences. In turn, their thought answers some of these key questions. Their positions can be summarized as follows.

Wolfhart Pannenberg

According to Pannenberg, God has created the universe with the incarnation as its chief goal and crown. The history of the universe is focused towards incarnation, and comes to fruition in Jesus Christ. His resurrection confirms that he is Son of God incarnate. He legitimizes the creaturely independence of reality from God, and is the model for creation's dependence upon God. In his incarnate union with creation, Jesus is the means for the cosmos to transcend its mortality, which will be realized in the eschaton. In light of the incarnation, Pannenberg declares that "we humans can be called the goal of creation." In this incarnational perspective, the history of the universe is "a prehistory to the coming of humanity."[1]

The significance of the image of God in humanity, most fully realized in the incarnate Jesus, is that it represents God's self in the cosmos. Though God is a mystery, when he once and forever unites with his creation, it is as a *human being*. Thus with Barth, the incarnation al-

---

1. Pannenberg, *Systematic Theology*, 2:74.

lows us to assert the *humanity* of God.² As such, human nature as the *imago Dei* can only be understood holistically, in light of Christ's own life. Humanity represents God to the cosmos, and the cosmos to God. While the Sabbath rest may image the completion of creation with God himself, humans are an essential part of that completion. "The destiny of all creation is at stake," because the whole creation waits "for the manifestation of divine sonship in the human race."³ Only then will the corruptibility of all creation end. Thus humanity is the key to the cosmos' salvation. Representing realist Protestant Trinitarian theology, Pannenberg's thought, centered on the "human-divine representative," is intrinsically anthropocentric.

Karl Rahner

For Rahner, human transcendentality and the incarnation give humanity crucial cosmic importance. In them God has become incarnate into his creation once and for all time. Human nature alone is ready and adoptable to become God in Christ, because it alone is indefinable without transcendence. Humanity is *the* material creature that transcends the material cosmos, and who can be regarded—as both a material and spiritual being—as the "goal of nature." The incarnation shows that ontologically, transcendent causality has guided the creation and evolutionary processes towards their human end from the very beginning. The scientist may not admit this teleological and theological conclusion, but must admit the distinctiveness of the end result of the natural processes in the rational consciousness of humanity.

Rahner also believes that in humanity, properly located within the life of God in Christ, the cosmos finds "final consummation."⁴ Thus humanity is of vital cosmic significance. Human nature and the incarnation, as aspects of the life of the Triune God occurring in and for cosmic destiny, confirm an anthropocentric universe. Rahner sometimes seems open to de-anthropocentrizing possibilities, like extraterrestrials and multiple incarnations. However, theology seems unlikely at present to need to adapt to these speculative possibilities. Rahner's overall program, representative of post-Vatican II Roman Catholic theology,

---

2. Barth, *Humanity of God*, 49–50.
3. Pannenberg, *Anthropology*, 12.
4. Rahner, *Theological Investigations*, 5:168.

remains in its human transcendent and incarnational focus deeply anthropocentric.

John Zizioulas

For Zizioulas, humanity is unique in creation because it is the image of the Triune God. Humans alone of all creatures are created as *persons*, modeled after God's *personhood*, and capable of *theosis*—the Orthodox concept of potentially being made into the likeness of God in Christ. Only humans are capable of transcending the given law-bound nature of the cosmos in freedom, creativity, and love. As the *imago Dei*, human nature is not to be understood in substantive terms, but only in relation to God. Because of the person and work of Christ, humanity is offered a share in divine personhood, to be fulfilled eschatologically. The cosmos is prepared from its foundations for the incarnation, so that humanity is the fulcrum that unites the nature of God with the cosmos. Christ, in whom the communion of the divine and human natures is restored, turns the cosmos into a realm where God is present rather than absent.

God's divine life is extended through redeemed humanity, his corporate body the church, so that they become "the very core and nucleus of the destiny of the world." Ecclesial humanity is priest in Christ for the creation, representing the cosmos to God and God to the cosmos, bringing the two into communion. The hope of the universe rests upon them because only in them will it gain immortality. So Zizioulas says, "Man . . . is the only being responsible for the fate of creation."[5] Insofar as he represents the Orthodox Christian tradition, that stream of Christianity remains deeply anthropocentric, correlating divine and human personhood at the center of cosmic history.

Conclusion

Having critically considered the thought of Pannenberg, Rahner, and Zizioulas on the *imago Dei* and the incarnation, and the interaction of their ideas with many other theologians, a general theological position on human significance in the cosmos may now be framed. The two doctrines work together to reveal, in a perspective that spans the work

---

5. Zizioulas, "Mystery of the Church," 296; "Preserving God's Creation (3)," 3; "Preserving God's Creation (2)," 45.

of God across cosmic history, that humanity is made in and as the image of God, and that this image finds its restoration, culmination, and fulfillment in the incarnation of God in Jesus Christ, the perfect image of God. Pannenberg, Rahner, and Zizioulas all agree on the preeminent distinction revealed by the incarnation for humanity—of all creatures, only it was prepared for and then did receive very God into its flesh and blood existence.

From this foundational understanding of the full *imago Dei*, several things may be inferred about human significance. Humanity is God's chosen vessel in the cosmos for most clearly and openly revealing himself. While potentially present in created human nature, the fullness of the image is only realized in the incarnate Christ. He reveals God's self to the whole creation once and for all time in human form. It is humanity's role in the cosmos to receive this incarnate union between creation and Creator, to reveal the transcendent God in the created cosmos. For this reason, humanity can be called the goal of creation; in incarnational perspective, the history of the universe is a prehistory to the coming of humanity.

Humanity is also vital to the universe's fulfillment. Human beings are God's covenant partners, representing the entire cosmos. In them the cosmos becomes conscious of itself, conscious of God, and finally one with God. In Christ, humans are priest to and for the cosmos. The destiny of creation is fulfilled through humanity's relationship to God in Christ. The whole creation waits—even longs—for the revealing of the children of God in the human race, for only then will its mortality and corruptibility end. This focus on humanity has limits, especially as only God can finally save the world, and humans are liable by themselves to destroy it. However, it is the union of Christ with humanity that gives the cosmos its ultimate future, when its consummation at the wedding feast is eschatologically realized. In that union, the cosmos will be liberated from its frustration and bondage to decay, and brought into the glorious liberty of the children of God.

While nuances of approach are evident in these three ecumenical theologians, their position, insofar as it is representative of Christianity in general, suggests that incarnational and Trinitarian theology is intrinsically human centered. Humanity is the representative and image of God, the focal point of God's fulfillment of cosmic history in the incarnation, realizing in Trinitarian fellowship a goal of creation (there may be other goals), and acting as the key upon which the redemption of nature depends. This significance can only be understood within a properly theocentric horizon. All this shows that an anthropocentric focus is more than just a passing feature of contemporary ecumenical theology. It is embedded in its deep structure, part of its warp and woof, the inevitable result of Trinitarian and incarnational thought. Christianity believes humanity is at the heart of cosmic destiny in Christ.

The Scientific Perspective

Recall the scientific questions and problems posed at the beginning. Does modern science prove that foundational features of theology like incarnation and resurrection are unreal? Is reductionistic naturalism the ultimate rationality it claims to be, so that human significance is purely metaphorical or symbolic? Has science eliminated the absolute barrier separating humans from the non-human creation? Does it prove that humans are only different in degree from animals? Has it proved that humans are nowhere near the center of the universe, either physically or metaphorically? Does it really destroy the belief that God's providence has led to human existence, and show that human beings are a cosmic triviality? Is bad anthropocentric theology at the root of the ecological problem? Is the theological portrait of humanity just fluff on top of what we know to be true from science?

While science by definition is unable to answer meaning-type questions, the analysis suggests that science nevertheless sees human beings as unique and significant. This becomes clear not so much in light of the specifics of human origins, or a full scientific definition of the human person, as in what science sees as unique about human existence and nature. Despite being unable to determine humanity's geographical place in the universe, the evidence suggests some non-geographical ways of describing human significance. Science supports at least three interrelated senses in which human beings are of central significance on the cosmic stage: (1) The human mind is unique among all types of known and speculative minds. (2) Humanity is the pinnacle of complexity in the known universe—the final and highest result of the universal processes of sequential complexity. Finally, (3) science reveals a universe in which earth, and hence humanity, is likely to be extremely rare, possibly one of a kind. All these features are visible to science.

The Boundary of Science with Theology

The collapse of Enlightenment foundationalism has shown the ultimate irrationality of materialistic naturalism. The methodological naturalism of the scientific method cannot claim epistemic hegemony in the theological realm; science cannot describe the whole of reality. The revelation of religion is not reducible to or understandable in terms of the naturalistic method of science, focused as it is on the repeatable regularities of nature. Science can say nothing about historical and/or supernatural events like the incarnation and resurrection. In this sense, theology is independent of science, and yet may still say true things about physical and spiritual reality. Discovering coherence between the two disciplines on the thesis of *critical anthropocentrism* helps bolster its validity, and shows that it is more than just a metaphorical truth that is only useful within a limited theological milieu.

Non-human Intelligence

Does non-human intelligence cast doubt on human uniqueness? While it is true that modern science has closed some of the gap separating human beings from other creatures, it has also illuminated how wide and fixed the gap remains, and how truly unique the human mind is. The fact that no kind of linguistic mastery ever arises in other animals' natural condition, is difficult at best to inculcate, and never reaches the level sufficient for moral reasoning, indicates the deep gulf between human and non-human intelligence. Only with anatomically modern humans does the record show a sudden and massive *mental* explosion. With our symbolically structured minds, human language supports a host of other uniquely human characteristics, including art, culture, religion, moral reasoning, and responsible interpersonal relationships. If this is what we mean by personhood (and this would seem to be a minimalist definition), then science agrees that in all the animal kingdom, only human beings are truly *persons*. Human symbolic reasoning, language, moral-relational capacity, and spiritual awareness are not even potentially present in other material creatures. Thus the claim of human uniqueness appears to be coherent with the current state of scientific knowledge.

Humans appear to be unique not only on the earth, but also in the cosmos as a whole. Artificial intelligence is unlikely to copy human nature anytime soon; in fact, it may be impossible both practically and theoretically to establish true human-like self-consciousness and volition in a machine. Extraterrestrial intelligence also appears unlikely to challenge human uniqueness. Although it may not be theoretically impossible—depending on one's position on evolutionary inevitability—ETI may be statistically improbable, especially in light of the rarity of earth's bio-friendly environment. Until concrete evidence emerges of higher life in other solar systems, it seems prudent to remain skeptical about its existence, and prudent to resist wholesale changes to our theology based on speculation.

Cosmic Evolution, Human Existence, and Providence

Because the very existence of science depends on an orderly and intelligible universe, science is rooted in metaphysics. The scientific data of the big bang, the anthropic conditions, and cosmic evolution have revitalized the cosmological argument. Other explanations for cosmic order, such as multiple universes, lucky chance, or brute fact, fail to have the same logical weight as the transcendent solution; the best explanation remains divine design. The development of the cosmos from its beginnings to the present has manifested remarkable order, the potentiality for and actualization of life, and the propensity to develop in the direction of sequential complexity. These features of the cosmos are strongly suggestive of teleology. Science by its methods might be unable to detect God's activity at a certain level, but could not circumscribe it, including such causation or inspiration on earth. What science describes in the anthropic principle and in the processes of cosmic evolution may in theological perspective be aspects of God's care and providential guidance of the cosmos.

The concept of *sequential complexity* suggests a fruitful way to describe humanity's place in the cosmos. Out of all observed levels of material reality, human being is the pinnacle of complexity. The human brain is the most complex object in the known universe. If specially created by God, humans can think of their existence in teleological terms. But even if human existence is an emergent result of non-predetermined natural processes, it could be regarded as accidental only in a limited sense. Its appearance would be an outcome of possibilities built into the cosmos by God, and therefore ultimately intentional. The doctrine of providence can encompass either interpretation.

Whether or not the universe has been designed to culminate simply in a *conscious* being or in *human* being, it is only humans, as Rahner observed, who open up fully to the absolute transcendent.[6] Only humans are able to relate consciously to God, and are the creatures in which the universe is finally prepared to relate to and receive *God's* being. It is a theological datum of faith that the universe has been designed to culminate in the incarnation, but this seems to be coherent with the scientific portrait of human complexity and consciousness; even science sees that humans are uniquely open and oriented to the transcendent realm.[7] Thus the idea that humanity might be a goal of the creation, while theological rather than scientific, is coherent with scientific discourse.

Ecological Concerns

Are ecological concerns damning to critical anthropocentrism? The relationship between humans and creation highlighted in Pannenberg, Rahner, and Zizioulas points to the ideas of stewardship and servanthood. These are only properly imaged and understood in the life and ministry of Jesus Christ, who shows that loving stewardship is the proper mode of that relationship. The incarnation is a realization of servanthood on behalf of the entire cosmos. Further, humans are the agent for the redemption of the cosmos, not the sole purpose for its redemption. All this suggests a role for the church in instructing human stewardship of creation.

Furthermore, efforts to eliminate anthropocentrism from solutions to the ecological crisis seem to ignore some fundamental realities. It is clear that ascribing significant moral status and value to animals is only meaningful to and for humans. Animals cannot return the favor. Regardless of whatever pre-moral behavior animals are said to possess, no one in the animal-rights discussion ever talks about giving animals moral responsibility, because they are incapable of it. In this sense, the attempt to evade "anthropocentric condescension" ends up highlighting uniquely human capacities and responsibilities. This potential for responsibility makes possible human efforts to protect and save the environment. Thus a high view of human significance need not be seen

---

6. Rahner, *Theological Investigations*, 4:107; *Foundations*, 188.
7. Morowitz, *Emergence of Everything*, 195.

as ecologically insensitive, and can in fact support environmental concerns. Nevertheless, there are limits to the human priestly relation to creation: only God can ultimately save the world. With such correction and sensitivity, an anthropocentric position is reasonable, perhaps even necessary, in light of ecological concerns.

Conclusion

The natural sciences are often presumed to show that humans are nowhere near the "center" of the universe, either physically or metaphorically. However, the scientific portrait of human existence and uniqueness suggests a very different conclusion. While a geographical center is meaningless, it appears that humans may occupy a place at the center of the spatio-temporal cosmic stage in terms of their uniqueness, their complexity, their socially and symbolically mediated mental capacity, and their orientation to the transcendent. The natural sciences converge to emphasize human uniqueness on the earth and in the entire cosmos, and underline those features that make human I-Thou relationships possible. As the one creature in the cosmos made in the image of the Creator, this is not a surprise to theology. What is meaningful in this context is the coherence of the scientific understanding with the theological understanding of human being. We appear to be unique, the most complex material life form in the cosmos, and significant for that alone. It is not only the case that the scientific evidence is consistent with the theological position; it is also in its own way indirect confirmation. This approach integrates the findings of science and theology, and is stronger than mere consistency without insisting one domain must prove conclusions in the other. Together, they form a broader, integrated interdisciplinary perspective on the truth of human significance.

Some Unresolved Issues

While a high view of human significance remains reasonable in the contemporary setting, there are a number of unresolved issues and questions requiring further investigation. For instance:

1. Given that theology is very much concerned with community in human, divine, and human-divine relations, contemporary insights on human nature from the natural sciences and anthropology ought to provide theology with some fruitful insights, for

instance in studies of social Trinitarianism, of Jesus' humanity and divinity, or in the role of the church in relation to community.

2. The connection between the human body, mind, and spirit remains an open question for both science and theology. The mind-body problem deserves more careful attention. Research into AI and consciousness still has much to discover, with perhaps as-yet-unimagined paradigms opening the way for further insight.

3. The debate by evolutionary theorists about whether life is inevitable or improbable, a result of chance, necessity, or both, as typified by the approaches of Monod vs. De Duve, will likely continue. Theoretical laws of emergent complexity and so-called evidence for intelligent design both deserve further exploration.

4. The extraterrestrial intelligence debate is far from over. Concrete exploration of space may be the only definitive way to answer the question.

5. Worldviews heavily influenced by the scientific vision may well be tempted to idolize the human mind and rationality. What correctives and responsibility towards culture does theology have? What are the ethical implications of *critical anthropocentrism*?

6. In a world with seven-plus billion people, the human relation to the environment is ever more critical. What should stewardship of the environment entail? What role ought the church have in relation to the problem?

These deserve fuller unpacking, and there are no doubt many other questions that could be raised, but those are beyond the scope of this work.

Summary and Conclusion

It is clear from the evidence unpacked in this project that a high view of human significance is built into Christian theology, and this special position is tightly coherent with contemporary natural science. Christianity, insofar as it is Trinitarian and incarnational, is, even in the modern ecumenical setting, deeply and inevitably anthropocentric. Such a conclusion is best grounded and understood theocentrically, in God's action toward the world in Jesus Christ, both in the creation of human beings as the creature made to image God, and in the incarnation, when the Son of God joins with creation as a human being. This inate theological anthropocentrism restores the dignitiy of human personhood, and can be sensitive to current ecological and justice issues, especially in light of the moral and stewardship dimensions of the image of God.

Contrary to the pervasive and degraded stereotype so prevalent in sci-fi movies and pop culture, contemporary science also agrees that something very special has appeared in the universe in human beings. The human mind appears to be unique in the cosmos; we are the one being "in whom the universe has become conscious of itself," and conscious of God.[8] Our capacity for personal relationships and communion is unrivaled in the known material realm, scientifically visible in our unique symbolic and relational intelligence, with its accompanying moral, ethical, and creative freedom.

The two disciplines of theology and science show a remarkable integration on human distinction and significance. Though each discipline has its own unique perspective, and neither view proves the findings of the other, together they provide a complementary picture of human dignity and importance. Awareness of this complementarity should provide some fruitful avenues of further discussion across the science-theology dialogue, as well as challenge the stereotype of antipathy often presented as the only way the two disciplines can engage.

Further, a renewed appreciation for humanity's cosmic significance may have profound implications not only in theology and science, but in ethics and moral philosophy. God's love for creation has a fulcrum in humanity. Human dignity and eternal worth are at the heart of the gospel proclamation of the incarnate Son. Today it is more vital than ever that the disciplines of both science and theology inform the decision-making processes of our human community. Our various cultures' increasing use of developing genetic and medical technology without sufficient ethical or spiritual foundation cries for the integration of these two disciplines, if we are not to reap unforeseen and possibly disastrous consequences.

Both the garden of Eden and the tower of Babel stories are about humans reaching towards heaven without regard for God, and the dire consequences that follow. The gospel, on the other hand, is about God in Christ coming down to us, to make us like him in love and so fit us for

---

8. Polkinghorne, *Science and Theology*, 56.

an eternal destiny. Bringing the theological truths of that knowledge to the table alongside scientific truth may help us to keep our knowledge and technology in their proper place as our tools, not our masters. This will call us to be good stewards of the world with which we have been entrusted, understanding that creation will continue to groan as it waits for God's children to be fully revealed. And it will help preserve and protect human dignity and eternal worth, telling us who we are, and who we are called to be, because all creation waits for its consummation in *us*.

Bibliography

Academic Press Dictionary of Science and Technology. Edited by Christopher Morris. San Diego: Academic, 1992.
Acuna, M. H., et al. "Magnetic Field and Plasma Observation at Mars: Initial Results of the Mars Global Surveyor Mission." *Science* 279 (1998) 1676-80.
Aichele, George, et al., editors. *The Postmodern Bible: The Bible and Culture Collective.* New Haven: Yale University Press, 1995.
Akazawa, Takeru, Kenichi Aoki, and Ofer Bar-Yosef, editors. *Neandertals and Modern Humans in Western Asia.* New York: Plenum, 1998.
Alston, William P. *Perceiving God: The Epistemology of Religious Experience.* Ithaca: Cornell University Press, 1991.
Alter, Robert, and Frank Kermode, editors. *The Literary Guide to the Bible.* London: Collins, 1987.
Aminoff, Michael J., et al. "Electrocerebral Accompaniments of Syncope Associated with Malignant Ventricular Arrhythmias." *Annals of Internal Medicine* 108 (1988) 791-96.
Anderson, Ray S. "On Being Human: The Spiritual Saga of a Creaturely Soul." In *Whatever Happened to the Soul? Scientific and Theological Portraits of Human Nature,* edited by Warren S. Brown et al., 175-94. Minneapolis: Fortress, 1998.
Anderson, Robert A. *Daniel: Signs and Wonders.* Edinburgh: Handsel, 1984.
Archer, Margaret S. *Culture and Agency: The Place of Culture in Social Theory.* Cambridge: Cambridge University Press, 1996.
Ariansen, Per. "Anthropocentrism with a Human Face." *Ecological Economics* 24 (1998) 153-62.
Armstrong, David M. *A Materialist Theory of the Mind.* London: Routledge/Kegan Paul, 1968.
Athanasius of Alexandria. "Four Discourses against the Arians." In *Select Treatises of S. Athanasius, Archbishop of Alexandria, in Controversy with the Arians,* translated by J. H. Newman, 1:177-555. Library of Fathers of the Holy Catholic Church 8. Oxford: J. H. Parker, 1842.
Atkins, Peter. *Creation Revisited.* London: Penguin, 1994.
Ayala, Francisco J. "Human Nature: One Evolutionist's View." In *Whatever Happened to the Soul? Scientific and Theological Portraits of Human Nature,* edited by Warren S. Brown, Nancey C. Murphy, and H. Newton Maloney, 31-48. Minneapolis: Fortress, 1998.
―――. "The Myth of Eve: Molecular Biology and Human Origins." *Science* 270 (1995) 1930-36.
Ayer, A. J. *Language, Truth, and Logic.* 2nd ed. London: V. Gollancz, 1946.
Bader-Saye, Scott. "Imaging God through Peace with Animals: An Election for Blessing." *Studies in Christian Ethics* 14 (2001) 1-13.

Badham, Paul. "Do Animals Have Immortal Souls?" In *Animals on the Agenda: Questions about Animals for Theology and Ethics*, edited by Andrew Linzey and Dorothy Yamamoto, 181–89. London: SCM, 1998.

Bailey, Derrick Sherwin. *The Man-Woman Relationship in Christian Thought*. London: Longmans, 1959.

Bandura, Albert. "Reflexive Empathy: On Predicting More Than Has Ever Been Observed." *Behavioral and Brain Sciences* 25, no. 1 (Feb 2002) 24–25.

Barbour, Ian G. *Ethics in an Age of Technology*. Gifford Lectures, 1990–91. San Francisco: HarperSanFrancisco, 1993.

———. *Nature, Human Nature, and God*. Minneapolis: Fortress, 2002.

———, editor. *Western Man and Environmental Ethics: Attitudes toward Nature and Technology*. Reading, MA: Addison-Wesley, 1973.

Barr, James. *The Garden of Eden and the Hope of Immortality: The Read-Tuckwell Lectures for 1990*. London: SCM, 1992.

———. *Holy Scripture: Canon, Authority, Criticism*. Oxford: Clarendon, 1983.

Barr, Stephen M. "Anthropic Coincidences." *First Things* 114 (2001) 17–23.

Barrett, C. K. *The Gospel According to St. John: An Introduction with Commentary and Notes on the Greek Text*. London: SPCK, 1958.

Barrow, John, and Frank J. Tipler. *The Anthropic Cosmological Principle*. Oxford: Oxford University Press, 1986.

Barth, Karl. *Church Dogmatics* I/2. Translated by G. T. Thomson and H. Knight. Edinburgh: T. & T. Clark, 1956.

———. *Church Dogmatics* III/1. Translated by J. W. Edwards et al. Edinburgh: T. & T. Clark, 1958.

———. *Church Dogmatics* III/2. Translated by G. W. Bromiley et al. Edinburgh: T. & T. Clark, 1960.

———. *Church Dogmatics* IV/1. Translated by G. W. Bromiley. Edinburgh: T. & T. Clark, 1956.

———. *Church Dogmatics* IV/3. Translated by G. W. Bromiley. Edinburgh: T. & T. Clark, 1961.

———. *The Humanity of God*. London: Collins, 1961.

Barth, Markus, and Helmut Blanke. *Colossians: A New Translation with Introduction and Commentary*. Translated by Astrid B. Beck. AB 34B. Garden City, NY: Doubleday, 1994.

Bartholomew, David J. *God of Chance*. London: SCM, 1984.

Bauckham, Richard. *God and the Crisis of Freedom: Biblical and Contemporary Perspectives*. Louisville: Westminster John Knox, 2002.

———. "Jesus and Animals I: What Did He Teach?" In *Animals on the Agenda: Questions about Animals for Theology and Ethics*, edited by Andrew Linzey and Dorothy Yamamoto, 33–48. London: SCM, 1998.

———. "Joining Creation's Praise of God." *Ecotheology* 7 (2002) 45–59.

BBC News. "Life after near death." February 4, 2000. Online: http://news.bbc.co.uk/1/hi/health/629710.stm.

BBC2. "The Day I Died." Documentary, February 5, 2003.

Behe, Michael J. "A Functional Pseudogene?: An Open Letter to Nature." Discovery Institute Web site, May 13, 2003. Online: http://www.discovery.org/a/1448.

———. *Darwin's Black Box: The Biochemical Challenge to Evolution*. New York: Free Press, 1996.

Bekoff, Marc. "Considering Animals—Not "Higher" Primates: Consciousness and Self in Animals. Some Reflections." *Zygon* 38 (2003) 229–45.
Benedict XVI (Joseph Ratzinger). *In the Beginning—: A Catholic Understanding of the Story of Creation and the Fall.* Translated by Boniface Ramsey. Edinburgh: T. & T. Clark, 1995.
Berry, R. J. "Divine Action: Expected and Unexpected." *Zygon* 37 (2002) 717–27.
Bertorelle, Giorgio, et al. "Evidence for a Genetic Discontinuity between Neandertals and 24,000-Year-Old Anatomically Modern Europeans." *Proceedings of the National Academy of Sciences* 100, no. 11 (May 27, 2003) 6593–97.
Bickerton, Derek. *Language & Species.* Chicago: Chicago University Press, 1990.
Blackmore, Susan J. *Beyond the Body: An Investigation of Out-of-Body Experiences.* London: Heinemann, 1982.
———. *Dying to Live: Science and the Near Death Experience.* London: HarperCollins, 1993.
Boehm, Christopher. "Segmentary 'Warfare' and the Management of Conflict: Comparison of East African Chimpanzees and Patrilineal-Patrilocal Humans." In *Coalitions and Alliances in Humans and Other Animals*, edited by Alexander H. Harcourt and Frans B. M. de Waal, 137–73. Oxford: Oxford University Press, 1992.
Bornkamm, Günther. *Jesus of Nazareth.* Translated by Irene and Fraser McLuckey and James M. Robinson. London: Hodder & Stoughton, 1960.
Bowker, John, editor. *The Oxford Dictionary of World Religions.* Oxford: Oxford University Press, 1997.
Braaten, Carl E., and Philip Clayton, editors. *The Theology of Wolfhart Pannenberg: Twelve American Critiques, with an Autobiographical Essay and Response.* Minneapolis: Augsburg, 1988.
Bradley, Walter L. "The 'Just So' Universe." *Touchstone* 12, no. 4 (1999) 70–75.
Braine, David. *The Human Person: Animal and Spirit.* Notre Dame: University of Notre Dame Press, 1992.
———. "The Impossibility of God Being Incarnate More Than Once." Paper first delivered to the Aberdeenshire Theological Club in the 1990s, revised for later publication.
Brenz, Johannes. *De personali unione duarum naturam in Christo.* Tübingen, 1561.
Brooks, Rodney A. "Intelligence without Representation." *Artificial Intelligence* 47 (1991) 139–59.
Brown, Warren S. "Conclusion: Reconciling Scientific and Biblical Portraits of Human Nature." In *Whatever Happened to the Soul? Scientific and Theological Portraits of Human Nature*, edited by Warren S. Brown et al., 213–28. Minneapolis: Fortress, 1998.
———, et al., editors. *Whatever Happened to the Soul? Scientific and Theological Portraits of Human Nature.* Minneapolis: Fortress, 1998.
Brueggemann, Walter. *Genesis.* IBC. Atlanta: John Knox, 1982.
Brun, Rudolf B. "Cosmology, Cosmic Evolution, and Sacramental Reality: A Christian Contribution." *Zygon* 37 (2002) 175–92.
Brunner, Emil. *The Christian Doctrine of Creation and Redemption.* Translated by Olive Wyon. London: Lutterworth, 1952.

———, and Karl Barth. *Natural Theology: Comprising "Nature and Grace" by Emil Brunner and the Reply "No!" by Karl Barth.* Translated by Peter Fraenkel. London: Centenary, 1946.

Buber, Martin. *I and Thou.* Translated by Walter Kaufmann. Edinburgh: T. & T. Clark, 1970.

Budziszewski, Jay. "The Second Tablet Project." *First Things* 124 (2002) 23–31.

Buller, Cornelius A. *The Unity of Nature and History in Pannenberg's Theology.* Lanham, MD: Littlefield Adams, 1996.

Bultmann, Rudolf. *Existence and Faith: Shorter Writings of Rudolf Bultmann,* edited and translated by Schubert M. Ogden. London: Hodder & Stoughton, 1960.

Buss, Martin. "The Meaning of History." In *Theology as History,* edited by James M. Robinson and John B. Cobb Jr., 135–54. New Frontiers in Theology 3. New York: Harper & Row, 1967.

Cabaud, Jacques. *Simone Weil: A Fellowship in Love.* London: Harvill, 1964.

Cantor, Geoffrey. "Does Religion Impede the Progress of Science?" "Theology and Science" lecture series, University of Edinburgh, May 8, 2003.

Carlyon, Richard. *A Guide to the Gods.* London: Heinemann, 1981.

Carmody, Denise Lardner, and John Tully Carmody. "Christology in Karl Rahner's Evolutionary World View." *Religion in Life* 49 (1980) 195–210.

Carr, Anne E. *The Theological Method of Karl Rahner.* AARDS 19. Missoula, MT: Scholars, 1977.

Carr, Edward Hallett. *What Is History?* New York: Random House, 1953.

Carter, Brandon. "The Anthropic Principle and Its Implications for Biological Evolution." *Philosophical Transactions of the Royal Society of London. Series A: Mathematical and Physical Sciences* 310 (1983) 347–63.

———. "Large Number Coincidences and the Anthropic Principle in Cosmology." In *Confrontation of Cosmological Theories with Observational Data,* edited by Malcolm S. Longair, 291–98. Symposium—International Astronomical Union 63. Dordrecht: Reidel, 1974.

Cassuto, Umberto. *A Commentary on the Book of Genesis.* Pt. 1: *From Adam to Noah.* Translated by Israel Abrahams. Jerusalem: Magnes, 1961.

Cheney, Dorothy L., and Robert M. Seyfarth. *How Monkeys See the World: Inside the Mind of Another Species.* Chicago: University of Chicago Press, 1990.

Clark, Andy. *Being There: Putting Brain, Body, and World Together Again.* London: MIT Press, 1997.

Clark, Stephen R. L. *Animals and Their Moral Standing.* London: Routledge, 1997.

———. *Biology and Christian Ethics.* New Studies in Christian Ethics 17. Cambridge: Cambridge University Press, 2000.

Clarke, Adam. *A Commentary with Critical Notes,* vol. 1: *Genesis through Deuteronomy.* AGES Digital Library. Albany: AGES, 1997. Print ed.: New York: Methodist Espiscopal Church, (1831).

Clarke, William Newton. *The Christian Doctrine of God.* Edinburgh: T. & T. Clark, 1909.

Clatworthy, Jonathan. "Let the Fall Down: The Environmental Implications of the Doctrine of the Fall." *Ecotheology* 4 (1998) 27–34.

Clayton, Philip. "Anticipation and Theological Method." In *The Theology of Wolfhart Pannenberg: Twelve American Critiques, with an Autobiographical Essay and

Response, edited by Carl E. Braaten and Philip Clayton, 122-50. Minneapolis: Augsburg, 1988.
Clute, Holly L., and Warren J. Levy. "Electroencephalographic Changes During Brief Cardiac Arrest in Humans." *Anesthesiology* 73 (1990) 821-25.
Coakley, Sarah. "'Persons' in the 'Social' Doctrine of the Trinity: Gregory of Nyssa and Current Analytic Discussion." Presentation at the Boston Theological Society, Boston Theological Institute, February 8, 1999.
Cobb, John B., Jr. "All Things in Christ?" In *Animals on the Agenda: Questions about Animals for Theology and Ethics*, edited by Andrew Linzey and Dorothy Yamamoto, 173-80. London: SCM, 1998.
Collins, John Joseph. *Daniel: A Commentary on the Book of Daniel*. Hermeneia. Minneapolis: Fortress, 1993.
Cone, James H. *God of the Oppressed*. New York: Seabury, 1975.
Connor, Steve. "Sheep cannot be accused of woolly thinking, say scientists." *The Independent*, November 8, 2001. Online: http://www.independent.co.uk/news/science/sheep-cannot-be-accused-of-woolly-thinking-say-scientists-616276.html.
Conway Morris, Simon. *The Crucible of Creation: The Burgess Shale and the Rise of Animals*. Oxford: Oxford University Press, 1998.
———. *Life's Solution: Inevitable Humans in a Lonely Universe*. Cambridge: Cambridge University Press, 2003.
———. "The Paradoxes of Evolution: Inevitable Humans in a Lonely Universe?" *Borderlands* 2 (2003) 6-9.
Cooper, John W. *Body, Soul and Life Everlasting: Biblical Anthropology and the Monism-Dualism Debate*. Grand Rapids: Eerdmans, 1989.
Cope, David. "Experiments in Musical Intelligence." Online: http://arts.ucsc.edu/faculty/cope/experiments.htm.
———. "One Approach to Musical Intelligence." *IEEE Intelligent Systems* 14 (May-June 1999) 21-25.
Coyne, George V. "The Evolution of Intelligent Life on the Earth and Possibly Elsewhere: Reflections from a Religious Tradition." In *Many Worlds: The New Universe, Extraterrestrial Life, and the Theological Implications*, edited by Steven J. Dick, 177-88. Philadelphia: Templeton Foundation Press, 2000.
Craig, William Lane. *Reasonable Faith: Christian Truth and Apologetics*. Wheaton, IL: Crossway, 1994.
———. "Theism and the Origin of the Universe." *Erkenntnis* 48 (1998) 47-57.
Crick, Francis. *The Astonishing Hypothesis: The Scientific Search for the Soul*. London: Simon & Schuster, 1994.
Crowe, Michael J. *The Extraterrestrial Life Debate, 1750-1900: The Idea of a Plurality of Worlds from Kant to Lowell*. Cambridge: Cambridge University Press, 1986.
Cummins, Robert, and Denise Dellarosa Cummins, editors. *Minds, Brains, and Computers: The Foundations of Cognitive Science*. Blackwell Philosophy Anthologies 10. Oxford: Blackwell, 2000.
Darrach, Brad. "Meet Shaky, the First Electronic Person." *Life* 69:21 (November 20, 1970) 58B-68.
Darwin, Charles. *The Descent of Man and Selection in Relation to Sex*. London: J. Murray, 1901.

Davies, Brian. *An Introduction to the Philosophy of Religion.* Oxford: Oxford University Press, 1993.

Davies, P. C. W. *The Fifth Miracle: The Search for the Origin and Meaning of Life.* London: Penguin, 1998.

———. *The Mind of God: The Scientific Basis for a Rational World.* London: Penguin, 1992.

Davis, John Jefferson. "Search for Extraterrestrial Intelligence and the Christian Doctrine of Redemption." *Science and Christian Belief* 9 (1997) 21–34.

Dawkins, Richard. *The Blind Watchmaker: Why the Evidence of Evolution Reveals a Universe without Design.* London: Penguin, 1991.

———. *The Selfish Gene.* New ed. Oxford: Oxford University Press, 1989.

De Duve, Christian. "Constraints on the Origin and Evolution of Life." *Proceedings of the American Philosophical Society* 142 (1998) 525–32.

———. "Lessons of Life." In *Many Worlds: The New Universe, Extraterrestrial Life, and the Theological Implications*, edited by Steven J. Dick, 3–13. Philadelphia: Templeton Foundation Press, 2000.

Deacon, Terrence. *The Symbolic Species: The Co-Evolution of Language and the Human Brain.* London: Allen Lane/Penguin, 1997.

Deane-Drummond, Celia. "Editorial: Creation Spirituality." *Ecotheology* 7 (2002) 5–9.

———. "Navigating the Maze: Biology and Animal Ethics." Theology and Science Lecture Series, University of Edinburgh, February 25, 2003.

Del Colle, Ralph. "'Person' and 'Being' in John Zizioulas' Trinitarian Theology: Conversations with Thomas Torrance and Thomas Aquinas." *SJT* 54 (2001) 70–86.

Dembski, William A. *Intelligent Design: The Bridge between Science & Theology.* Downers Grove, IL: InterVarsity, 1999.

Dennett, Daniel C. *Consciousness Explained.* London: Allen Lane, 1991.

———. *Darwin's Dangerous Idea: The Evolution and Meanings of Life.* London: Allen Lane Penguin, 1995.

Descartes, Rene. *Discourse on the Method of Rightly Conducting the Reason, and Seeking Truth in the Sciences*, 1637. Translated by John Veitch. Edinburgh: Sutherland & Knox, 1850.

Dick, Steven J. "Cosmotheology: Theological Implications of the New Universe." In *Many World*, edited by Steven J. Dick, 191–210. Philadelphia: Templeton Foundation Press, 2000.

———, editor. *Many Worlds: The New Universe, Extraterrestrial Life, and the Theological Implications.* Philadelphia: Templeton Foundation Press, 2000.

Dodwell, P. C. *Brave New Mind: A Thoughtful Inquiry into the Nature and Meaning of Mental Life.* Oxford: Oxford University Press, 2000.

Donald, Merlin. *A Mind So Rare: The Evolution of Human Consciousness.* New York: Norton, 2001.

———. *Origins of the Modern Mind: Three States in the Evolution of Culture and Cognition.* Cambridge: Harvard University Press, 1991.

Drees, Willem B. *Religion, Science, and Naturalism.* Cambridge: Cambridge University Press, 1996.

Dreyfus, Hubert L., and Stuart E. Dreyfus. *Mind over Machine: The Power of Human Intuition and Expertise in the Era of the Computer.* New York: Free Press, 1986.

Duffy, Stephen. "Our Hearts of Darkness: Original Sin Revisited." *TS* 49 (1988) 597–622.

Dyson, Freeman J. *Disturbing the Universe*. London: Pan, 1981.

Eichrodt, Walther. *Theology of the Old Testament*. Vol. 2. Translated by J. A. Baker. OTL. London: SCM, 1967.

Eisenberg, Leon. "The *Human* Nature of Human Nature." *Science* 176 (1972) 123-28.

Eldredge, Niles. *Fossils: The Evolution and Extinction of Species*. London: Aurum, 1991.

Ellis, George F. R. "The Theology of the Anthropic Principle." In *Quantum Cosmology and the Laws of Nature: Scientific Perspectives on Divine Action*, edited by Robert J. Russell et al., 367–405. 2nd ed. Berkeley: Center for Theology and the Natural Sciences, 1999.

———, and William R. Stoeger. "Introduction to General Relativity and Cosmology." In *Quantum Cosmology and the Laws of Nature: Scientific Perspectives on Divine Action*, edited by Robert J. Russell et al., 33–48. 2nd ed. Berkeley: Center for Theology and the Natural Sciences, 1999.

Everett, Hugh, III. "'Relative State' Formulation of Quantum Mechanics." *Reviews of Modern Physics* 29 (1957) 454–62.

Feenstra, Ronald J., and Cornelius Plantinga Jr., editors. *Trinity, Incarnation, and Atonement: Philosophical and Theological Essays*. Library of Religious Philosophy 1. Notre Dame: University of Notre Dame Press, 1989.

Ferguson, Sinclair B. *The Communicator's Commentary. Daniel*. Communicator's Commentary Series, Old Testament 19. Waco, TX: Word, 1988.

Fergusson, David. *The Cosmos and the Creator: An Introduction to the Theology of Creation*. London: SPCK, 1998.

Fields, Stephen M. *Being as Symbol: On the Origins and Development of Karl Rahner's Metaphysics*. Washington, DC: Georgetown University Press, 2000.

Flanagan, Owen J. *Consciousness Reconsidered*. London: MIT Press, 1992.

Foerst, Anne. "Artificial Intelligence: Walking the Boundary." *Zygon* 31 (1996) 681–93.

———. "COG, a Humanoid Robot, and the Question of *Imago Dei*." *Zygon* 33 (1998) 91–111.

Foley, Robert. *Another Unique Species: Patterns in Human Evolutionary Ecology*. Essex: Longman Scientific & Technical, 1987.

Fortes, Andrew Dominic. "Magnetic Fields of the Planets" and "Magnetic Fields at Mars." Undergraduate report, University College London, September 18, 1997. Online: http://www.es.ucl.ac.uk/research/planetary/undergraduate/dom/magrev/magtoc.htm.

Fossey, Dian. "Vocalizations of the mountain gorilla (*Gorilla gorilla beringei*)." *Animal Behavior* 20 (1972) 36–53.

Fowler, Dean R. "A Response to Fr. O'Donovan." In *Theology and Discovery: Essays in Honor of Karl Rahner, SJ*, edited by William J. Kelly, 303–5. Milwaukee: Marquette University Press, 1980.

Fuller, Michael. *Atoms and Icons: A Discussion of the Relationships between Science and Theology*. London: Mowbray, 1995.

Galloway, Allan Douglas. *Wolfhart Pannenberg*. Contemporary Religious Thinkers. London: Allen & Unwin, 1973.

Gallup, Gordon G., Jr., and Steven M. Platek. "Cognitive Empathy Presupposes Self-Awareness: Evidence from Phylogeny, Ontogeny, Neuropsychology, and Mental Illness." *Behavioral and Brain Sciences* 25, no. 1 (2002) 36–37.

Garaudy, Roger. "The Meaning of Life and History in Marx and Teilhard de Chardin: Teilhard's Contribution to the Dialogue between Christians and Marxists." Translated by N. Lindsay. In *Evolution, Marxism & Christianity: Studies in the Teilhardian Synthesis*, edited by Bernard Towers and Anthony Dyson, 58–72. Teilhard Study Library 2. London: Garnstone, 1967.

Gee, Henry. *Deep Time: Cladistics, the Revolution in Evolution*. London: Fourth Estate, 2000.

Geertz, Clifford. *The Interpretation of Cultures: Selected Essays*. New York: Basic, 1973.

Gellner, Ernest. *Postmodernism, Reason and Religion*. London: Routledge, 1992.

Gerstenberger, Erhard S. *Yahweh—the Patriarch: Ancient Images of God and Feminist Theology*. Translated by Frederick J. Gaiser. Minneapolis: Fortress, 1996.

Gibellini, Rosino. "The Theological Debate on Ecology." In *Ecology and Poverty: Cry of the Earth, Cry of the Poor*, edited by Leonardo Boff and V. Elizondo, 125–34. Concilium 1995, 5. London: SCM, 1995.

Gibson, Kathleen R., and Tim Ingold, editors. *Tools, Language, and Cognition in Human Evolution*. Cambridge: Cambridge University Press, 1993.

Gilkey, Langdon. *Nature, Reality, and the Sacred: The Nexus of Science and Religion*. Minneapolis: Fortress, 1993.

Godlovitch, Stan. "Descriptive and Normative Anthropocentrism." PHIL 302 class notes, Lincoln University, Christchurch, New Zealand, 1998. Online: http://www.lincoln.ac.nz/emd/subjects/phil302/notes/1998/anthcent.htm.

Goodall, Jane. *In the Shadow of Man*. Rev. ed. London: Phoenix, 1996.

Gore, Rick. "The first pioneer? A new find shakes the human family tree." *National Geographic Magazine* 202, no. 2 (August 2002) xxiv–xxxiii.

Gould, Stephen Jay. *Wonderful Life: The Burgess Shale and the Nature of History*. London: Hutchinson Radius, 1990.

Graham, Gordon. *Evil and Christian Ethics*. New Studies in Christian Ethics 20. Cambridge: Cambridge University Press, 2001.

———. "Playing God." "Theology and Ethics" lecture, New College, University of Edinburgh, October 22, 2002.

Green, Joel B. "'Bodies—That Is, Human Lives': A Re-Examination of Human Nature in the Bible." In *Whatever Happened to the Soul? Scientific and Theological Portraits of Human Nature*, edited by Warren S. Brown et al., 149–73. Minneapolis: Fortress, 1998.

Greene, Brian. *The Elegant Universe: Superstrings, Hidden Dimensions, and the Quest for the Ultimate Theory*. New York: Norton, 1999.

Gregersen, Niels Henrik. "Autopoiesis: Less Than Self-Constitution, More Than Self-Organization." *Zygon* 34 (1999) 117–38.

———. "A Contextual Coherence Theory for the Science-Theology Dialogue." In *Rethinking Theology and Science: Six Models for the Current Dialogue*, edited by Niels Henrik Gregersen and J. Wentzel van Huyssteen, 181–231. Grand Rapids: Eerdmans, 1998.

———, et al., editors. *The Human Person in Science and Theology*. Edinburgh: T. & T. Clark, 2000.

———, and J. Wentzel van Huyssteen, editors. *Rethinking Theology and Science: Six Models for the Current Dialogue*. Grand Rapids: Eerdmans, 1998.
Gregory Nazianzus. "To Cledonius against Apollinaris (Epistle 101)." In *Christology of the Later Fathers*, edited by Edward Rochie Hardy, 215-24. LCC 3. London: SCM, 1954.
Gregory of Nyssa *Against Eunomius* 1. AGES Digital Library. Albany, OR: AGES, 1997.
Grenz, Stanley J. "The Appraisal of Pannenberg: A Survey of the Literature." In *The Theology of Wolfhart Pannenberg: Twelve American Critiques, with an Autobiographical Essay and Response*, edited by Carl E. Braaten and Philip Clayton, 19-52. Minneapolis: Augsburg, 1988.
———. *Reason for Hope: The Systematic Theology of Wolfhart Pannenberg*. Oxford: Oxford University Press, 1990.
———. *The Social God and the Relational Self: A Trinitarian Theology of the* Imago Dei. London: Westminster John Knox, 2001.
Grey, Mary. "Falling into Freedom: Searching for New Interpretations of Sin in a Secular Society." *SJT* 47 (1994) 223-43.
Grey, W. "Anthropocentrism and Deep Ecology." *Australasian Journal of Philosophy* 71 (1993) 463-75.
Gribbin, John R. *The Birth of Time: How Astronomers Measured the Age of the Universe*. London: Weidenfeld & Nicolson, 1999.
———, and Jeremy Cherfas. *The First Chimpanzee: In Search of Human Origins*. London: Penguin, 2001.
———, and Martin Rees. *Cosmic Coincidences: Dark Matter, Mankind, and Anthropic Cosmology*. London: Black Swan, 1991.
Groves, J. Alan, Dale Wheeler et al. *Westminster Hebrew Morphology*. Release 3. BibleWorks, 1998. Print ed.: Philadelphia: Westminster Theological Seminary, 1998.
Grube, Dirk-Martin. "Religious Experience after the Demise of Foundationalism." *RelS* 31 (1995) 37-52.
Gruen, Lori. "Revaluing Nature." In *Ecofeminism: Women, Culture, Nature*, edited by Karen J. Warren, 356-74. Bloomington: Indiana University Press, 1997.
Gunton, Colin E. "The Spirit Moved over the Face of the Waters: The Holy Spirit and the Created Order." Presentation at the 9th Edinburgh Conference on Christian Dogmatics, Free Church College, Edinburgh, August 28, 2001.
———. "Trinity, Ontology and Anthropology." In *Persons, Divine and Human: King's College Essays in Theological Anthropology*, edited by Christoph Schwöbel and Colin E. Gunton, 47-61. Edinburgh: T. & T. Clark, 1991.
———. *Yesterday and Today: A Study of Continuities in Christology*. 2nd ed. London: SPCK, 1997.
Haeckel, Earnst H. P. A. *The History of Creation, or The Development of the Earth and Its Inhabitants by the Action of Natural Causes*. Translated by E. Ray Lankester. Vol. 1. London: H. S. King, 1876.
Hall, Douglas John. *Imaging God: Dominion as Stewardship*. Grand Rapids: Eerdmans, 1986.
Hamilton, Victor P. *The Book of Genesis: Chapters 1–17*. NICOT. Grand Rapids: Eerdmans, 1990.

Hardy, Daniel W. *God's Ways with the World: Thinking and Practising Christian Faith.* Edinburgh: T. & T. Clark, 1996.

Hardy, Edward Rochie, editor. *Christology of the Later Fathers.* LCC 3. London: SCM, 1954.

Harré, Rom. *Varieties of Realism: A Rationale for the Natural Sciences.* Oxford: Blackwell, 1986.

———, and Michael Krausz. *Varieties of Relativism.* Oxford: Blackwell, 1996.

Harris, William S., et al. "A Randomized, Controlled Trial of the Effects of Remote, Intercessory Prayer on Outcomes in Patients Admitted to the Coronary Care Unit." *Archives of Internal Medicine* 159 (1999) 2273–78.

Hartle, J. B., and S. W. Hawking, "Wave Function of the Universe." *Physical Review D* 28 (1983) 2960–75.

Hartman, Louis F., and Alexander A. Di Lella. *The Book of Daniel.* AB 23. Garden City, NY: Doubleday, 1978.

Hauerwas, Stanley, et al., editors. *Theology without Foundations: Religious Practice and the Future of Theological Truth.* Nashville: Abingdon, 1994.

Haugeland, John, editor. *Mind Design II: Philosophy, Psychology, Artificial Intelligence.* 2nd ed. Cambridge: MIT Press, 1997.

Hauser, Marc D. "A Primate Dictionary? Decoding the Function and Meaning of Another Species' Vocalizations." *Cognitive Science* 24 (2000) 445–75.

Hawking, Stephen W. *A Brief History of Time: From the Beginning to Black Holes.* New York: Bantam, 1996.

———, and Roger Penrose. *The Nature of Space and Time.* Princeton: Princeton University Press, 1996.

Hefner, Philip. *The Human Factor: Evolution, Culture, and Religion.* Minneapolis: Fortress, 1993.

———. "The Role of Science in Pannenberg's Theological Thinking." In *The Theology of Wolfhart Pannenberg: Twelve American Critiques, with an Autobiographical Essay and Response,* edited by Carl E. Braaten and Philip Clayton, 266–86. Minneapolis: Augsburg, 1988.

Herzfeld, Noreen L. *In Our Image: Artificial Intelligence and the Human Spirit.* Minneapolis: Fortress, 2002.

Heschel, Abraham Joshua. *Man Is Not Alone: A Philosophy of Religion.* New York: Octagon, 1951.

Hess, Richard S. "Genesis 1–2 and Recent Studies of Ancient Texts." *Science & Christian Belief* 7 (1995) 141–49.

Hick, John. "Christology at the Cross Roads." In *Prospect for Theology: Essays in Honour of H. H. Farmer,* edited by F. G. Healey, 137–66. Welwyn: Nisbet, 1966.

———. *The Metaphor of God Incarnate.* London: SCM, 1993.

Hiebert, Paul G. *Cultural Anthropology.* 2nd ed. Grand Rapids: Baker, 1983.

Hillstrom, Elizabeth L. *Testing the Spirits.* Downers Grove, IL: InterVarsity, 1995.

Hirotsune, Shinji, et al. "An expressed pseudogene regulates the messenger-RNA stability of its homologous coding gene." *Nature,* May 1, 2003, 91–96.

Hocket, Charles F. "The origin of speech." *Scientific American* 203(9) (1960) 89–96.

Hockett, Charles F., and Stuart A. Altmann, "A Note on Design Features." In *Animal Communication: Techniques of Study and Results of Research,* edited by Thomas A. Sebeok, 61–72. Bloomington: Indiana University Press, 1968.

Hocket, Charles F., and Robert Ascher. "The Human Revolution." *Current Anthropology* 5(3) (1964) 135–68.

Hofstadter, Douglas R. *Gödel, Escher, Bach: An Eternal Golden Braid*. Harmondsworth: Penguin, 1980.

―――, and Daniel C. Dennett, editors. *The Mind's I: Fantasies and Reflections on Self and Soul*. Harmondsworth: Penguin, 1981.

Holwerda, David. "Faith, Reason, and the Resurrection in the Theology of Wolfhart Pannenberg." In *Faith and Rationality: Reason and Belief in God*, edited by Alvin Plantinga and Nicholas Wolterstorff, 265–316. Notre Dame: University of Notre Dame Press, 1983.

Hopkins, William D., and E. Sue Savage-Rumbaugh. "Vocal communication as a function of differential rearing experiences in Pan paniscus." *International Journal of Primatology* 12 (1991) 559–83.

Humphrey, Nicholas. *The Inner Eye*. Oxford: Oxford University Press, 2002.

―――. "The Private World of Consciousness." *New Scientist*, January 8, 1994, 23–25.

Isham, Chistopher J. "Quantum Theories of the Creation of the Universe." In *Quantum Cosmology and the Laws of Nature: Scientific Perspectives on Divine Action*, edited by Robert J. Russell et al., 49–89. 2nd ed. Berkeley: Center for Theology and the Natural Sciences, 1999.

Jamieson, Robert, A. R. Fausset, and David Brown. *Commentary, Critical and Explanatory, on the Old and New Testaments*. Old Testament, vol. 1: *Genesis–Psalms*. AGES Digital Library. Albany: AGES, 1997. Print ed.: Hillsdale, MI: J. B. Names, 1871.

Jayawardhana, Ray. "No Alien Jupiters." *Science* 265 (1994) 1527.

Jenson, Robert W. "Creator and Creature." *International Journal of Systematic Theology* 4 (2002) 216–21.

―――. "Jesus in the Trinity: Wolfhart Pannenberg's Christology and Doctrine of the Trinity." In *The Theology of Wolfhart Pannenberg: Twelve American Critiques, with an Autobiographical Essay and Response*, edited by Carl E. Braaten and Philip Clayton, 188–206. Minneapolis: Augsburg, 1988.

―――. *Systematic Theology*. 2 vols. Oxford: Oxford University Press, 1997–1999.

Jobling, David, et al., editors. *The Postmodern Bible Reader*. Oxford: Blackwell, 2001.

John Paul II. Address to the Pontifical Academy of Sciences, October 23, 1996, reported in John Tagliabue, "The Pope Pronounces Evolution Fit," *New York Times*, October 27, 1996, sec. 4, p. 2, online: http://www.nytimes.com/1996/10/27/weekinreview/the-pope-pronounces-evolution-fit.html?scp=1&sq=Pope%20Pronounces%20Evolution%20Fit&st=cse.

Johnson, Aubrey Rodway. *The One and the Many in the Israelite Conception of God*. Cardiff: University of Wales Press, 1942.

―――. *The Vitality of the Individual in the Thought of Ancient Israel*. Cardiff: University of Wales Press, 1949.

Johnson, Elizabeth A. "Redeeming the Name of Christ." In *Freeing Theology: The Essentials of Theology in Feminist Perspective*, edited by Catherine Mowry LaCugna, 115–27. San Francisco: Harper, 1993.

Kano, Takayoshi. "A pilot study on the ecology of Pygmy Chimpanzees, *Pan paniscus*." In *The Great apes: Perspectives on Human Evolution*, Vol. 5, edited by David A

Hamburg and Elizabeth R. McCown, 123–35. Menlo Park: Benjamin/Cummings, 1979.

Kauffman, Stuart A. *At Home in the Universe: The Search for Laws of Self-Organization and Complexity.* London: Penguin, 1995.

Kazlev, M. Alan. "Anthropocentrism." 2004. Online: http://www.kheper.net/topics/worldviews/anthropocentrism.html.

Kelly, Geoffrey B., editor. *Karl Rahner: Theologian of the Graced Search for Meaning.* Edinburgh: T. & T. Clark, 1992.

Kelly, William J., editor. *Theology and Discovery: Essays in Honor of Karl Rahner, SJ.* Milwaukee: Marquette University Press, 1980.

Kendall, Stuart. "Intratextual Theology in a Postmodern World." In *Postmodern Theologies: The Challenge of Religious Diversity*, edited by Terrence W. Tilley, 91–113. Maryknoll, NY: Orbis, 1995.

Kendrick, Keith, et al. "Sheep don't forget a face." *Nature*, November 8, 2001, 165–66.

Kenny, Anthony. *The Five Ways: St. Thomas Aquinas' Proofs of God's Existence.* London: Routledge/Kegan Paul, 1969.

Kerr, Fergus. *Immortal Longings: Versions of Transcending Humanity.* London: SPCK, 1997.

Kim, Eun-Chul. *Honor Be to God the Father: Patrology in Biblical Texts.* Unpublished paper, Edinburgh, 2003.

Knibb, Michael A. "Life and Death in the Old Testament." In *The World of Ancient Israel: Sociological, Anthropological, and Political Perspectives. Essays by Members of the Society for Old Testament Study*, edited by Ronald E. Clements, 395–415. Cambridge: Cambridge University Press, 1989.

Koertge, Noretta, editor. *A House Built on Sand: Exposing Postmodernist Myths about Science.* Oxford: Oxford University Press, 1998.

Korsmeyer, Jerry D. *Evolution and Eden: Balancing Original Sin and Contemporary Science.* Mahwah, NJ: Paulist, 1998.

Kortenkamp, Katherine V., and Colleen F. Moore. "Ecocentrism and Anthropocentrism: Moral Reasoning about Ecological Commons Dilemmas." *Journal of Environmental Psychology* 21 (2001) 261–72.

Kuhn, Thomas S. *The Structure of Scientific Revolutions.* 3rd ed. Chicago: University of Chicago Press, 1996.

Laats, Alar. *Doctrines of the Trinity in Eastern and Western Theologies: A Study with Special Reference to K. Barth and V. Lossky.* Studies in the Intercultural History of Christianity 114. Frankfurt: Lang, 1999.

LaCugna, Catherine Mowry. "The Baptismal Formula, Feminist Objections, and Trinitarian Theology." *JES* 26 (1989) 235–50.

———. *God for Us: The Trinity and Christian Life.* San Francisco: Harper, 1991.

———. "God in Communion with Us: The Trinity." In *Freeing Theology: The Essentials of Theology in Feminist Perspective*, edited by Catherine Mowry LaCugna, 83–114. San Francisco: Harper, 1993.

Laitman, Jeffrey T., et al. "The Basicranium of Fossil Hominids as an Indicator of Their Upper Respiratory Systems." *American Journal of Physical Anthropology* 51 (1979) 15–34.

Lakatos, Imre. *Philosophical Papers.* Vol. 1: *The Methodology of Scientific Research Programmes.* Edited by John Worrall and Gregory Currie. Cambridge: Cambridge University Press, 1978.

Laland, Kevin N. "The Evolution of Culture." In *Neanderthals and Modern Humans in Western Asia*, edited by Takeri Akazawa et al., 427–38. New York: Plenum, 1998.

Landa, Keith. "Humans and the Environment: Environmental Ethics." Lecture outline. Online: http://darwin.cord.edu/courses/B170F97/sessions/ethics.html.

Larkin, Lucy. "Douglas John Hall—The Stewardship Symbol and the Image of God." *Theology in Green* 3, no. 7 (1993) 13–19.

Lash, Nicholas. *The Beginning and the End of 'Religion.'* Cambridge: Cambridge University Press, 1996.

———. "Up and Down in Christology." In *New Studies in Theology 1*, edited by Stephen Sykes and J. Derek Holmes, 31–46. London: Duckworth, 1980.

Leahy, Michael P. T. *Against Liberation: Putting Animals in Perspective*. Rev. ed. London: Routledge, 1994.

Lemaire, André. "Burial Box of James, the Brother of Jesus." *BAR* 28, no. 6 (2002) 24–33.

Leslie, John. *Universes*. London: Routledge, 1989.

Lieb, Elliott H., et al. "Stability of Matter in Magnetic Fields." *Physical Review Letters* 75 (1995) 985–89.

Lindbeck, George A. *The Nature of Doctrine: Religion and Theology in a Postliberal Age*. London: SPCK, 1984.

Linzey, Andrew. *Animal Theology*. Urbana: University of Illinois Press, 1995.

———. "Reverence, Responsibility and Rights." In *The Status of Animals: Ethics, Education and Welfare*, edited by David Paterson and Mary Palmer, 20–50. Wallingford: CAB Int'l, 1989.

———. "Unfinished Creation: The Moral and Theological Significance of the Fall." *Ecotheology* 4 (1998) 20–26.

———, and Dan Cohn-Sherbok. *After Noah: Animals and the Liberation of Theology*. London: Mowbray, 1997.

———, and Dorothy Yamamoto, editors. *Animals on the Agenda: Questions about Animals for Theology and Ethics*. London, SCM, 1998.

Lock, Andrew, and Michael Colombo. "Cognitive Abilities in a Comparative Perspective." In *Handbook of Human Symbolic Evolution*, edited by Andrew Lock and Charles R. Peters, 596–643. Oxford: Clarendon, 1996.

Lommel, Pirn van, et al. "Near-death experience in survivors of cardiac arrest: a prospective study in the Netherlands." *The Lancet* 358, no. 9298 (2001) 2039–45. Online: http://www.thelancet.com/journals/lancet/article/PIIS0140-6736(01)07100-8/fulltext.

Longair, Malcolm S., editor. *Confrontation of Cosmological Theories with Observational Data*. Symposium—International Astronomical Union 63. Dordrecht: Reidel, 1974.

———. *Our Evolving Universe*. Cambridge: Cambridge University Press, 1996.

Losinger, Anton. *The Anthropological Turn: The Human Orientation of the Theology of Karl Rahner*. Translated by Daniel O. Dahlstrom. Moral Philosophy and Moral Theology 2. New York: Fordham University Press, 2000.

Lossky, Vladimir. *Orthodox Theology: An Introduction*. Translated by Ian and Ihita Kesarcodi-Watson. Crestwood, NY: St. Vladimir's Seminary Press, 1978.

Lucas, J. R. "Minds, Machines, and Gödel." In *Minds and Machines*, edited by Alan R. Anderson, 43–59. Englewood Cliffs, NJ: Prentice-Hall, 1964.

Ludlow, Morwenna. *Universal Salvation: Eschatology in the Thought of Gregory of Nyssa and Karl Rahner.* Oxford: Oxford University Press, 2000.

Lynch, Tony, and David Wells, "Non-Anthropocentrism? A Killing Objection." *Environmental Values* 7 (1998) 151–63.

MacKinnon, John. "The behavior and ecology of wild orang-utans (*Pongo pygmaeus*)." *Animal Behaviour* 22(1) (Feb 1974) 3–74.

The Macquarie Dictionary. Melbourne: Macmillan Australia, 2005.

Manson, Neil A. "Anthropocentrism and the Design Argument." *RelS* 36 (2000) 163–76.

Manson, Thomas Walter. *The Teaching of Jesus: Studies of Its Form and Content.* 2nd ed. Cambridge: Cambridge University Press, 1943.

Marler, Peter R. "Social organization, communication and graded signals in the chimpanzee and the gorilla." In *Growing Points in Ethology*, edited by Patrick P. G. Bateson and Robert A. Hinde, 239–80. Cambridge: Cambridge University Press, 1976.

Marshall, Bruce D. *Trinity and Truth.* Cambridge Studies in Christian Doctrine 3. Cambridge: Cambridge University Press, 2000.

Marshall, I. Howard. *The Gospel of Luke: A Commentary on the Greek Text.* NIGTC. Grand Rapids: Eerdmans, 1978.

Martin, Civilla D. "His Eye Is on the Sparrow." Hymn. 1905.

Masao, A. B. E. "The Problem of Self-Centeredness as the Root-Source of Human Suffering." *Japanese Religions* 15 (1989) 15–25.

Mayr, Ernst. *Toward a New Philosophy of Biology: Observation of an Evolutionist.* Cambridge: Harvard University Press, 1988.

McArthur, Jane. "Memory at the Eschaton: Erased or Transformed." Presentation at the postgraduate conference, New College, University of Edinburgh, June 7, 2002.

McCarthy, John. "Some Expert Systems Need Common Sense." *Annals of the New York Academy of Sciences* 426 (1984) 129–37.

McCormick, Richard A. "Gustafson's God: Who? What? Where? (ETC.)" *JRE* 13 (1985) 53–70.

McFadyen, Alistair I. *Bound to Sin: Abuse, Holocaust, and the Christian Doctrine of Sin.* Cambridge Studies in Christian Doctrine 6. Cambridge: Cambridge University Press, 2000.

———. "Child Killers, Sin & Forgiveness." "Theology and Ethics" lecture, New College, University of Edinburgh, February 18, 2003.

———. *The Call to Personhood: A Christian Theory of the Individual in Social Relationships.* Cambridge: Cambridge University Press, 1990).

McFague, Sallie. *The Body of God: An Ecological Theology.* London: SCM, 1993.

McFarland, Ian A. *Listening to the Least: Doing Theology from the Outside In.* Cleveland: Pilgrim, 1998.

McGinn, Bernard, and John Meyendorff, editors. *Christian Spirituality: Origins to the Twelfth Century.* World Spirituality 16. London: Routledge/Keegan Paul, 1985.

McGrath, Alistair. *The Foundations of Dialogue in Science and Religion.* Oxford: Blackwell, 1998.

McHarg, Ian L. "The Place of Nature in the City of Man." In *Western Man and Environmental Ethics: Attitudes toward Nature and Technology*, edited by Ian G. Barbour, 171–86. Reading, MA: Addison-Wesley, 1973.

McKnight, Edgar V. *Postmodern Use of the Bible: The Emergence of Reader-Oriented Criticism*. Nashville: Abingdon, 1988.

McMullin, Ernan. "Life and Intelligence Far from Earth: Formulating Theological Issues." In *Many Worlds: The New Universe, Extraterrestrial Life, and the Theological Implications*, edited by Steven J. Dick, 151–75. Philadelphia: Templeton Foundation Press, 2000.

Meer, Jitse M. van der, editor. *Facets of Faith and Science*. Vol. 1: *Historiography and Modes of Interaction*. Lanham, MD: University Press of America, 1996.

Mellars, Paul. "The Impact of Climatic Changes on the Demography of Late Neandertal and Early Anatomically Modern Populations in Europe." In *Neanderthals and Modern Humans in Western Asia*, edited by Takeru Akazawa et al., 493–507. New York: Plenum, 1998.

———. *The Neanderthal Legacy: An Archaeological Perspective from Western Europe*. Princeton: Princeton University Press, 1996.

Mellor, Philip A., and Chris Shilling. *Re-forming the Body: Religion, Community and Modernity*. London: Sage, 1997.

Meyendorff, John. *A Study of Gregory Palamas*. Translated by George Lawrence. London: Faith Press, 1964.

Michaels, Patricia A. "Ecocentrism vs. Anthropocentrism." Online: http://environment.miningco.com/newsissues/environment/library/weekly/aa033097.htm. Accessed 2003.

Midgley, Mary. "Animals and Why They Matter." *Theology in Green* 5, no. [3] (1995) 22–32.

———. *Animals and Why They Matter*. Athens: University of Georgia Press, 1983.

Migliore, Daniel L. *Faith Seeking Understanding: An Introduction to Christian Theology*. Grand Rapids: Eerdmans, 1991.

Minsky, Marvin. *The Society of Mind*. London: Heinemann, 1986.

Mitani, John C. "Comparative studies of African ape vocal behavior." In *Great Ape Societies*, edited by William C. McGrew, Linda F. Marchant, and Toshisada Nishida, 241–54. Cambridge: Cambridge University Press, 1996.

———. "Singing behavior of male gibbons: field observations and experiments." In *Topics in Primatology*, vol. 1: *Human Origins*, edited by Toshisada Nishida et al, 199–210. Tokyo: University of Tokyo Press, 1992.

Mithen, Stephen J. *The Prehistory of the Mind: A Search for the Origins of Art, Religion, and Science*. London: Thames & Hudson, 1996.

Moberly, R. W. L. *The Bible, Theology, and Faith: A Study of Abraham and Jesus*. Cambridge Studies in Christian Doctrine 5. Cambridge: Cambridge University Press, 2000.

Molnar, Paul D. "Some Problems with Pannenberg's Solution to Barth's 'Faith Subjectivism.'" *SJT* 48 (1995) 315–39.

Moltmann, Jürgen. "Christianity and the Values of Modernity and the Western World." Lecture, Fuller Theological Seminary, Pasadena, CA, April, 1996.

———. *God in Creation: An Ecological Doctrine of Creation*. London: SCM, 1985.

———. *The Way of Jesus Christ: Christology in Messianic Dimensions*. London: SCM, 1990.

Monod, Jacques. *Chance and Necessity: An Essay on the Natural Philosophy of Modern Biology*. Translated by Austryn Wainhouse. London: Penguin, 1971.

Morey, Robert A. *Death and the Afterlife*. Minneapolis: Bethany House, 1984.

Morgan, John H. "Karl Barth in Pursuit of God's Humanity." *Religion in Life* 45 (1976) 324–38.

Morito, Bruce. "Value, Metaphysics, and Anthropocentrism." *Environmental Values* 4 (1995) 31–47.

Morowitz, Harold J. *The Emergence of Everything: How the World Became Complex.* Oxford: Oxford University Press, 2002.

Morris, Henry M., and John C. Whitcomb Jr. *The Genesis Flood: The Biblical Record and Its Scientific Implications.* London: Evangelical, 1969.

Müller, Julius. *Die Christliche Lehre von der Sünde.* Breslau: Josef Max, 1849.

Murphy, George L. "Cosmology and Christology." *Science and Christian Belief* 6 (1994) 101–11.

Murphy, Nancey. "Introduction." In *Theology without Foundation: Religious Practice and the Future of Theological Truth*, edited by Stanley Hauerwas et al., 9–31. Nashville: Abingdon, 1994.

Nagel, Thomas. "What Is It Like to Be a Bat?" In *Mortal Questions*, 165–80. Cambridge: Cambridge University Press, 1991.

Nass, C., et al. "Anthropocentrism and Computers." *Behavior & Information Technology* 14 (1995) 229–38.

Newman, Barclay M. *A Concise Greek-English Dictionary of the New Testament.* BibleWorks, LLC, 1998. Print ed.: London: United Bible Societies, 1971.

Newton-Smith, W. H. *The Rationality of Science.* London: Routledge, 1981.

Nichols, Terrence L. "Miracles in Science and Theology." *Zygon* 37 (2002) 703–15.

Niebuhr, Reinhold. *The Nature and Destiny of Man: A Christian Interpretation.* Vol. 1: *Human Nature.* Gifford Lectures, 1939. London: Nisbet, 1941.

Noble, William, and Iain Davidson. *Human Evolution, Language, and Mind: A Psychological and Archaeological Inquiry.* Cambridge: Cambridge University Press, 1996.

Northcott, Michael S. *The Environment and Christian Ethics.* Cambridge: Cambridge University Press, 1996.

Nouwen, Henri J. M. *Finding My Way Home: Pathways to Life and the Spirit.* New York: Crossroad, 2001.

Novak, Michael. "The Embodied Self." *First Things* 130 (2003) 18–21.

O'Donnell, John J. *The Mystery of the Triune God.* London: Sheed & Ward, 1988.

O'Donovan, Leo J. "Making Heaven and Earth: Catholic Theology's Search for a Unified View of Nature and History." In *Theology and Discovery: Essays in Honor of Karl Rahner, S.J.*, edited by William J. Kelly, 269–99. Milwaukee: Marquette University Press, 1980.

Olson, Roger. "The Human Self-Realization of God: Hegelian Elements in Pannenberg's Christology." *PRSt* 13 (1986) 207–23.

———. "Trinity and Eschatology: The Historical Being of God in Jürgen Moltmann and Wolfhart Pannenberg." *SJT* 36 (1983) 213–27.

Oomen, Palmyre M. F. "On Brain, Soul, Self, and Freedom: An Essay in Bridging Neuroscience and Faith." *Zygon* 38 (2003) 377–92.

Page, Ruth. "The Animal Kingdom and the Kingdom of God." Occasional Paper, Center for Theology and Public Issues, University of Edinburgh, 26. Edinburgh: University of Edinburgh, 1991.

———. "The Fellowship of All Creation." *Theology in Green* 3, no. 7 (1993) 4–13.

———. *God and the Web of Creation.* London: SCM, 1996.

———. "Theology and the Ecological Crisis." *Theology* 99 (1996) 106–14.
Paine, Thomas. *The Complete Writings of Thomas Paine.* Edited by Philip S. Foner. Vol. 1. New York: Citadel, 1945.
Paley, William. *Natural Theology, or Evidences of the Existence and Attributes of the Deity: Collected from the Appearances of Nature.* London: R. Faulder, 1803.
Palmer, Clare. Review of *God and the Web of Creation* by Ruth Page. *JTS* 48 (1997) 750–53.
Pannenberg, Wolfhart. "The Anthropic Principle and Creation Theology." Lecture. Online: http://www.counterbalance.net/physics/ap-body.html.
———. *Anthropology in Theological Perspective.* Translated by Matthew J. O'Connell. Edinburgh: T. & T. Clark, 1985.
———. *Basic Questions in Theology.* Vol. 1. Translated by George H. Kehm. London: SCM, 1970.
———. *Basic Questions in Theology.* Vol. 3. Translated by G. H. Kehm and R. A. Wilson. London: SCM, 1973.
———. "Die Bedeutung des Christentums in der Philosophie Hegels." In *Gottesgedanke und menschliche Frieheit*, 72–113. Göttingen: Vandenhoeck und Ruprecht, 1972.
———. "The Concept of Miracle." *Zygon* 37 (2002) 759–62.
———. "God the Spirit—and Natural Science." Lecture at Lutheran School of Theology, Chicago, cosponsored by the Zygon and CTNS Science and Religion Centers, March, 2001. Electronic video file, online: http://www.counterbalance.net/pberg/index-frame.html.
———. "Der Gott der Geschichte, der trinitarische Gott und die Wahrheit der Geschichte." *KD* 23 (1977) 76–92.
———. *Human Nature, Election, and History.* Philadelphia: Westminster, 1977.
———. *An Introduction to Systematic Theology.* Edinburgh: T. & T. Clark, 1991.
———. *Jesus—God and Man.* Translated by Lewis L. Wilkins and Duane A. Priebe. London: SCM, 1968.
———. *Metaphysics and the Idea of God.* Translated by Philip Clayton. Edinburgh: T. & T. Clark, 1990.
———. "Response to John Polkinghorne." *Zygon* 36 (2001) 799–800.
———. "Response to My American Friends." In *The Theology of Wolfhart Pannenberg: Twelve American Critiques, with an Autobiographical Essay and Response*, edited by Carl E. Braaten and Philip Clayton, 313–36. Minneapolis: Augsburg, 1988.
———. "Response to the Discussion." In *Theology as History*, edited by James M. Robinson and John B. Cobb Jr., 221–76. New Frontiers in Theology 3. New York: Harper & Row, 1967.
———. "Resurrection: The Ultimate Hope." In *Ancient and Postmodern Christianity: Paleo-Orthodoxy in the 21st Century. Essays in Honor of Thomas C. Oden*, edited by Kenneth Tanner and Christopher A. Hall, 254–62. Downers Grove, IL: InterVarsity, 2002.
———, editor. *Revelation as History.* Translated by David Granskou and E. Quinn. London: Sheed & Ward, 1969.
———. *Systematic Theology.* 2 vols. Translated by Geoffrey W. Bromiley. Edinburgh: T. & T. Clark, 1991–94.
———. "Theological Questions to Scientists." *Zygon* 16 (1981) 65–77.
———. "Theology and Science." *Princeton Seminary Bulletin* 13 (1992) 299–310.

———. *Toward a Theology of Nature: Essays on Science and Faith*, edited by Ted Peters. Louisville: Westminster John Knox, 1993.

———. *What Is Man? Contemporary Anthropology in Theological Perspective*. Translated by Duane A. Priebe. Philadelphia: Fortress, 1970.

Pasquini, John J. *Atheism and Salvation: Atheism from the Perspective of Anonymous Christianity in the Thought of the Revolutionary Mystic and Theologian Karl Rahner*. Lanham, MD: University Press of America, 2000.

Paul VI/Vatican Council (2nd: 1962–65). "Pastoral Constitution on the Church in the Modern World" (*Constitutio pastoralis de ecclesia in mundo huius temporis*). In *The Documents of Vatican II*, edited by Walter M. Abbott and Joseph Gallagher, 199–308. London: Chapman, 1966.

Peacocke, A. R. "Biology and a Theology of Evolution." *Zygon* 34 (1999) 695–712.

———. "The Challenge and Stimulus of the Epic of Evolution to Theology." In *Many Worlds: The New Universe, Extraterrestrial Life, and the Theological Implications*, edited by Steven J. Dick, 89–117. Philadelphia: Templeton Foundation Press, 2000.

———. *Creation and the World of Science*. Bampton Lectures, 1978. Oxford: Clarendon, 1979.

———. "The End of All Our Exploring: Paths from Science towards God?" "Theology and Science" lecture series, University of Edinburgh, November 19, 2002,.

Penrose, Roger. *The Emperor's New Mind: Concerning Computers, Minds, and the Laws of Physics*. London: Vintage, 1989.

———. *Shadows of the Mind: A Search for the Missing Science of Consciousness*. Oxford: Oxford University Press, 1996.

———. "Singularities and Time-Asymmetry." In *General Relativity: An Einstein Centenary Survey*, edited by Stephen W. Hawking and W. Israel, 581–638. Cambridge: Cambridge University Press, 1979.

Peters, Ted. "Editor's Introduction: Pannenberg on Theology and Natural Science." In *Toward a Theology of Nature: Essays on Science and Faith*, by Wolfhart Pannenberg, edited by Ted Peters, 1–14. Louisville: Westminster John Knox, 1993.

———. "On Creating the Cosmos." In *Physics, Philosophy, and Theology: A Common Quest for Understanding*, edited by Robert J. Russell et al., 273–96. Notre Dame: University of Notre Dame Press, 1997.

———. "Truth in History: Gadamer's Hermeneutics and Pannenberg's Apologetic Method." *JR* 55 (1975) 36–56.

Peterson, Gregory R. "Are We Unique? The *Locus Humanus*, Animal Cognition and the Theology of Nature." PhD diss., University of Denver and Iliff School of Theology, 1996.

———. "Being Conscious of Marc Bekoff: Thinking of Animal Self-Consciousness." *Zygon* 38 (2003) 247–55.

———. "The Evolution of Consciousness and the Theology of Nature." *Zygon* 34 (1999) 283–306.

———. *Minding God: Theology and the Cognitive Sciences*. Minneapolis: Fortress, 2003.

———. "Nature as the Image of God: Reflections on the Signs of the Sacred." *Zygon* 29 (1994) 489–505.

Philips, D. Z. *Faith after Foundationalism: Plantinga-Rorty-Lindbeck-Berger, Critiques and Alternatives.* Boulder, CO: Westview, 1995.

Piaget, Jean. *The Moral Judgement of the Child.* Translated by Marjorie Gabain. London: Kegan Paul, 1932.

Picard, Rosalind W. *Affective Computing.* London: MIT Press, 1997.

———, and Jonathan Klein. "Computers that recognize and respond to user emotion: theoretical and practical implications." *Interacting with Computers* 14 (2002) 141–69.

Pius XII. "Theology and Modern Science: Pope Pius XII on the Harmony of the Work of God." *Bulletin of the Atomic Scientists* 8 (1952) 143–46, 165.

Plantinga, Alvin. "Methodological Naturalism." In *Facets of Faith and Science*, edited by Jitse M. van der Meer, 1:177–221. Lanham, MD: University Press of America, 1996.

———. "Reason and Belief in God." In *Faith and Rationality: Reason and Belief in God*, edited by Alvin Plantinga and Nicholas Wolterstorff, 16–93. Notre Dame: University of Notre Dame Press, 1983.

———. *Warranted Christian Belief.* Oxford: Oxford University Press, 2000.

———, and Nicholas Wolterstorff, editors. *Faith and Rationality: Reason and Belief in God.* Notre Dame: University of Notre Dame Press, 1983.

Plantinga, Cornelius, Jr. "Gregory of Nyssa and the Social Analogy of the Trinity." *The Thomist* 50 (1986) 325–52.

Plumwood, Val. "Androcentrism and Anthropocentrism." In *Ecofeminism: Women, Culture, Nature*, edited by Karen J. Warren, 327–55. Bloomington: Indiana University Press, 1997.

Polanyi, Michael. *Personal Knowledge: Towards a Post-Critical Philosophy.* 2nd ed. London: Routledge/Kegan Paul, 1962.

Polkinghorne, John C. *The Faith of a Physicist: Reflections of a Bottom-Up Thinker.* Gifford Lectures, 1993–94. Princeton: Princeton University Press, 1994.

———. "Fields and Theology: A Response to Wolfhart Pannenberg." *Zygon* 36 (2001) 795–97.

———. "The Friendliness of Science and Religion." Chaplain's lecture, Herriot Watt University, February 4, 2002.

———. *Science and Christian Belief: Theological Reflections of a Bottom-Up Thinker.* London: SPCK, 1994.

———. *Science and Creation: The Search for Understanding.* London: SPCK, 1988.

———. *Science and Providence: God's Interaction with the World.* London: SPCK, 1989.

———. *Science and Theology: An Introduction.* London: SPCK, 1998.

———. "A Scientist's View of Religion." *Science and Christian Belief* 2 (1990) 83–94.

———. *Serious Talk: Science and Religion in Dialogue.* London: SCM, 1995.

———, editor. *The Work of Love: Creation as Kenosis.* Grand Rapids: Eerdmans, 2001.

Povinelli, Daniel J., et al. "Towards a Science of Other Minds: Escaping the Argument by Analogy." *Cognitive Science* 24 (2000) 509–41.

Powers, John. *A Concise Encyclopedia of Buddhism.* Oxford: Oneworld, 2000.

Preston, Stephanie D., and Frans B. M. de Waal. "Empathy: Its Ultimate and Proximate Bases." *Behavioral and Brain Sciences* 25 (2002) 1–20, 49–71.

Purcell, Michael. *Mystery and Method: The Other in Rahner and Levinas.* Marquette Studies in Theology 15. Milwaukee: Marquette University Press, 1998.
Rabut, Olivier A. *Dialogue with Teilhard de Chardin.* London: Sheed & Ward, 1961.
Rahner, Karl. *Christian at the Crossroads.* Translated by V. Green. London: Burns & Oates, 1975.
———. *The Content of Faith: The Best of Karl Rahner's Theological Writings.* Edited by Karl Lehmann and Albert Raffelt, translation edited by Harvey D. Egan. New York: Crossroads, 1992.
———. *Foundations of Christian Faith: An Introduction to the Idea of Christianity.* Translated by William V. Dych. London: Darton, Longman & Todd, 1978.
———. *Hearers of the Word.* Translated by R. Walls. London: Sheed & Ward, 1969.
———. *Hominisation: The Evolutionary Origin of Man as a Theological Problem.* Translated by W. T. O'Hara. London: Burns & Oates, 1965.
———. *I Remember: An Autobiographical Interview with Meinold Krauss.* Translated by Harvey D. Egan. London: SCM, 1984.
———. *Nature and Grace and Other Essays.* Translated by Dinah Wharton. New York: Sheed & Ward, 1964.
———. *Theological Investigations.* 23 vols. Translators vary. London: Darton, Longman & Todd, 1961–.
———. "Theology and Anthropology." In *The Word in History: The St. Xavier Symposium,* edited by T. Patrick Burke, 1–23. New York: Sheed & Ward, 1966.
———. *The Trinity.* Translated by Joseph Donceel. London: Burns & Oates, 1970.
———, and Wilhelm Thüsing. *A New Christology.* Translated by David Smith and Verdant Green. London: Burns & Oates, 1980.
Rauch, Catherine. "Probing the power of prayer." WebMD Inc. CNN.com, January 18, 2000. Online: http://www.cnn.com/2000/HEALTH/alternative/01/18/prayer.power.wmd/.
Rees, Martin. "Life in Our Universe and Others: A Cosmological Perspective." In *Many Worlds: The New Universe, Extraterrestrial Life, and the Theological Implications,* edited by Steven J. Dick, 61–77. Philadelphia: Templeton Foundation Press, 2000.
———. *Our Universe: The Tenth Leverhulme Memorial Lecture.* Liverpool: Liverpool University Press, 2000.
Richardson, Alan. "Adam, Man." In *A Theological Word Book of the Bible,* edited by Alan Richardson, 14–15. London: SCM, 1950.
Ring, Kenneth, and Sharon Cooper. *Mindsight: Near-Death and Out-of-Body Experiences in the Blind.* Palo Alto, CA: William James Center for Consciousness Studies, 1999.
Roberts, Louis. *The Achievement of Karl Rahner.* New York: Herder & Herder, 1967.
Robinson, H. Wheeler. *Corporate Personality in Ancient Israel.* Rev. ed. Edinburgh: T. & T. Clark, 1981.
Robinson, Howard. "The General Form of the Argument for Berkeleian Idealism." In *Essays on Berkeley: A Tercentennial Celebration,* edited by John Foster and Howard Robinson, 163–86. Oxford: Oxford University Press, 1985.
Robinson, James M., and John B. Cobb Jr., editors. *Theology as History.* New Frontiers in Theology 3. New York: Harper & Row, 1967.
Robinson, John A. T. *The Human Face of God.* London: SCM, 1973.

Rodd, Cyril S. "Introduction." In *Corporate Personality in Ancient Israel*, by H. Wheeler Robinson, 7–14. Rev. ed. Edinburgh: T. & T. Clark, 1981.

Rolston, Holmes, III. *Environmental Ethics: Duties to and Values in the Natural World*. Philadelphia: Temple University Press, 1988.

———. *Genes, Genesis, and God: Values and Their Origins in Natural and Human History*. Gifford Lectures, 1997–98. Cambridge: Cambridge University Press, 1999.

Ronen, Avraham. "Domestic Fire as Evidence for Language." In *Neanderthals and Modern Humans in Western Asia*, edited by Takeru Akazawa et al., 439–47. New York: Plenum, 1998.

Rorty, Richard. *Philosophy and the Mirror of Nature*. Princeton: Princeton University Press, 1979.

Ross, Hugh. "Design Evidences in the Cosmos." Reasons to Believe, 2008. Online: http://www.reasons.org/resources/apologetics/#design_in_the_universe.

Roush, Sherrilyn. "Copernicus, Kant, and the Anthropic Cosmological Principle." *Studies in History and Philosohpy of Modern Physics* 34 (2003) 5–35.

Rowan-Robinson, Michael. *The Nine Numbers of the Cosmos*. Oxford: Oxford University Press, 1999.

Rumbaugh, Duane M. "Animal Thinking—by Stimulation or Simulation?" In *Primate Ontogeny, Cognition, and Social Behaviour*, edited by James G. Else and Phyllis C. Lee, 31–42. Selected Proceedings of the Tenth Congress of the International Primatological Society 3. Cambridge: Cambridge University Press, 1986.

———. *Language Learning by a Chimpanzee: The Lana Project*. London: Academic Press, 1977.

Ruse, Michael. "From Belief to Unbelief—and Halfway Back." *Zygon* 29 (1994) 25–35.

———. *Darwinism Defended: A Guide to the Evolutionary Controversies*. Reading, MA: Addison-Wesley, 1982.

Russell, Robert J. "Finite Creation without a Beginning: The Doctrine of Creation in Relation to Big Bang and Quantum Cosmologies." In *Quantum Cosmology and the Laws of Nature: Scientific Perspectives on Divine Action*, edited by Robert J. Russell et al., 293–329. 2nd ed. Berkeley: Center for Theology and the Natural Sciences, 1999.

———, et al., editors. *Quantum Cosmology and the Laws of Nature: Scientific Perspectives on Divine Action*. Berkeley: Centre for Theology and the Natural Sciences, 1993 (2nd ed. 1999).

Rybarczyk, Edmund J. "What Are You, O Man? Theo-Anthropological Similarities in Classical Pentecostalism & Eastern Orthodoxy." In *Ancient and Postmodern Christianity: Paleo-Orthodoxy in the 21st Century. Essays in Honor of Thomas C. Oden*, edited by Kenneth Tanner and Christopher A. Hall, 83–105. Downers Grove, IL: InterVarsity, 2002.

Sabom, Michael B. *Recollections of Death: A Medical Investigation*. London: Corgi, 1982.

Sagan, Carl. *Cosmos*. London: Futura, 1980.

Santmire, H. Paul. *Nature Reborn: The Ecological and Cosmic Promise of Christian Theology*. Minneapolis: Fortress, 2000.

Santos, Raymond. Personal conversation with author, May 27, 2003.

Sarna, Nahum. *Genesis = Be-reshit: The Traditional Hebrew Text with the New JPS Translation*. JPS Torah Commentary. Philadelphia: Jewish Publication Society, 1989.

Savage-Rumbaugh, E. Sue. *Ape Language: From Conditioned Response to Symbol*. Oxford: Oxford University Press, 1986.

———, et al. *Apes, Language, and the Human Mind*. Oxford: Oxford University Press, 1998.

———, et al. *Language Comprehension in Ape and Child*. Monographs of the Society for Research in Child Development 58, no. 3–4. Chicago: University of Chicago Press, 1993.

———, and Roger Lewin. *Kanzi: The Ape at the Brink of the Human Mind*. London: Doubleday, 1994.

———, and Duane M. Rumbaugh. "Ape-Language Research: Past, Present and Future." In *Ape Language: From Conditioned Response to Symbol*, edited by E. Sue Savage-Rumbaugh, 398–404. Oxford: Oxford University Press, 1986.

———. "The Emergence of Language." In *Tools, Language, and Cognition in Human Evolution*, edited by Kathleen R. Gibson and Tim Ingold, 86–108. Cambridge: Cambridge University Press, 1993.

Scheffczyk, Leo. *Creation and Providence*. Translated by Richard Strachan. London: Burns & Oates, 1970.

———. *Einführung in die Schöpfungslehre*. 3rd ed. Darmstadt: Wissenschaftliche Buchgesellschaft, 1987.

Schmaus, Michael. "Materie und Leben in theologischer Sicht." In *Materie und Leben: Vorträge und Diskussionen, gehalten anlässlich der 6. Arbeitstagung des Institutes der Görres-Gesellschaft für die Begegnung von Naturwissenschaft und Theologie*, 255–68. Naturwissenschaft und Theologie 7. Freiburg/Munich: Alber, 1966.

Schoonenberg, Piet J. A. M. *God's World in the Making*. Dublin: Gill, 1965.

———. *Man and Sin: A Theological View*. Translated by Joseph Donceel. London: Sheed & Ward, 1965.

Schüssler Fiorenza, Elisabeth. *Jesus: Miriam's Child, Sophia's Prophet. Critical Issues in Feminist Christology*. New York: Continuum, 1994.

Schwöbel, Christoph, and Colin E. Gunton, editors. *Persons, Divine and Human: King's College Essays in Theological Anthropology*, edited by Christoph Schwöbel and Colin E. Gunton, 47–61. Edinburgh: T. & T. Clark, 1991.

———. "Rational Theology in Trinitarian Perspective: Wolfhart Pannenberg's *Systematic Theology*." *TS* 47 (1996) 498–527.

Searle, John. "Minds, Brains, and Programs." *Behavioral and Brain Sciences* 3, no. 3 (1980) 417–24, 450–57.

———. *Minds, Brains, and Science*. 1984 Reith Lectures. Cambridge: Harvard University Press, 1984.

Seed, John. "Beyond Anthropocentrism." In *Thinking Like a Mountain—Towards a Council of All Beings*, by John Seed et al., 35–40. London: Heretic, 1988.

Sellars, Wilfred. "Empiricism and the Philosophy of Mind." In *Minnesota Studies in the Philosophy of Science*, vol. 1, edited by Herbert Feigl and Michael Scriven, 253–329. Minneapolis: University of Minnesota Press, 1956.

Senesi, Nicola, James A. Rice, and Teodoro M. Miano. "Preface" to *Matter and Energy Fluxes in the Anthropocentric Environment: Selected Papers Presented at the XIII International Symposium on Environmental Biogeochemistry, Monopoli (Bari),*

Italy, 21–26 September, 1997. *Chemosphere* 39, no. 2 (special issue, July 1999) 165–66.
Shafer, Ingrid. "What Does It Mean to Be Human? A Personal and Catholic Perspective." *Zygon* 37 (2002) 121–36.
Sheehan, Thomas. *Karl Rahner: The Philosophical Foundations*. Series in Continental Thought 9. Athens: Ohio University Press, 1987.
Shults, F. LeRon. *The Postfoundationalist Task of Theology: Wolfhart Pannenberg and the New Theological Rationality*. Grand Rapids: Eerdmans, 1999.
Simpson, George G. *The Meaning of Evolution, a Study of the History of Life and of Its Significance for Man*. Terry Lectures. New Haven: Yale University Press, 1949.
Singer, Peter, editor. *Ethics*. Oxford: Oxford University Press, 1994.
———. *Practical Ethics*. 2nd ed. Cambridge: Cambridge University Press, 1993.
Sinkewicz, Robert E., editor and translator. *The One Hundred and Fifty Chapters*. By Gregory Palamas. Studies and Texts 83. Toronto: Pontifical Institute of Mediaeval Studies, 1988.
Smith, Peter K., et al. *Understanding Children's Development*. 3rd ed. Oxford: Blackwell, 1998.
Sober, Elliot, and David Sloan Wilson. *Unto Others: The Evolution and Psychology of Unselfish Behavior*. Cambridge: Harvard University Press, 1998.
Sobrino, Jon. "Spirituality and the Following of Jesus." In *Systematic Theology: Perspectives from Liberation Theology, Readings from Mysterium Liberationis*, edited by Jon Sobrino and Ignacio Ellacuría, 233–56. Maryknoll, NY: Orbis, 1996.
Soskice, Janet M. "Can a Feminist Call God Father?" In *Women's Voices: Essays in Contemporary Feminist Theology*, edited by Teresa Elwes, 15–29, 159–61. London: Pickering, 1992.
Southgate, Christopher. "God and Evolutionary Evil: Theodicy in the Light of Darwinism." *Zygon* 37 (2002) 803–24.
———, et al., editors. *God, Humanity, and the Cosmos: A Textbook in Science and Religion*. Edinburgh: T. & T. Clark, 1999.
Stanley, Charles K. "The Transcendental Method of Karl Rahner: A Response to Creationist Naiveté." *Encounter* 48 (1987) 195–206.
Stannard, Russell. *The God Experiment*. London: Faber & Faber, 1999.
Stenmark, Mikael. *Scientism: Science, Ethics, and Religion*. Aldershot, UK: Ashgate, 2001.
Stewart, Jacqui A. *Reconstructing Science and Theology in Postmodernity: Pannenberg, Ethics and the Human Sciences*. Aldershot, UK: Ashgate, 2000.
Stonier, Tom. *Beyond Information: The Natural History of Intelligence*. London: Springer-Verlag, 1992.
Stork, David G. "The End of an Era, the Beginning of Another? HAL, Deep Blue and Kasparov." IBM Research. Online: http://www.research.ibm.com/deepblue/learn/html/e.8.1.html.
Swinburne, Richard. *The Existence of God*. Rev. ed. Oxford: Oxford University Press, 1991.
Tanner, Kenneth, and Christopher A. Hall, editors. *Ancient and Postmodern Christianity: Paleo-Orthodoxy in the 21st Century. Essays in Honor of Thomas C. Oden*. Downers Grove, IL: InterVarsity, 2002.

Tattersall, Ian. *Becoming Human: Evolution and Human Uniqueness.* Oxford: Oxford University Press, 1998.

———. *The Last Neanderthal: The Rise, Success, and Mysterious Extinction of Our Closest Human Relatives.* Rev. ed. Boulder, CO: Westview, 1999.

Teilhard de Chardin, Pierre. *The Phenomenon of Man.* Translated by Bernard Wall. London: Collins, 1959.

Templeton, John. *The Humble Approach: Scientists Discover God.* London: Collins, 1981.

TeSelle, Eugene. *Christ in Context: Divine Purpose and Human Possibility.* Philadelphia: Fortress, 1975.

Teske, John A. "That Haunting of the Human Spirit." *Zygon* 34 (1999) 307–22.

Thomas Aquinas. *Summa Theologica.* Translated by Fathers of the English Dominican province. AGES Digital Library. Albany, OR: AGES, 1997. Print ed.: New York: Benziger, 1911–25.

Thunberg, Lars. "The Human Person as Image of God: Eastern Christianity." In *Christian Spirituality: Origins to the Twelfth Century,* edited by Bernard McGinn and John Meyendorff, 291–312. World Spirituality 16. London: Routledge/Kegan Paul, 1985.

Tipler, Frank. "Omega Point as Eschaton." *Zygon* 24 (1989) 217–53.

Tomasello, Michael. "Primate Cognition: Introduction to the Issue." *Cognitive Science* 24 (2000) 351–61.

Toronto Airport Christian Fellowship Web site. Online: http://www.tacf.org.

Torrance, Alan J. *Persons in Communion: An Essay on Trinitarian Description and Human Participation, with Special Reference to Volume one of Karl Barth's Church Dogmatics.* Edinburgh: T. & T. Clark, 1996.

Torrance, Thomas F. *The Christian Doctrine of God: One Being Three Persons.* Edinburgh: T. & T. Clark, 1996.

———. *Divine and Contingent Order.* Oxford: Oxford University Press, 1981.

———. "The Transcendental Role of Wisdom in Science." In *Facets of Faith and Science,* edited by Jitse M. van der Meer, 1:131–49. Lanham, MD: University Press of America, 1996.

———. *Theological Science.* Edinburgh: T. & T. Clark, 1996.

———. *The Trinitarian Faith: The Evangelical Theology of the Ancient Church.* Edinburgh: T. & T. Clark, 1988.

———. "Ultimate and Penultimate Beliefs in Science." In *Facets of Faith and Science,* edited by Jitse M. van der Meer, 1:151–76. Lanham, MD: University Press of America, 1996.

Troxell, Eugene. "Environmental Ethics: Philosophy 332. Class Overheads." Course materials, San Diego State University, Fall 1997. Online: http://www-rohan.sdsu.edu/faculty/troxell/332_f97/332overheads.html.

Tupper, E. Frank. *The Theology of Wolfhart Pannenberg.* London: SCM, 1974.

Turing, Alan M. "Computing Machinery and Intelligence." *Mind* 59 (1950) 433–60. Online: http://www.loebner.net/Prizef/TuringArticle.html.

Tuttle, Russell H. *Apes of the World: Their Social Behavior, Communication, Mentality and Ecology.* Park Ridge, NY: Noyes/William Andrew, 1986.

Van Buren, Paul Matthews. *Discerning the Way.* Vol. 1 of *A Theology of the Jewish Christian Reality.* New York: Seabury, 1980.

Van Huyssteen, Wentzel. *Essays in Postfoundationalist Theology*. Grand Rapids: Eerdmans, 1997.
———. "Rethinking the *Imago Dei*: Theology and Science on Human Uniqueness." "Theology and Science" lecture, New College, University of Edinburgh, November 7, 2002.
VanGemeren, Willem. *Interpreting the Prophetic Word*. Grand Rapids: Academic, 1992.
Vanhoozer, Kevin. "Human Being, Individual and Social." In *The Cambridge Companion to Christian Doctrine*, edited by Colin E. Gunton, 158–88. Cambridge: Cambridge University Press, 1997.
Vass, George. *A Pattern of Christian Doctrines 1: God and Christ*. Vol. 3 of *Understanding Karl Rahner*. London: Sheed & Ward, 1996.
———. *A Theologian in Search of a Philosophy*. Vol. 1 of *Understanding Karl Rahner*. London: Sheed & Ward, 1985.
Vawter, Bruce. *On Genesis: A New Reading*. London: G. Chapman, 1977.
Volf, Miroslav. *After Our Likeness: The Church as the Image of the Trinity*. Grand Rapids: Eerdmans, 1998.
Von Rad, Gerhard. *Genesis: A Commentary*. Translated by John H. Marks. Rev. ed. OTL. London: SCM, 1972.
Vorgrimler, Herbert. *Karl Rahner: His Life, Thought and Work*. Translated by E. Quinn. London: Burns & Oates, 1965.
Waal, Frans B. M. de. "Chimpanzee Justice." In *Ethics*, edited by Peter Singer, 67–69. Oxford: Oxford University Press, 1994.
———. *Good Natured: The Origins of Right and Wrong in Humans and Other Animals*. Cambridge: Harvard University Press, 1996.
Wainwright, Geoffrey. "Pannenberg's Ecumenism." In *The Theology of Wolfhart Pannenberg: Twelve American Critiques, with an Autobiographical Essay and Response*, edited by Carl E. Braaten and Philip Clayton, 207–23. Minneapolis: Augsburg, 1988.
Walsh, Michael J. *The Heart of Christ in the Writings of Karl Rahner: An Investigation of Its Christological Foundation as an Example of the Relationship between Theology and Spirituality*. Analecta Gregoriana 209. Rome: Università Gregoriana Editrice, 1977.
Ward, Graham, editor. *The Postmodern God: A Theological Reader*. Oxford: Blackwell, 1997.
Ward, Keith. "Believing in Miracles." *Zygon* 37 (2002) 741–50.
———. *In Defense of the Soul*. Oxford: Oneworld, 1998.
———. *God, Chance & Necessity*. Oxford: Oneworld, 1996.
———. *Religion and Creation*. Oxford: Clarendon, 1996.
Ward, Peter Douglas, and Donald Brownlee. *Rare Earth: Why Complex Life Is Uncommon in the Universe*. New York: Copernicus, 2000.
Warren, Karen J., editor. *Ecofeminism: Women, Culture, Nature*. Bloomington: Indiana University Press, 1997.
Watson, Francis. *Text, Church and World: Biblical Interpretation in Theological Perspective*. Edinburgh: T. & T. Clark, 1994.
Watts, Fraser. "The Multifaceted Nature of Human Personhood: Psychological and Theological Perspectives." In *The Human Person in Science and Theology*, edited by Niels Henrik Gregersen et al., 41–63. Edinburgh: T. & T. Clark, 2000.

———. "Psychology and Theology." In *God, Humanity, and the Cosmos: A Textbook in Science and Religion*, edited by Christopher Southgate et al., 173–96. Edinburgh: T. & T. Clark, 1999.

Weger, Karl-Heinz. *Karl Rahner: An Introduction to His Theology*. Translated by David Smith. London: Burns & Oates, 1980.

Weil, Simone. *La Connaissance Surnaturelle*. Paris: Gallimard, 1950.

Weinberg, Steven. *Dreams of a Final Theory*. London: Vintage, 1993.

Welker, Michael. *Creation and Reality*. Translated by John F. Hoffmeyer. Minneapolis: Fortress, 1999.

———. "Is the Autonomous Person of European Modernity a Sustainable Model of Human Personhood?" In *The Human Person in Science and Theology*, edited by Niels Henrik Gregersen, et al., 95–114. Edinburgh: T. & T. Clark, 2000.

———. "Das theologische Prinzip des Verhaltens zu Zeiterscheinungen." *EvT* 36 (1976) 225–52.

Wesley, John. *The Works of John Wesley, Complete and Unabridged*, vol. 1: *Journals from October 14, 1735, to November 29, 1745*. 3rd ed. AGES Digital Library. Albany, OR: AGES, 1997. Print ed.: London: Methodist Connection, 1872.

Westermann, Claus. *Genesis 1–11*. CC. Minneapolis: Fortress, 1994.

Westphal, Merold. "Hegel, Pannenberg, and Hermeneutics." *Man and World* 4 (1971) 276–93.

Wetherill, George. "How Special Is Jupiter?" *Nature*, February 9, 1995, 470.

White, Jr., Lynn. "The Historic Roots of the Ecologic Crisis." In *Western Man and Environmental Ethics: Attitudes toward Nature and Technology*, edited by Ian G. Barbour, 18–30. Reading, MA: Addison-Wesley, 1973.

Wicken, Jeffrey. "Theology and Science in the Evolving Cosmos: A Need for Dialogue." *Zygon* 23 (1988) 45–55.

———. "Toward an Evolutionary Ecology of Meaning." *Zygon* 24 (1989) 153–84.

Wiles, Maurice. Review of *The Triune Creator: A Historical and Systematic Study* by Colin E. Gunton. *Zygon* 37 (2002) 220–22.

Williams, Michael. *Problems of Knowledge: A Critical Introduction to Epistemology*. Oxford: Oxford University Press, 2001.

Williams, Patricia A. *Doing Without Adam and Eve: Sociobiology and Original Sin*. Minneapolis: Fortress, 2001.

Wilson, Allan C., and Rebecca L. Cann, "The Recent African Genesis of Humans." *Scientific American* 266 (April 1992) 68–73.

Wilson, Edward O. *The Diversity of Life*. London: Penguin, 1992.

———. *On Human Nature*. Cambridge: Harvard University Press, 1978.

Winograd, Terry, and Fernando Flores. *Understanding Computers and Cognition: A New Foundation for Design*. Reading, MA: Addison-Wesley, 1987.

Wolterstorff, Nicholas. "Can Belief in God Be Rational If It Has No Foundation?" In *Faith and Rationality: Reason and Belief in God*, edited by Alvin Plantinga and Nicholas Wolterstorff, 135–86. Notre Dame: University of Notre Dame Press, 1983.

World Council of Churches, Faith and Order Commission. *Faith and Order Paper 140: Confessing One Faith. Towards an Ecumenical Explication of the Apostolic Faith as Expressed in the Nicene-Constantinopolitan Creed (381)*. Geneva: WCC Publications, 1987.

———. *Reason within the Bounds of Religion*. 2nd ed. Grand Rapids: Eerdmans, 1984.

Wynn, Mark. *God and Goodness: A Natural Theological Perspective*. Routledge Studies in the Philosophy of Religion 1. London: Routledge, 1999.

Zizioulas, John. "On Being a Person: Towards an Ontology of Personhood." In *Persons, Divine and Human: King's College Essays in Theological Anthropology*, edited by Christoph Schwöbel and Colin E. Gunton, 33–46. Edinburgh: T. & T. Clark, 1991.

———. *Being as Communion: Studies in Personhood and the Church*. Contemporary Greek Theologians 4. Crestwood, NY: St. Vladimir's Seminary Press, 1985.

———. "The Contribution of Cappadocia to Christian Thought." In *Sinasos in Cappadocia*, 23–37. London: Agra Publications, 1985.

———. "Human Capacity and Incapacity: A Theological Exploration of Personhood." *SJT* 28 (1975) 401–48.

———. "The Mystery of the Church in Orthodox Tradition." *OiC* 24 (1988) 294–303.

———. "Preserving God's Creation: Three Lectures on Theology and Ecology: Lecture One." *King's Theological Review* 12, no. 1 (1989) 1–5.

———. "Preserving God's Creation: Three Lectures on Theology and Ecology: Lecture Two." *King's Theological Review* 12, no. 2 (1989) 41–45.

———. "Preserving God's Creation: Three Lectures on Theology and Ecology: Lecture Three." *King's Theological Review* 13, no. 1 (1990) 1–5.

———. "Reflections of an Orthodox." *Evangelical Review* 23 (1971) 30–34.

Zycinski, Joseph M. "The Weak Anthropic Principle and the Design Argument." *Zygon* 31 (1996) 115–30.

Subject Index

Adam, 35, 48, 49, 50, 53, 64, 123, 128, 135–36, 156, 159, 167–72, 285
afterlife, 215, 233–34
altruism, 169, 219–20
androcentrism, 6, 12
angels, 59, 69, 113–16, 120–21, 238, 280, 290
animal(s), 36, 93, 96, 126, 127, 149, 150, 165, 166, 179, 182, 203–43
   communication, 203, 205–10, 219
   instinct, 170, 219–20
   intelligence, 204–7, 214
   and language, 205–14
   and morality, 170, 218–22
   rights, 38, 204, 222, 287–89, 291–92, 302
anthropic principle, xiii–xiv, 8, 10, 18, 30, 60–63, 84–85, 248, 249, 250, 255–58, 262, 263, 270, 275, 276, 301
anthropocentrism, xiii–xiv, 2–13
   critical, 2, 11–13, 17, 84–85, 141–42, 183–84, 145, 148, 188, 243–45, 278–79, 292–93, 294, 300–304
   cosmic, 5, 8, 9–10
   epistemic, 5, 9–10, 94
   medieval, 2, 3, 8–9, 11
   pernicious, 7, 8–9, 290
   radical, 4, 8–9, 12
   strong and weak versions, 7

anthropocentric hypothesis, 8–9, 11
anthropology, cultural, 191
apes (*see* chimpanzee/Kanzi)
apocalyptic milieu, 26, 53, 71–73
apocalyptic expectations, 182, 236–37
Apostles, 75, 90, 105, 162
Arianism, 136, 181
aritifical intelligence (AI), xiii, 18, 224–37, 300
art, 215, 216, 300
astrophysics, 235, 251
atheism, 193

baptism, 155, 164, 177
beginning (*see* origins: cosmic; human), 16, 36, 100, 109, 159, 260, 281
Bible (*see* Scripture), 38, 175, 197
big bang theory, 57, 156, 248, 249–56, 260–61, 262, 270, 276, 301
Black-American experience, 80
bonobo (*see* chimpanzee/Kanzi), 205, 208
brain, human, 64–65, 205–6, 210, 225, 233, 239, 248, 262, 301
brain/mind problem, 227, 231, 232, 236
Buddhism, 7
burial-human, 215
burial-Neanderthal, 215

Cappadocian Fathers, 174–75

Subject Index

causation, 28, 61, 110, 174–76, 189, 258–59, 262, 265, 273, 276, 301
cave paintings, 215
chimpanzee (*see* also Kanzi), 203, 205, 211–12, 213
   and intelligence, 211, 212, 213, 214
   and language, 205–9
   and morality, 211, 218–19, 221
Christology (*see* Jesus Christ), 28, 79–80, 83, 91, 102, 108, 111, 112, 115, 121–22, 131, 132, 133–42, 143, 144, 154, 168, 179, 180, 238, 263
   degree, 136, 137, 138, 140, 142, 285
church, 7, 46n12, 49–52, 80–81, 90, 119, 144, 145, 151, 153, 155–56, 161–63, 177, 179–80, 183–84, 292–93, 297, 302, 304
COBE, 253
COG, 229
cogito ergo sum, 65, 66
cognition, 68, 87, 95, 126, 166, 178, 212, 230
coherence, 2, 15–16, 19, 23, 30, 34, 56, 58, 91, 95, 107, 117, 142, 188
communication, xiii
   animal, 203, 204–5, 207–10, 219
   human, 46, 64, 67, 69, 115, 207–10, 222, 224
   search for alien (SETI), 60, 238–39, 240
communion, 42, 46, 47, 64, 81, 91, 93, 100, 103, 127, 143–44, 146–47, 153, 155, 159, 160–61, 163, 167, 173–74, 177, 183–84, 244, 279, 280, 283, 284, 286, 287, 297, 305
community, 14, 45, 47, 49, 51–52, 68, 76–77, 146, 147, 149, 151, 154, 174, 176, 195, 208–9, 244, 303–5
complexity theory 110
computers 6, 192, 224–31
consciousness, 262, 263, 270–75
   animal, 213, 224
   human, 63, 92–93, 109, 142, 172, 178, 224, 229–34, 248, 296, 302
   computers, 229–34, 304
   extra-terrestial, 17, 117
conservation, 7
contingency, 25, 29, 56–57, 63, 72, 79, 95, 126, 137, 159, 175, 238, 260, 271, 273, 284, 287
Copernican revolution, 1, 10
cosmological argument, 247, 251–61, 262
cosmology, 18, 27, 60, 66, 250, 254, 260, 281, 285, 287
creatio ex nihilo, 156, 157, 250, 258–61
creation, xii, 11, 14n51, 27–29, 42, 52–56, 63, 87, 110, 114, 135, 156–60, 164, 258, 260, 265, 278, 288
   Christ in creation, 32–33, 49–50, 62, 79, 81–82, 83, 99–100, 102–3, 111–13, 120–22, 124, 134, 142, 162, 172, 275, 298
   humans as goal/crown of, 1, 6, 17, 30–31, 33–34, 40–41, 46–47, 55, 61, 63–69, 84, 95, 109, 121, 148, 160, 222, 246, 249, 271–73, 274, 277, 297–99, 302
   humans as representative of, 43–45, 84, 118, 148, 151–55, 163–64, 177, 182–83, 279–87, 290–93, 302
   new creation 26, 55, 67, 124, 134, 161–63
Creator (*see* God)
critical realism 15, 198–201

Subject Index   337

Cro-Magnon man, 217
cross-crucifixion (*see* Jesus Christ), 120, 134–35
culture, 71, 80, 90–91, 115, 117, 132, 188, 191, 192, 193, 200, 204, 212–14, 216, 218, 220, 237, 238, 300, 304, 305

Darwinism (*see* evolution), 167, 246
death
   mortality, 62, 121, 124, 139, 156–57, 159–60, 161, 172, 179, 284, 286, 289
   near-death experiences (NDE), 129, 232–35
   human, 73, 128, 129, 172, 184, 282, 287
   and Jesus Christ, xii, 24, 67, 75, 105–6, 118, 120, 122, 123, 124, 133, 134–36, 140, 141, 153, 155, 165, 272
Deep Blue, 225, 226, 228
deification (*theosis*), 158, 184, 297
Deism, 111, 148, 188, 260, 273, 282
design argument (*see* teleology), 261, 266
destiny
   cosmic, 42, 43, 61–62, 83, 133, 153–56, 161–62, 184, 296, 299
   creation, 45, 60, 62, 84, 151, 296, 298
   human, 39, 42, 43, 44, 53, 84, 104, 112, 150, 152, 161–62, 184, 284, 299, 306
   the church, 145, 183, 297
determinism, 56, 199
dignity, human, 44–45, 69, 95, 96, 104, 204, 224, 232, 236, 305–6
DNA, 203, 217, 267–67, 284
dolphins, 203, 205, 211

dominion, 3, 17, 35–41, 45, 47, 50–51, 52, 64, 158, 179, 293

Earth, 128, 225, 240, 250, 263, 265
Easter, 74, 81, 140
Eastern Orthodoxy, 175
ecclesiology, 144
ecocentric, 7, 291
ecology, 2, 143, 209
ecopathy, 291
Eden, 159, 171, 244, 305
egotism, 6
eikon, 144
ekstasis, 147, 155
emergent complexity, xiii, 114, 210, 238, 239, 268–72, 304
emotion, 66, 67, 69, 80, 203, 214, 218–19, 229–231, 268
Enlightenment, 12, 25, 56, 66, 71, 76–77, 144, 164, 165, 188–92, 196–97, 290
   Foundationalism (EF), 188–91, 196–98, 300
   worldview, 12, 25n12, 56, 66, 76–77, 165–65, 187–97
   naturalism, 18, 56, 73, 76, 77, 144, 165, 187–88, 189–90, 192, 193–97, 198, 201, 299–300
entropy, 114, 159, 270
environment, xiv, 7, 12, 38–39, 152–53, 210, 214, 241, 267, 291, 293, 301, 302–3, 304
epistemology
   foundationalism (*see also* Enlightenment Foundationalism), 191, 197
   postmodernism, 13, 76, 196–98
   postfoundationalism, 13–14, 73, 190, 196, 198
   critical realism, 15–16, 73, 198–201
   naïve realism, 192
   instrumentalism, 254

Subject Index

eschaton/eschatology, 30, 34, 67, 62, 72, 82, 92, 96, 129, 135, 150–51, 177, 288–89
ethnocentrism, 6, 191–93
ETI (*see* extraterrestrial intelligence)
Eucharist, 163–65, 177, 182, 289
Euclidean geometry, 196
Eve (*see* Adam), 48, 53, 135–36, 167, 172
evil, 39, 66, 134, 150, 157, 159, 169–72, 221–22, 264, 281–83, 287
evolution
    animal, 1, 209, 210, 213, 223, 280
    human, 1, 53, 54, 63, 91, 95, 96–97, 106, 108, 109, 133, 160, 171, 172, 209, 210, 213, 217, 218–19, 223, 241, 280, 296
    cosmic, xiv, 18, 28, 33, 61, 62, 110, 160, 238–240, 242–44, 246–77, 294, 301–2
exocentricity, 35–37
extraterrestrial intelligence (ETI), x, xiii, 8, 18, 30, 59, 84, 91, 113–16, 121–23, 142, 162, 237–40, 243–44, 250, 276, 295–96, 301, 304

faith, 14–16, 24–27, 31, 39, 58, 68, 70, 72, 73, 74, 75, 77, 78, 79, 88, 89, 91, 95, 101, 105, 107, 108, 113, 132, 142, 163, 194, 196, 200, 201, 238, 257, 260, 277, 278, 291, 302
Fall, the, 42, 99, 135–136, 150, 152, 154, 156, 158–59, 167, 168, 170–72, 179, 197, 282, 287
fatherhood
    human, 180
    of God, 179–81
feminist theology, 179–80
fideism, 201

fine-tuning, 61, 63, 240, 249, 261–64, 266, 268, 270, 273 (*see* anthropic principle)
forgiveness, 51, 89, 163
foundationalism (*see* Enlightenment), 13, 188–91, 196–97, 300
freedom 36, 41, 69, 72, 93, 97–98, 118, 141, 145–46, 148–53, 163, 167, 171, 219–24, 243, 264, 271–72, 276, 281–84, 286–87, 305
    animal vs. human, 36, 69, 72, 91, 97, 98, 106, 141, 149–52, 155–57, 159, 163, 165, 167, 172, 179, 183, 219–24, 276, 283, 286, 305
    moral, 41, 69, 219, 222, 284, 287, 305
    personal, 36, 41, 49, 69, 86, 118, 146, 171, 220, 224, 272, 284, 286, 305

Genesis, 17, 27–28, 34, 35, 39, 41, 45, 46, 47, 50, 53, 54, 55, 64, 66, 124, 133, 136, 157, 159, 167, 170, 172, 219, 236
genesis, 253, 273
genetics, 7, 169, 171, 217, 219, 268
geocentric, 3, 10
Gnosticism, 130
God
    Creator, 62, 127, 164, 276
    the Father, x, 24, 32, 49, 78, 81, 100, 120, 145–46, 155, 173–76, 179–81
    the Holy Spirit, 59, 163, 173, 176
    immutability, 116, 117, 124
    and personhood, 41, 46, 48, 52, 64, 119–20, 143–44, 145–50, 154–55, 161, 173–76, 181
    the Son (*see also* Jesus Christ), 145, 244

God (cont.),
    the Trinity, 32, 36, 44, 144,
        145–48, 150, 173–79
    inner-Trinitarian relations,
        72, 83, 174, 176
    communion, 42, 46, 64, 81,
        100, 127, 143–44, 146–47
    immanent, 78, 79, 140
    economic, 78
god-of-the-gaps problem, 283
God-consciousness, 130
grammar (*see* language features),
    207, 209

Hartle-Hawking theory, 254, 260
heaven, xi, 33, 42, 50, 98, 119,
    120–21, 125, 161–62, 184,
    279, 289, 305
Hellenistic thought, 65, 79–80
Hermeneutics, 70, 74–80
historical-criticism, 70, 73, 197
history, 15, 24–26, 28–34, 41, 53, 55,
    58, 60–62, 71–73, 75, 77–79,
    81–85, 89–91, 98, 108–13,
    118, 121, 126, 134–36, 141,
    143, 144, 159, 164, 184, 194,
    197, 210, 213, 242, 244, 260,
    264, 265, 271–72, 281, 283,
    286, 295, 297–98
Holy Spirit, x, 59, 163, 173, 176
hominids, 36, 216
hominization, 95
homo sapiens, 5, 8, 10, 36, 63, 117,
    123, 133, 171, 217, 219, 223
hope, 36, 37, 67, 97, 105, 129, 134,
    149, 156, 172, 177, 182, 184,
    297
horror, 267
Hubble Space Telescope, 247
human
    body, 65, 67, 116, 127
    brain, 205, 206, 210, 248, 262,
        301
    destiny, 39, 284

    divine ambassador, 39, 40–41
    divine image, 48, 67
    evolution, 137, 217
    freedom (*see* freedom, personal)
    imago dei (*see* separate entry)
    mind-brain problem, 64–65,
        225, 227, 231–40
    morality, 135, 147, 156, 157,
        160–62, 169, 172–73, 177,
        184, 298
    nature, xiii, 6, 12, 17, 63, 65,
        67–69, 80, 92–96, 97, 99,
        100–105, 107, 109, 111–12,
        119, 122, 124, 209, 296–97
    nonmaterial aspects, 232–35
    openness, 92, 188
    origins, 60–63, 107–13, 167–73,
        239, 299
    religious character, 36, 43, 89,
        93, 97–98, 107, 127, 139, 166,
        224
    significance, xi, xii, xiv, 2, 10,
        16–19, 35, 37, 145, 148, 165,
        166, 203, 204, 223–25, 237,
        240, 244, 300–301, 303
    soul, 45, 65, 96, 127–29, 145,
        149–50, 156, 231, 282, 288
    spirit, 17, 41, 72, 91, 95, 97,
        126–28, 235
    uniqueness, xii, 18, 35, 37, 145,
        148, 165, 166, 203, 223,
        224–25, 240, 244, 300–301,
        303
hypostatic union, 102, 104, 112, 130

icon, 147, 148, 237
idolatry, 64
image vs. likeness and the *imago
    dei*, 158
imagination, xii, 10, 94, 122, 257
imago dei, 12, 16, 35–37, 39, 41,
    42–43, 45, 46–47, 49–52,
    63–66, 68–69, 94, 123, 145,
    148, 153–54, 167, 174, 177,

Subject Index

imago dei (cont.),
179, 181, 183, 203, 223,
232, 236, 244–45, 285, 294,
296–98
immortality, 127, 149, 157, 161,
172, 184, 297
immutability (*see* God), 116, 117,
124–25
incarnation (*see* also Jesus Christ),
and human signficance, xii, 3,
16, 30–34, 42–43, 59, 61–63,
84, 93, 99–105, 121, 141,
153–55, 159, 162, 164, 184,
274, 276–77
and Pannenberg, 42–45, 47, 54,
59, 61–63, 69, 78, 79, 82–85
and Rahner, 89, 91–92, 93, 98,
99–104, 108–13, 116–26,
130, 132–33, 137–42
and Zizioulas, 144–45, 153–55,
157, 159, 160, 162, 164,
172, 173, 176, 178–79, 181,
183–84
possibility of multiple, 91,
116–19, 121–25, 139, 142,
238, 296
individualism, 147, 153
information theory, 269
instincts (*see* animals), 170, 219
instrumentalism (*see*
Epistemology)
intelligence
alien, xiii
animal, xiii, 18, 204, 214, 224,
235
scaffolded intelligence, 214
artificial, xiii, 18, 59, 224–37,
243, 300
degree vs. *kind* and animals, 18,
96, 149, 166, 203, 204–14,
218–24
extraterrestrial, 59–60, 113–16,
122, 237–43

human, 8, 18, 37, 59, 62, 115,
149, 205, 214, 218, 219, 221,
223–28, 230, 232, 241, 243,
266, 276, 291, 300, 305
intelligent design theory (ID), 108,
110, 269, 273, 304
intelligibility, 57, 62, 137, 178, 197,
202, 274–75
intercessory prayer, 257
interpretation (*see* hermeneutics)
Israel, 24, 26, 72, 73, 83, 134, 265
I-Thou, 48, 52, 222, 236, 244, 303

Jesus Christ
and history, 15, 24, 25, 27, 30, 34,
71, 77, 80, 81, 83, 89, 134
and human nature, 112, 122,
126, 141
and salvation, 104, 121, 125, 291,
293
and the cross, 75, 128, 134, 175
as *imago dei*, 16, 39, 42, 49, 50,
52, 154, 179
as *logos*, 30, 59–60, 83, 100, 102,
119, 121, 123
as Son of God, 24, 32, 70, 78–79,
82, 83, 84, 136, 138, 180
birth, 82, 144, 165, 188,
death/crucifixion, 140, 272
future rule, 34, 82–82, 150–51
incarnation, 16, 24, 31, 32, 33,
34, 78, 79, 82, 84, 89, 99, 101,
117, 118, 123, 140, 176, 183,
284, 285, 295, 298, 302
pre-incarnate existence, 75, 78,
80, 138
resurrection, 24, 26, 27, 28, 33,
34, 55, 61, 67, 69, 74, 75, 105,
119, 140, 144, 154, 162, 165,
188, 194–95, 272, 285
Jubilee, 53, 55
Jupiter, 241
justice, 36, 51, 52, 53, 55, 64, 66, 72,
218, 221, 305

justification, 4, 111, 161, 193, 291

Kanzi, 205–8, 214
kenosis, 80
kingdom of God, 54, 163, 177

language/linguistics, 205–23
    and animals, 205–10, 224
    and children, 205–6, 221
    and Kanzi, 205–6
    and Neanderthals, 215–16, 218
    features of human, 207–10, 213–14, 224
liberation theology, 66
life
    eternal, 32, 79, 84, 105, 121, 159, 173, 184,
    origins (*see* human: origins; creation; evolution)
life-friendly environment, 240–43, 263–66
logos (*see* Jesus Christ), 31, 33, 47, 50, 59–60, 64, 71, 79, 80–83, 99–104, 112, 115, 116, 119, 121–22, 123, 124, 126, 130, 131, 139, 140–41, 154, 244, 275
love, ix, 32, 44, 47, 49, 50–52, 55, 56, 80, 83, 87, 89, 90, 100, 104, 106, 110, 129, 132, 133, 134–36, 146, 147, 148, 149, 150, 166, 173, 175–76, 179, 180, 183, 204, 219, 247, 265, 275, 280, 283, 285, 288, 292, 297
lunar tides, 241

machines, 6, 131, 225, 227, 228, 231, 269, 288
many-worlds interpretation of quantum mechanics, 116
Marxist thought, 160
mathematics, 94, 114, 224, 227, 255
medieval

worldview, xi, 1, 8, 247, 294
    synthesis, 3, 8, 11
messiah (*see* Jesus Christ), xii, 75, 161
metaphysics, 87, 88, 200, 202, 247, 301
microwave background radiation, 253
mind (*see* human; animal), 17, 59, 63–67, 69, 72, 87–88, 114, 115, 126, 128, 129, 131, 133, 138, 140, 144, 145, 153, 169, 176, 178, 181, 201, 204, 211, 212, 213, 216, 218, 220, 224, 227, 231, 232, 233, 234, 235, 236, 269, 271, 274, 275, 294, 295, 299, 300, 304, 305
mind-body-brain problem, 232, 236
miracles, 14, 15, 25, 74, 77, 187, 190, 192–93, 194, 201–2, 283
mitsein, 282, 285
modernism (*see also* the Enlightenment), 68, 71, 111, 142, 144, 184
monkeys (*see* chimpanzees), 209, 211–12
monophysitism, 102
monotheism, 175
morality, 68, 149, 166, 169, 218, 222, 298
mortality (*see* death), 84, 127, 135, 147, 149, 156–57, 159–60, 161, 162, 169, 172–73, 177, 184, 286, 295, 297, 298
multiple universes (*see* multiverse), 255, 257, 301
multiple-incarnations (*see* incarnation), 91, 116–19, 121–25, 139, 142, 238, 296
multiverse, 256–58
music, 216, 228–29

mystery, 69, 87–88, 90, 92, 97, 112, 137, 155, 200, 216, 259, 268, 295
myth/mythology, 27, 31, 73, 75, 76–77, 144, 158, 167–68, 171, 189, 191, 192, 196, 199

naturalism
    materialistic/ontological, 56, 70, 73, 76, 115, 144, 187, 193–96, 197, 202, 299–300
    methodological, 18, 115, 141–42, 193–96, 202, 299–300
nature (as in human or animal, or mother nature)
Neanderthals, 63, 215–19
near-death experience (NDE), 129, 232–35
necessity (see also contingency), 1, 32, 133, 148–49, 151, 154, 220, 238–39, 259, 267, 304
neuroscience, 234
Newtonian physics, 199
Nicene Creed, 119
Nineveh, 288
noetic nonmaterial realm, 234
nous, 65, 66

obedience, 122, 134, 135, 157
objectivity, 9, 73, 76, 87, 104, 189, 192, 197, 201
Ockham's Razor, 131
ontological argument, 96, 108, 111, 252, 258–61, 270, 273–74
ontology, 146, 176, 178, 197, 258
original sin (see also sin), 135, 145, 165–68, 170, 173
origins (see also creation; life)
    cosmic, 60, 246–61
    human (see human: origins)
orthodoxy (see Eastern Orthodoxy), 76, 83, 90, 106, 156, 175

out-of-body experiences, 233

Paleolithic Age, 217
paleontology, 215–18
panentheism, 127
Pannenberg, Wolfhart
    anthropic principle, 30, 59, 60–63, 84–85
    biography, 23
    Christ's divinity, 24, 30, 31, 33, 44, 45, 50, 70, 78–84
    extra-terrestrial life, 30
    hermeneutics, 70, 74, 78, 83
    human dominion, 35, 37, 38–41, 45, 47, 50, 52
    human uniqueness, 35, 37
    imago dei, 36, 37, 39, 41–47, 49–52, 63–66, 68–69
    incarnation, 24, 31–34, 42–45, 54, 59, 61–63, 69, 78–80, 82–85
    resurrection, 24–30, 34, 42, 45, 55, 56, 58, 61, 67, 70, 71, 73–80, 82–85
    and science, 24, 29–31, 36, 37, 56–59, 61, 62, 64, 66, 75, 81, 84
pantheism, 72
patriarchalism, 179–81
pattern-making and the Logos, 122, 139
perception, 10, 91, 191, 193, 194, 196, 199, 210, 213, 214, 233, 234
personal agency, 259
personhood, 41, 48, 52, 59, 62, 64, 67–68, 69, 119–20, 143–51, 154, 158, 160–61, 162, 164, 166–67, 171, 173–77, 179–84, 203–4, 222, 236, 244–45, 274, 286, 293, 297, 300, 305
Planck time, 249

postfoundational (*see* epistemology), 13, 70, 73
postmodernism (*see* epistemology)
prayer, 69, 148, 179, 193, 257, 286
predator animals, 170, 221, 291
predestination, 82, 84, 159, 173
priesthood
  of Christ, 122, 144, 155
  of humanity, 145, 152, 155, 164, 182-83, 279-93
primates, 204-8, 211, 213, 214-15, 216, 218
properly basic, 189-91
providence, 18, 63, 247, 250-51, 274-76, 295, 299, 301
Ptolemaic worldview 2, 3

quantum cosmology, 253-56, 260

Rahner, Karl
  angels, 91, 103, 113-16, 120-21, 123-24
  biography, 86
  Christology, 91, 102, 103, 108, 111, 112, 115, 121, 122, 131-42
  evolution, 90, 91, 95, 96-97, 106, 108-14, 131-38, 141-42
  extra-terrestrials, 151
  human nature, 92-105, 107, 109, 111-12, 119, 122, 124, 127-29, 134, 138, 139, 141-42
  imago dei, 94, 123
  incarnation, 89, 91-92, 93, 98-104, 108-15, 117-26, 130, 132-33, 137-42
  multiple incarnations, 116-25
  philosophy, 87, 97, 108, 132
  spirituality, 88, 127, 129
rare Earth hypothesis, 240, 250, 263, 265
rationalism, 27, 70, 74, 76, 81, 108, 132, 165, 188

rationality, xiii, 12, 17, 18, 30, 41, 63-66, 68-69, 70-71, 73, 76, 80, 112, 114, 125, 126, 127, 129-30, 136, 138, 144, 149, 151, 153, 164, 165-66, 178, 188-89, 190-91, 195-96, 197, 199-201, 204, 224, 225, 226, 227, 274, 288, 299, 304
reality, xiii, 4, 14-15, 16, 23-24, 27, 29, 31, 32-33, 35-36, 56-58, 65, 71, 75, 76, 78, 79, 81, 83, 84, 87, 88, 89, 90, 91, 93, 96, 98, 99, 101-2, 103, 105, 107, 109, 111-12, 113, 114, 115, 118, 120, 131, 134, 140, 141, 142, 143-44, 145, 147, 159, 164, 165, 168, 179, 180, 187-88, 189, 191-92, 193, 194, 195, 196, 198-200, 201-2, 211, 214, 219, 221, 222, 234-35, 236, 247, 248, 254, 255, 258-59, 262, 263, 271, 275, 279, 292-93, 295, 300, 301
rebellion (*see* sin), xi, 136, 157-59, 169, 287
redemption, 45, 53, 59, 62, 96, 98, 121, 123, 124, 125, 130, 134-35, 153, 156, 159, 161, 163-65, 177, 182, 188, 282, 284, 286, 289, 293, 299, 302
reductionism, 200, 231
reincarnation, 150
relationality, 36-37, 46, 52, 140, 147, 151, 175, 178
relationship
  human, 12, 38, 48, 68, 129, 161, 172-73, 203, 226, 286
  inter-Trinitarian (*see* God, Trinity)
relativism, 13, 77, 89, 197
relativity, 196, 235, 251, 252, 254

religion, xiii, 7, 14, 36, 45, 64, 71, 72, 77, 94, 187, 193, 195–96, 202, 224, 300
Renaissance, 290
responsibility, xiv, 37, 39–40, 43, 64, 153, 160, 161, 163, 164, 167, 183, 184, 218, 222–23, 224, 236, 237, 284, 290, 291, 292, 293, 302, 304
resurrection, 18, 24–28, 30, 34, 42, 55, 56, 58, 61, 67, 70, 71, 73–85, 105–6, 119, 120, 122, 123, 126, 128–30, 134–35, 138, 140, 144, 165, 177, 181, 188–89, 194, 201, 257, 272, 282, 284, 285, 295, 299–300
revelation, 3, 15, 17, 24–26, 27, 28, 30, 67, 70, 71, 73, 74, 78, 83, 89, 90, 93, 108, 109, 113, 114, 115, 117, 118, 124, 131, 132, 140, 142, 159, 179–80, 181, 182, 188, 194, 195, 236, 260, 275, 285, 287, 295, 300
righteousness, 45, 49, 52, 285
robotics, 228–30
Romans, 34, 124

sabbath, 17, 28, 52–56, 295–296
sacraments (*see* also Eucharist, baptism, communion), 143–44, 155, 163, 177
sainthood, 193
salvation, 17, 25, 31–32, 85, 89, 100, 104, 116, 117, 120, 122, 124, 130, 133, 134, 138, 155, 160, 161, 162, 177, 182–83, 272, 284, 286, 291, 293, 295, 296
Saturn, 241
scientism, 195
Scripture, 14, 25, 27, 29, 34, 35, 45, 46, 53, 54, 70, 73, 89, 90, 100, 113, 115, 116, 117, 119, 121, 122, 124, 127, 128, 138, 139, 161, 236, 244, 279–80, 287, 288, 290
self-awareness, 68, 109, 140, 148, 211, 220, 232
self-consciousness, 37, 74, 95, 107, 109, 126, 204, 211, 229, 244, 301
self-determination, 148, 222, 283
selfishness, 169–70, 173, 219
self-organizing principle, 61
self-revelation, God's, 25, 103
self-transcendence, 35–36, 44, 109–13, 134
sentience, 68, 242, 288
serpent, 66, 135, 159, 288
servanthood, 133, 293, 302
SETI, 60, 116, 238, 239, 240
sexuality, 46
sheep, 35, 122, 204
significance, human, xi, xii, xiv, 2, 10, 16–19, 23, 55, 85, 142, 145, 165, 183, 184, 187, 202, 250, 285, 297, 298, 298, 302, 303
silicon-based life, 231
sin (*see* also original sin), 33, 35, 50, 52, 102, 123, 130, 135–36, 137–38, 145, 147, 154, 158, 159, 163, 165, 167–73, 183, 287
singularity, 120, 125, 174, 252–53, 260
smoothness problem, 249
sociality, 68, 81
sociobiology, 169, 219
something-from-nothing problem, 253, 254
sonship, Christ's, 24, 79, 104
soteriology (*see* salvation; Jesus Christ:salvation)
soul, 44–45, 64, 65, 96, 127–29, 145, 149–50, 156, 164, 231, 282, 288
spirituality, 41, 88, 127, 224,

Subject Index   345

steady-state theory, 251–53
stewardship, xiv, 7, 37, 39, 163, 293, 302, 304, 305
subjectivity, 4, 10, 27, 71, 73, 76, 97–98, 113, 146, 230–31, 236
suffering, 122, 135, 138, 149, 162, 180, 282, 283, 288
supernatural, 25, 74, 93, 125, 127, 165, 187–90, 193–94, 200, 201, 300
symbolic reasoning, 37, 64, 69, 220, 222, 224, 226, 244, 300
syntax (*see* features of language), 207, 209

technology, 37, 118, 305–6
teleological argument, 248, 262, 276
teleology, 107, 239, 240, 247, 250, 251, 261, 262, 263, 265, 266–67, 269–70, 272, 273, 276, 295, 301
teleomorphy, 271, 272,
Tetragrammaton, 244
theocentrism, 103
time
    beginning of, 248–50, 252–53, 255, 258
    and Christ, 50, 75, 81–83, 123–24, 139, 141, 155
    and creation, xi, 27, 58, 63, 109, 111, 118, 238–39, 248–53, 267
    and eternity, 24, 46, 124, 248, 275
    and God, 53, 120, 81–82, 260, 284, 286
    and human existence, 60, 85, 99, 111, 121, 150, 155, 170, 217, 242–43
    Planck's, 249
Toronto Airport Christian Fellowship, 193

transcendentality, 88, 89, 93, 96, 97–98, 100, 105, 109–10, 125, 130, 136, 141, 296
Trinity (*see* also God), 32, 36, 44, 63, 78, 79, 140, 144–47, 148, 150, 173–79
truth, xiii, 14, 15, 16, 23–25, 27–31, 61, 71, 74, 76, 77, 81, 85, 86–87, 89–90, 95, 103, 107–8, 142, 143–44, 157, 168, 169, 171, 192, 195, 197–201, 224, 274, 275, 288, 300, 303, 306
Turing test, 229

uniqueness, human, xii, 18, 35, 37, 145, 148, 165, 166, 203, 204, 223–25, 237, 240, 244, 300–301, 303
universalism, 92
universe (*see* cosmos), xi, xii, xiv, 1–6, 8–11, 13, 16, 17, 18, 31, 41–42, 43, 50, 55, 57, 58, 60–61, 62–63, 82, 84–85, 91, 94–95, 97, 103, 106–7, 113, 114, 115, 117–18, 119, 120, 121–22, 124–25, 137–39, 141, 142, 153, 156–57, 159, 160, 162, 173, 178, 184, 196, 202, 238–44, 246–77, 280, 282, 294, 295–96, 297–99, 301–3, 305

vocalization (*see* features of language), 207, 209, 216
vocation, 39, 40

Weltoffenheit, 36
Western thought, 107, 116, 144, 165, 188
whales, 203
will
    human (*see* freedom: personal; animal vs. human)
    God's, 55, 273, 275, 293

wisdom, 66, 183, 274
woman, 46, 48, 67, 97
Word of God, 14, 26, 28, 30, 81, 89, 102, 104, 118, 244
worldview, xi, 1, 3, 15, 38, 56, 77, 90, 91, 108, 115–16, 126, 128, 132, 135, 144, 164, 165, 184, 188, 192, 194, 197, 199–200, 290, 294, 304
worship, 38, 54, 55, 103, 121, 163, 224, 236–37, 276, 280, 286, 288

Zizioulas
  biography, 143
  cosmic destiny, 150, 153, 184
  and ecology, 143
  human priesthood, 144–45, 152, 164, 182–83
  human uniqueness, 145, 148, 164–65, 166, 167
  imago dei, 145, 147–48, 152, 153, 154, 167, 174, 177, 179, 181, 183
  incarnation, 144–45, 150, 153–54, 155, 157, 159, 160, 162, 164, 172–73, 176, 179, 181, 183, 184
  personhood, 143–55, 158, 160–61, 162, 164, 166–67, 171, 173–76, 177, 179–84
  sacraments, 155
  sin, 145, 147, 154, 158, 159, 163, 165, 167–73, 183
  the Trinity, 144–48, 150, 173–76, 178–79

Author Index

Alston, William P., 77, 192, 194, 196
Anderson, Ray S., 43, 46, 47–48, 65, 127, 128
Aquinas, Thomas, 12, 14, 87, 200, 259, 288, 289
Ariansen, Per, 8, 292
St. Athanasius of Alexandria, 49, 181
Atkins, Peter, 246, 247, 270, 273,
Ayala, Francisco J., 36, 37, 220, 223
Ayer, A. J., 190

Badham, Paul, 234, 235
Bailey, Derrick Sherwin, 47
Barbour, Ian G., 19, 209, 224–25, 228, 231, 232, 236, 244
Barr, James, 128, 172
Barr, Stephen M., 106–7
Barrow, John, 5, 10, 255, 256
Barth, Karl. T., 23, 25, 41, 42–43, 48, 52, 53, 69, 93, 98, 103, 104, 113, 125, 135–36, 160, 162, 168, 295–96
Barth, Markus, 50, 80
Bauckham, Richard, 281, 289, 290
Behe, Michael J., 267–68
Bekoff, Marc, 166, 211
Benedict XVI (aka Joseph Ratzinger), 14, 41, 147, 152, 265
Blackmore, Susan J., 233
Blanke, Helmut (see Markus Barth)
Boehm, Christopher, 218
Bornkamm, Günther, 74

Braine, David, 65, 100, 119, 123–24, 224, 285
Brownlee, Donald (see Peter D. Ward)
Brueggemann, Walter, 53, 54
Brun, Rudolf B., 264, 271–72, 282, 285
Brunner, H. Emil, 25, 222
Buber, Martin, 48
Budziszewski, Jay, 68, 69
Buller, Cornelius A., 32, 33, 38, 44, 72
Bultmann, Rudolf, 25, 189

Cantor, Geoffrey, 192
Carmody, Denise Lardner and John Tully Carmody, 93, 100–101, 104, 109, 112
Carter, Brandon, 242
Cassuto, Umberto, 47, 64
Cheney, Dorothy L., 211–12
Clark, Andy, 64–65, 227
Clark, Stephen R. L., 182, 183, 290
Clarke, Adam, 287
Clayton, Philip, 71–72
Coakley, Sarah, 175
Cobb, Jr., John, 39, 182, 183, 290
Cohn-Sherbok, Dan, 287, 288–89
Cone, James H., 80, 193
Conway Morris, Simon, 239–240, 242–43, 263, 271
Coyne, George V., 116
Craig, William Lane, 25
Crick, Francis, 230, 231, 282

347

Darwin, Charles, 1, 203, 204, 213, 224, 246, 282
Davidson, Iain (*see* William Noble)
Davies, Brian, 259, 261
Davies, Paul, 1, 246, 258
Dawkins, Richard, 187, 188, 219, 239, 246, 247, 266, 268, 269, 270, 273
de Duve, Christian, 126, 224, 231, 235, 239, 240, 266, 269, 275, 304
de Waal, Frans B. D., 218, 221
Deacon, Terrence, 206-7, 209, 210, 239, 240, 266
Deane-Drummond, Celia, 178, 221, 289, 290, 292
Del Colle, Ralph, 14
Dembski, William A., 269
Dennett, Daniel C., 187, 213-14, 219, 229, 268, 269, 270
Descartes, Rene, 4, 12, 65, 66, 196, 288, 289
Dick, Stephen J., 116
Dodwell, Peter, 213
Donald, Merlin, 214, 223
Drees, Willem B., 187, 251, 258
Dreyfus, Hubert and Stuart Dreyfus, 226, 227
Dyson, Freeman, 246, 269, 274

Eichrodt, Walther, 47, 148, 158
Eisenberg, Leon, 219
Ellis, George F. R., 248-49
Everett, III, Hugh, 256

Feenstra, Ronald J., 285
Fergusson, David, ix-xii, 53, 157
Fields, Stephen M., 87, 126
Flores, Fernando (*see* Terry Winograd)
Foerst, Anne, 229, 232, 236
Foley, Robert, 203
Fortes, Andrew D., 241-42

Galloway, Allan D., 44, 72, 78
Gallup, Jr., Gordon G., 206
Geertz, Clifford, 191-92
Gibellini, Rosino, 4, 12, 37-38
Gilkey, Langdon, 178, 179
Godlovitch, Stan, 8
Goodall, Jane, 218-19
Gould, Stephen Jay, 238, 282
Graham, Gordon, 13, 169
Green, Joel B., 127
Greene, Brian, 235
Gregersen, Niels Henrik, 134, 283
Gregory of Nazianzus, 122, 137, 176
Gregory of Nyssa, 175
Grenz, Stanley J., 47
Gribbin, John R., 203, 263
Grube, Dirk-Martin, 189
Gruen, Lori, 7, 10, 290
Gunton, Colin E., 34, 40, 53, 62, 70, 71, 79-80, 115, 130, 138, 139, 151-52, 192, 285

Haeckel, Earnst, 3
Hall, Douglas John, 12, 16, 38, 39-40, 146, 204, 278, 285-86
Hamilton, Victor, 47
Hardy, Daniel W., 80-81
Harré, Rom, 198, 199, 200
Hartle, J. B., 253, 254, 255, 260
Hartman, Louis F., 115
Hawking, Stephen W., xi, xiii, 247, 251, 252, 253, 254, 255, 256, 260
Hegel, G. W. F., 71-73, 83, 87-88, 126
Hefner, Philip, 169, 171, 219-20
Herzfeld, Noreen L., 64-65, 178, 225-26, 227, 228
Heschel, Abraham J., 3-4
Hick, John H., 74, 215
Hiebert, Paul G., 6
Hillstrom, Elizabeth L., 234
Hirotsune, Shinji, 267-67

Hockett, Charles F., 207
Hofstadter, Douglas R., 227
Holwerda, David, 73, 194
Humphrey, Nicholas, 230

Isham, Chistopher J., 254–55

Jayawardhana, Ray, 241
Jenson, Robert W., 36, 78, 120, 127, 159–60, 166
St. John the Apostle, 32, 49–51, 80, 102, 119, 122–24, 129, 130, 148, 157, 172, 180–81, 195, 204
John Paul II (aka Karol Wojtyla), 46, 67
Johnson, Elizabeth A., 179
Johnson, Aubrey, 127–27

Kauffman, Stuart, 110
Kendall, Stuart, 197
Kenny, Anthony, 270
Kerr, Fergus, 38–39, 69
Knibb, Michael A., 128
Koertge, Noretta, 198
Kortenkamp, Katherine V., 291
Krausz, Michael (*see* Rom Harré)
Kuhn, Thomas, 198

Laats, Alar, 149, 150, 179
LaCugna, Catherine Mowry, 146, 175–76, 181
Laitman, Jeffrey T., 216
Laland, Kevin N., 204
Larkin, Lucy, 177, 204, 223
Lash, Nicholas, 14, 79, 136
Leahy, Michael P. T., 219, 221, 222–23, 289
Lemaire, André, 74
Leslie, John, 8, 254–55, 256, 257, 263
Lindbeck, George A., 189
Linzey, Andrew, 182, 279, 287–91
Lock, Andrew, 214

Lommel, Pirn van, 233
Longair, Malcolm S., 248
Losinger, Anton, 94, 140
Lossky, Vladimir, 149, 150, 179
Lucas, J. R., 227
Ludlow, Morwenna, 93

Marshall, Bruce D., 90, 91, 115, 136, 168
Masao, A. B. E., 7
Mayr, Ernst, 238, 266
McArthur, Jane, 67
McFadyen, Alistair I., 48
McFague, Sally, 177–78
McFarland, Ian, 180
McGrath, Alistair, 189–91, 199
McHarg, Ian L., 278
McKnight, Edgar V., 197
McMullin, Ernan, 117, 123
Mellars, Paul, 210, 215, 216
Mellor, Philip A., 65
Meyendorff, John, 160–62
Michaels, Patricia A., 7–8
Midgley, Mary, 211
Migliore, Daniel L., 173, 176
Minsky, Marvin, 226
Mithen, Stephen, 206, 216
Moberly, R. W. L., 197
Molnar, Paul D., 70–71, 73
Moltmann, Jürgen, 11–12, 40, 53, 54, 134, 149, 152, 157, 180, 285
Monod, Jacques, 238, 239, 266–67, 268, 304
Morito, Bruce, 5
Morowitz, Harold J., 210–11, 220
Murphy, George L., 121–22, 139
Murphy, Nancey, 195

Nagel, Thomas, 211, 216, 320–31
Newton-Smith, W. H., 198, 199
Nichols, Terrence L., 193
Niebuhr, Reinhold, 169

Noble, William, 206, 207, 208–10, 213–14, 215, 216
Northcott, Michael, 7, 291
Nouwen, Henri, 129
Novak, Michael, 46

O'Donnell, John J., 146
O'Donovan, Leo J., 97–98
Olson, Roger, 71, 79
Oomen, Palmyre M. F., 283–84

Page, Ruth, 10, 12, 38, 61, 187, 264, 278, 279, 280, 281, 282, 283, 284, 285, 286, 287, 292
Paine, Thomas, 116
Paley, William, 261, 266
Palmer, Clare, 282
Pannenberg, Wolfhart, 17, 23–85, 113, 128, 129, 130, 143, 156, 163, 165, 179, 188, 193, 194, 201, 202, 203, 237, 265, 274, 293, 294, 295–96, 297–98, 302. See also subject index under "Pannenberg"
St. Paul the Apostle, 26, 49, 80, 120–21, 128–30, 135, 180, 183
Paul VI, 148
Peacocke, Arthur, 19, 57, 116, 127, 167, 170, 172, 177, 188, 211, 239, 251, 264, 269, 271, 274–75, 281, 283, 285
Penrose, Roger, 233, 234, 252, 270
Peters, Ted, 79, 260
Peterson, Gregory R., ix, 64–65, 169, 178, 204, 214, 220, 230, 231, 232
Philips, D. Z., 195
Piaget, Jean, 205
Piccard, Rosalind W., 230, 231
Pius XII, 260
Plantinga, Alvin, 165, 188, 190–91, 192, 247
Plantinga, Jr., Cornelius, 145, 146

Platek, Steven M. (see Gordon Gallup, Jr.)
Plumwood, Val, 6
Polanyi, Michael, 194, 195
Polkinghorne, John, 234, 251, 254, 255, 257, 258, 260, 265, 283
Povinelli, Daniel J., 212, 213
Purcell, Michael, 88, 93, 126, 140

Rabut, Olivier A., 111
Rahner, Karl, x, xiii, 15, 17, 57, 78, 86–142, 143, 157, 165, 168, 188, 201, 203, 237–38, 259, 293, 294, 295, 296–97, 298, 302. See also subject index under "Rahner."
Ratzinger, Joseph (see Benedict XVI)
Rees, Martin, 263
Richardson, Alan, 168–69
Ring, Kenneth and Sharon Cooper, 233
Robinson, H. Wheeler, 171
Robinson, John A. T., 112
Rolston, III, Holmes, 219, 221, 223, 238, 263–64, 265, 266, 269, 290
Ronen, Avraham, 215
Rorty, Richard, 192, 198
Ross, Hugh, 241, 242, 249
Rowan-Robinson, Michael, 60, 106
Rumbaugh, Duane M. (see E. Sue Savage-Rumbaugh), 205, 212
Russell, Robert J., 260, 280
Rybarczyk, Edmund J., 123, 154, 158, 159, 160

Sabom, Michael, 233, 234
Sagan, Carl, 8, 11, 106, 187, 188, 246, 247, 273
Santmire, H. Paul, 164
Sarna, Nahum, 28, 47, 55
Savage-Rumbaugh, E. Sue 205–6, 207, 209

Scheffczyk, Leo, 273, 283
Schmaus, Michael, 111
Schoonenberg, Piet, 168
Schwöbel, Christoph, 32, 76
Searle, John, 226, 230
Seed, John, 6, 7–8, 10
Sellars, Wilfred, 191
Seyfarth, Robert M. (*see* Dorothy L. Cheney)
Shults, F. LeRon, 13–14, 73, 190, 201
Shilling, Chris (*see* Phillip A. Mellor), 65
Simpson, George G., 218
Singer, Peter, 204, 218, 222–23
Smith, Peter K., 206
Sober, Elliot, 219
Sobrino, Jon, 66
Southgate, Christopher, 264, 267, 280–81, 283, 286
Stanley, Charles K., 126
Stannard, Russell, 280
Stenmark, Mikael, 195
Stewart, Jacqui A., 36, 38, 52, 59, 62, 67–68, 72–73, 75, 80, 198–99
Swinburne, Richard, 256, 270

Tattersall, Ian, 208–9, 214, 215, 216, 223
Teilhard de Chardin, Pierre, 111, 112, 137, 170, 263
Templeton, John, 6
TeSelle, Eugene, 132
Thunberg, Lars, 67, 123, 154, 158
Tipler, Frank, 5, 10, 60, 248–49, 252, 253, 255, 256
Torrance, Alan J., 174, 176–77
Torrance, Thomas F., 43, 62, 175, 176, 180, 227, 274
Tupper, Elgin Frank, 40
Turing, Alan M., 229

Van Buren, Paul M., 34

Van Huyssteen, J. Wentzel, 15–16, 36–37, 39, 51, 191, 196, 199–200, 201
Vanhoozer, Kevin, 4
Vass, George, 87, 100, 101, 103, 105, 140
Vawter, Bruce, 158
Volf, Miroslav, 154
Von Rad, Gerhard, 158
Vorgrimler, Herbert, 131

Wainwright, Geoffrey, 180
Walsh, Michael J., 92, 93, 95, 101, 102,
Ward, Graham, 190
Ward, Keith, 95, 96, 263, 264, 265, 270, 271
Ward, Peter D., 240–41, 243, 263
Watson, Francis, 46
Watts, Fraser, 129, 171, 219, 234
Weger, Karl-Heinz, 87, 125
Weil, Simone, 265
Weinberg, Steven, 252, 253
Welker, Michael, 13, 28, 48, 68
Wesley, John, 193
Westermann, Claus, 41, 47, 53, 168
Westphal, Merold, 72
Wetherill, George, 241
White, Jr., Lynn, 7, 38
Wicken, Jeffrey, 57, 59, 247
Wiles, Maurice, 66
Williams, Michael, 194
Williams, Patricia A., 167, 168, 169
Wilson, David Sloan, 219
Wilson, Edward O., 219, 268, 269
Winograd, Terry, 192, 226–27, 228
Wojtyla, Karol (*see* John Paul II)
Wolterstorff, Nicholas, 189

Zizioulas, John, xiii, 17, 143–184, 188, 201, 203, 204, 222, 225, 236, 238, 285, 285, 290, 293, 294, 295, 297, 298, 302. *See also* subject index under "Zizioulas."

www.ingramcontent.com/pod-product-compliance
Lightning Source LLC
Chambersburg PA
CBHW071149300426
44113CB00009B/1145